Love,
Greg & Lauren

Love, Greg & Lauren

Greg Manning

BANTAM BOOKS

NEW YORK   TORONTO   LONDON   SYDNEY   AUCKLAND

LOVE, GREG & LAUREN

PUBLISHING HISTORY

Bantam hardcover edition published March 2002
Bantam trade paperback edition/September 2002

COVER PHOTO BY SIGRID ESTRADA
COVER DESIGN BY BELINA HUEY AND JIM PLUMERI
BOOK DESIGN BY GLEN EDELSTEIN

"Travelin' Prayer" Copyright © 1973, renewed 1999, Impulsive Music.
All Rights Reserved. Used by Permission.
All Rights Reserved Used by Permission Dovan Music, Inc.
"I Can See Clearly Now" written by Johnny Nash.
"I Got You" by Dwight Yoakam. © Coal Dust West Music. All rights
administered by Warner-Tamerlane Publishing Corp. All Rights Reserved Used by
Permission WARNER BROS. PUBLICATIONS US, INC. Miami, FL 33014..

Library of Congress catalog card number: 2002074206

Library of Congress Cataloging-in-Publication Data is on file with the publisher.

ISBN 0-553-38189-X

Published simultaneously in the United States and Canada

Bantam Books are published by Bantam Books, a division of Random
House, Inc. Its trademark, consisting of the words "Bantam Books" and the
portrayal of a rooster, is Registered in U.S. Patent and Trademark Office
and in other countries. Marca Registrada. Bantam Books, 1540 Broadway,
New York, New York 10036.

PRINTED IN THE UNITED STATES OF AMERICA

10 9 8 7 6 5 4 3 2 1

BVG

Love,
Greg & Lauren

PROLOGUE

As midnight came on September 11, 2001, I stood at my wife's bedside in the William Randolph Hearst Burn Center at New York-Presbyterian Hospital.

Webs of plastic tubing fed her intravenous fluids and medications. Over the next twenty-four hours she would receive approximately twenty liters—forty-two pounds—of fluids to replace those she was losing through her wounds. She was heavily sedated and would remain in this drug-induced sleep for weeks. She was on a ventilator to support her breathing; there was a feeding tube in her nose. Her body was wrapped in white gauze, and she was draped in sheets and blankets to keep her warm. At 8:48 that morning, she had been burned over 82.5 percent of her body as she entered the lobby of 1 World Trade Center.

At 8 that morning she had been a vibrant, athletic, and beautiful woman, decisive and demanding and the picture of health.

At about 8:30 she had breezed through our living room telling me how she'd solved a scheduling problem, making phone calls that delayed her normal departure about fifteen minutes. She lingered in the hallway, saying good-bye to our ten-month-old son, Tyler, and then she headed off to work, going downstairs and hailing a cab to take her to the World Trade Center, where she was (and is) a senior vice president, partner, and director of global data sales for Cantor Fitzgerald.

Less than twenty minutes later, listening to the "Imus in the Morning" program as I was about to leave for work, I heard Imus break in and say, "What's this? A plane hit the World Trade Center?"

I ran to our terrace, which looks down Manhattan's West Street toward the twin towers, and saw a vast hole billowing black smoke from the top of Tower One. I could see that the plane had hit at or just below Cantor Fitzgerald's offices and that the impact had been huge. I tried to persuade myself that Lauren, that anyone at Cantor, could still be alive. I kept calling her telephone numbers but her office line was busy and her cell phone wasn't ringing. I paced the apartment, pounding the wall and calling her name, then watched as the second plane hit Tower Two, seemingly right at the 84th floor, my office at Euro Brokers.

I felt like the man on a battlefield who leaves his unit for a moment, only to look back as it is blown up before his eyes.

Friends and family kept calling our apartment to make sure we were all right. I could not say whether Lauren was alive; I was almost certain she was dead.

But she wasn't.

Arriving at the World Trade Center, she'd heard a whistling sound, entered the lobby to investigate, and been met by an explosive fireball. She ran outside in flames. A bond salesman over at the World Financial Center saw her and two others as they ran from the building, raced across West Street, and put out the flames that were consuming her. Lauren was lucid enough to tell him her name and our phone number. People had fled and there was no one else around for blocks. As heavy pieces of steel debris fell from a thousand feet above them, he stayed with Lauren until the ambulance came.

At 9:35 our phone rang once and went silent. A moment later it rang again. A breathless voice said, "Mr. Manning, I'm with your wife. She's been badly burned but she's going to be OK. We got her in an ambulance." The phone cut off before he could tell me where she was being taken. I was to learn later that the caller was a bond trader. His buddy, the bond salesman, had just saved Lauren's life.

Lauren's parents called from Savannah, Georgia; they literally dropped the phone when I told them the news, got in their car, and took off for New York.

Twenty minutes later a nurse called to tell me Lauren was at St. Vincent's Hospital, eight blocks away. Fighting tears, not knowing what to expect, I made my way there through the stunned crowds headed north on Hudson Street. At one point I turned around and saw Tower One wreathed in black smoke. I did not realize Tower Two had already come down.

I entered St. Vincent's moments before it was closed to all but patients and medical personnel. I found Lauren in a bed on the 10th floor, all but her face covered in white sheets. She looked normal, though as if she had a deep tan, but her eyebrows had been burned off and her beautiful blond hair was charred.

The first thing she said was "Get me to a burn unit."

2

Then she said, "Greg, I was on fire. I ran out. I prayed to die. Then I decided to live for Tyler and for you."

She asked me to apply balm to her blistered lips. Her pain grew and she begged for morphine. She became less aware. Her face began to swell. They transferred her to a private room and asked me to step out. For the next two hours the nurses dressed her wounds.

At 5 that afternoon, Dr. Edmund Kwan, a plastic surgeon affiliated with St. Vincent's and New York-Presbyterian, secured Lauren a bed in the Burn Center and ordered her sedated and intubated to protect against respiratory arrest during the transport. The ambulance driver headed across 14th Street, up an FDR Drive closed to all but emergency vehicles, and rolled to a stop in the hospital's ambulance bay. Within minutes we were in the Burn Center on the 8th floor. Lauren was wheeled to a glass-walled room and doctors and nurses surrounded her bed. Someone led me to the waiting room and I sagged into a chair. My friend Mary White arrived a short time later.

The hours passed. With the city locked down, home seemed far away, unreachable. Joyce, Tyler's nanny, stayed with him that night as I dozed on the floor of the waiting room just down the hall in case I was called to Lauren's bedside. My friend Bill Fisher kept the vigil with me. Members of other patient families slept there too, in chairs or on cots. Lauren's mother and father arrived at noon on Wednesday. They would stay in our apartment for the next three months and be there for Lauren and Tyler. Lauren's sister came in from New Jersey and her brother drove up from North Carolina. I asked my own family in Florida—my mother and father and sister—to remain at home; I did not have a place for them to stay if they came, and I promised to keep them continually posted on Lauren's condition.

On Thursday evening, a gray-haired man in a white coat met with us in the waiting room. He was Dr. Roger Yurt, the medical director of the Burn Center, Lauren's doctor in the pages that follow. In a calm voice he described what she was up against. The first seventy-two hours were the resuscitation phase, during which she was receiving an extraordinary quantity of fluids to replace those her body was dumping. If she survived this phase, Dr. Yurt would perform numerous grafts in the ensuing weeks to close her wounds and control her injury. Only after she was "closed" would she be out of danger; until then, infection would be a constant threat.

The prognosis was bleak, but the meeting with Dr. Yurt brought me the first twinge of hope. If there was anyone on earth who could save her, I thought, he was the one.

Late Saturday night, September 15, another critical patient, who had been brought in at the same time as Lauren, died, reducing by one the cadre of bereft and shattered families who had bonded in the waiting room since Tuesday. Dr. Palmer Bessey, Dr. Yurt's associate director, had to deliver the news to the patient's family, and as I was leaving the Burn Center that night he looked up and told me, "She's hanging in there pretty well." He paused. "She's going to get sicker before she gets better." He paused again, then said with quiet ferocity, "But we're going to do everything we can to pull her through. I don't want those bastards to get another person."

In the early afternoon of Sunday, September 16, I was told that Lauren's chances were less than 50-50, probably far less. (I was later to learn they were about 15 percent.) I found solace with a rabbi who was in the waiting room visiting another patient. He was not on the hospital staff, but at my request he came in to pray by Lauren's bedside so that she might hear the holy language and know that we were praying for her.

That night, another World Trade Center burn patient died.

Day after day the phone at home never stopped ringing; friends, colleagues, and family called from around the world. It grew difficult to repeat the full story, but I realized that the short version was becoming little more than a medical summary and said nothing of her courage.

So on the afternoon of September 19, I sat down to type an e-mail update on Lauren's condition. I wanted to thank everyone for their prayers and for their support, and to tell them how she was doing in ways that would convey just how hard she was fighting. So many things I was seeing deserved to be remembered: the resolve and morale of the medical staff, the love of friends and family, the bravery that was already evident as I stood by Lauren's bed.

As a token of my faith in her, I signed both of our names at the end of that first note, and to every one that followed.

The daily e-mails became a compulsion.

On November 19, I wrote:

"As you all know, I am doing two meaningful things: I am being there for Tyler and Lauren (with an enormous assist from her mother and father), and I am writing these e-mails, which represents, after caring for my family, the most valuable thing I have ever done. I have wanted it to build a network of love for Lauren so that when she needs it, the embrace that will take her in will encircle the globe. I have also appreciated hearing from people that my words have been inspiring; it is equally inspiring to have them read. But the soul of inspiration in this story is, of course, Lauren."

This book is for her.

From: Greg
To: Everyone
Date: Wednesday, September 19, 2001 5:30 PM
Subject: Lauren Update

First of all, I want to thank all of you, and all of the others to whom you speak about Lauren. The love that has flooded in and the prayers that are being uttered on her behalf have helped us immensely.

She is still heavily sedated due to her condition, but they say she can hear my voice, so I tell her about everyone I have spoken to, that they send their love and best wishes, and their prayers, including numerous congregations across the spiritual spectrum, both synagogues and churches around the world. I have been informed that this evening the Baptists will be added to this group.

Lauren is putting up a heck of a fight. She has been through two surgeries and continues to hold on. She has a long road in front of her, but she is hanging in there, and we are by her side constantly. As of 5 PM Wednesday she remained stable.

For those of you who may not know the story, she was entering the lobby of the North Tower of the World Trade Center when a fireball exploded from the elevator shaft. She and two others managed to run out of the building, all three of them on fire. A passerby across the street ran to them, reaching Lauren first, and put the flames out. He then put Lauren in an ambulance, so she was the first person evacuated. He certainly saved her life.

She was at St. Vincent's, where I joined her, and then at 5 PM Tuesday rode in the front of the ambulance when she was transferred to the Burn Center at NY-Presbyterian.

When I got to St. Vincent's, she told me that she had decided to live for Tyler and for me; so I am taking her at her word.

Thank you for all your support and prayers.

Love,
Greg & Lauren

Lauren had a good day today—they are easing back on the ventilator support and she is tolerating that well; she is maintaining her blood pressure, and her stomach is functioning normally. She is looking good, too. She is showing encouraging signs of healing on her own in places that were not as seriously affected.

We need to keep our expectations on an even keel because she still has a very long road in front of her. But all of these are good signs.

Yesterday I mentioned that Lauren had already had two surgeries. Several hours after she reached the Burn Center on September 11, they incised the burned skin along the entire length of her left arm to relieve swelling and preserve the pulse to her left hand. On Tuesday the 18th, her surgeon grafted the backs of her legs and most of her back using her own skin.

Her next graft surgery will be early next week if she remains stable and continues to exhibit encouraging signs. Tomorrow she is scheduled for her first visit to the "tank," the room where patients are given a water bath that helps in removing the burned tissue and promoting healing.

We appreciate all of your prayers; we are thankful (I am thankful) that Lauren is loved by so many people. I continue to admire her strength. She really is a tough lady.

The hour is late but I wanted to share this news with you all.

Love,
Greg & Lauren

Hello All—

Lauren continues to hang on. She did not visit the tank today after all, but she continued to do OK—her blood pressure was lower in the morning but it was back to 110 when I left the hospital at 9 tonight. She will probably go to the tank tomorrow. One of the nurses did say that her grafts looked good today during "burn care," a changing of the bandages and washing of the wound areas that is done every twelve hours by a team of nurses.

I had the opportunity today to meet with the gentleman who helped rescue one of the other patients on the ward, Jennieann. He was at the hospital visiting with her family. I forgot his name, unfortunately!

He was in the Marriott World Trade Center hotel (formerly the Vista) when the first plane hit. For those of you who know the former World Trade Center layout, he was just beyond the revolving door between the WTC lobby and the Marriott. He helped Jennieann as she emerged from the smoky haze on the WTC side of the revolving door, the 1 World Trade Center (North Tower) lobby. But when the second plane hit, he sat down; she urged him to get on his feet and leave the hotel with her. They left through a side exit to Liberty Street (for the experts, through the Tall Ships Bar).

It later turned out that this man had lost his sister and his niece on that second plane—and lost another family friend on the first! There is a lot of tragedy sitting in that waiting room at various times of day.

Lauren's parents are doing the day shift at the hospital. I think that schedule will help make it possible for me to go back to work, at least for a couple of hours a day, starting next week. But don't worry— Lauren is still priority one.

Tyler is also doing well, prospering from the care he is receiving from the child care team of Joyce Monday to Friday and Lauren's parents during evenings and weekends. I am back on my regular morning duty, waking up with Tyler and feeding him his morning bottle, changing him, and hanging with him until it's time to feed him his cereal.

Thank you again for your best wishes and prayers.

Love,
Greg & Lauren

From: Greg
To: Everyone
Date: Saturday, September 22, 2001 11:32 PM
Subject: Lauren Update for Sept 22 (Saturday)

Lauren had another good day. The way the nurses tell it, she is not giving them as much work as she did on previous days. Of course we are still in the early stages, with many more to go, both surgeries and general healing, before she can be declared out of the woods. But every gradual step is important.

Now that she is off "paralytic" agents, she can contribute to her own breathing. This is a step down from the mandatory ventilator setting she had been on. She is maintaining her blood pressure well, and has been weaned off several other medications.

Though she is still sedated and on heavy pain medication, her eyelids are beginning to open slightly, and I touched her arm and stroked her beautiful hair as I spoke to her tonight. She is more aware than she has been.

She is finally due to visit the tank tomorrow, which is the fifth day after her second surgery. The doctors will check how the graft has done on her buttocks.

I read to her from the book *A Poem a Day*, brought to me with a lovely inscription from my friend Dan Gold. Unfortunately, most of the poems are pretty depressing, being mostly about leaving this mortal coil; but there are some great ones about love, including several Shakespeare sonnets. My favorite to read to her today is Robert Burns's "My Love Is Like a Red, Red Rose."

> *My Love is like a red, red rose*
> *That's newly sprung in June:*
> *My Love is like the melodie*
> *That's sweetly play'd in tune!*

As fair thou art, my bonnie lass,
So deep in love am I:
And I will love thee still, my dear,
Till a' the seas gang dry:

Till a' the seas gang dry, my dear,
And the rocks melt with the sun;
I will love thee still, my dear,
When the sands of life shall run.

And fare thee weel, my only Love,
And fare thee weel a while!
And I will come again, my Love,
Tho' it were ten thousand mile.

OK, put down the Kleenex.
Again (and again), thank you for your prayers and support.

Love,
Greg & Lauren

From: Greg
To: Everyone
Date: Sunday, September 23, 2001 11:55 PM
Subject: Lauren Update for Sept 23 (Sunday)

Lauren visited the tank today, and her grafts looked pretty good. Some areas did not take on her legs, not unexpected and primarily due to the sheer size of the graft that was done, but those areas can be regrafted. Her back looked good. Her face also looks good. Her vital signs continue mostly stable.

The process of weaning her off the ventilator support and reducing the sedation is gradual, over time. Today this resulted in her being more aware of her surroundings, including turning her head very slightly in response to my voice, moving her eyes under her eyelids.

She was also taking on more responsibility for her breathing, a good sign but too big a step right now; her breaths were shallow, and she was not oxygenating as well as with the 100 percent ventilator support.

The nurse managed the situation, and that is mostly what happens. Lauren is still very critical, so the days are a continual process of managing every event, whether a slight drop in blood pressure, a spike in fever, falling out of sync with the ventilator, to get her back to a normal setting.

While Lauren was more aware, I read her some poems again, referred to a number of her friends by name while conveying their best wishes to her, and again told her about the pictures we've taped to the wall of her room (pictures of the two of us with Tyler, a picture of Tyler, a picture sent by Leslie of Lauren, Deirdre, and Leslie when we all got together in December). Someone has written on the whiteboard in there, "We love you Lauren!"

A number of you have written back asking how I'm doing ("how are YOU doing," like in that beer commercial). I am doing OK. I could do without all of this, but I have much to hope for. It is sometimes hard to maintain an even keel (well, almost all the time) but I give it my best shot. I have been eating and sleeping, and last week actually went to an Off Wall Street Jam jam session and rehearsed with the Rolling Bones (I play bass). It's a long road, but mostly, right now, I am focused on being there for Lauren.

Thank you again for all your prayers and for all the offers of help.

Love to all,
Greg & Lauren

From: Greg
To: Everyone
Date: Tuesday, September 25, 2001 12:27 AM
Subject: Lauren Update for Sept 24 (Monday)

Another good day. Lauren was stable throughout the last twenty-four hours. The grafts on her back and legs looked good, except for one area on the top of her right thigh, but that may yet be OK; the part that didn't take was the outer layer of skin-bank skin, not Lauren's own, so there may still be good news underneath.

As I've mentioned, last week she received extensive grafts to her back, the backs of her legs, and her buttocks. There are three ways that burn sites can be grafted: with cadaver skin from a skin bank, called a homograft, a temporary measure since it is rejected within two to three months; with artificial skin, a silicone rubber material with a matrix underneath to help the growth of the foundation layer of skin, the dermis (which later receives a graft of the outer layer, or epidermis); and with the patient's own skin, called an autograft. The autograft is the only permanent solution; it is harvested from the patient's undamaged skin areas, called donor sites, which heal normally within about two weeks, at which point they can be used again.

Lauren's back and legs received autografts; her buttocks were grafted with artificial skin. During her visit to the tank this morning, she did lose the graft of artificial skin, but this is not as much of a concern, since it can be replaced.

She is due for her second major surgery at 7:30 AM on Tuesday, a one-and-a-half-hour procedure that should be over by midmorning (give or take some time to go down to the OR and be returned to the burn unit floor). Her left arm will be regrafted (this was always expected) and they may attempt to graft her left hand, all with her own skin.

Lauren is unlikely to remember any of this period. She remains deeply sedated, although there are moments where she is more aware. In both cases, she is very stubborn. For example, over time, they try to wean her off the ventilator, permitting her to breathe more on her own. Yesterday, this led to a period of rapid and shallow breathing that was out of sync with the ventilator. The ventilator had been set to deliver a certain number of breaths per minute, which the nurse said Lauren "did not like," adding, "You told us she was strong-willed, didn't you?" Her efforts to breathe were conflicting with the ventilator's attempts, leading to sub-par blood oxygen.

The settings on the ventilator were then changed. Now the machine senses the increase in pressure when Lauren seeks to breathe on her own, and assists to ensure that she gets a complete breath. She seemed much more comfortable this evening.

I was able to buy her a boom box today, which means less poetry and more Willie Nelson in the room. Tomorrow, I will bring a few CDs to vary the selection. I think the music will be very helpful, some easy blues mixed with classical. Overnight I left the radio tuned to Lite 106.7; I hope someday she forgives me for this.

As far as the report on me, I went to a friend's tonight for an informal dinner. There were around ten people there, most of them connected in some way to the tragedy. Two of them were in 2 World Trade Center when the first plane hit Tower One, saw the rain of debris, and recognized that they had to get out. Another person watched the attacks from a New Jersey ferry pier, feeling sick and helpless as he followed the arc of the second plane.

We talked about people who had been lost, many of them close friends of the people there; while it was occasionally somber, mostly people had a good time, which we all needed. Many congratulations to the hostess (you know who you are), who also made some excellent stars and stripes cookies.

I thank everyone for their responses to these updates—even if I don't have the chance to respond individually, I read every piece of e-mail, and I am grateful for everyone who is lending their love and support.

Thanks from both of us!!!
Greg & Lauren

From: Greg
To: Everyone
Date: Wednesday, September 26, 2001 12:32 AM
Subject: Lauren Update for Sept 25 (Tuesday)

Lauren's surgery went well today. She went down to the OR promptly at 7:30. She was the first case. The operation took a little longer than expected and she did not come back up until noon, but the reasons were good—the doctor was able to do a little more than he anticipated, grafting her left arm, the back of her left hand, and a spot on her right arm with her own skin.

Today's sites won't heal for two weeks; last week's sites will heal in about seven more days. Therefore, she is not due for more graft surgery until at least a week from today. If these grafts take, the size of her burn will have been reduced from 82.5 percent to 30 percent. Based on these grafts healing, her doctor says that her prognosis has improved, though she remains in highly critical condition. Nevertheless, this is an important step.

I can't remember if I've written the analogy I use to describe her situation, but it's this—she is expected to spend a day in the unit for every percent burn, meaning close to three months. For that entire time, she is highly critical, with the greatest risks posed by infection. I see it as comparable to an eighty-three-mile journey through enemy territory. Anything can happen at any time, but we are now fourteen miles in, and we don't have to repeat that part of it. So we hope for the best.

This was, therefore, another good day. Her vital signs remain strong. Her body temperature dropped a bit during surgery, but well within the range of the expected. Her lungs continue to oxygenate well, which is vital for her healing process.

I have seen troops in camouflage at the unit several times; this morning I asked one of them if he was National Guard, and he said he was regular army. I shook his hand, telling him my wife was in the unit and wishing him good luck with every part of his mission. It turns out he was a colonel, the top guy coordinating the disaster health services deployment from around the country.

The two nurses who have taken care of Lauren for the past five days are actually part of this deployment. In total, fifteen nurses from this team are at the Burn Center.

Lauren's day nurse is from a burn unit in Minnesota. Her night nurse is from Boston, and I believe she is the overall coordinator/manager of the deployment team. They are rotating out in the next several days, though the night nurse says she expects to rotate back in a couple of weeks. Both nurses have been terrific in letting me spend time with Lauren, and in keeping me informed when I call in for updates during the day and overnight. Also in climbing around me while they tend to Lauren so I can sit by her side, touch her arm, and read to or talk to her.

The regular staff nurses from the unit have also been great.

Lauren's day nurse for the first few days came by to check on her and me today, dressed in a shirt and tie; when he is not tending to patients, he is an instructor in the hospital's nursing education program.

It turns out that the nurses on the unit are rooting very strongly for Lauren, and for all the other critically ill patients from the WTC attacks. There is something about these injuries being deliberately inflicted that has deeply affected everyone.

In my view, there are two Ground Zeros in New York; the one at the disaster site, where rescue teams are combing through the rubble in a desperate search for living survivors, now against odds where survival would be well beyond miraculous. The other Ground Zero, or "Grounds" Zero, are at the NY-Presbyterian Burn Center and at every other hospital ward in the city where critically injured patients from this tragedy are being treated.

The doctors and nurses in these wards—of course I'm extrapolating from what I see in my own little part of this world—work around the clock and incredibly hard. The difficulty of what they do, and the grace with which they do it, is incredible. The most remarkable visible part of it is the bedside manner—everyone is courteous, polite, full of information, and as completely attentive to the emotional welfare of the families as to the moment-to-moment well-being of the patients.

Whether or not this is their training protocol, they are terrific at it, which means that at one key level the families are able to relax, knowing that their loved ones—including my Lauren—are at the place they need to be to have the best chance for survival and recovery.

Some related facts:

1. Yesterday a young woman who had been mentored by Lauren at Cantor Fitzgerald came by to offer her love and support. She had been let go from eSpeed the night before the attack. She is still here but she lost a number of her closest friends; she was grateful to Lauren, who she said was always good to her and looked out for her. (Of course, I went in and told Lauren that she'd been there, as I tell her of every visitor.)

   About an hour earlier, I had been given a teddy bear by one of the staff at the Burn Center who had been trying for days to get me to accept one. I had finally relented. But it quickly became clear that this young woman was meant to have the teddy bear, so I gave it to her and said she should consider it as coming from Lauren.

   It seemed a little silly but also appropriate because it probably really WAS from Lauren, in some way, and it was clearly ready to be hugged. And it must have been the right thing to do, because she took it.

2. A picture of our wheaten terrier, Caleigh, with her paws crossed on a pillow, which Lauren had taken, has been added to the family gallery on the wall.

As of this evening, Lauren was doing well, "holding her own," and that's a nice way to go off to sleep.

Love,
Greg & Lauren

Tonight has been difficult for Lauren; she needed more fluids than expected to keep her blood pressure up, she has a touch of pneumonia, and also a blood infection. Her need for fluids had stabilized by the time I left, however, and she is on three different antibiotics.

As I noted yesterday, infection may be the greatest obstacle to a successful recovery from a significant burn injury. In addition to making the patient sick, infection can decrease blood flow to the skin, which can undermine recent skin grafts as well as limit the regrowth of skin at donor sites. For someone with the massive burn injury Lauren suffered, eventual infection is certain. In fact, she has been fortunate not to have shown evidence of a significant infection before this.

Antibiotics are used to fight the infection when it is discovered, and the patient's blood is cultured to identify the specific infectious agent. But antibiotics can't kill anything by themselves; they require the assistance of the patient's own immune system. In the case of a patient with Lauren's level of injury, the immune system may not have much to contribute.

Fortunately, these doctors have many years of experience treating this particular problem. Lauren also benefits from being well along in her treatment course, having had three surgeries in all and having done pretty well after them. Depending on whether she remains stable and the infection can be controlled, she is still due to have her next surgery next Tuesday.

We are at fifteen and a half days and counting.

During the afternoon, there was a tea party in the waiting room. A woman named Claire has been doing these weekly tea parties at Columbia Presbyterian for years, in the pediatric neurology and cardiology wards. She moved the gathering down to the NY-Presbyterian Burn Center temporarily, following the September 11 attacks. She and a group of volunteers bake about fifteen different desserts, then come in with urns of hot water and coffee, trays of tea sandwiches, tablecloths, silverware and china teacups, golden doilies, and stars-and-stripes napkins, and proceed to serve this feast to the family members of patients on the ward.

All the women were wonderful to talk to. One of them had several pictures of her own sister, who had been badly burned in a propane explosion (60 percent, including face and hands), but two years later has returned to running a construction company with her husband, who was also burned, but not as badly, and who goes biking, cross-country skiing, and rock climbing! The pictures and the story were an inspiration.

At sundown, I began my Yom Kippur fast—I have already lost ten pounds since this began, but I think I will lose another few tomorrow—and at pretty much that same moment a gospel choir arrived and sang. A large group of friends of one of the WTC burn patients, who was not as seriously burned, held a brief prayer meeting with him in the waiting room, and then a dozen donuts and a huge tray of chocolate chip cookies appeared. Someone offered me a cookie; I declined, telling him I was fasting, and he said, OK, here, have a donut.

I'm not sure the donut part is in the Bible. (I passed.)

That's really it for today; we continue to admire the way Lauren is hanging in there, and we hope for a better tomorrow.

And I am exhausted, so good night!

Love,
Greg & Lauren

From: Greg
To: Everyone
Date: Friday, September 28, 2001 2:01 AM
Subject: Lauren Update for Sept 27 (Thursday)

Lauren had a good day today, which was very good news following her not so good day on Wednesday.

At that time, as I wrote, she needed more fluids than expected to keep up her blood pressure, and there were signs of infection. Fortunately she rallied, and started to maintain her pressure on a fairly low dose of dopamine, with a normal body temperature. The infection was cultured so they could be sure she was on the correct antibiotic. As of early Thursday evening, she had been stable for most of the day.

I just spoke to her night nurse (I am up very late—more on that in a moment) and her pressure is now a little low, but they are raising her dopamine dose to see if that will improve it.

That's the way it goes all day long—they manage her condition so that she can continue to heal.

This is important; the better she fights the infection, the better her grafts will do, the better her donor sites will heal, and the better the prognosis for her next graft surgery early next week.

I attended Yom Kippur services in the hospital, joined by my friends Mitch and Wendi. The service was in an auditorium on the 11th floor, and was designed for hospital patients and their families. It was a short-duration service, but it brought a taste of the entire liturgy, and I was able to say Lauren's name during the prayer for healing. My record of attending services has not been terrific over my life, but I am glad I did the right thing this time around, with the help of friends.

The walls at the Burn Center are beginning to be covered with huge posters sent by school classes around the country, hundreds of in-dividual greeting cards drawn by elementary-school kids, and a box of individual get-well notes, each of which had a bag of Hershey's Kisses taped to it.

Good Samaritans continue to donate food and other assorted good-ies to the families in the waiting room; today's snacks included brown-ies and granola bars and bottles of Poland Spring water.

I had an enjoyable dinner out to break my fast, and then tonight I played that gig at the Red Lion.

I did that with some trepidation; I was nervous about doing some-thing so frivolous, but everyone told me it was important that I not stop doing things I enjoy, so I decided to play.

We opened with a short version of "You Can't Always Get What You Want," segueing into "Street Fighting Man"; Billy, our band leader, framed these tunes with some choice words regarding the ter-rorist attacks.

Midway through the set I stepped up to the microphone to dedicate a song to Lauren. At first, I couldn't get people to quiet down for my announcement, but they stopped once I mentioned where Lauren was. Briefly, I said that we had all been affected in different ways by the tragedy, as a city but also individually to varying degrees. I said that my wife was in the Burn Center at New York-Presbyterian, fighting for her life as a result of the attacks.

I told everyone that I had searched for a Stones song that would be appropriate to dedicate to her and chose "Wild Horses" but wanted to point out that I was not dedicating certain of the lyrics. First of all, Lauren is not a graceless lady—she is extremely graceful. Secondly, the last line of the song says "Let's do some living after we die"; I told everyone we weren't going to do that, we were going to do some living before we die. That drew some applause.

We played a passionate version of "Wild Horses" and I felt very good about having dedicated it to her.

Other than that, we actually rocked tonight; we had twenty people dancing right in front of us, and everyone was performing—our singer went into the audience, as did our lead guitar player. Everyone in the band was dead-on.

By the end of the set, I was very glad I had played—it felt nice, for an hour or so, to have different, far more trivial concerns, such as remembering the chords and notes to a song. Following the set, a number of people came up to me to give me their best wishes for Lauren's recovery.

Actually, I think the Stones themselves might have been satisfied with the way we played tonight.

Another friend came by the Red Lion this evening, after helping to hold a memorial for his good friend who was missing from my firm, Euro Brokers, in the disaster. The service was held in Stamford, Connecticut. My friend had printed 200 to 300 programs but close to a thousand people showed up. This man had three children; his death, like all the others, was an outrage.

The CEO of my firm, Gil Scharf, came by the hospital today to ask about Lauren and told me how the firm is rebuilding in its temporary space. He also told me stories of some of the employees who were lost, including staffers who helped people down to the lower floors and then, because of the PA announcements stating that the building was secure and appeals on their walkie-talkies from colleagues who were still upstairs and needed help, went back up to our floor (84) and were never seen again. The fact that so many people died while trying to help others makes their deaths doubly tragic.

Howard Lutnick, Lauren's CEO, also stopped by the Burn Center today. It seems more and more as if all the good works in Lauren's life, and the modest good works that I have accomplished, have affected many people who are now visiting the hospital and rooting for her. I appreciate all these visits. They truly mean a lot. I tell her about everyone who writes or comes by. She's the one who is doing all the heavy lifting.

Love,
Greg & Lauren

From: Greg
To: Everyone
Date: Friday, September 28, 2001 9:52 AM
Subject: Followup Message, Sept 27

I apologize for writing last night's update in a state where my faculties were to a good degree on sabbatical. I think I left out a very important piece of news:
Tyler was eleven months old yesterday.
Happy eleven months, Tyler!!!!

Best—
Greg

From: Greg
To: Everyone
Date: Saturday, September 29, 2001 12:40 AM
Subject: Lauren Update for Sept 28 (Friday)

Today was a stable day. Lauren still has the septic infection, which they are fighting with antibiotics, but her lungs are functioning well, as is her stomach, two very important factors. The oxygen and the protein intake she is receiving through a feeding tube are needed to build new tissue and for her skin to heal.

I have a better understanding now of something the doctor told me about doing Lauren's grafts. He said he would "mesh 3-to-1" when doing autografts. Basically, a special machine is used to create a mesh pattern in the donor skin—her own skin—that permits it to cover an area three times as large as the site from which it was taken.

The homograft, or skin-bank skin, is then placed over this mesh, creating a layer that enables the autograft beneath to heal better. The goal is for the mesh to take and for healing to occur in the open spots. More than one graft is often necessary to finish each site.

The grafts already done look good, which means the majority have probably taken. Unfortunately, the infection does have an adverse effect on the healing process, both of the grafts and of the donor sites. That is why Lauren's time in the burn ICU is such a balancing act. Negative factors have to be controlled so that positive factors can win out. The good aspect for Lauren is that she was strong and healthy going in, so she has managed to keep herself mostly stable, a word that has become very important for the families of all the burn patients.

I may have mentioned this before, but the best any of us can say to each other when we first arrive in the morning, search for the other families, and ask about the condition of their sister/husband/ son/daughter/wife, is the one-word answer "stable," followed by a shrug.

Her nurse explained to me tonight how Lauren's various systems were adjusting on their own to maintain stability. For example, her heart was pumping faster to maintain her blood pressure despite a slight dilation of blood vessels due to infection. A glass-half-full type of sign.

I put two pictures, of Lauren and of Lauren, Tyler, and my dad, up on her wall. The pictures are an important way for the nursing staff to make a connection to her. They are all looking forward to meeting her when she is more awake, later in her treatment course.

That alone should tell you how difficult the work is that these nurses do; the patients arrive gravely injured, frequently unable to communicate, and highly critical. The medical and nursing staffs often fight for weeks to keep the patient improving; this is well before they have a chance to encounter the patient's personality. The staff first gets to know the patient through the family visitors, and the photographs help the staff connect with the life they are trying to help the patient return to.

The WTC disaster families have been there for seventeen days now, and we know each other well. We watch one another's bags, and I have a running joke with one family, who always ask me if I have a million dollars in my briefcase. One day I apologized and said, actually, just under a million; I was told that wouldn't be worth stealing. The next day I said I had two million.

This bonding between families is due to the utter stress of the situation; we have all spent days, now weeks, and hopefully will spend months, worrying minute to minute about a loved one's condition. It is the same as if a surgical procedure were to last for weeks on end. We learn to read the facial expressions and voices of doctors and nurses; if new nurses come on the rotation, I have found I need to speak with them for at least fifteen minutes before I feel I have a good gauge of how they assess Lauren's condition. While they are all using the same objective standard, each has a slightly different way of communicating. Eventually, though, it all comes down to how many different ways they define "stable."

So we, the waiting, speak to each other, and to the staff psychologists and chaplain and the Red Cross volunteers who wander through, and we are visited by Good Samaritans of all types who provide food and candy and water and magazines. And in the end, we alone understand what we are going through: we are the loved ones of critically injured patients from a massive tragedy in which most victims either died or walked out under their own power.

We, the waiting, are therefore at somewhat of a disconnect from the world at large, which is pursuing closure (not my favorite word), whether coping with loss of a family member; coming to terms with having one's life saved by something so trivial as arriving late for work; or honoring the heroism of lost firefighters, and police, and managers who made sure their staffs got out of the building first, as well as support staff in many companies who helped coworkers out and were still doing this when the buildings came down.

Most of the world is already viewing the attacks from a distance, but we are pretty much still there at Time Zero, with the outcome unknown.

The bonds we have formed are deep. One of the family groups that were there the first few days were the mother and sister and boyfriend of a woman, "D," who had walked down from the 78th floor of Tower Two (the South Tower) with severe burns. I got to know D's sister "M" pretty well (sorry about the code names!). As I was leaving on the fifth night, one of the attending doctors was gathering D's family in a small waiting room. The next day, they were no longer among the waiting.

I had wanted to find out their names and send a card; but yesterday, almost two weeks later, M came to the waiting room to see us, to talk about how she and her family were coping with losing D, and how D's fourteen-year-old son was taking it. At one point we actually did a group hug, even laughing just a little while we did it. But that didn't hide how hard it was for M, or how difficult the day-to-day remains for the rest of us.

However, we are all making it through, with the help of the huge support networks that have sprung up all around us. Including y'all. I thank everyone again for all your encouraging responses. It really does help us, me and Lauren, to know how many people care.

Love,
Greg & Lauren

From: Greg
To: Everyone
Date: Sunday, September 30, 2001 1:12 AM
Subject: Lauren Update for Sept 29 (Saturday)

Lauren remains stable. Her nurse this evening extended her hand in a flat line to indicate that she had been very stable for the past several days. While she continues to receive antibiotics to manage the continuing infection, she is clocking through the twelve-hour shifts in intrepid style.

She remains sedated, though when I spoke to her today, I could see her eyes moving under her eyelids in a way similar to REM sleep, so I think she was hearing me. I made sure to tell her that Tyler loves her very much.

The music of choice today was a Bach CD featuring Dirk Freymuth, a name that sounds as if it had to have been thought up by Douglas Adams for *Hitchhiker's Guide to the Galaxy*. The music, however, is very good (well, of course Bach is good), by which I mean consistent in modulation; no selections are jarringly different from the others on the CD, so the listening experience is soothing.

Given that I am in charge of the music, the Bach CD is in a rotation with Dwight Yoakam, Eric Clapton, Sting, Willie Nelson, and Patsy Cline. I know, you're thinking that this will speed her recovery by provoking Lauren to get out of bed tomorrow and smack me. On some level, though, I think I know what I'm doing.

The calendar told me that this was a Saturday, but the days have really begun to blend together; there is little variation from one to the next, and they are all pretty much lousy.

But as I noted to one of the other families as I was leaving the hospital tonight, what we need are more lousy days like these—lots more.

I talked about bonding with other patients' families yesterday. Each of the patients is highly critical, so the news from hour to hour for any one of them can vary pretty sharply. Any deviation from stable (followed by a shrug) causes your mood to drop, while any return to stable from a serious problem can trigger elation. Each patient is fighting a very different and very private war against any number of potential dangers. A patient with a smaller burn area but a more severe lung injury may have far less need for grafts but is far more vulnerable to lung infections or a collapsed lung. Lauren is fortunate that while her burn is very severe, her lungs are permitting her to oxygenate her blood and so promote healing. Another patient struggles with a very severe burn, 90 percent, and has yet to be taken to surgery.

The relative need for a hug passes from family to family based on the most recent status report, and the status during any twelve-hour period can often be determined just from reading the faces and the body language of each patient's family. We all struggle to give each other reassurance, but we are all vulnerable to a sustained feeling of helplessness very similar to the feelings of most of the world as they watched the towers fall on September 11. We know the outcomes we want, but all we can do is watch, wait, and hope for the best.

Today I spent most of the day with Tyler. I am helping him to learn to walk holding only one of my hands (actually, I am continuing Joyce's work on this project). Today I had his right hand in my left, and as he stood next to me, I took a single step and he imitated me, and then I took another with the other foot and he followed me again. We took a number of steps in this manner—first my foot, then his much smaller one, almost in a rhythm. I am aware of the high sugar content of this story, but it was very cute if you were there.

Thanks again, everyone, for all your prayers and support.

Love,
Greg & Lauren

From: Greg
To: Everyone
Date: Tuesday, October 2, 2001 1:12 AM
Subject: Lauren Update for Oct 1 (Monday)

This was a good day. Filled with some emotional and some extraordinary experiences, but for Lauren, an encouraging twenty-four hours.

Regarding her grafts, as I have noted, when she receives an autograft, her own skin, there is a layer of skin-bank skin placed on top of that to promote healing. Until the skin-bank skin sloughs off, they do not know the status of the autografts. In Lauren's case, the skin-bank skin was coming off possibly a little early, so the nurses were not positive on the status of the autografts. Hence my mood yesterday.

It turns out that 80 to 90 percent of the autografts have adhered. Within the context of what remains a highly critical situation, that is truly excellent news. She is maintaining her blood pressure without support, she is oxygenating well, and her other major organ systems are also functioning. She is able to absorb sufficient nutrition to promote healing and the growth of new tissue. This is a very important factor and explains the encouraging news regarding the autografts. She is no longer receiving any paralytic agents, and she is being weaned off some other medications. For someone in her situation, while she remains at high risk, she has a number of factors pointing ever so slightly in her favor.

In her second surgery her buttocks were grafted with artificial skin; these did not take. And the 10 to 20 percent of autografts that did not take will have to be redone. Also, certain areas that were not touched in her three previous surgeries have not healed on their own, so they will have to be addressed.

Lauren's next surgery is scheduled for Wednesday. At that time the doctor will also take another look at her hands, which have so far not been touched. This is a good thing; she has strong pulses to her hands, and the longer she has a chance to heal on her own, the better her prognosis in that area.

Today was also the day of the Cantor Fitzgerald firm-wide memorial. Cantor Fitzgerald lost 658 employees, and a total of 698 people, including workmen, visitors, and contract employees, died on the Cantor floors. The service was held in Central Park and it drew thousands, all somber. People I had not seen in years, people who left Cantor years ago, streamed in. A woman who worked for me years ago, and had been based at Cantor Fitzgerald's corporate bond desk when she reported to me, saw me and hugged me, crying, and I realized she had not known until then that I was OK. She also did not know that Lauren and I were married, had an eleven-month-old, or that Lauren was in the hospital from this dastardly attack. She will be praying for Lauren, but I should add one other detail.

This same woman had attended an event some years earlier at which both Lauren and I were present. That very night, this woman said she thought we were an item. This was news to me, since absolutely nothing had happened yet between us. But then something did, so yesterday I told her that she had called it all those years ago. Her response: she wasn't surprised; she has always been intuitive. This was a brief moment of levity in what was a solemn afternoon.

Many, many people came up to me and asked about Lauren, including many I had never met but who worked with her or had an office near hers. And one person said, "Lauren is our hope."

There was a wall of remembrance at the entrance, where photographs and collage memorials of the missing were posted; note cards were provided so that people could post their own reminiscences beside the picture of someone they loved. The wall was very moving; there were many photographs, and loving notes, but it did not bespeak the desperation of searching families the way a similar wall of "missing" posters had done at the Plaza Hotel crisis center that Cantor had set up just a couple of weeks earlier. To me, this meant that the business of the day was not to memorialize specific individuals, but to come to terms with and accept the collective loss while paying a fitting tribute.

Thousands of seats were arranged in rows beneath a huge tent; on each of the seats was a teddy bear, with the name of the schoolchild who had sent it. Those who spoke were on a raised, covered stage, with a podium diagonally to their left. Behind them were the Harlem Boys Choir and their accompanists, and draped across the very back of the stage was a huge American flag.

Mayor Giuliani spoke movingly; he eulogized Cantor's employees as everyday heroes who made a key aspect of the economy, the bond market, function as a result of their hard work. And he said a very simple thing: "We're right, and they're wrong." Meaning that our society is about freedom, the exchange of ideas, the rule of law, and respect for human life; and that the terrorists are against those things. He spoke of his admiration for the way Cantor had staggered back onto its feet in two days, and the example this was for all Americans.

He received a number of ovations, but none bigger than when he arrived and when he finished speaking. It was very clear that he has risen to be a figure of global prominence because of his leadership in the wake of the disaster; he has also become a father figure to the injured of his city, and through his physical presence alone has helped soothe the pain of thousands of us in mourning. His resolute voice, and his unambiguous pride in the city and its people, gave all our spirits a lift.

Three wives and one husband of lost employees spoke; each gave a moving eulogy of their lost spouse, and the lives they had lived. Two priests and a rabbi led us in prayers and gave brief remarks.

Howard Lutnick spoke of how proud he was of the people who had been lost, and also of the people who survived. Of the unimaginable pain and sorrow that had been experienced, but also of the hope that had risen from it almost immediately, and of how he felt that the firm had bonded almost into a single entity, a "family of one." He said that gave him faith that the firm could face the future well, functioning as a business while continuing to help the families of those who had died. He spoke of how after the tragedy new widows had called to make HIM feel better, and that he found this utterly beyond his experience of human behavior.

The choir sang all the songs of the moment, and beautifully: "God Bless America," "We Shall Overcome," and "The Battle Hymn of the Republic." In two other songs, "America the Beautiful" and "Amazing Grace," they were led by Judy Collins, whose voice remains clear and haunting.

And then it was over and I walked to the hospital, knowing that Lauren had been stable earlier but still hoping to speak to her doctor to allay my fears from the previous night. Once I had that conversation, I learned of something else that was happening that evening: the Emir of Qatar would be visiting the Burn Center to show his support. The Weill-Cornell Medical College is building the Weill Medical College of Qatar in Qatar, so the head of state was coming to pay his respects to the victims of a terrible tragedy.

I was in Lauren's room when the entourage came through, their passage highlighted by repeated flashes of cameras and flanked by a large security detail. I was seated on a swivel chair at Lauren's side, facing the hallway; this is the perch from which I read and speak to her. And then the Emir was passing the room, and Lauren's doctor gestured toward us and the Emir looked at Lauren and at me and dipped his head. I nodded at him, and he nodded at me, and they moved on.

A full day and a good day, and most of all for Lauren. And that may be because the prayers being uttered on her behalf had a significant boost, according to this e-mail from my mother:

"By the way, I don't know if you were informed of this, but ___ told me that her niece lives in Ireland six months of the year and in the U.S. the other half. When she heard of Lauren's misfortune [her niece] called her priest in Ireland and asked that a prayer be made for Lauren from her church over there. The priest was so touched by the request that he telephoned every priest in Ireland and asked that prayers be dedicated to Lauren Manning this day, so congregants in churches all over Ireland dedicated their prayers to ask God to protect and keep Lauren Manning. I thought it was a magnificent gesture. I hope it helped."

I think it did.

Best to all,

Love,
Greg & Lauren

From: Greg
To: Everyone
Date: Wednesday, October 3, 2001 1:15 AM
Subject: Lauren Update for Oct 2 (Tuesday) (plus Greg's visit to a special site)

Lauren continues to hang in there; another stable day. She is still scheduled for her next operation tomorrow at just after noon. In addition to several new grafts, she will also receive a tracheostomy, where the breathing tube is placed through the upper chest. After about three weeks, breathing tubes that run through the mouth, as hers does now, can begin to cause serious problems.

They are also backing off a bit more on Lauren's sedation; she is still not very aware of her surroundings and her eyes are still closed, but she has the ability to try to lift her arms, and I felt her doing that with her right arm today. This is better for her, as it gives her a chance to move, though very slightly, and helps her lungs. It is a very tiny step in the direction they want to take her.

Today I retrieved a book of Mark Twain's humorous sketches, which our friends Milena and Frank had left for me with their doorman. I was finally able to read Lauren some amusing material, and started with "Punch, Brothers, Punch," an essay I'm sure none of you have ever heard of but which is very funny.

Lauren also received several new cards and prayers from her friend Leslie. We had a number of visitors in the waiting room, including Lauren's friend Harvey, whom I had never met. Harvey's son interned for Lauren this past summer.

Earlier this morning, before I left for the hospital, I took a look at Tyler and could not believe how cute he has become. He is so expressive, so active, and when he is happy, he has this extra-powerful smile where he ratchets up the happiness quotient to an almost intolerably adorable level. He is completely uninterested in crawling—he wants to stand, he wants to cruise around, he wants to get into the kitchen cabinets and the stereo cabinets, and he has reminded me that before all this nastiness went down, Lauren and I were ready to begin baby-proofing our apartment.

As the Rolling Stones song says, "Time Waits for No One." Certainly, Tyler is not waiting. I watch him develop and I want him to have his mother again as soon as possible. It is a blessing in one way that he is so young, but I also wish that Lauren could be sharing in these days. So we are trying to videotape him and to record this period so that she won't really miss it. (I should say that I would not have been organized enough to get any of this together; her family charged up the camcorder and a neighbor bought tapes; I just took the video once I was spoon-fed the supplies.)

Most of my morning was spent running an important errand that I did not want to wait too long before doing. If you find the description ponderous or depressing, just skip it!

I visited Ground Zero today, a visit arranged by a new contact, Lucie Ferell, a nurse from Minnesota who is with the American Red Cross. Over the past week, she has spent considerable time at the hospital coordinating Red Cross assistance with the various patient families. She has pointed out that this disaster is larger than anything the organization has experienced, and notes that we are all—patients, families, health care workers, and volunteers—writing the rules as we go: how to deal with individual loss and collective loss, and how to cope with the daily and long-term struggles that so many of us are facing.

As a senior Red Cross volunteer, she is entitled to an ID with a green stripe, granting full, unrestricted access to Ground Zero. This permits her to escort family members of the September 11 tragedy to the site. She arranged for me to see the site today. I invited my friend Mitch to accompany us.

The three of us rode to the World Trade Center in his car, retracing Lauren's and my typical daily commute: down Washington Street to Houston Street, right one block on Houston, then left down West Street to the Trade Center. Before the attacks this was a $4.70 cab ride, taking about five minutes; the distance was roughly one and a half miles.

Lauren would typically make the U-turn just past Vesey Street and pull into the turnaround for 1 World Trade, entering through the West Street revolving doors. That is what she did on September 11, suffering her injuries just inside the lobby of 1 World Trade (the North Tower).

I would ride my cab half a block farther, making a U-turn at Liberty Street by the Marriott World Trade Center, getting out at the corner, and then walking another half block to the entrance to 2 World Trade (the South Tower).

This morning, the first checkpoint heading south was at Canal Street. Lucie showed her green-stripe ID; we had to show a photo ID such as a driver's license, and proof of employment (in my case, my Port Authority World Trade Center ID). We were waved through, down a single southbound lane on the northbound side of West Street that was lined by orange traffic cones.

We passed three more checkpoints on the way south, each with successively more police (the final checkpoint had six), finally reaching the block north of Vesey Street. The last two southbound blocks on West Street were completely wetted down on both the northbound and southbound sides. We pulled over, climbed out of the car, and crossed Vesey Street to enter Ground Zero.

It was hard to believe that both towers were simply gone, that the streets themselves were gone, but it was all real. Mitch noted that the scene reminded him of nothing more than a post-apocalyptic movie, with the set built on an impossibly large scale.

I waited for emotion to sweep over me, but I was numb. Mostly, I served as tour guide, giving a detailed description of what had stood where, and where Lauren and I had gotten out of cabs, gone into the buildings, and gathered to go home at day's end. I realize now that while I had been visualizing the catastrophic destruction in my imagination, I still saw the buildings and the plazas as intact. That is no longer true.

Instead, there are rolling hills of rubble. The World Trade Center Plaza is a sea of debris. In the center you can still see the metal globe sculpture that formed the plaza's centerpiece; it has been badly dented. Heavy machinery was in action throughout the site. Firemen were gathered in several locations, as were demolition workers. Two K-9 officers passed, their rescue dogs on leashes.

At the World Financial Center, a corner of the American Express Building has been scraped off like the side of a cardboard box, and still has a piece of the Trade Center hanging from it. Smashed windows showing the impact zone extend in an inverted parabola up thirty or forty stories.

The surrounding buildings along the perimeter of what had been the Trade Center complex are charred on their faces like the sides of a fireplace where the flames have gotten out of control.

It was hard to tell where the sidewalks and bridges had been, since almost no original features remained. The pedestrian bridge from the World Trade Center to the World Financial Center atrium was completely gone, had already been cleared, except for its central concrete support. The entrance to the atrium was completely caved in.

And of course the towers were gone. The sun was shining on us from the east at 10 in the morning; buildings I used to look *over* to watch the ferries ply the Hudson now towered more than fifty stories above our heads.

Where there had been a modern urban landscape of giant office buildings and a newly paved boulevard flanked by nearly finished pedestrian and bicycle paths and freshly planted lawns on September 10, there was now a series of hillocks resembling a scrap-metal strip mine. The ground smoked from subterranean fires like smoke fields near an active volcano. Huge sections of the street were caved in. Steel framing hung down like pieces of rusted tinsel, from both the partially destroyed skeleton of the lower World Trade Center buildings and the collapsed sections of the street.

Seventy-foot-tall remnants of three side walls of 1 World Trade Center, blackened by flames and bent sideways by implosion, framed a pile of pulverized rubble that rose forty or fifty feet above grade. And this rubble pile fills underground shopping concourses, parking garages, and subway and PATH tunnels extending another seventy to eighty feet below grade. Structural beams poked from the debris pile, beams of steel and concrete more than twelve inches on a side. Other beams were twisted like matchsticks into U shapes.

The lobby windows of both towers had probably been fifty feet high. The steel framing of these windows is still there, creating an illusion of scale that makes the full-sized material handlers, with their eighty-foot-long jointed booms and hydraulic grabbing shovels, resemble Tonka trucks, toys rolled onto a dirt pile and scratching at its surface.

Huge flatbeds and double-length dump trucks wait in line to be loaded and dispatched. The material handlers seem to be making scarcely a dent in the debris, but nevertheless fill up one of these double-length trucks in about ten minutes. As each truck leaves, the next one backs in to take its place, and the crane crabs sideways on its treads and resumes loading. Towering over this scene are giant cranes with boom arms that rise thirty stories above us.

Lucie asked about obtaining hard hats, and soon after a Bronx fireman drove us on a cart around the outer perimeter, south along West Street, up Pine Street, and to the firehouse at the corner of Liberty and Greenwich. He went inside and brought out three white hard hats. We put them on and crossed to a row of sawhorse police lines forty feet from the wreckage of Tower Two. My office had been on the 84th floor.

I say crossed but there was no hint of a street. The pedestrian bridge from 2 World Trade to the Bankers Trust building had collapsed. I lost my bearings for a moment then, until I realized that the southernmost hundred feet of 3 World Trade were also gone. The surrounding buildings looked firebombed, with smashed windows and bent facades. The Millenium Hotel and several other buildings were draped in red construction mesh like a Christo wrapping gone horribly wrong.

A sinkhole thirty feet deep lay open in front of us. The main entrance of the building where smokers and tourists used to gather was an unrecognizable maze of collapsed supporting beams. Again, the steel framing of the lobby walls and the first few stories surrounded a mound of pulverized rubble.

More than fifty of my coworkers lay in that burial mound, and of course thousands of others. Mitch and I said Kaddish for them, then walked down what had been the south side of Liberty Street, past the shattered remains of the hotel and the Tall Ships Bar at the corner. The parking lot that had taken up the block south of Liberty is now a debris field; it was impossible to tell where the church had stood.

At the intersection of Liberty and West Streets we walked between huge cranes and past the remains of the entrance to the Marriott World Trade Center hotel, eventually returning to the front of the 1 World Trade Center wreckage. At that point I looked straight up and tried to imagine the tower that had risen more than fifteen hundred feet from this spot. All was clear blue sky.

We said Kaddish for the Cantor Fitzgerald employees who had perished there.

I then squatted down at the place where Lauren almost certainly was injured and then rescued, placed my palm on the ground, and said a prayer for her and another burn patient who had been standing close by, waiting for an airport bus, when the plane hit.

We stood there for a long while, then walked north on the west side of West Street, past fire and police department office trailers, and began our return to the world where buildings still stand and roads still exist. Back in Mitch's car, we passed though police cordons, and several blocks north of the site two men took high-pressure sprayers and cleaned the dust and ash off the car.

As we left the last checkpoint and headed uptown, one of the cops said, "There's no traffic."

Love,
Greg & Lauren

From: Greg
To: Everyone
Date: Thursday, October 4, 2001 2:14 AM
Subject: Lauren Update for Oct 3 (Wednesday)

Lauren's surgery went well. She did not go down until 4:30 PM, but the operation was done by 7:45 and I was able to see her back in her room, in bed for the night, at 9. She received grafts to the fronts of her feet, the side of her abdomen, and an area of her buttocks. These were all homografts, using skin from a skin bank. Her donor sites will not be ready to be reharvested until early next week.

As I've mentioned before, the homografts can adhere and grow, but will typically be rejected within two to three months. They are therefore a temporary measure but can be a critical one. They permit the doctors to excise damaged tissue and replace it with healthy tissue, giving the body a chance to heal on its own and provide a better foundation for the eventual autografts with the patient's own skin. In five days, the doctors will take down the surgical dressings and examine whether these new homograft sites have "taken," another simple word with a very significant meaning in the current context, similar to the impact of "stable" (said with a shrug).

I spent a long time at the hospital today, but one of the first things I did was check the status of the other very critical patient who had major surgery yesterday, and who faces a very difficult prognosis. It was good to learn that she was holding her own, proving that like Lauren, she is a fighter.

Before Lauren was taken down to surgery, she actually was able to just open her eyelids. When I saw this, I tried to think of all the things I had told her in recent weeks, during the time she has been heavily sedated, when I couldn't even be certain she could hear my voice, let alone understand or process the information. I tried to list those things again as completely as possible. The result, I think, is that I managed to agitate Lauren enough to elevate her blood pressure. But I was pleased that I managed to make very brief eye contact with her for the first time since September 11.

I have remarked how the nurses on the ward are rooting for the patients who came in from the Trade Center disaster and how determined the doctors are to save them, not because they are any more special or important than any other burn patient, but because they were all victims of a deliberate act. In fact, this attitude took root before the patients even arrived. The Burn Center implemented their disaster plan within a short time after the plane crashes, and the most appropriate metaphor is a military one. On September 11, the Burn Center received a wave of battlefield casualties, an extraordinary concentration of critically injured patients that taxed their resources to the utmost. In normal circumstances they may receive one, maybe two critical burn patients at once, but never fifteen.

The center began by freeing up all but one of the critical ICU beds.

They were able to do this because the eastern half of the wing is designed to be converted from what is called step-down care to intensive care in just such an emergency. One patient, a young boy, was too critical to move, but I believe about fourteen beds were freed up. One nurse told me that they then scavenged the hospital for spare supplies, including IV tubes, IV liquids, and presumably bandages and other items that would be needed in great quantities.

They were able to prepare the Burn Center for an onslaught of patients within two hours. But their work was really only just beginning.

All burn patients require triple-redundant 24/7 monitoring of all their vital organs, including heart, lungs, and kidneys. Two computer screens above each bed give constant readouts of heart rate, blood pressure, blood-oxygen, and ventilator settings, including lung pressures, flow rates, and type of breath (mandatory, spontaneous, assisted).

Electronic Baxter pumps, each with a small display screen and several horizontal slots for IV tubes to be fitted through, track the flow of all IV fluids and medications, including sedatives, analgesics, and liquid food, each with a different rate of administration. Blood work is done at least twice each shift, or more often if the nurse believes it is necessary (called "per RN").

Some patients, including Lauren, have air beds that can be inflated or deflated in different sections at the push of a button, so that the patient can be turned from side to side with little effort. These air beds can also give percussive shocks to the patient, which helps prevent fluid buildup in the lungs.

Any one of these devices—ventilator, heart rate monitor, feeders, even the air bed—can set off an alarm at any time, which the nurse needs to assess and respond to.

On top of this, twice a day most patients receive burn care, cleaning and redressing of their injury sites, and a visit from physical and occupational therapists, who exercise their limbs and position their bodies to ensure that they have the best chance to recover some, or all, of their functional capabilities.

To assist with this incredible workload, as I have written previously, FEMA deployed burn nurses from around the country, including Minnesota, Massachusetts, Florida, and Alabama. Each of these deployed nurses spent a shift with one of the regular staff nurses, then took on his or her own individual patients following this training. It is a tribute to the hospital's, and the country's, disaster planning that when the time came to mobilize, the nurses were ready.

The doctors also faced difficult challenges, having to create treatment plans for all these new patients and then find the time to perform the sheer number of necessary procedures. Normally, the burn unit runs one OR a day, with each of the attending surgeons operating on a different day. But for the past three weeks, until today, I believe, the Burn Center was running two ORs and all the surgeons were operating every day, each on two to three different patients per day. Doctors from other medical services within the hospital were also rotated in.

News organizations are beginning to understand that the story of the injured survivors is really being fought here.

As of the wee hours this morning, Lauren remains "rock stable." Which could be a great name for a rock-and-roll band.

Best to all.

Love,
Greg & Lauren

From: Greg
To: Everyone
Date: Thursday, October 4, 2001 11:57 PM
Subject: Lauren Update for Oct 4 (Thursday)

Lauren held stable today, with a slightly lower blood pressure but otherwise steady as she goes (literally). Her face had been relatively swollen during the past week and a half, after a brief respite where the swelling had gone down. The renewed swelling was caused by a septic infection, typical for burn patients, and also from saline solution injected under her scalp so that it could serve as a donor site. (The scalp is a good choice cosmetically because her hair, which is not harmed by the harvesting, grows back to cover any residual markings. The skin is harvested above the hair follicles so growth is not affected.)

Today the physical therapists sat her up in her bed as part of their daily repositioning regimen, and having her head raised helped reduce the swelling. Also, her face shows excellent signs of healing well on its own; as one of the nurses said the other day, "That face is PINK," meaning that it is recovering nicely. As I may have pointed out in a previous e-mail, the face can look the worst but it often recovers the best, and in Lauren's case, her face looked surprisingly good when I saw her in St. Vincent's on September 11, and the recovery has been very encouraging.

This means she looks more like herself—her features are more defined, and the rest of her, swathed in sheets, looks as though she had a really aggressive tuck-in when she went to bed. There were fewer bandages on her face, and one of the nurses encouraged me to stroke her forehead, saying he believed in the positive energy of touch. He gave me sterile gloves, and I very, very gently caressed her as I spoke to her.

A number of you have e-mailed me about the NPR report about the Burn Center that aired on "All Things Considered" yesterday. Today, someone e-mailed me a link so I could hear the report; it lasted about eight minutes, and was very well done. A number of you also asked whether the female patient being discussed was Lauren. It was—the percentage burn cited—82.5—the location of the grafts, and the status of the grafts all matched exactly.

Patient families are not allowed into the tank room—and we're always asked to step out when procedures are performed at the patient's bedside—but the correspondent clearly was there when they took Lauren in, and what she described was the way they often treat Lauren. While she is essentially in an induced coma, there is still some awareness, and the nurses make sure to tell her what they are doing as they do it: "Lauren, I'm going to touch your ear for a moment to take your temperature" or "Lauren, I'm going to raise your arm for a moment, sweetheart." So I heard, via NPR, the nurses talking to Lauren while they cleansed her wounds.

I could have done without hearing her doctor give the discouragingly low quantitative assessment of the survival rate for burns of her severity. (It is exactly what I thought: 100 minus the percentage burn, so I had already anticipated a similar figure.) But I realized that I had been sitting in the swivel chair, listening to music with Lauren, as that very part of the interview was conducted at the nurses' station right outside her room! One of the reporter's assistants was even looking into the room, at Lauren, during the conversation; I had no idea that he was doing this as the doctor was discussing her case.

Regarding that quantitative assessment, I console myself by thinking that Lauren faced those odds the moment she came through the door on September 11, but since then she has accumulated more positives than negatives on her side of the survival ledger. She continues to do everything she has to do to pull through, and, if she has a good result from her most recent surgery (specifically if her grafts "take" and start to grow), it is possible that she could actually turn a corner. This wouldn't mean that she was out of the woods, but it might mean that she had at least found the path, and it would mean that the chances of survival had risen.

That hasn't happened yet; all she is doing now is being unbelievably strong, or as I told her two nurses today (one male, one female), Lauren is one tough hombre.

Another person featured during the NPR report was a stock trader who had been discharged from the hospital within the past few days, after coming in on September 11 with a 34 percent burn. (He also appeared on "Good Morning America" and in a number of newspapers.) He was back at the unit today, walking down the hall, and I spoke to him. I told him I was glad that he was OK and I congratulated him for already being discharged. He said he too was glad to be out, but he almost wanted to come back because at the hospital they had taken such good care of him. As he said this, his arms were still swathed in webbed bandages, and the burn could be seen on his face and hands. He was back today to be measured for the pressure garments he will wear for some time to help control scarring as he continues to heal.

I told him that I had once been debilitated from a medical procedure; you notice that the rest of the world is healthy, and it takes a lot more effort to keep up with the everyday than you ever realized. I also said that my illness had been a hangnail compared to a severe burn (though it was serious enough), but I told him that even if he found himself discouraged, he had to have the faith that he would make it all the way back.

He gave me his best wishes for Lauren; we discussed her briefly, and I sent regards to his cousin, with whom I'd had some lengthy conversations in the waiting room. She is a Muslim woman from Pakistan, and she had spent a long time explaining to me her perspective on the attacks beyond her revulsion at their sheer barbarity; namely, that they were a complete violation of the teachings of her religion. Nevertheless, the presence, and street-level power, of extremists in her native country are very real, as is the presence of Afghani refugees; those people who favor liberal change in that society, or oppose its more extreme teachings, face daunting problems and must cope daily with very real menace from fanatics.

Some more good news—the woman with the 90 percent burn, the woman who was facing a very difficult prognosis, has surprised the doctors and held stable since what was a very risky operation Tuesday. She is scheduled for another operation tomorrow, midmorning. Her name is Jennieann—I've mentioned her before, and if you can, throw in a prayer for her.

My friend Dan stopped by the hospital today, bringing two CDs, one Enya and one Sinatra with Jobim, for Lauren's CD collection. That collection has become a fringe benefit for Lauren's nurses; they find the CDs they like and spin them throughout the day and night. The music spans classical, country, blues, pop, and jazz, but—believe it or not—no rock and roll, unless you count Stevie Ray or Sting.

Dan also brought a book of selected poems by e. e. cummings, and at my request turned down the corners of pages for about twenty of his favorite poems in the collection. Over Bach, I read every one of the flagged poems to Lauren, and I could again see her eyes doing their REM flutter. She's in there.

Love,
Greg & Lauren

From: Greg
To: Everyone
Date: Saturday, October 6, 2001 1:23 AM
Subject: Lauren Update for Oct 5 (Friday)

I will have to write later—I am too tired to finish tonight.

My apologies,
Greg

Lauren remains "rock stable," according to her day nurse. She had her eyes open a few times today; when I was reading to her I sensed that she reacted to my voice, and I think she certainly reacted when I told her that I had been high-fiving Tyler. (She also had her eyes open several times during the day while her parents were in with her.)

Brief digression: Lauren taught him to high-five when he was very young, maybe six months old, but he did it tentatively, hesitating, as if wondering if he was doing the right thing throughout the entire sequence. He would also pick and choose when to do it. However, something must have stuck, because today I put my hand in front of his and said "High-five!" and he gave me one. He then laughed his little half giggle—just saying ha, and then a second later, ha again—and did it about ten times in a row. I could see that he was really proud of figuring this one out, so I kept doing it back. Then, when I held up both hands and said "Double high-five," he slapped both hands. This was probably the first clear communication I've had with him where it seemed he understood the words I was saying.

These developing social skills will be valuable to him, as he is proving quite popular—he has been invited to several birthday parties during the month of October, and will have his own on the 27th!

Lauren is two days post-op from her most recent surgery, so she did not have as much planned for her schedule Friday. The biggest event was the arrival of new arm splints, which have her arms raised in a steeper angle above her bed.

In a way that I, as a healthy person, would never have imagined, your overall flexibility is actually determined not just by your muscle extension (keep up those stretching exercises!) but by how you have grown into your skin and how it has grown around you. This happens over a lifetime; your skin accommodates your movement—it's you, and its shape is the result of every movement you've made your entire life to get to this moment.

Critically ill burn patients have suffered severe damage to their skin. During the initial stages of their treatment, they spend a long amount of time on their back, and during that time, because of the sedation, they really do not move much on their own. Yet this is the time that the vast majority of their skin is healing. If a patient's body were left unsupported, the skin would heal into the position you or I would assume if we lay on a bed on our backs (you can try this at home to see what I mean). This has the potential to significantly affect locomotion and posture.

Thankfully, this is a widely known aspect of burn recovery, and making sure that the patient is healing in the correct position is the responsibility of the staff occupational and physical therapists, who not only exercise Lauren but also fabricate the splints that she requires to support herself in what they describe as a "functional position." The therapists start their work almost immediately after the patient arrives at the Burn Center, even for the most critical patients. In fact, it may be most important for those who are most critical.

Since she arrived at the Burn Center, Lauren has had day splints and night splints that support her arms and ankles and hands in the correct posture to ensure that she will be able to regain a normal range of motion. In fact, the instructions for taking these splints on and off morning and night are posted in large Magic Marker on the wall of her room.

The physical therapists also come in at least once a day to exercise her limbs through an appropriate range of movement, including sitting up, reaching with her arms, and raising her legs. By appropriate, I mean that they use a limited range at this point, and will gradually increase the range by tiny steps as the patient can tolerate it.

Earlier this week, I had a very long discussion with an occupational and a physical therapist. The OT was a woman who is the senior OT for the unit; the PT, a man, barely spoke—when we parted I said, nice talking to you, though you didn't do much talking; he smiled very broadly and pointed out he was a good listener.

Like so many of the staff on the unit, this woman spoke with determination and animation. She talked about how impressed she is already by Lauren's strength. She noted that Lauren had actually resisted the movements a couple of times. She said that that was unsurprising since they were painful, but through the resistance she could feel Lauren's physical strength, and felt that this would be a tremendous asset during her future rehabilitation.

The occupational therapist also talked about a debilitating illness she herself had had as a young person, and how she had dedicated herself to her own therapy and rehabilitation to overcome the physical restrictions it imposed. Clearly, that led her to a passion for occupational therapy as a career. And she explained that this is why she loves all these patients—she kept referring to the WTC patients as "these patients" and then adding, "and all the patients on the ward"—she loves to help them; she understands how discouraged they feel when they lose faith that they can get back to normal, but that it is her job to get them there.

I told her that I always felt reassured because the staffers at the Burn Center were so dedicated, and that her attitude and commitment would be invaluable to Lauren when her spirits flagged.

After a while the two therapists had to move on to help other patients, but then both of them came back to the waiting room to finish the conversation with me!

It is that level of passion—the nurses do the same thing, connecting with the caregivers as strongly as with the patients, in fact using the connection they form with the families of the critically ill patients to create an early connection to the patient themselves—that lets me relax when I am home, late at night, thinking of Lauren in her hospital bed, and knowing that she is being aggressively, and conscientiously, cared for.

Love, and thanks again for all the prayers!!!
Greg & Lauren

From: Greg
To: Everyone
Date: Sunday, October 7, 2001 2:12 AM
Subject: Lauren Update for Oct 6 (Saturday)

(Please accept in advance my apology for the length of the novella you are about to read.)

Lauren remains rock stable, so we are grateful. In fact, her heart rate has slowed down somewhat from the hypermetabolic levels it has maintained for most of the last twenty-five days (today, for the first time that I saw, it dipped below 100). Her blood pressure hovered over 100, her pulse oxygen was at 100; everything where it needed to be.

When I spoke to her nurse by phone this morning, Lauren was being a little more responsive, opening her eyes and moving very slightly. Later in the afternoon she took another trip to the tank room, a two-hour procedure; so for that they increased her sedation and her pain medication. By the time I showed up late tonight, at 9, she was no longer opening her eyes, though I did see them moving beneath her lids.

I sat in the swivel chair and looked at Lauren. (The nurses use this same chair to type her chart information straight into their workstations. It is usually set at the height of a barstool, since the workstation is on a raised table, and this permits me to be at the same level as Lauren's hospital bed.) I realized that she has not spoken for almost four weeks, since that first morning at St. Vincent's. Time has begun to add up, and while I am still there every day, as are Lauren's mom and dad (and her sister on weekends), she has not been truly around for almost a month.

Her body is there, but not her voice. Her injuries sent her on a journey far away; we have been trying to get her back, and she has been struggling to come back, ever since. I am looking very much forward to her fond return.

I can work very hard to help with her recovery during this stage, but I still have no idea of how she will approach it (other than with determination), or what any of her thoughts will be. It occurred to me that while this is all really her story, she doesn't know it and couldn't tell it. She may be able to tell the inner facts, certain impressions, someday, but will almost certainly remember nearly nothing of this period. Which is fine.

But when I see her lips move, or her eyelids, or her arm slightly, I know she is feeling something. She's still the same consciousness that she was. I'm impatient to hear about things from her side.

Lauren's nurse this evening is a man in his mid-thirties who has an interesting history—he enrolled in the seminary, seeking to become a priest, then became a fashion designer, then an EMT, and took that road to becoming a critical care nurse.

He observed that the entire experience since September 11 has been surreal. For him it was especially so—he was the nurse with the young boy who was too ill to be moved from the burn ICU on the day of the attacks, so he stayed with his patient and could only watch as the disaster plan was implemented, or, as he put it, "All hell was breaking loose out here," a statement that, in this case, can be taken absolutely literally.

He said, not with gloom but objectively, that the period since September 11 has changed everyone on staff at the Burn Center, just as it has changed the lives of the patients and their families. He noted that when he gets tired, he can go home and sleep, while the patient he is treating must struggle 24/7. But there is no doubt that the entire staff is working under more intense conditions than they could ever have imagined they would encounter in a major urban teaching hospital. (One of Lauren's nurses from the Midwest, part of those mobilized under the FEMA disaster plan, said she was told "Come, on, you'll never be deployed" by someone trying to coax her into applying for the FEMA position. And until September 11, that was probably a valid statement.) As will the patients' families, the staff will remember being challenged by these times like no others in their lives.

As the nurse spoke, he told me something that explained why the previous night I'd considered him somewhat standoffish.

As part of more general comments on burn patient management, he explained that when I had entered Lauren's room the night before, he was working with a doctor to recalibrate her ventilator settings to permit her to blow out more carbon dioxide. While I was showing him how to operate Lauren's CD player and asking what type of music he liked, he was in the middle of important actions to keep Lauren stable. As I was trying to make sure he maintained the right atmosphere in the room, he was actively working to maintain the proper atmosphere in her lungs! And I hadn't a clue.

Tonight, I talked about how well Lauren's face appears to be healing, and since he hadn't heard it before, told him the story of the morning of September 11, the phone call that told me Lauren was in an ambulance, the things she and I said to each other at St. Vincent's. It dawned on me that she probably could not drop and roll immediately when she ran from the lobby (a question that has nagged me), because she had to keep running some distance through the flames that came down the outside of Tower One. Which means she may have been even braver, and tougher, than I had thought. We may never know the details, but that is probably a fair assumption.

So I said, "God has something in mind for her." And then I said I didn't want to sound arrogant about a recovery that was still in the early stages. And he said he didn't think it was arrogant; he believed that too, and he thought it was humbling. I repeated my thought that nothing good can come from evil, but good things can happen after evil.

I then told him about the two rosaries, the mass cards, the stamp of

Padre Pio in an envelope on the windowsill in Lauren's room, the blessed water from the Kabbalah Center and the holy water from Lourdes. Since he'd studied to be a Catholic priest, I figured he would know how to properly apply that last item (I had placed it in her room, but being Jewish, quite honestly didn't know what to do with it). He said, it's all the same God. So he will do that tonight.

As a quick note, the reason I got to the hospital so late was that I actually made tremendous headway catching up on paperwork (including a fair amount from before September 11) and straightening out the apartment, with an enormous—enormous—assist from Fran, who also baby-proofed our wrought-iron and glass coffee table in a very aesthetically appealing way. Lauren, even in her sedated condition, must have felt some positive karma from that.

I also brought Lauren Dolly Parton's recent bluegrass CD, "The Grass Is Blue." It starts with a kickin' version of Billy Joel's "Travelin' Prayer" (though of course when Dolly sings about her baby, he's a he). Pretty much every time I listen to the song, I start to cry, but it expresses my thoughts about Lauren exactly (Dolly's version, word for word, with a sex change, and Billy Joel's copyright):

Hey Lord, take a look all around tonight
And find out where my baby's gonna be.
Hey Lord, would you look out for her tonight
For she is far away from me.
Hey Lord, would you look out for her tonight
Make sure that she's gonna be all right
And things are gonna be all right with me.

Hey Lord, would you look out for her tonight
And make sure all her dreams are sweet.
Say now that you got her on the road
Would you make it softer for her feet.
Hey Lord, would you look out for her tonight
Make sure that she's gonna be all right
Until she's home and here with me.

Hey Lord, would you look out for her tonight
For she is sleepin' under the sky.
Hey Lord, make sure the ground she's sleepin' on

Is always warm and dry.
Ooh, don't give her too much pain,
And keep her away from planes,
'Cause my baby hates to fly.

Hey Lord, would you look out for her tonight
For it gets rough along the way.
And if it all sounds strange just because I don't know how to pray.
Ooh, won'tcha give her peace of mind,
And if you ever find the time
Tell her I miss her every day.

Hey Lord, take a look all around tonight
And find out where she's gonna be.
Hey Lord, would you look out for her tonight
For she is far away from me.
Hey Lord, would you look out for her tonight
Make sure that she's gonna be all right
Until she's home and here with me.
Here with me.

Almost every word of this song resonates.

Speaking of pop songs, most of you probably know that I am in the Rolling Bones, but probably didn't know that the Bones had a gig playing at the Rock and Roll Hall of Fame in Cleveland today. Yes, THAT Rock and Roll Hall of Fame. Since September 11, I had debated whether to go or not, and every time decided I couldn't; late Friday night I was still debating and still deciding not to go, with an assist from Lauren's sister. It finally came down to one deciding factor: if Lauren was not awake to tell me to go, then I had to stay by her side. So I did.

Finally, a couple of notes and clarifications:

Scottish songs—I received a booklet of Scottish songs to read to Lauren, from the person everyone receives Scottish songs from, of course: their Israeli uncle. The songs are excellent, except that you cannot sail through a single one completely without running aground on a line that is utterly and humorously incomprehensible. And wouldn't you know the first song I opened to was one I knew the melody to, namely, "Loch Lomond"? My singing of it could probably be unfavorably compared with Bugs Bunny's, and I stopped my performance quickly because I didn't want to raise Lauren's blood pressure.

Ground Zero—The front of the firehouse at the intersection of Liberty and Greenwich, from which we retrieved the hard hats, had been turned into a shrine, just like so many other firehouses in the city: covered with posters of the smiling faces of those who were lost, and with bouquets of flowers laid at the base of the walls or hanging beside the posters. We were right near the firehouse, but I did not look at it until I had crossed to the wreckage of Tower Two, because I think I was restricting myself to the "appropriate path" the way one feels compelled to do in a cemetery; not to wander, but to pay tribute to the ceremony that has brought you here. I do not know how many firefighters were lost from that company.

Survival rate for serious burn patients—As I mentioned earlier, last week's NPR report cited a very low survival rate for patients with a burn as severe as Lauren's. I mused that perhaps her chances along that curve had improved as she achieved some distance from the initial injury. According to a physician friend who responded via e-mail: "Your analysis of Lauren's percentage chances is exactly right; statistics start from the minute patients walk through the door. Second, the resuscitation stage, which she has already flown through, is one of the highest mortality periods. Third, and you would have to confirm this with the folks there, is that smoke inhalation may be an independent contributor to these mortality rates, esp the high-percentage burn patients." In fact, Lauren's lung injuries were thankfully not that severe and she is oxygenating normally; one of those factors on the plus side of her ledger.

Surgery—Lauren will not undergo a tracheostomy until her next surgery, expected for this coming Tuesday. She had been on her stomach for much of last Wednesday's procedure, and this caused increased swelling at the site where the tube was to be placed; it was therefore safer to wait until this week, so that procedure was not performed.

Love to all, and thank you all for your love and prayers.
Greg & Lauren

Lauren took a late trip to the tank today, and continued to sail on steady. Her vital signs are stable as she approaches two big days. Tomorrow the status of her grafts of last Wednesday will be checked; on Tuesday, she is scheduled to have another surgery, which should include the tracheostomy. That would remove the ventilator tube from her mouth, and give her the opportunity, as she becomes more awake, to mouth words and seek to communicate.

Despite the sedation, her eyes still flashed beneath her lids at my mention of Tyler's name. I told her I loved her and that she was beautiful.

The other patients in the critical zone with Lauren continue to hang in, and the family members all told each other tonight, See you tomorrow.

Again today I arrived at the hospital late, so I did not spend a lot of time with Lauren. I will make up for that tomorrow. Her family was there throughout the day, keeping her company. My lateness excuse this time was my first visit to the Family Assistance Center at Pier 94, 54th Street and the Hudson River.

To enter requires showing ID to four successive police checkpoints, each about fifty feet apart, in order to approach the reception table. There, NYPD representatives sit behind a banquet table covered with printouts listing relief agencies, important phone numbers, and location maps for the facility. They ask what brings you there. Family members of victims receive a special yellow stick-on tag that says "FAMILY" in big black letters and entitles you to skip lines and go directly to a claims officer.

Almost immediately, there was a slight disconnect. I explained to the officer that my wife was in the burn unit and had been badly injured. He heard me, gave me a tag, and sent me inside in what I thought was a helpful way. It was volunteers at the Cantor cubicle who noticed that I did not have a Family tag. I returned to the table, asked him for one, and he looked at me but didn't react; the woman beside him gave me one right away, so I didn't think much of it. About an hour later I realized that he had not given me a Family tag at first because he thought they went only to those whose family members had died. I have to say I think the oversight was unintentional; because there are very few seriously injured survivors, there seems to be no policy governing how to handle their families. This issue came up repeatedly.

The facility itself is a long, high-ceilinged warehouse space. To the right as you enter is a huge food service area, with a buffet worthy of a corporate cocktail party; rows of sliding-glass-door refrigerators filled with bottled water and soft drinks; huge coffee urns; soda fountains; tables with baskets of Power Bars and piles of desserts; and rows of round, linen-covered dining tables. Food service employees wander about this area working hard; they are all wearing Red Cross vests. Just past this dining area are kiosks for interpreters.

Radiating outward from the entrance to fill the cavernous space in all directions are curtain-partitioned aisles and cubicles reminiscent of a huge technology trade show—except that instead of company names, the signs display names like "Crime Victims Board," "FDNY," "Social Security," "Workers' Compensation." There is only one actual company sign, at the front of the long aisle to the right: "Cantor Fitzgerald / eSpeed / TradeSpark."

I decided to start there, and received some instructions and materials from the volunteers, who gave me a list of agencies arranged in the order that Cantor families are instructed to visit (I'll explain the asterisks in a moment):

Legal*
Crime Victims Board (CVB)
Safe Horizons
CAN*
Met Life*
Social Security
FBI
Department of Labor
Workers' Compensation Board
Tzu Chi Foundation
HRA
American Red Cross
Salvation Army

The following agencies take registration by phone:

The asterisks identify companies that deal solely in death benefits. Legal is listed first because that is where you receive the death certificate, which you then show to each successive agency. Legal was not on my list, nor were the life insurance companies.

My first stop was the FDNY; I am trying to get the names of the EMS crew who brought Lauren to St. Vincent's. They did not have these records. When I told them my wife was at the Cornell Burn Center, they told me it was the best in the world. They immediately understood the severity of Lauren's injury and one of them stood up and spoke to me for a few minutes, offering me a stick of gum and giving me his best wishes for Lauren.

I decided to begin my claims tour with the CVB, where I met with a rep who seemed quite helpful. While sitting at his desk, I saw a name on a list on his screen, and realized that a former Euro Brokers employee, whom I had known, had gone to work at Cantor and had died there on September 11. I remembered that his computer screen-saver had always been a collage of pictures of his young daughter, now probably four or five years old. These surprises keep happening; one of those in my industry circle (similar to many of you on this cc list) said that for many months we can keep expecting another shoe to drop each time we discover that someone we hadn't even thought was affected had died.

I filled out a CVB claim for benefits on behalf of Lauren (CVB supplements insurance and Workers' Compensation and has no medical cap) but was told that without a legal power of attorney (POA) I could not sign for her; she had to sign for herself. I pointed out that she was on a ventilator and could not speak, might remain in an induced coma for some time, and may not be able to write for some time after that. He said, when she wakes up, maybe she can mouth her approval of the POA. I asked that he confirm I couldn't sign, given the situation; he checked, and I was turned down.

I went to the Safe Horizons table, which was right beside the CVB table. I picked up the Safe Horizons handout and asked the man there if I could talk about Safe Horizons with him. He looked to his left, saw that the other two people at the table were not free, and said OK. After speaking with me for a couple of moments, he too got up to see if I could sign for Lauren; after a few minutes, he too came back and said no.

Next stop was Workers' Compensation. When the rep asked what company Lauren worked for, I said Cantor Fitzgerald; the woman rolled her eyes, as so many now do at that name, and I thought she was going to put her hands to her face and say how sorry she was. Instead, she smiled. Then she said, "I have done so many claims for Cantor, and this is the first person who is still alive." She instructed me how to sign on Lauren's behalf, with my signature and printed name and the word "husband" beside it.

I wondered why it wasn't that easy with CVB and Safe Horizons. She told me she could not answer that for another agency, but that if they required it, I should probably get a POA from the Legal people at the back.

I returned to the Cantor table and one of the volunteers offered to walk me back to Legal. She explained the situation. Legal was closed but she got a lawyer anyway; that lawyer knew only death certificates, however, so it was no use.

The Cantor volunteer seemed surprised that I hadn't gotten more assistance from Safe Horizons. She walked me back over to them; the woman behind the Safe Horizons table was much more responsive than the man had been. It quickly emerged that this was because al- though he was sitting at the Safe Horizons table and agreed to talk about Safe Horizons, he was really from CVB and talking about CVB, and had made me wait five minutes while he went back to the same dry well to get the same refusal.

The actual Safe Horizons woman immediately walked me back about a hundred feet to the row of Safe Horizons cubicles, an entirely different area, where the Cantor volunteer and I sat down with a young, energetic, and quite flabbergasted Safe Horizons volunteer who lives three blocks away from me in the West Village. She could not believe the runaround CVB had given me.

She stalked down there and dressed the guy down, asking what he was thinking when he told me this. Then she came back and told me that the commissioner of CVB wanted to meet me. It turned out that he was right there, less than fifty feet away from the dead end kids. He shook my hand, called Albany, and had the CVB general counsel make a ruling that spouses of critically injured victims could sign on their behalf. Within four minutes the commissioner's top deputy had walked me to the notary, called Albany and secured a claim number, and filed my claim.

The result was that I got a state agency to make a ruling that changed its policy. I may have been the first spouse of a living victim to check in; there had been no policy in place to deal with such as me. As much as this is a tale of bureaucratic madness, it is equally a tale of bureaucratic sanity.

My thanks to the Cantor volunteer and the SH volunteer, as well as to the commissioner of CVB and his lieutenant.

There is one other feature of the Family Assistance Center. The wall that lines the aisle leading back to Legal, about 150 feet long, is covered with missing posters from top to bottom. At the far end, I had two more nasty shocks; two more guys I'd known by face at the office, but not by name, had died.

I will be at the hospital tomorrow from about 2 PM. But before that, I will be attending the Euro Brokers company memorial service, where we will pay tribute to our sixty lost colleagues.

I thank God every moment now, every moment, that I still have that glimmer of hope.

Love,
Greg & Lauren

From: Greg
To: Everyone
Date: Tuesday, October 9, 2001 12:04 AM
Subject: Lauren Update for Oct 8 (Monday)

Tomorrow will mark four weeks since the World Trade Center disaster, and Lauren continues to hold stable with a couple of tweaks to her liquids and medications to manage infection. I spent a long while sitting by her bed and stroking her hair, which shows every sign of remaining healthy.

There was some good news concerning previous grafts. As a reminder, homografts use skin from a skin bank, autografts use her own skin, and she is not "out of the woods" until she is fully grafted with her own skin.

When Lauren went to the tank room today (I was mistaken yesterday; this was actually her first visit to the tank in two days), her doctor reviewed the condition of the autografts on her back, legs, and arms done three weeks ago. Her back is almost completely healed, except for some small spots that haven't closed but are expected to do so on their own. Her legs have done well, as has her left arm. This is good news, because all these grafts are permanent.

The homografts done last Wednesday have not done as well, but since they are not her own tissue, they would have to be redone at some point anyway. Fortunately, her first set of donor sites is now healed and ready to be harvested again.

So Lauren is now scheduled for her next surgery early tomorrow. She will have the tracheostomy to remove the ventilator tube from her mouth. She will receive 1½-to-1 (a tighter mesh pattern) autografts to replace the homografts on the front of her feet, and she will receive 1-to-1 autografts on her hands, including the first grafts to her fingers.

At the same time that her surgeon grafts her fingers, he will "cross-pin" her finger joints, inserting temporary metal pins to preserve functional position in the fingers as Lauren heals. You can see this functional position for yourself if you gently tap the tip of your index finger against your thumb, holding the index finger as straight as it can for the fingertip and thumb to still meet.

It is a measure of the degree to which we have become armchair experts in burn care that we can receive all this information about grafts, vital signs, and infection and make a general assessment that things are going well. However, Lauren faces huge challenges in coming weeks. I keep referring to this as a journey, and noting that she has to pass through all points on the map to get from here to a safe recovery. It's better that she is at this point than to not have reached it yet, but she still has a long way to go.

Earlier this morning I returned to the Family Assistance Center, completed paperwork with Safe Horizons, and registered with the FBI, which is assisting victim families with transportation and lodging. When I looked around this time, rather than a warehouse, the facility is better described as a huge Quonset hut, with one-yard-diameter ducts, sagging in places, stretching for hundreds of feet along the ceiling. The wall of missing posters is closer to 250 feet long than 150, and every inch of the base is lined with donated teddy bears featuring the tag of the schoolchild who sent it.

Here, as in so many places during this strange time, I have seen a new kind of offering on the meeting tables: tissue kiosks, baskets full of tissue packets, Red Cross–branded tissues, trays of cough drops, evidence that there is a grief industry that knows exactly which supplies are truly needed where grieving families gather by the hundreds.

From Pier 94, I received a ride in a sheriff's car to Grand Central, where I attended the Euro Brokers memorial service at the Grand Hyatt hotel.

Several hundred employees, family members, and friends were in attendance to remember and pay tribute to sixty Euro Brokers employees who died September 11. The crowd also included a number of former employees who were there to remember old colleagues and friends. The service was deeply moving.

It began with the top desk and department managers being called up to read aloud the names of the employees who had been lost from their group (in several cases newly promoted desk heads read the names of the people they had worked for). This was far more intimate than a simple reading of the entire list would have been, and powerfully brought home the loss of each individual.

There was a beautiful speech by the wife of one of the desk heads who had been lost; she had worked at Euro Brokers and met her husband there, and now she has returned to the firm. She spoke of feeling lost and devastated after September 11, then finding strength in her husband's memory, and in the memory of his faith. She said that this strength seemed to grow in her, and had given her the power to sustain herself and to set about rebuilding her life. She put it much better than that, of course; she was both tearful and inspiring.

Two priests and a rabbi then spoke, talking of how survivors should not turn from God because this evil did not come from God, and how faith can give us strength to face the future as our moment of grief recedes with time, even while the memories of lost loved ones do not.

The rabbi closed by comparing the horrors of September 11 to his own experience as a Holocaust survivor, when countless innocent lives were taken not by God but by men. In such a situation, it is pointless to ask why God would take someone to him because it was not God who performed these acts. Instead, he said, we should seek a purpose based on the remembered lives of those who have been senselessly murdered; in his case, upon the death of a beloved grandfather, he resolved to become a rabbi himself when he grew up. He encouraged all of us to find some meaning, some positive purpose to which we can dedicate ourselves.

Then Gil Scharf, our CEO, spoke movingly of the quality of the people who were gone, and how important it would be to rebuild the business in their memory. He read a card that had been sent by our London office, urging this rebuilding and exhorting us, "Don't Quit." He thanked the employees, business partners, and customers who had worked around the clock starting September 11 to help the company return to operation. He also spoke of the creation of the Euro Brokers Fund, including plans to hold an annual charity event to ensure continued contributions. But most of all he spoke with emotion about the incomprehensible losses the firm had suffered. The firm, in the end, was and is nothing more than its people. Repeatedly referring to the lost employees as family, he said we should try to remember the positives in their lives, and how much they had contributed to all of us who remained.

The service was followed by a reception featuring many hugs and more intimate sharing of memories. Yet again I discovered more people I knew who had died, including several "hallway" guys I would see in the lunch line or in the hallway and with whom I had shared many jokes without ever being sure of their names. Family members of missing employees searched for any account of their loved ones' last moments. Surviving employees told simple stories of how they had escaped from the building before it fell.

Several of them were true heroes—one man had carried a woman all the way downstairs on his back. In particular, a friend of mine added details to his account of how he had rescued a man from the rubble on the 81st floor, one of the impact floors, and helped him down to safety. My friend remembers hearing the man calling from far away, seeing a hand reaching out from beneath the debris, pushing a shattered wall out of the way, climbing over twenty or thirty feet of rubble, and lifting construction materials and parts of a broken desk off the trapped man. That man has since told my friend that when he appeared, he had seemed to float above the rubble.

The rescued man also told of how he had watched the second jet approach, had actually seen the men piloting the plane as it hurtled into the building. The plane had dipped its left wing just a split second before impact. I think this man has also given my friend an account of how the tip of the airplane wing that hit his floor had snapped off and gone hurtling through their floor, not on fire, just a few tons of steel traveling 300 to 400 miles per hour through office cubicles.

It is important to remember that this happened in an ordinary business office, that the men who struck us sought to kill tens of thousands, and that they are the purest form of evil in the world, one that has no respect for any human life, including their own. And when I think of this, I think of my wife, entering her building, hearing a whistling sound, and having her life changed forever.

Thank God she still has a chance to return to it.

Love,
Greg & Lauren

From: Greg
To: Everyone
Date: Wednesday, October 10, 2001 1:15 AM
Subject: Lauren Update for Oct 9 (Tuesday)

Lauren was in the OR from 7:30 AM to 1:30 PM, and received new autografts to the front of her feet and to her right hand, with homografts for her left hand. We learned that her right hand is in better shape than her left. Her right-hand fingers only needed wires to stabilize them for a week or so until the autografts can adhere, while her left-hand knuckle joints did need to be cross-pinned, as originally expected. She also received the tracheal tube, so she no longer has the ventilator tube in her mouth.

She remains vulnerable to infection, and currently has a resistant strain of pneumonia. (The longer she has been on antibiotics, the more likely it has been that a resistant infection will appear.) As of Tuesday morning, she remained stable, but this bacterium bears watching. It does not respond to any of the antibiotics Lauren is already receiving, and may need to be treated with an older antibiotic that has not been widely used for about ten years. The older antibiotic has a higher risk of toxicity, so they are watching the infection for another twenty-four hours to see whether she can shake it herself. But if she stays puffy, or deteriorates, they are likely to have to take some type of action to combat it.

Following her surgery today, she has had issues with her blood pressure, temperature, and liquid management, and they have had to give her additional medications to stabilize her. This night has not been as smooth as others have been, but it is also not her first rocky night.

Every night since September 11, I have made sure to give the reception desk the phone number at which I can be reached to be summoned back to the hospital. I have done this so often that I had almost forgotten why I have been doing it.

My pre-op routine is to be in the room with her and talk to her until the OR calls her down. It takes four or five nurses to move her: one squeezing the vent bag, one wheeling the rolling stand of IV drips, and two wheeling the bed. They are escorted by an OR doctor. I always watch them go down the hall until they turn the corner and I can catch a final view of her face. I don't think too much about what happens after that; just that she has to be moved from the gurney to the table, positioned, and then have some major, very thorough work done.

The OR-related suspense ends when her surgeon appears in the hallway back on the Burn Center floor to tell us how things have gone. And then we hear the truth: a procedures inventory that frankly would have been horrifying even to contemplate before all this happened but now comprises the checklist of necessary steps to fix her up.

When Lauren is the first surgical case, I am usually the first member of a patient family to arrive at the hospital and am alone in the waiting room. Once she goes down to the OR I usually face several hours alone. This morning I noticed that the wife of a third Cantor Fitzgerald patient, from the Cantor accounting department, was already there, asleep in a chair. I turned on the television softly, then at 8 AM wrote the following into a new BlackBerry that a friend has been strikingly generous in buying for me:

"In forty minutes it will be exactly twenty-eight days since the attacks—we really should call them crashes—an utterly meaningless anniversary except in one way. It is another clear day, and most of us woke up and got ready much as we had on September 11. I took a shower, went downstairs, got into my car, and drove to the hospital, no more expecting violence and destruction to rain from the sky than I had back then."

Before I could continue, the wife of the third Cantor patient, who had woken up, came over and told me that one of the other burn patients had died at 5:30 that morning.

This was a patient whose family had presented a resolute front, especially one woman, a performer and teacher, who had long been this patient's closest friend. On Monday night, as the patient's condition worsened, her friend's composure had shown signs of buckling under a flood of stronger emotions; tears started to bead at the corners of her eyes. Moments like this have happened time and again for each family as the outlook falls from a peak to a trough and the sorrow is as relentless as the tide.

On Monday night a different group of volunteers had served a hot dinner of fresh carved turkey, rice, potato salad and corn, and a banquet-sized rectangular carrot cake in the staff room. I had sat with this closest friend, who had been there almost every evening since September 11. Normally a fount of positive energy, she was preparing herself for what she saw as the inevitable, feeling certain that the patient had made a final choice, and that as her closest friend she needed to be strong enough to "respect her decision." Being a performer, she said that she felt "completely centered." But as she braced herself for loss, she seemed to shake from the sheer physical effort. Sometime around 5:30 Tuesday morning, she had the chance to respect her friend's decision.

The wife of the third Cantor patient was there to tell me all this because she herself had left the hospital late Monday only to be summoned back and told to stay close. She had slept the night in that waiting room chair. She had been there for the events at 5:30 AM, and as of 8:30, her husband's prognosis had not improved. As we spoke, his nurse came out to speak to her about his condition. It seemed that one by one, fates were being decided.

She was shaken by this conversation, as was I. We paced the hall together until I asked whether she needed to call anyone, and she focused on this task, phoning a number of family and friends and asking them to come to the hospital. We sat together for several hours until they began to arrive; and she spent the day maintaining her highly stressful vigil. When I left the hospital this afternoon at 4 PM, we told each other, as we always do, that we would see each other tomorrow.

So I keep the faith, in Lauren's strength and in her destiny, and ride the waves as they rise and fall, and hope that they will deliver her to safe harbor, even as she steers singly across a merciless ocean.

Love,
Greg & Lauren

P.S. The Burn Center hallway is papered with more and more hand-drawn cards from young schoolchildren, longer letters from older children written on ruled paper in painstaking script, large posters, and long banners with messages of support from schoolchildren and adults alike.

Early on, a synagogue sent a twenty-foot banner filled with children's handwritten wishes, mostly variations on: Get Well Very Soon, Thank You for Saving America, Sorry This Happened to You, Hope You Get Better. A recent addition to an end wall of the waiting room proper was a ten-foot-long white banner from a hospital in Richmond, Indiana, covered with handwritten wishes from adults written in bold blue script. As on the children's banner, almost every one echoed one of several themes: God Bless You, You Are Loved, Our Thoughts and Prayers Are With You, in two hundred different handwritings.

For the past month there was a third type of wall covering at the Burn Center: posters of the missing. One had been one of the hallway guys at Euro Brokers, someone I knew in life only in passing, but whom I came to know more intimately through the smiling photograph on his posters at the hospital—there had been one next to the ground floor elevator, one at the elevator bulletin board on the Burn Center floor, and one high up on the wall behind the center's reception desk. The last of the missing posters were taken down Monday. It was one more coincidence that his posters came down on the day of the Euro Brokers memorial service, the day you could say that he was suitably mourned.

From: Greg
To: Everyone
Date: Thursday, October 11, 2001 9:24 AM
Subject: Lauren Update for Oct 10 (Wednesday)

One trivial note before the serious stuff: my band, the Rolling Bones, plays tonight at the Red Lion, on Bleecker Street, at 10 PM. Fans of the Rolling Stones and dive-y bars are welcome.

I have been saying that the next few days are critical for Lauren, and that is only becoming more so; there is more discussion of this toward the end of this piece, which I am finishing Thursday morning because I was simply too tired last night. Please forgive the disjointedness of what follows; I thought you might want to read it sooner rather than wait forever for me to reorganize it.

I peeked into Lauren's room late last night, at 10:30, just as her evening burn care was due to begin. Her vital signs were stable and had been most of the day (there had been an episode where her pressure and heart rate slipped when she was turned over for her burn care earlier in the day, but she had recovered on her own). Her stability was reassuring, but she remains very puffy from the resistant infection that has taken hold in her. (I discuss this infection and her treatment later. Overnight—early Thursday morning—Tyler woke up at 3 AM, so I checked in with the hospital. She did better with her burn care than she had Wednesday morning; her vital signs did not start to drop, and that was about as encouraging as any news I received in the last twenty-four hours.)

When I stepped into Lauren's room yesterday afternoon at 5, I found I could not speak to her without my voice breaking. I had to grab the e. e. cummings anthology and read to her from that before I could get words out without sadness. Many of cummings's poems also resonate with Lauren's condition, notably, "i thank You God for most this amazing day."

I should tell you the story of the princess. Since early in our relationship, Lauren would often turn to me and say: "Tell me a story," and I might spin some humorous and often corny tale of the blond princess of Perry Street. Over the past year I felt that I had run out of these stories.

Tonight, after I finished the cummings, I began to tell her of a princess in a city by the waters (not a kingdom by the sea; this was not derivative of Poe and didn't rhyme), who journeyed daily to a castle with two towers where she did good works and was widely loved. One day as she entered the castle, two evil dragons descended on it and she was consumed by dragon's breath. And the story kept going, and soon it developed that the princess was in a deep sleep, like Sleeping Beauty or Snow White, and needed to be brought back, not just by her prince, but also by her healers; and that what brought her out was the love of the whole world, concentrated prayer, that formed into the vessel of her husband (I have to tinker with how a fairy tale princess could be married and have a son), who stood beside her and laid his hand upon her and transferred love into her at each of those spots, until the princess had no more blood, but only pure love coursing through her veins.

And it was that love that touched every part of her, from the inside out, and brought her back to her prince and their infant son. And she felt that love in the depths of her sleep; and that was how she managed to return.

I have never willed anything more strongly than I have willed that to be true.

When I walked out to the waiting room, the woman I wrote about yesterday morning was seated beside a chaplain and stroking a large purple teddy bear. (I told her about what I wrote Tuesday and she was fine, and said I could mention her husband's name today, which I do lower down.) He is still hanging on. She had already named the teddy bear. We joked about how this could seem ridiculous but utterly comforting at the same time.

Speaking about Lauren, I again had to stop for a moment, so she put the bear down, stood up, and hugged me, pointing out that she was there for me, just as I had been there for her the day before. We are all there for each other; especially as the stress we all feel takes on a grim desperation.

At about 8:30, after the nursing shift change, some friends took me out for another dinner at the Beach Café: Mary and Chris, Marian and Bill, and Kitty. We talked about Lauren, and then about the war, and came to the conclusion that we were in general agreement: Lauren should get better and the war should be fought, and there wasn't a place to hide on the planet Earth from the concentrated might of the United States of America.

We will win this war. I only wish that this could do something, anything, for Lauren herself; because in truth, a successful military campaign does not really help her unless she feels satisfaction to know that our government, and others, are chasing to the ends of the earth the people who did this to her. And she may feel that way in the future.

But what a disconnect—I have not spoken with Lauren now for four weeks; I have only talked to her.

We are in our own little world, but the world is coming to us. (At this point, and as I expected early on, some major news organizations are speaking with the Burn Center about doing long-term stories on the patients and their recovery.) Since the incident, and in part because they cannot speak for themselves or even give authorization to others to speak for them, the critical patients are being reported on as statistics; this is their condition, this is what they face, but nothing about their lives. They are the last group to remain anonymous, and admittedly a very tiny one in number. Yet since the morning of September 11, I have believed that Lauren and those like her are the embodiment of this disaster, the ones who will bear the physical scars of the incident for the rest of their lives. Rather than statistics, I want these people to be acknowledged for the sacrifice imposed on them, because it is only slightly less great than those who lost their lives. These critical patients have lost their lives as they knew them. The only difference is that they have hope, however faint in some cases, and that there is a point to fighting as long as that hope still exists.

Lauren has lost Tyler, and he has lost her, for at least six months to a year, possibly longer, and we cannot know now whether she will ever be the same woman who sang to him and fed him and carried him in the pool, changing him and bathing him and teaching him to walk.

Her whole life was about having this baby, and now she will not be around to see some very special moments. The only thing that gets me through is that there will be so many more special moments as Tyler gets older, and when he can learn about it he will know what happened to his mother, and, I hope, hope fervently, she will be there to love him and to laugh with him.

There are just a few critical patients now, and most of their families have allowed their names to be in this e-mail: Jennieann, Elaine, René (a man), Donovan, Harry, and of course Lauren. Those are the families whom I know, who support each other. Each of the patients fights alone for now; down the road, I hope all of them can go through their rehabilitation together.

There is a difficult calculus; the longer the battle continues, the odds do not necessarily improve. People who entered the battle strong after lives spent eating well and exercising have now become people who have spent a month on their back; the strength they came in with is dissipated, and now what they have primarily is momentum. Their odds improve significantly only when they are fully grafted with their own skin.

But they are still fighting for every moment.

That is what Lauren was doing last night. This is a true crisis, but on the other hand, where she is healing she looks good, and the important grafts have done so well. The resistant bacterium that she has, which colonizes intensive care units even when sterile protocols are religiously followed, was cultured over the weekend and tested responsive to one of the two new antibiotics she is now being given.

It is all a balancing act, of course. Her doctor now has to judge the best mix of medicine and surgery to manage her from moment to moment. At this point, I believe, he has to run as much on feel as on science, because the science can take you only so far. He has to make the best decisions he can based on the evidence, but also taking into consideration the subjective ways that she is different from any other patient. Over my lifetime I have heard this described as being a "classic clinician" (I have, perhaps, hung around too many doctors), as distinguished from a diagnostic computer program that may be capable of crunching endless statistics but perhaps not capable of grasping a unique nuance of a particular patient's condition, and using that additional understanding to arrive at a unique treatment that may well help the patient to beat the disease.

Once I had told Lauren the story of the princess, I sang to her, played CDs, did everything I could to remind her that I was there and that Tyler loves her.

I love her, and I love all of you, and please keep writing back to me, because it sustains me, makes it easy for me to be there for her because I know that we are not alone, and my little story of the princess may be a true one, because even as I told it, I placed my hand on her hands, and over her, and believed to the depths of my being that I was laying the concentrated love of thousands upon her wounds.

When you pray for her, please also put in a good word for the others. Speak to you tomorrow!

Love,
Greg & Lauren

This day will go down in the annals of the more encouraging, except for Tyler, who has a cold.

But there are other things he has: the ability to high-five on command; the ability to raise his arms when asked How big is Tyler?; the ability to crawl, which he has finally adopted instead of his commando-style skootching; the ability to focus intense concentration on the act of picking up individual Cheerios and eating them. He also has the ability to laugh, and loves to show off this skill in particular.

I arrived at the hospital to learn that Lauren's signs were strong and stable, and that she had done better today than the day before. The doctors were preparing to back off on her dopamine and her fluids, and that is a good sign. It is too early to tell whether the two new antibiotics are having an effect on the resistant infection, but it is certainly good to see her really holding her own.

When I spoke to her tonight, she opened her eyes and tried to speak to me. She was only able to move her lips slightly, soundlessly, and her eyes did not turn toward me, but she was definitely trying to respond.

This is a good thing, but to a family member who doesn't understand the circumstances, it can be somewhat alarming, because the patient is wrapped in bandages and largely immobilized, so it seems when the patient fails to significantly move their arms or legs and their blood pressure starts to rise that they are agitated and unhappy. My greatest fear was that Lauren would turn to me and begin to speak in a perfectly clear voice and tell me exactly how she felt, and I did not want her to be that alert at that moment.

I asked the nurse about this, and she went over to Lauren, introduced herself, and asked Lauren repeatedly if she was in pain. She told Lauren, open your eyes if you are in pain. Lauren kept her eyes shut.

The nurse, another FEMA nurse, from Tampa, Florida, then explained to me that Lauren was on a lot of drips, so she probably did not feel pain, and probably did not remember from moment to moment. But she said Lauren definitely heard me and was certainly trying to respond. The nurse said, She's comfortable; she's probably just happy to hear your voice.

So I went back to Lauren and spoke to her some more, very simply, telling her that Tyler loves her, I love her, and all her friends, everyone she's touched in her life, loves her, and that thousands of people were praying for her and rooting for her, and that all her old friends are waiting for their first chance to see her and undoubtedly hug her.

I told her she was loved by many, many people, me most of all, and I asked her to rest.

The other families of patients were all there in the waiting room, and we all said See you tomorrow—knowing as always that when we say it to each other, it means a lot more than see you tomorrow.

There are more cards on the walls; there was more rotisserie chicken in the staff room; there were piles of Rice Krispies Treats in the waiting room; a never-ending supply of gowns, masks, gloves, and hats in the gown room; and another day went into the books: thirty days and counting since September 11, 2001.

So let's say another prayer for Lauren, René, Elaine, Jennieann, Donovan, and Harry; their families all want to see them tomorrow.

Love,
Greg & Lauren

From: Greg
To: Everyone
Date: Saturday, October 13, 2001 12:35 AM
Subject: Lauren Update for Oct 12 (Friday) **CORRECTED**

Lauren had a good day today, and that is a direct quote from her day nurse. Her signs were stable, she took a swim (a visit to the tank room), and she did fine. Her donor sites look very good, and her swelling has gone down some. Her face looks as if it is healing very well. The doctors are slowly backing off on drugs and fluids. The balancing act continues.

This morning she again seemed to be more responsive, and I am told she opened her eyes when asked, though she did not do that for me tonight. She did try to move her arms a bit, though they were immobilized by splints. I read the usual poems to her and played Enya in the background (a gift from—Dan?). The theme was soothe.

Say that three times fast.

One of the other critical patients has actually taken a turn for the better; she went from a very high risk surgery a week ago to showing significant improvement in her lungs in the past few days. The elation among the families can barely be measured at moments like that, though we are quick to remind ourselves, as Tom Wolfe memorably said in *The Right Stuff,* that it can blow at any seam. Even the baby steps are giant steps—as long as they keep coming.

By the way, speaking of baby steps, Tyler is in full-fledged crawl mode, and crawls back and forth across the floor, laughing, from one end of the room to the other, whenever you wave him toward you. It is sometimes easy to forget that this is a twenty-or-so-pound human being. His babbling is taking on a new sense of purpose.

Today I returned to Euro Brokers for the first time since September 11. Of course I didn't return to the office; that's gone. Instead, I found my way downtown to One New York Plaza, where the firm is temporarily based on a vacant floor. The experience was far more unsettling than the visit to Ground Zero.

Ground Zero was a disaster site, and the destruction was so total and so unimaginable, and I had seen it so much on TV, that I was really more an observer than a mourner. My mood was dialed down and I did not have any overwhelming reaction. I felt solemnity but not fear. Today was different.

I came out of the south end of the Bowling Green station of the 4 and 5 subway trains into the middle of a bomb scare: fire trucks and police cars with their lights flashing, and yellow caution tape, cordoned off all the streets to my left. There were crowds of office workers who I assume had been evacuated, and Battery Park was a National Guard bivouac: troops and Humvees in camouflage, military tents behind barricades. I walked the perimeter of the scare area for several blocks.

Then came the time to enter the office. I received a security tag listing me as a Prudential employee (we are guests of Prudential). I went up to our floor and was hammered by the disconnect: our people in the wrong place, our security guards at a reception desk, our brokers and executives and IT people seated in consecutive rows of workstation positions throughout what had been a large trading floor. The view through the windows of the ferries plying New York Harbor was impossibly close, sixty-eight floors and about ten blocks closer than it had been from our previous location, and you wouldn't think this detail would make an impression, but it reminded me of what an aerie the Trade Center had been, and how far we had been thrown from it.

There was none of the lived-in feel of an office that has evolved around a functioning business, with familiar art (no matter how dismal), bulletin board signs, clearly delineated functional areas, and a complete cadre of staff. We were guests in someone else's vacant office space, and while we could do our business there, it felt nothing at all like home.

Many colleagues stepped up to shake my hand and I received a very gentle welcome, with many sincere inquiries about Lauren's condition. Still, I had a queasy feeling that I could not put my finger on. Finally, someone else articulated it: there were people missing. They should have been there but they died. The company had moved, but there were sixty of us who could not make the trip. There is a grimness about continuing, a lingering headache.

I was glad to reconnect, but after several conversations I started to feel the burden of my story. Every conversation was solemn. People who had known Lauren at Cantor, whom I'd never really spoken with since they moved to Euro Brokers, came to me in shock and sat down to talk about her and say how sorry they were and to send their best wishes to her.

In talking with others, I had a strange sensation every time I changed the subject that I was somehow trivializing things. Except for the company meeting and subsequent memorial, I had not seen anyone from the office other than our CEO. Those had all been ceremonial venues, or at the hospital; this was the first time I'd been back in the business context, and without ceremony or prayer the sense of tragedy and absence was palpable. The process today was about rebuilding daily contacts, and acknowledging the tragedy within the fabric of daily ritual.

There will be a pop sociology quiz at the end of this e-mail.

Now for the architecture review.

There is an aesthetic undercurrent that is never mentioned with respect to Ground Zero, understandably in view of the gravely injured survivors and the thousands of dead. Lives were lost, a nation's psyche was forever changed, utter devastation was wreaked—but beneath it all, we also lost a newly recognized and utterly enjoyable civility, a minor triumph of evolving taste that had replaced most of the institutional sterility that had come with the WTC when it opened.

The World Trade Center really was being spruced up. It had just been sold by the Port Authority to a real estate developer who was going to do more enhancements, but few realize how almost finished it was. It seems almost idiotic to mention it now. But the survivors who lost it as a workplace lost the order in their lives, and that started with the landscaping.

The bike path paralleling West Street was almost finished by then, with cobblestone drainage channels on either side and a hand-laid stone wall beside it. Green lawns had been planted along the World Financial Center, providing a decorative greensward, though how heavily they would have been used for sunbathing, with the river on the other side of the building, is a mystery.

West Street had been newly paved, the traffic light timings worked out, the traffic flows balanced, the left turn east on Vesey finally legal again. This was the culmination of several years of effort, and it had been very well done.

The World Trade Center concourse had been entirely reworked; the claustrophobic 1970s concourses, and the "food court" (I seem to remember some orange-mustardy tile paving and low-hanging yellow ceiling clocks, the Market Bar, and a place that sold burritos made from vinyl and foam rubber) had been converted to a much brighter, raised-ceiling 1990s/2000s environment. The bank branches, airline ticket counters, and courier services had been moved to 5 World Trade, so instead of large branch offices with industrial carpeting and teller lines, the space between the two towers was becoming a more stylish arcade with a Banana Republic, a recently opened Cole Haan, and an Ann Taylor Loft and Thomas Pink on the way.

Restaurants and cafés had opened on the edges of the WTC Plaza, which was less and less a concrete desert of T-shirt kiosks and more and more a place where summer concerts were performed, tourists shot the inevitable straight-up photographs, and people sat and watched the world go by from linen-covered tables.

But instead of wrapping up the finishing touches, the people who built the foundations are back to dig them out a second time.

My apartment is near some highly priced new construction in the West Village. Twin seventeen-story towers are rising next door to us. They are still in the concrete-pouring stage; they have two more floors to go, so the crews are still the structural contractors and the crane operators. When the World Trade Center was hit, I could see it from my terrace, and I looked down to see the construction crews from the sites milling in the street and staring at the smoke coming from the gaping hole in Cantor Fitzgerald's floors.

One of the guys who are always on our street is the foreman for the mechanical operators; he supervises the operation of two crawler cranes with twenty-story booms. I met him months ago when the fuel pump on my car failed, and he had helped steer it as it was winched onto a flatbed tow truck. Today I asked whether a lot of his guys had gone down to volunteer.

He said his union had sent down a bunch of guys in the immediate aftermath, and now it is all paid workers running the cranes in twelve-hour shifts. He said he had worked on the Trade Center more than twenty years ago when it went up, he knew how deep it went down, how big the hole was. He knew about the slurry wall, how it had been pinned when the site was originally excavated, and how the crews are now facing problems with leakage and with the threat of the Hudson River rushing in and filling the hole. That event would create a far more serious situation, not only with the removal effort but with a washout effect created by huge quantities of water coming and going with the tide.

Battery Park City is stable, built on piles that rest on the same bedrock that permitted the construction of the Trade Center in the first place. A washout effect, which is not currently present, could prove a major problem over time; you don't have to be an expert in the field to see that it would be a bad thing.

As the rubble is being removed, the slurry wall surrounding the World Trade Center can travel, and could move or collapse if not properly braced. The pressures are unimaginable. As a result, the structural engineers must repin, or reanchor, the slurry wall as they go down, using the same cabling technique that was used when the hole was initially constructed. Stabilizing the slurry wall would enable them to clear the hole under controlled conditions.

The cranes lifting and moving large debris are huge, and the one I described, the red one with two sets of ten vertical feet of cast iron counterweights, has a 1,200-ton lifting capacity. It is not there primarily for strength, however, but reach, so they are using its 300-foot boom, which limits its lifting capacity somewhat but permits it to reach an entire football field into the rubble.

The machines I described as looking like Tonka trucks on the rubble pile are backhoe excavators, with two types of grabbing buckets (clamshell, I think they are called)—one that simply grabs debris, and another type of bucket that can bite through steel. The tractor-trailer-length dump trucks I described drive their debris loads over to barges stationed off Battery Park City, where more cranes lift the debris into 30-by-60-foot material buckets, which are floated to the Fresh Kills landfill on Staten Island, where more grabbers lift the material out and spread it around so that it can be sifted by federal investigators, because it is still part of a crime scene.

This foreman's daughter is a friend of a woman who is at another hospital with a different type of catastrophic injury: a portion of landing gear—from a commercial jet—fell on her and gravely injured her back and legs. At first, the doctors thought she would lose her legs, but one doctor insisted that her legs could be saved, and she is still waging that fight.

When I told the foreman what had happened to Lauren, he said, Oh, you're the fella—he knew about it.

This is New York in October 2001—savage injuries suffered by friends and family, horrors visited on the people next door, a web of tragedy that extends unbroken through every community from Ground Zero out to the farthest reaches of the suburbs, characterized by pockets of social affiliation: one community has lost firefighters and cops, another brokers and traders, another has sent demolition workers to hold back the river and to carefully lift out millions of tons of debris, including large sections of white-hot metal.

Okay, enough of this.

Lauren continues to do well.

Love,
Greg & Lauren

"She's having an awesome day." This is the type of comment we want to hear from Lauren's nurse, because awesome is a word not casually used at the burn unit. This is absolutely the first time that it has been used in connection with Lauren.

It means things are not just rock stable, but improving. Three days ago Lauren received two strong antibiotics to combat the resistant bacterium in her system and was in crisis. Today the swelling has gone down in her face, she looks more and more like herself, her signs have been strong, they have backed off on other medications and fluids, and she has been closer to awareness than at any time since September 11.

This morning, while her family was with her (remember, I'm on the night shift), Lauren had her eyes open and seemed reactive. When they returned to our apartment before I left for the hospital, they were more cheerful than since I'd seen them last April. It was as if a great burden temporarily had been lifted, because one had; she had gone from being in real danger to a state where, for her level of criticality, she could legitimately be described as, well, awesome.

The staff at the burn unit does not sugar-coat anything. The medical staff won't tell you a patient is going to pull through when the odds are strongly against that, and they would also want to avoid creating a false complacency among a critically ill patient's family, especially one that ran counter to the data. When I got the first statement from a nurse that they had a good feeling about Lauren, I felt that at that moment, some objective threshold of expectation had been crossed, however incrementally.

That doesn't mean they don't tell each other; one of the nurses has told me that her doctor had a feeling about Lauren from the beginning, something he never could have told me himself. Because when he shares that impression with a member of the nursing staff, it means something entirely different: that a certain percentage of patients survive this level of injury, and that this patient may meet the statistical criteria to fit within that group.

Lauren's awesome day must fit in that context. It doesn't mean that she is leaving the hospital next week, or even that she will not be critical for another two months; it just means that she has dealt with the crisis, and that all her trends, which were beginning to look negative, have begun to turn positive.

It is too early to say whether the new antibiotic regimen has conquered the resistant bacterium. But it is not too soon to say she had an awesome day.

The beauty of words like awesome in an ICU is that the professional people who feel free to say them get a bounce, too. They care about their patients, and it must be a relief to be able to deliver bona fide good news.

Or, as Simon and Garfunkel once sang: Elation.

I can't describe how it feels when someone is beginning to return to her regular visage from something not so close (well, maybe I can). It is the sorrow of disease that it changes your appearance, so you are no longer yourself. Part of Lauren's being so ill is that sometimes she does not look at all like herself; but she battles, and seems to be winning when she herself, looking the way she looks, starts to reemerge. It is the battle as real and metaphorical simultaneously.

Directions to Caveat City: it is a long journey, there will be danger again, but when you have an open road in front of you, for however brief a period, revel in it.

This morning I did an innocuous errand that gained meaning only because it was not quite as innocuous as the last time I'd done it. I mean, of course, going to the Costco in Brooklyn, the same place Lauren and I shopped on Sunday, September 9. That day Lauren had to get her own Costco ID; it is a fact that the last good photograph taken of her is the grainy black-and-white thumbnail on her Costco Gold membership card.

On September 9 we drove past the World Trade Center, zipped through the Brooklyn Battery Tunnel, popped down the BQE, and reached Costco in less than ten minutes. We had Tyler with us. We bought huge quantities of Pampers and the largest container of Bertolli olive oil that I had ever seen (if need be, I can now make pasta with olive oil and garlic for 300). Today, my friend Wendi and I went back to the same place to get a same-sized box of Pampers, and we had to cross Manhattan to the Williamsburg Bridge, wander through local streets to the BQE, and then drive a fair distance to the store, which we reached after about thirty minutes.

Once inside, we shopped for excessively large packages of various goods. Wendi was great company (better than Lauren, strictly speaking, if you count the times she complained), but it was a very different experience. There was no one helping me choose between products, reminding me what I needed to get, thinking of stuff of her own that I would see in the medicine cabinet or linen closet later that night. Not to get maudlin, but I could really tell she wasn't there, and it was another reminder of the everyday that we have lost, for some yet undefined period of time.

Tyler likes to feed himself his own Cheerios. They get sprinkled on the shelf of his high chair. He reaches out, carefully picks one up, and slowly, very deliberately, places it in his mouth. If he notices you watching him do this, he smiles very broadly; but if he's not self-conscious, he will just keep lifting Cheerios, one after the other, eating each one with the same level of concentration. At Costco today, I bought him enough Cheerios to continue this until his sophomore year in college.

Tonight I told Lauren about it because I always talk about Tyler. I could see her eyes moving under her lids. I also saw her try to form words. She wasn't able to make any sounds; her vocal cords could not vibrate because the endotracheal tube diverted the airflow away from her larynx. But she was doing more than just breathing reflexively. Her mouth opened wide and once her lower jaw moved slightly to the side, as if she were pausing before trying to speak.

I moved to the other side of her bed, and sneaked in behind the rolling trees of IV tubes and pumps, and leaned over her and stroked her hair, and could see that she knew I was doing it. I leaned close and I started to name friends of hers, and saw continued reaction, this time without the agitation. She did not try to move her arms, she did not seem upset, and I think it was because finally, without the ventilator tube in her mouth, she was communicating to the best of her ability, and maybe felt that this time there were no obstacles to her getting through.

Then they needed to sedate her to fix her feeding tube, and that was OK because she needs the protein to heal. So I left the room, and when I came back, she was asleep again. For the moment, there would be no flickers of awareness. So I pulled over the swivel chair and settled in beside the bed, watching her. The Willie Nelson "Stardust" CD had been playing since I'd arrived. The CD had reached the last track, a bonus tune that had not been on the original LP, perhaps because the bass just didn't sound country enough for the '70s. But when the CD was remastered and reissued, two of the original studio tracks had been added back, so I listened to Willie's version of the Johnny Nash tune "I Can See Clearly Now."

Pop-song lyrics always mean something to everyone, that's what they are written to do, but as we experience different life events, the same words can take on powerful new depths of meaning. So while I watched Lauren I heard these lines:

> I think I can make it now, the pain is gone
> All of the bad feelings have disappeared
> Here is the rainbow I've been prayin' for
> It's gonna be a bright, bright
> Sunshiny day.
>
> Look all around, there's nothin' but blue skies
> Look straight ahead, nothin' but blue skies.

There are always reminders of every aspect of our lives in the world around us; you can sometimes tell the truth of your own mood just by what you choose to notice.

Out in the waiting room the moods of the other families varied.

One patient faces a lengthy and risky operation on Monday because of a persistent problem. Her family is again worried, but they continue to show the same powerful support and belief in her, and despite some hints of tears, they ask about Lauren and Tyler and tell me to kiss him for them.

Another patient finally had his breathing tube removed from his mouth, but not in favor of a tracheostomy. Instead, he was extubated and given the chance to breathe on his own rather than automatically undergoing another invasive procedure. And he is breathing on his own for now (if he requires assistance, he can still undergo the tracheostomy). This man used this first opportunity to speak to tell his wife he loved her, and to tell her (barely audibly) that it was wonderful to see her.

Tonight I introduced myself formally to still another family member I have seen in the waiting room since September 11, a man whose son worked at 1 World Trade and was also in the lobby when the fireball burst from the elevator shaft. The man and I had spoken many times, but I had not recalled the specific knowledge of his patient relationship. He told me about his son, and he had this to say about all the patients, "including [pointing to me] your wife":

"They got such a will to live. The will to live is so powerful."

Amen.

Thirty-two days.

Love
Greg & Lauren

From: Greg
To: Everyone
Date: Monday, October 15, 2001 12:37 AM
Subject: Lauren Update for Oct 14 (Sunday)

And I thought I would have nothing to write about today.

When I reached the hospital tonight, with the Yankees already ahead 7–2, both of Lauren's eyes were open, and not just a bit, like before, but most of the way. The swelling that had been present in her face only four days earlier had mostly dissipated, so she looked more like her old self than at any point since September 11. I leaned over, looked her right in the eyes, and said, "Honey, it's Greg, and I love you."

Her eyes moved ever so slightly, and then the barest, most subtle upturn came at the corners of her mouth; she was trying to smile. I told her again that I loved her and that Tyler loved her, and then I said, "It's really great to see you," and I burst into tears, the first happy tears since for what seems like a thousand years.

I apologized for crying, but I told her it was because I was just so happy to see her.

For thirty-one days, what mattered when I walked into her room were her blood pressure, her heart rate, her pulse oxygen, her vital signs as they appeared on the data screen above and beside her bed. These were the instant checklist that in the absence of any other feedback quantified how she was doing.

I grew adept at reading the screen, looking for good oxygen wave patterns, understanding what lay behind her active heart rates, and having it explained to me that the most important figure for her blood pressure was not the systolic (the high number, representing the pressure as blood is pumped out from your heart) or the diastolic (the low number, the pressure when your heart relaxes), but the MAP, or Mean Arterial Pressure (a function of cardiac output, the volume of blood pumped per minute; and systemic vascular resistance, or the resistance put up by the systemic vasculature excluding the pulmonary vasculature—and why the pulmonary vasculature is excluded is something you can ask an actual doctor). The MAP appears in parentheses to the right of the systolic and diastolic numbers, and what I learned about it is that it needs to remain above 60.

I would also check the percentage oxygen setting on her ventilator and get a brief report from the nurse. Then I would know how she was doing, and it was time to play a CD or pick up a book and start reading to her.

For the past two days, I haven't been checking the screen; the numbers are there, of course, but they aren't the focus anymore. The focus is her face and her eyes and her perfect teeth, visible again now that the ventilator tube is out of her mouth. And most of all, as of tonight, the way she can shape her features to indicate how she feels, otherwise known as showing emotion; making a face.

It was a very faint effort that she managed; she was mouthing something but not making a sound, and she did not really look at me, though her eyes were open. When I leaned into her field of view, her gaze did not lock on. Instead, she seemed to be staring at the ceiling, looking past me into some middle distance, and maybe not absorbing any of the situation in front of her.

But when I spoke my name, and Tyler's, there was an effort to animate her features that simply wasn't there the past month. She blinked, she moved her head very slowly to the side, her cheeks moved, and the shape of her mouth changed. Just like a faint sound heard in the distance, or the ringing of a telephone that intrudes on a dream, she did just enough to make it clear that she was doing something, and that something was to smile. Several times the smile made it into her cheekbones and her eyes gently narrowed.

And there was a hint of the other difficult aspect of the journey, the part where the heroine not only has to run from danger, but with a twisted ankle (not just running from the bad guy in high heels, but with an actual physical injury). Twice, tears were visible toward the corners of her eyes, once when the nurse spoke to her very sincerely of how lucky she was, the other time when I listed the people who were praying for her and rooting for her. These tears were tiny hints of the emotional struggles to come, when her return to awareness will include learning what happened to her and to those she knew.

It is important to remember that she is not emerging into consciousness on her own, without permission; she is being maintained at a certain level of awareness by medication, which controls both her perception of her surroundings and her pain. It is joyful to see her, as if through the window of a passing train, but she is still on a very different track and has quite a journey before the tearful hug of reunion.

She will not be allowed merely to snap awake, and it would not be kind to let her. On the other hand, they are not going to push her down any farther than absolutely necessary, because they need her strength and her will to help her get better. The more time she spends on her back, the more she needs to draw on mental strength to balance a very real physical decline. So they need to start keeping her closer to the world. She will reenter it with tightly calibrated gradations. Inevitably, with the regaining of full consciousness will come the ability to ask, and to be told about, the state of that world.

Even so, just with this stage, this step above absence, she seemed as if she had surfaced from the depths of the deep ocean, shaken her head for a moment, and taken her first breath of air.

I had a lot to tell her about, by the way. Tyler took his first two stumble-steps today. He was holding on to Fran's beautifully baby-proofed coffee table, saw his mega saucer (nonparents: this is the self-contained bouncy seat where the baby is supported in a vertical position at the center of a plastic circle and can rotate to play with all sorts of cute gadgets), let go of the table, took two steps, and made it to the saucer without falling. These weren't his true first steps, but he's rehearsing.

He has no fear of walking, that's certain; in a way, today he was just like his mom. She took her first steps back from a dream and he took his first free steps on his own. He didn't know enough to be scared, and he didn't really know what he had done; but I was shocked, and stared at his little back, jumped, and got the video camera. I then photographed him cruising (nonparents: the act of walking some fair distance while holding on to a piece of furniture for balance) three times around the perimeter of the coffee table. She took the first big step on her journey back to standing on her own; he began his.

He didn't just begin it, actually; he notched the first leg. For several hours he stayed with a family down the hall. Instead of carrying him the sixty or so feet to their door, I held his hand and he walked the whole way. (They have two boys, which means that they have had to fit their fairly large apartment around a substantial toy collection. From the moment Tyler arrives there, he commences examining each and every one of these toys, to the powerful amusement of their youngest, who instantly becomes the seasoned veteran of Toyland.)

For me, today was therefore basically the crying game. I cried at the end of the day, when I spoke to Lauren and told her it was great to see her again. In the middle of the day, I caught the end of the movie *The Crying Game*. And at the beginning of the day, I read a brief passage that also and instantly brought tears to my eyes, not of sadness, or even happiness, but of gratitude.

Without giving too much explanation, let me say, simply, that one person who receives this daily e-mail has spoken about Lauren to a member of our armed forces deployment, and the captain wrote back (to her, not to me) as follows:

"I'm sure it's not much consolation for Lauren but tell her to rest assured that a world-class combat search-and-destroy outfit is on a mission to bring to justice those that would infringe on our right to freedom. They will pay back ten times for the wrongs they committed against Lauren and we will hunt them down and eliminate them from society. We will not sleep and we will never go away. These people and those who support them will have to sleep with one eye open for the rest of their lives.

"We will do this in honor of Lauren.

" 'These Things We Do That Others May Live.' "

I don't really have anything to add to that, except thanks.

Love,
Greg & Lauren

I wrote yesterday that I cried as I told Lauren, It's good to see you. That's true—but it would be more accurate, in retrospect, to report that I cried not because it was good to see her, but because it was good that she could see me.

Tonight there was no doubt about it. When I arrived, her eyes were open, and she was blinking. I said hi, told her the usual (love, Tyler, etc.), and then said, Honey, you look great, give me a big smile.

And she smiled, not once but twice. It was the same as yesterday, just a hint, but it was there, indisputably. I can't tell you how much joy there is in just having that connection with her, after the month she has spent. It's really as simple as the switch, which had been turned off, being turned on; there's something there, and the act of communicating with her is more than just voice therapy. It's communication again.

I don't want to belabor the point; she is this aware because this is where the doctors want her to be, but it is still an incredibly emotional thing. I won't build my hopes up excessively. She is not even halfway through her critical stage, her wounds are still not completely closed, and she faces continued risks of infection and major surgery. Then once her wounds are closed, the big challenge will be weaning her off the drugs she has needed to make it to this point. She is allowed to be made more aware because they are already in the process of reducing levels of some of her medications.

She has done well by empirical measures.

The antibiotics she is receiving appear to have made an impact on the resistant bacterium. Her facial swelling is well down from five days ago (though up slightly since yesterday). Her face continues to look great. She appears to have changed "metabolically"—she is healing well, and faster. Her upper back is almost completely healed except for three spots about one by three inches in size. Her right-hand autograft is doing OK, and her left-hand homograft appears to be doing well.

Then there is the literal flip side. Her buttocks have yet to be successfully grafted, and she was scheduled to undergo that procedure Thursday or Friday, by which time she was expected to have recovered enough from her crisis. But she has done well enough since last

Friday that they have moved the surgery up to tomorrow. (She will again be the first case in the OR.)

During this surgery, she will be placed in the prone position (on her stomach), and then will remain prone for five days to permit the grafts to adhere and start to heal. When I wrote last week that she faced a critical ten days, it was because of this surgery.

I noted to her doctor that the last time the Yankees won a playoff series, Lauren had a baby the next morning. He said he hadn't run any tests to confirm this, but he did not believe that Lauren was likely to have a baby tomorrow. I clarified that what I meant was that when the Yankees play a clinching game, Lauren tends to have a good medical night. But I liked that he showed some humor; this was another in a series of tea leaves that could be read to indicate that Lauren's situation really was coming along.

Later, I spoke to another doctor, the one who had said five days after September 11, regarding Lauren, that she was hanging in there pretty well, would get sicker before she got better, but they would do everything they could to pull her through, because they didn't want "those bastards to get another person."

This evening, he came over to ask how I was doing (he knew quite well how Lauren was doing). He again pointed out that she was doing well for such a critical case.

I reminded him of his earlier comments, noting that while I knew they devoted the same lifesaving effort to every patient on the unit, not just to the WTC victims, his determination had lifted one worry from my shoulders weeks earlier, because since then I had never doubted that her doctors were as dedicated to saving her as I was.

Regarding the WTC patients, he said that the doctors and nurses do take the situation personally—the victims were friends, neighbors, colleagues, and all they were guilty of was going to work.

There were very few days off at the Burn Center in the days following the WTC tragedy; for weeks the staff did little but come into work to ensure that their patients got the best possible care. And the disaster plan is still in effect. Lauren has had FEMA nurses from Florida, Utah, and now Seattle in the last several days. Nothing is being left undone to make sure that the care of these patients is properly managed.

When it came time to leave this evening, it was actually easier than it had been in the past. In the days immediately after September 11, I didn't even want Lauren to know I had left the room, figuring that since she couldn't keep meaningful track of time, she would be better off to think I was always there. Then I realized that this tactic might be creating some anxiety, so I started saying good night. But I felt that the more aware she was, the less willing she would be to see me leave, even for a good night's sleep.

Instead (and probably predictably), the more aware she is, the easier it is to leave for the night because I can now tell that she is trying to get some sleep!

So I left the hospital, and joined my friend Bill at the Beach Café, my frequent hangout at Second Avenue and 70th Street, to watch the Yankees beat the blue-collar boys from the East Bay. It was a nice way to end the evening, and to look with optimism toward tomorrow.

Love,
Greg & Lauren

From: Greg
To: Everyone
Date: Wednesday, October 17, 2001 12:58 AM
Subject: Lauren Update for Oct 16 (Tuesday)

Lauren did well in her surgery today and continues to do well tonight. She received a 3-to-1 autograft to her buttocks, covered by a 1½-to-1 homograft. She went down at 7:30 AM on the minute, and came back up at 12:30 PM on the minute.

Her doctor informed me that the operation went well by saying "We're back" with a certain restrained ebullience; he said she did fine, and that he was able to do what he set out to do, which was to apply an autograft to the site, which would be permanent, rather than a homograft, which would have been temporary and would have needed to be replaced within two to three months.

The deciding factor was whether the site was healthy enough for the autograft of her own skin to adhere. Were it not, then he risked wasting the autograft. In that case he would have applied the homograft, and then gone with an autograft when some healing had been achieved. But a pure homograft had already failed at this site before; a successful autograft would be a far, far better outcome.

The good news for Lauren is that this will be a permanent solution if it adheres; the bad news is that as mentioned, she must remain prone for five days to maximize the chances of adherence. This is something I would want to do only under sedation and with full-time pain management, but I don't think she is enjoying it even with those mitigating factors.

Still, her nurse reports that she is resting comfortably; her heart rate is lower, and her blood pressure is normal rather than elevated. When she gets agitated, it does not seem to be her position, but merely that she wants to know that someone is there with her. When she is reassured that she is not alone, she relaxes. They have the lights off so she can sleep, and they are spinning Enya-type music to help her stay relaxed.

And, like the tough mother she is, she is doing what she needs to do to get by.

Each step is a little step, but at some point we will look back and realize we're more than halfway to being out of the woods.

One benefit of the prone position is that I can caress the other parts of her back (too gently to be called a rub) for quite some time. This is something she always enjoyed (who doesn't?), but it was the first time I'd been able to do it since September 11. I stood there and eavesdropped on just a small part of the nurses' report.

As the nurses change shifts, they "make report." When doctors do rounds, they discuss each patient's care and maintain or modify the treatment plan. The nurses are responsible for carrying out that plan, while monitoring the patient for every moment he or she is under their care. So when the nurses make report, they agree on where the patient was when handed off, and then exhaustively review the flow rate of every drop of fluid, making sure that ample supplies of fluids and medications are on hand, that IV lines are clean, and that the nurse on the incoming shift knows what to watch for, and any other idiosyncrasies of that patient's care (including which CDs the husband wants to be playing in the background).

A lot of information is exchanged; as one of the nurses explained tonight, they "make sure that everyone is speaking the same language when it comes to caring for the patient."

When I left tonight, Lauren seemed calm and relaxed, and I felt hopeful about the next few days. There is that word again, hope. It has been a precious, and finite, commodity since September 11.

Early Sunday morning, another critical patient died; I did not hear of this until Tuesday. The news, even though it was more than forty-eight hours old, was heartbreaking. The man's wife, who had been in the waiting room constantly for days, had not been there the previous two, but I hadn't been arriving until the early evening so I thought maybe I was just missing her. When I learned the truth, it merely confirmed what I think I had guessed at but not spoken. This battle is for real, and the stakes are very high. Sunday provided another stark reminder.

But with every story of sadness comes another story of inspiration. Today I learned that the staff chaplain of the Burn Center was in the World Trade Center when it was hit. This is something she had told none of the families, even though she has been here, helping to comfort each and every one of us, from the beginning; not to mention stuffing us with comfort food (she is the source of the Rice Krispies Treats, the cookies, and the chips).

She was in 2 World Trade Center on the 16th floor when Tower One was hit. She heard a tremendous boom, the building shook, and she turned to the window to see vast quantities of debris raining down on the World Trade Center Plaza. Her first instinct was to get out of the building, but the instructor of the course she was attending said to wait where they were for instructions.

There were PA announcements that Tower One had been hit but that Tower Two was secure. She kept insisting the building was not secure. Her position as staff chaplain at the Burn Center is sponsored in part by the New York City Fire Department; she had learned through contact with firemen that what they all needed to do was to get the hell out of the building. She and some other people made their way down to the lobby.

When they got there, people were milling about inside, not getting out because of the continued PA announcements to stay put. She kept shouting, We have to get out, and left the building, literally dodging her way through falling debris and fireballs that were cascading down from Tower One.

She headed south from 2 World Trade, so was directly underneath the flight path of the second plane when it hit. She said the sound was so enormous that she thought she would die right there; I believe her, because none of us have ever heard from up close the sound of a jumbo jet with its engines fully revved flying at an airspeed of over 400 knots.

(The vibrations are so intense, they vibrate all your internal organs—I was at an air show and stood under fighter jets as they flew less than 200 feet above our heads. The volume is deafening and the grinding vibration overwhelming.)

There was another huge boom and series of explosions, and she began to run, all the way to the firehouse close to Beekman Downtown Hospital. The hospital was a madhouse; injured were streaming in from the disaster, and many people were irrational and screaming. There was another chaplain there too who knew her, and who told her she had to get to the Burn Center.

But the subways were closed down as soon as Tower Two fell. She started walking north, and at City Hall found an off-duty cop who was able to give her a lift to the Upper West Side, where she caught a crosstown bus to the hospital. It was on the bus that for the first time she had a moment to relax and think about what happened, and she broke down in tears. But she made it to the hospital and was ministering to patients and their families by 11 that terrible morning. Like so many others at the Burn Center, she feels she is doing her life's work. She was there and she was spared, and she is sure that this was for a reason, and who can possibly argue with her?

In many ways, I feel the same way myself.

As I send this off, I hope that Lauren is sleeping gently, soothed by calm, serene music; just four and a half days to go, honey.

Love,
Greg & Lauren

P.S. Wednesday's *New York Times* will feature a story on Lauren; I think the reporter did a good and thorough job, capturing the essence of why Lauren has managed to survive: Love and Grit.

From: Greg
To: Everyone
Date: Wednesday, October 17, 2001 10:07 AM
Subject: NYTimes.com Article: A Fireball, a Prayer to Die, Then a Hard Battle
         to Live

This article from NYTimes.com has been sent to you by Greg.

A FIREBALL, A PRAYER TO DIE, THEN A
HARD BATTLE TO LIVE
BY LESLIE EATON

This is the story of a woman who decided to live. No one knows yet if she will.

Her name is Lauren Manning, and on the morning of Sept. 11 she had just walked into the north tower of the World Trade Center when the first plane hit. She was engulfed in a fireball.

"I heard a whistling sound and I was on fire," she told her husband, Greg, when he found her at St. Vincent's Manhattan Hospital that morning. "I prayed to die. Then I decided to live, for Tyler and for you." Tyler is their 11-month-old son.

The terrible calculus of the catastrophe at the trade center seems to have divided the people there into two neat categories: the thousands who escaped with their lives (and their nightmares) and the thousands who did not. But there is a small third group, the gravely injured, for whom the road from ground zero will be very long, if they get to walk it at all.

Mrs. Manning is a member of that group. She was transferred to the burn unit at New York-Presbyterian Hospital. She was among 17 victims of the attack, all of whom had burns over 14 percent to 90 percent of their bodies; she was among the most seriously injured. Five of the others have died. Three have been released. Others have been taken off the critical list. And seven, including Mrs. Manning, remain in a deep, drug-induced sleep while doctors tend to their wounds.

Her doctors would not talk, even in the broadest terms, about the treatment that she and the other patients were receiving. But the hospital confirmed that generally, a patient's chance of survival is roughly equivalent to the percentage of the body that is not burned. Age also plays a role; Mrs. Manning is 40 and extremely fit.

Infection is a constant threat, and patients who survive face multiple skin grafts and months, even years, of physical therapy.

Some of those who are close to Mrs. Manning are reluctant to talk about her, because she has always been a very private person. "I suspect she knew far more about me than I knew about her," said an old friend, Harvey E. Rand. But he decided to talk about her, a woman he described as "a ray of sunshine," because, he said, "maybe more people will pray for her."

Her husband, Gregory P. Manning, said he wished his wife could speak for herself. But he wants to pay tribute to her strength and courage, and to bear witness to the enormity of the injury that was done to her. "She deserves it," he said simply.

And whether she wants it or not, Lauren Manning has become a symbol of hope for Cantor Fitzgerald, the bond-trading firm where she works. The firm lost 700 employees in the trade center disaster. Others were severely hurt, including one in the burn unit with Mrs. Manning who died over the weekend.

"There are 700 families who would give anything in the world for their loved one to be where Lauren is," said Howard W. Lutnick, the president of Cantor Fitzgerald, whose brother died in the collapse of the twin towers.

"She's got to pull through, because she's got 700 families' worth of love," he said. "It's not fair, but she's part of their hope."

He is also eager to have Mrs. Manning back on the job as director of market-data sales. (Cantor puts out the bond market equivalent of a stock market ticker.) "She is the quintessential sales person," Mr. Lutnick said. "Driven, determined, energetic, self-starting, organized." And, he added, very beautiful.

Even in college, Mrs. Manning knew that she wanted to go into business, said Deirdre N. O'Connell, who went to Fordham University with her and roomed with her for several years in Hoboken, N.J. "Lauren was always very focused, that was just her," Ms. O'Connell said. "Very determined, really determined."

She also worked hard at being a good friend. She was the first person Ms. O'Connell called with news of her engagement. She got an internship for Mr. Rand's son this summer, when jobs on Wall Street were hard to find.

And when a colleague on the 105th floor, Gary Lambert, needed help with his love life, she was there. "She certainly used to give me, from a female perspective, very good advice," he said. "I'm a single man, she's a married lady."

She and Mr. Manning have only been married a year and a half. They met on the job in 1996, and started dating the next year. They got engaged in August 1999, the night before Mr. Manning had surgery to remove a benign brain tumor. "She took care of me for the next two months," he said.

Now it is his turn to take care of her, as best he can.

He thinks she had some inkling of how seriously she was injured and how hard her recovery will be—when he found her at St. Vincent's, she told him she needed to go to a burn unit.

"She was really helpless, but she was still trying to take charge," he said. "I was so impressed with her, so desperate to do everything I could to make sure she pulled through."

She was able to tell him some of what had happened to her. She had been running a little late for work—she was usually at her desk by 8:30 a.m.—in part because she had been waving goodbye to her son.

She usually took a cab down to the West Street entrance of the trade center, where they both worked. Mr. Manning is not sure where she was in the building, but he thinks she had just entered the lobby when the fireball hit. A good Samaritan got her on an ambulance.

Mr. Manning, who took the morning shift with the baby, was still at home when the plane hit the north tower. He got a call from a man on the ambulance saying his wife had been burned, but the call was cut off before he could ask where she was going. At 10 a.m., he got a call from the hospital.

Since then, he has been spending his afternoons and evenings at the burn unit—he spent the first night wrapped in a sheet on the floor of the beige waiting room. Wearing surgical gown, mask and gloves, he reads poetry to her or plays music on a CD player, everything from Bach to Dwight Yoakam. And he has been sending friends long e-mail messages full of love and pain, grief and hope, messages he signs, "Love—Greg and Lauren."

He has been to a memorial service for Mrs. Manning's colleagues at Cantor, many of whom were his friends, and to one for the 60 missing people from Euro Brokers, where he is a senior vice president. He has also visited ground zero with a friend, to say kaddish. Last Friday, he went to the office for the first time, at the company's temporary quarters near the tip of Manhattan.

And he is trying not to become too excited. Because, after a tough week, Mrs. Manning has opened her eyes. She remains deeply sedated, but on Monday, she smiled at him.

"I pray for Lauren to be happy again," he said. "I don't know what form that will take. But I do believe good things will happen to her— and she will deserve every one of them."

From: Greg
To: Everyone
Date: Thursday, October 18, 2001 1:05 AM
Subject: Lauren Update for Oct 17 (Wednesday)

Lauren remains on her bed, facedown, to permit the new grafts on her back to heal, so it is probably accurate to say that she is stable but slightly annoyed. I saw her at midday today and she seemed relaxed, but she would occasionally move her head from side to side, mostly when I leaned in to speak to her. As of late tonight, while her blood pressure and heart rate were not showing signs of stress, her nurse had requested additional pain medication just to try to make her more comfortable.

It is a little disorienting that she has had to be turned over just as she was doing so well and becoming more alert, but it was that very improvement in her condition, and that strength, that led them to move up the surgery that required this position. For all that she is doing well, she is still in the survival stage of her treatment, and she needs these grafts to take; she has just about three and a half days to go before they can be evaluated, and if they are doing well, she will have cleared an important hurdle.

She is completely unaware of how many people became aware of her story today, when it ran on the front page of *The New York Times*.

I knew that the story would be running, but I did not expect to see it on the front page. Or, rather, I did not expect to have my judgment as to the story's worth confirmed by seeing it there.

The day after the tragedy, on September 12, I felt that Lauren's story was extraordinary. Since then, I have written about why: because she was so badly injured, yet survived; because she was remarkably lucky, within the context of a grave, grave injury, to be on the street where the ambulances literally pulled up (and to miss being hit by debris that fell from a thousand feet above her); and because despite her injuries and her fear and her pain, she made a clear decision to live, and then handed it off to me to make sure that everything was done to give her a fighting chance.

Hers is one of thousands of stories, and I thought it deserved to be told, and not just through my e-mails, though I have tried hard to tell it well. I did not want to be front and center in that story, though I would necessarily be the person explaining it from closest to the core of her life; and I did not want to exploit her vulnerability by telling it, though I think she deserved to be honored (there is no better word for it) for the sacrifice that was imposed on her, and which, when she had to choose, she did not permit to drive her to despair.

I was not surprised that a reporter would think the story worthy of writing. I was definitely surprised to learn that it really would be on the front page. But Lauren did something that made her story remarkable, the reporter focused on it, and even the hard-boiled editors at the *Times* ended up seeing it that way, too.

Lauren decided to live. From the very beginning, I told people what she said to me, that she first prayed to die, then changed her mind; and that I was taking her at her word. Even from her induced coma she has continued to fight, and to fight hard, against the brutal realities of a serious burn. And the story hasn't changed, never will change, from that simple fact, which has the beautiful simplicity of a Hollywood pitch line: from inside hell itself, a woman decides to live.

That was the lead of the story, and that will continue to be the lead, even ten years from now. Everything that happens from here on in has been defined by her.

It was a private moment when she told me that she had prayed to die, then decided to live—but the moment I heard it I thought that this was one of the greatest things ever said, absent rhetoric, by anyone to anyone.

I may be attributing too much to one statement. But I think that reporting this fact in a news story does create a legacy for Lauren, and for Tyler; when someone's actions merit respect, it's not a bad thing for them to receive it.

I think that Leslie Eaton did a fine job with the story; I think she understood it from the beginning, and I saw her do the necessary leg-work to get it right, then to write it right. By writing the truth she equipped the story to find its rightful place.

While Lauren is unaware of the impact her story had today (or even that the story was reported), I have heard from many, many people, some who are receiving Lauren's nightly e-mail, some whom I haven't spoken to in more than a decade. All the notes have been eloquent and heartfelt and appreciated.

And this is the irony of this ghastly situation; at first you believe that your life is taken away, and it indeed has been; but in the vacuum that follows, you find that your entire life, not just your present but your past, rushes in. In many ways, Lauren and I have the opportunity to get our lives back; not just the quotidian aspects, but a real passion and appreciation for life, as well as, one hopes, after the flood recedes, renewed friendships and a much stronger love.

I want Lauren to feel that way too, of course, so we need her to pull through. And even then, all this is years down the road. I do not underestimate what she confronts, and I take nothing for granted. The hardest part is the uncertainty; but considering the alternative, why even worry about that.

The next time you drink a toast, then, please join me in raising a glass to Lauren's good health and long life; she has given me so much more than I can ever give back to her.

Love,
Greg & Lauren

(Some of this was written at 3:30 AM Friday, some closer to 11 AM; if I speak of today or yesterday below, both of those terms refer to Thursday, October 18. Early this morning refers to 3:30 AM Friday.)

I checked with the hospital very early this morning and Lauren was still doing fine, her temperature controlled (she'd had a fever earlier in the day) and her vital signs stable.

This was a very late night for me; I played a gig, we went on thirty minutes late, played for two and a half hours, and I wound up in the open jam portion of the evening doing a bunch of Doors covers when I would probably have been better off going out the door. Let me reassure people, therefore, that I am remembering to have fun, too. In fact, there were probably twenty minutes where I just thought of music; and then I thought of where Lauren was right then, and I didn't feel bad about having been preoccupied, just that the entire situation was impossibly surreal. I'm onstage, and she is in her bed at the Burn Center.

I learned today how difficult Lauren's first seventy-two hours were following September 11. At the time, I was heartbroken and desperate, but unless I make a conscious attempt to place myself back there, I have already forgotten the intensity of the helplessness I felt. In fact, Lauren had a number of complications and risky moments. Her day nurse those first days, who has consistently checked back on her, told me something about that today. But the best evidence of that was how different his demeanor is now that he is teaching a course again and not working shifts on the Burn Center.

Now he is relaxed and cheerful and wears a white coat with a shirt and tie underneath. He could not be more different from the man dressed in gray scrubs and blue tieback surgical cap who spoke to us with almost a wild-eyed intensity during Lauren's first days in the hospital. At that time his voice was deliberate, but there was a steel edge to it as he explained with methodical clarity everything they were doing to manage Lauren's condition. At that time, I thought of him as someone with an almost fanatical devotion, and thought how fortunate Lauren was to have someone that crazy in her favor taking care of her.

Well, he's not crazy. In person, now, he is quite low-key and gentle. His fanaticism of mid-September was not for his profession but for saving Lauren. His fierce concentration was more comparable to the game face of a pitcher who has to stay in a close contest for every second or risk losing everything because of a simple mistake. The sheer physical and mental effort of what he was doing exhausted me at the time, and I learned now that it really was that close. But he (and the night nurses at that time, who worked just as hard and just as well) got it done.

The difference in him from that time to this is the single best gauge of how ill Lauren was when she arrived at the hospital and how hard she had to fight just to reach this moment, thirty-seven days later. To quote the former madman turned patient instructor: "She is waging an amazing fight. Just amazing."

My father arrived in town Tuesday and has been to the hospital every day since. It is good to have him here. Last night he joined us just as the regular volunteers—the singer-songwriter, the realtor, the journalist—brought in their thrice-weekly provisions promptly at 6 o'clock. Actually he had left at 5:45 PM, being more on a Florida schedule and not wanting to have to wait until 6 PM to have dinner, but I reached him on his cell phone at one minute after 6 sitting on the crosstown bus at 72nd and York as he waited for it to pull away from its origination stop. I told him: Get off the bus and come back here.

The menu was Chinese beef and vegetables, beef lo mein, rice, ravioli, rigatoni, Bundt cake, and karaoke. And this may have been the finest karaoke in the history of the planet.

Christine is the real deal. She is the singer-songwriter, she has recorded several CDs, and she has her own small label. She went to the back of the staff room on the Burn Center floor, popped in the karaoke CDs, and started to sing. She did Whitney Houston and others note for note, and by that I mean every single note, cascading lines, all-out, full-tilt performance. She had to modulate her power to fit the room; after all, her audience was the families of patients and the staff of the Burn Center—nurses and support people in gray scrubs—seated at three rectangular tables and on chairs that lined one wall only a few feet away from her. She did most of her singing with a broad smile and her eyes closed.

From the moment she started, more and more people came in and filled the room; the doors had been left open and people started to drift in from the hallway and gather at the back as she sang. We applauded after each selection; she sang songs about heroes, and then closed her first set with a very campy version of "I Will Survive," during which I tried to form a chorus line of backup dancers but was largely rebuffed. (We pulled it together for about twenty seconds, during which the girls in the line far outshone my long-dormant dancing skills.)

As I walked down the hall after the first set, I spoke to one of the staff managers in the hallway, and he said that was the BCDC—the Burn Center Dance Club. When I say first set, this was because Christine was coaxed into doing another set later, when a second group of volunteers arrived with another full meal! By the way, Christine's CD is called "Worth of My Soul," by Christine Graham.

From there, it was a step down in talent (mine only), if not fun, to the Rolling Bones at Le Bar Bat. Christine and several of her co-volunteers came, as did the burn patient who had been released from the hospital two weeks earlier. He had pressure gloves on his hands and wore a small hat, but he looked and sounded terrific; he was very cheerful, totally into having fun, and it was really great to see him there. I dedicated the entire set to him and to the Burn Center staff and patients; I told everyone, This night, the fun's for you.

In the end, we actually played three Stones songs that I had forgotten, but I still felt on—for the whole performance, felt I was able to punch the notes, get the bottom going, and sail on into the morning.

Twenty blocks away, Lauren was doing the same thing.

Love,
Greg & Lauren

From: Greg
To: Everyone
Date: Saturday, October 20, 2001 1:38 AM
Subject: Lauren Update for Oct 19 (Friday)

Lauren's latest grafts look good.

As a consequence of having played music late into the night before and a nap this afternoon, I did not hear this directly from Lauren's surgeon. I did not reach the hospital until 6 PM, so I missed his conversation with Lauren's parents. But I heard much of it from the nurse, and some fill-in information from other patients' family members in the waiting room who overheard him.

This happens; we don't try to listen, but every once in a while the doctors come in and we hear what they have to say to the other families. Mostly when this happens, the news is good. Bad news tends to be delivered quietly, and in a closed room, in a firm but soft voice. For the good news, there isn't the same effort to take people aside. I am guessing this is because there is less need for privacy when the news is good.

I did receive some bad news related to Lauren's condition a couple of weeks ago, and I heard it in the big waiting room rather than in the private room, with about five chairs and a telephone, that sits between the big waiting room and the chaplain's office. (This is bad news I have already written about; regarding how ill she was and the state of some grafts.) But we were the only people in the waiting room at that time; it was about 11 AM, so we had privacy. I remember that almost at the moment I heard the news the temperature in the room seemed to drop twenty degrees, and I had such a sudden chill I needed to put on my jacket and my hat, even though nothing had actually changed from one moment to the next.

The opposite happened a couple of weeks ago. One of the senior doctors, who had been forced to deliver a stream of difficult news to one of the patients' families over a period of weeks, came into the waiting room one evening, grabbed a fresh Krispy Kreme (the local shop donates donuts several times a week), sat down and said, "Her lungs are doing much better," accent on much. Compared to how I had seen him deliver harsher news (I had been on the phone one evening when he came to the door of the small waiting room and asked for use of the room, clearly to deliver news of a patient's death), that night he seemed positively buoyant.

Today, I am told, Lauren's doctor's mood was very positive, and he used the words "very pleased." As I understand it, this is because the homograft, the skin-bank skin that is covering the base autograft, has adhered, which is a very strong sign that the autograft has really taken hold and that he may have succeeded in grafting the last significant damaged area.

I need to stress again that this does not mean that Lauren is out of the woods; it will take three weeks for the graft to fully heal, and for that period she continues to be extremely vulnerable to infection. She had a high fever this morning and was placed on a new antibiotic today. All it means is that she is now in front of the danger, and may be able to outrun it if these grafts heal as well as some of the others have. We will not know the answer for several weeks; but we are now thirty-eight miles into an eighty-three-mile journey through enemy territory; that is, we are thirty-eight days into a period of eighty-three days during which Lauren is expected to remain in critical condition. The enemy can strike anywhere at any time, and sometimes when the safe border is in view. But if the graft has really taken, she may have emerged from the thickest part of the swamp.

I went in to spend some time with her. The room was dark. Her day nurse for the past few days usually had the curtain drawn and the lights off so that Lauren could rest. Normally the curtain being drawn indicates that some sort of procedure is being performed and that visitors cannot enter, but in this case it just meant peace and quiet. The day nurse explained to me what had happened.

For each of Lauren's surgeries, the procedure has been to "take a peek" at the grafts under their surgical dressings after three days, then to take the dressings down—remove them—after five days. This was the third day post-op so today was the day for the peek, and what they saw was the best possible outcome.

The plan now was to take the dressings down as scheduled in two more days, then "flip" Lauren back over and place her on a special air bed that approximates the performance of a water bed. It is designed to float the patient so that there are no pressure points; Lauren would remain on it for seven more days, taking out to twelve days the period during which her buttocks will have optimal conditions to heal. With no plans for any surgery next week, Lauren will then have some days to rest.

As I noted, this was the last big area that needed to be repaired. The other large areas—upper back and legs—are largely healed, having been grafted several weeks ago. I took a look at one of these spots today, and I have to say the appearance of the grafted skin was better than I expected. Of course, I had no objective criteria on which to build an accurate picture, so I had developed my own concept of what a healed 3-to-1 mesh graft would look like based on glimpses of those sites shortly after surgery. But of course, this was before any significant healing had taken place. So today, when I looked at how the back of her leg had healed, I was very encouraged. (Remember, that's my opinion; Lauren will have her own.)

So she will rest next week, and then the following week will undergo surgery to touch up the smaller open areas, procedures her nurse described as cosmetic.

Now, that is not how I had understood the word with respect to burn treatment. It had been made clear to me that Lauren's treatment would pass through several stages: survival, function, and then cosmetic. We are still very much in the survival stage, though we are overlapping the initial parts of the function stage (which will involve several years of physical therapy). The true cosmetic stage will occur much further down the road.

What cosmetic meant today was that the areas that remain to be grafted are cosmetic by comparison, spots where grafts may not have taken hold, or spots at the edge of larger areas, but not entire limbs or areas of her torso.

If all goes well, it is possible that in three weeks or so, Lauren may start spending part of her day in "the chair," essentially a large exercise mat with the angles of a chair in which burn patients are allowed to sit for some portion of the day, to get them back to vertical and really begin their journey back to "the norm."

When I see Lauren sitting up, then I will know things have taken a significant turn for the better.

Speaking of sitting up, standing, and/or walking, Tyler today attended the first birthday party of a playmate of his. As we got off the elevator, there was a valet-parking line of empty strollers lined up along the hallway wall. Inside at the party, where the action was, Tyler was one of about ten year-old babies on the living room floor, crawling randomly around, some sitting, some kneeling, some standing up holding on to furniture or a nanny, one actually standing and taking several steps on his own before sitting down gently and then repeating the process. Some were crying, some were laughing, some were playing with toys on their own, some were fighting over toys and refusing to share, some wore the birthday hats, some wouldn't tolerate them even for a moment.

The menu was cupcakes, pizza, and Doritos. Pretty much all of it was for the adults.

At one point we lined up all the babies for a picture, and there was a period of between one to two seconds where they all sat there together, waiting for the photo to be taken. Then several babies started to cry, a couple crawled toward their nannies, and the neatly composed portrait of America's future scattered to the four corners of the rug.

I met the parents of Tyler's friends, and even have a play date Sunday at the home of one of them. This particular mother had reached out to me after hearing what happened to Lauren, and had actually gone so far as to buy on behalf of Tyler a present for today's guest of honor, vastly simplifying my life. There are favors and offers of help everywhere.

The only thing missing at the party was Tyler's mom; but she has a shot to be at the next one.

Another day enters the books. As all the families of the Burn Center patients say to each other every night: See you tomorrow.

Love,
Greg & Lauren

From: Greg
To: Everyone
Date: Sunday, October 21, 2001 3:25 AM
Subject: Lauren Update for Oct 20 (Saturday)

I had the conversation with Lauren's doctor today that I missed yesterday, but my report was accurate; the grafts she received four days ago, and for which she has lain facedown for four days, look "as good as can be expected." The autograft underneath cannot be seen because the homograft that was laid on top of it has adhered. This is excellent news; by comparison, the homografts had actually sloughed off the autografts on her arms and legs, yet those autografts have also adhered and have mostly healed. These most recent grafts are in better shape than that.

The question then becomes when does Lauren "turn the corner"? That point will not come for at least two more weeks, when these most recent grafts have not only adhered but healed and closed. (They were 3-to-1 mesh, which permitted a larger area to be covered but which requires tissue to "bud" and fill in the gaps.) We need to keep holding our breath, but for the first time, we can see the date on which we may be permitted to exhale.

Yesterday I mentioned the air bed that had been requisitioned for Lauren. I saw it today in the hallway, where it has waited on standby in case she could not tolerate the facedown position. But as of tomorrow she will have tolerated it for the optimal five days after surgery; her reward is to be "flipped over" and to get the special bed.

The special bed is just like a normal bed except that the area beneath the patient's body from the arch of the lower back to the heels features a special air suspension technology that floats the lower body, allowing wounds on the legs and backside to heal without being compromised by the pressure of the patient's own body weight.

When the bed is turned off, the suspension area is a beige rectangle six inches deep, approximately four feet long by two feet wide, carved out of a normal-sized rust-colored hospital mattress. (The patient's body above the lower back is supported by a regular mattress.) The bottom of the rectangle consists of sections of plastic membrane filled with a sandlike material. Even with the air mechanism off, this area felt extremely soft and gentle.

When the bed is turned on, air is blown into the membrane, which rises to a level flush with the rest of the mattress. The patient's upper body is supported, while the combination of air and sand floats the lower body with a uniform lift that prevents localized pressure points.

When they get her into this new bed, Lauren will be able to relax and heal, and I am relaxed myself just by the thought of how comfortable she will be after five uncomfortable days. Of course, she may not get too comfortable; she is penciled in for surgery Wednesday just in case; her doctor wants to keep her on the calendar in case there is an opportunity, for example, to close some of the smaller openings in the grafts on her back and legs. But the key consideration will be to encourage healing of the grafts she received this week.

Meanwhile, the fight on Lauren's behalf continues from "somewhere in the Middle East." I have continued to correspond with the captain who sent the message a week ago, describing how his unit would fight their battles in honor of Lauren. They have maintained an active interest in her condition since, complaining when they don't receive the update in a timely manner. I am happy to provide it.

Of course, the war is being waged on behalf of all who were injured or killed on September 11. The list of those who were lost continues to stagger, and memorial services are still being held throughout the

New York area more than five weeks after the attack. This sadness is the strongest assertion of the deep feelings of hope I have invested in Lauren. It is all too easy to imagine what it would have felt like losing her on September 11. I try to remember this as the conversations regarding her condition turn more positive, and I am preparing myself to completely surrender to a feeling of hope, and faith in the future, the moment she turns the corner.

Love,
Greg & Lauren

From: Greg
To: Everyone
Date: Monday, October 22, 2001 1:31 AM
Subject: Lauren Update for Oct 21 (Sunday)

Lauren is on her back again, lying on that special air bed, and her face is greatly improved. The swelling that she had from surgery and excess fluids has largely gone down, and so her delicate facial features have returned.

With her eyes closed, she looks as though she is merely asleep, and it is possible to look at her and forget where she is.

But of course, that is a momentary illusion. She is in the Burn Center, and over the next several weeks she will become aware of that. While she was in her drug-induced sleep, she was fighting on a primeval physical level; the harder fight will come on the conscious level. I experienced the first signs of that tonight.

Lauren was more awake than she has been since her injury. I arrived in the evening, and stayed very late. I had the Yankee game on, with the volume muted, and sat beside her. But shortly after I sat down, she started to open her eyes.

She had been lying there with her eyes closed; first they opened a crack, and then a little more. I spoke to her then, saying my name and that I was there, and she opened her eyes and they moved toward me. I don't think she could focus, but she was clearly understanding some part of what I said. The nurse said she was mostly reacting to my voice, but I saw a little more than that in her expression.

When I mentioned Tyler and told her I loved her, she did smile. But she also seemed to realize where she was, and her face moved from a smile to the squeezed eyes and downcast mouth of someone on the verge of tears.

I started stroking her hair, and told her that she was doing great and that she would be fine. I told her I would take care of her, that the doctors and nurses would all be taking care of her, that they were doing a great job, that she had done terrifically herself. I told her also of the people who had been there, Howard Lutnick, her office mate, her parents; but then I felt that might be too abstract, so I returned to telling her that she would be fine, that it would be OK to rest, that Tyler wanted to have her home again soon.

I think she heard me; I stroked her hair and she seemed to relax. But it will be so difficult for her, and that difficulty is no longer in the future—it is here.

When I left, instead of saying good night to Lauren and then taking my leave of the night nurse, I said I was leaving and she looked scared. So I told her she would not be alone, and I asked the night nurse to step over and introduce himself by name and reassure her, which he did. It was difficult, yet it was also easier to leave tonight than it had been any other night, because this time I was able to tell her that I would be giving Tyler a great big hug for her when I got home and know that at some level she would understand me.

I know that she is strong, a fighter, tough as nails; but she is also a person who has been grievously hurt, and she is about to make the transition from being asleep for over a month into rejoining the world. None of us can possibly imagine what that might be like.

Despite such forebodings, these are all still good developments; her signs are strong and today they reset the ventilator to see how well she would manage to breathe on her own. The answer was pretty well; the numbers on the machine (expiratory pressure, inspiratory pressure) were all at optimal settings, and left to her own resources, her pulse oxygen remained at 100 percent.

Lauren's nurse tonight had an interesting story. In June he had founded a long-term-disability insurance firm, using his nursing experience as a knowledge base that would help him better understand how to structure those types of policies.

On September 11, he had been at his new insurance office when he heard about the first jet hitting the World Trade Center. He made plans to leave by midday; when the second jet hit the second tower, he left immediately and went right to the hospital. Later that morning he was the admitting nurse for Jennieann, the severely burned patient I have mentioned previously.

He said that the admitting nurse is responsible for all the paperwork for a particular patient, securing a medical record number so that "everything interfaces" within the hospital's online chart system. In general, the admitting team consists of several nurses and doctors. They check a new patient's vital signs, check the fluids the patient is receiving, check the IV lines, check the wounds, and hook the patient up to all the monitoring machines. This is the team that surrounded Lauren when she was transferred to the Burn Center on September 11.

Lauren's most recent grafts have not done as spectacularly as I had been hoping, based on the reports from the third day post-op. However, they may still perform well; the special bed will give them a chance to continue healing. I hope to clarify the true prognosis for these grafts after speaking with her surgeon tomorrow. There is also the chance that he will give a more optimistic report than the nursing staff has; that's what happened with the grafts on her legs and on her back, and those have taken beautifully.

Finally, back in the West Village, Tyler and his dad had a swell day. Tyler did some very serious walking leaning on a sort of toddler's pushcart made by Fisher Price that's designed to help babies learn to walk by permitting them to balance on the handle of the pushcart as they motor onward. He walked about sixty feet down our building hallway and back, twice.

In the late morning, Tyler and his dad (me) went to that play date we set up at last week's birthday party. It was three blocks away, and we arrived on time.

There were four babies, three couples, and me. The babies wandered about as babies do, without really acknowledging each other much, just flailing toys and scampering off to the far reaches of the living room. This living room was in the basement of a town house and extended back for probably more than sixty feet— the result of an addition that was put on the brownstone at some point in history before this practice was outlawed, and certainly before the current owner moved in. Seven years ago, in 1994 (a good time to buy real estate), he bought this town house; he told me he had set out to buy a two-bedroom apartment but could not pass up the deal on this place once he saw what it was and where it was:

namely, a town house in one of the hottest neighborhoods in Manhattan.

The couples were very nice; the jobs inventory included among others a derivatives trader, a PR person, a wine connoisseur, an editor, and little old me. Our hosts provided bagels and smoked salmon and we spent two hours hanging out. I wanted Lauren to be there, and soon. So I will keep praying for that.

Love,
Greg & Lauren

From: Greg
To: Everyone
Date: Tuesday, October 23, 2001 9:47 AM
Subject: Lauren Update for Oct 22 (Monday)

(Much of this was written late at night Monday, October 22.)

Lauren remains stable, continuing her streak (begun on October 26 of last year, when Tyler was born) of sleeping overnight in the hospital on the day that the New York Yankees clinch a playoff series. She was less involved today in rooting for the team, but they won nonetheless.

While I was with her last night, she mostly rested. She did open her eyes several times, and I leaned in and told her, very clearly and slowly, that I was there, and that I loved her, and that many, many other people loved her, especially Tyler.

There were a couple of moments of real sadness, when it was clear that for a moment she understood where she was, and why I was wearing a surgical gown, cap, and mask when I talked to her. I realized that she could not see me smile, so I told her I was smiling. Reassurance seemed to work; that she has done well, that she looks great, and that the nurses are taking good care of her. But there was one thing that worked a little better.

I removed a picture of Tyler from where it had been taped onto the wall and held it eighteen inches from her face. It was the printout of a scanned photograph, just Tyler's face as he sat at a table in a restaurant, with his bottle in front of him. He was looking over his left shoulder. I asked her if she knew this was Tyler, her baby, and she smiled, indicating she did. She smiled again a few moments later when I showed her a picture of our dog, Caleigh. And it seemed that after this connection, she was content to go to sleep; she rested with her eyes closed for most of the evening.

Not only Lauren seems to do well when the Yankees are clinching some sort of postseason series. There is someone else in the family whose particular good fortune seems to correlate to the Yankees reaching a milestone: last year, Tyler was born at 6:25 on the morning after the Yankees won the World Series. This year, at 8:15 in the morning after the Yankees won their fourth consecutive pennant, Tyler took his first real steps—two in a row, from his nanny to me.

Camera crews scrambled to capture additional footage, and these exploits were successfully documented for future generations.

In the days following September 11, crowds of family members and friends overflowed the waiting room at the Burn Center. Discussion groups, mediated by the staff psychologist, were held for family members to discuss how they were coping; they could become a bit unwieldy because at any given time the group might involve more than thirty people. Some family members had asked to meet a recovering burn patient to hear the story from a patient's side, so they would know what to expect, so one day the group was addressed by an Asian man, an electrician, who had been burned over 65 percent of his body in June. He was working on an electrical riser in a new office building, a riser that was to supply power to thirty-two floors of a major financial services company, and someone had turned it on while he was in contact with it. He was not expected to survive, but he did.

He spoke about his struggle and, most of all, his recovery, and I was told he was inspirational. (I had not been able to stay to listen to him; I had become suddenly concerned about Lauren and had run to check that she was all right, which, within the context of her injury, she was.) His wife had spent every day by his side, even as she was pregnant with their child. He was discharged a little over a month ago; the new baby, a boy, came three weeks ago.

I had a long conversation with him and his wife today. He talked about how important the presence and support of family were; how the thought of his baby had carried him through; how he felt very changed by the experience, and very much wanted to help others who were going through a similar situation. Less than six months after the injury, walking around with a huge smile on his face, with a new baby at home, and with contagious enthusiasm, he was inspirational again.

And once again the contrasts were stark. Even as I was speaking to him about the joy of his own survival and hearing his words about how best to support Lauren, another patient on the ward took a significant turn for the worse.

Jennieann had begun to deteriorate the previous night; her family had been called first thing Monday and asked to come to the hospital earlier than has been their routine. They came early, prayed for her, and struggled to maintain hope.

Last night, right around midnight, she died.

I had grown close to her family over forty-one days, getting to know her mother and father, aunt and uncle, and especially her sister. I have experienced their moments of elation and moments of apprehensiveness; they have shared mine. I have met their friends, they have met my family. We have talked about our beloved patients' conditions constantly. They are a close and wonderful family, and now they are devastated.

Since September 11, the game at the Burn Center has been real. The truth is what it is; as the doctors themselves say, there are only so many arrows in the quiver. The doctors fight each setback until they run out of answers, and then keep fighting until the battle is lost. I have never in my life been in a situation where the presence of life and death was so real, where hopes were so strictly circumscribed, where so much tragedy resulted from deliberate harm.

We have prayed, we have been attentive to the words of the doctors, finding positives where we can, hoping for the best possible outcome regardless of the bleakness of a situation. There have never been any guarantees or certainties, and there still are not. Only in hindsight has it been inevitable that certain patients would survive through the current day. Tonight, tragically, another miracle story ends, and without a miracle at its end.

Someone in her family voiced a question last night, one I myself had struggled with mightily in the days immediately following the attacks: why endure such suffering, only to lose the struggle; why have to go through such an ordeal of prolonged suffering and uncertainty only to become another ultimate victim of the demonic attacks of September 11? Those of us in the waiting room have continued to exist at Time Zero, the moment of this horrible tragedy; and Time Zero has again proven that it will not easily surrender its grasp on those whom it first clutched on that day.

I have known the families of five patients who have died since September 15; I mourn each of them, even as I, and their families, continue to pray for Lauren. Every prayer, every minute, still counts.

Love,
Greg & Lauren

From: Greg
To: Everyone
Date: Wednesday, October 24, 2001 2:01 AM
Subject: Lauren Update for Oct 23 (Tuesday)

Lauren had a "very good day," and this was part of the nurse's report to the next shift. It means she was stable, no surprises, she did well with her fluids, her medications, and her protein intake.

Last night she slept for five hours.

This simple statement is actually quite remarkable; because she has to be able to be awake to go to sleep, and for her to sleep, truly sleep, without a boost from sedation (she is still receiving medications but has been weaned to a point where, as has been noted, she can open her eyes and look around) means that she is getting the first real rest she has had in more than a month.

In fact, I left last night as I saw her sleeping peacefully, and her nurse told me she would turn the lights down. I did the same thing tonight, seeing her eyes closed, but not clamped shut, as they had been; when she lies there resting, she now looks relaxed, as you or I would, rather than submerged, at an unknown distance from awareness.

It is interesting how my behavior has changed. I used to sit or stand next to her bed, reading poetry, telling her stories, talking incessantly to let her know that I was there and she was not alone. Now that she can see me, I have taken to sitting quietly beside her, watching to see if she opens her eyes; and then I stand up and talk to her, but far more simply, and caress her head; far less effort is required to let her know that I am there.

But far more effort is actually required to communicate with her because she is no longer a passive presence in the room; she has feelings, and is beginning to express them, however slightly. I was correct in assuming that reassurance was what she needed; her day nurse pointed out that too much talking can overstimulate her, make her anxious, that she needs to be managed with the sensitivity one would give a child, with simple words, soothing tones, and a gentle touch.

Even though it seems that she has awakened after a long sleep, it is more accurate to say that she has awakened to find that she has just run a marathon and is overcome by weariness. The most natural thing for her now is to fall back to sleep, to get the rest she missed. It is so calming to me now when she gently closes her eyes.

I learned a lot tonight during a conversation in the staff room. The thrice-weekly smorgasbord was laid out: tubs of pasta, rectangular tins filled with mesclun, three soups, three containers of Chinese vegetables, dessert breads, brownies, two buckets of KFC. Two weeks ago, there were as many family members as staff in the room when the food came, but three patients have died since October 10 and the cadre of family members is dwindling.

I spoke to one of the most experienced nurses on the ward, a man I have seen and smiled at and even been introduced to once, but never known much about. He is always on the unit, wearing gray nursing scrubs; he helps set up Lauren for transport to the OR, always seems busy, but had never rotated in to take care of Lauren.

This is because he is the "clinician," a senior nurse and instructor, who gives new nurses their orientation, helps troubleshoot patient management procedures, and otherwise gives the nurses and the patients the benefit of fifteen years of experience and knowledge.

As we spoke, I heard again how driven the staff was to save the victims of September 11; again, not as a slight to any other patients, but more as an acknowledgment that the fifteen critical cases were the victims of deliberate harm, so stood not only for themselves but also for all those harmed that day. Many Americans felt the need to "do something" in the wake of the attacks; many have volunteered, and many more have donated funds and services. But it is the staff at the Burn Center that has been most able to help the people most injured by the attacks. Some of the most critically wounded have died, but not before the medical staff did everything humanly possible to save them.

As the strain of the work wore on the staff in the early days, this man said, one of the senior doctors at the unit had told them to take pride in their ability to contribute in the most concrete sense to the healing of a city after a terrible tragedy. And the sheer intensity of the work—fifteen highly critical patients, all requiring triple-redundant, twenty-four-hour management—led someone at the unit to say, "If the disaster site is Ground Zero, then this is Sub Zero."

I also heard my worst fears of September 11 confirmed; that Lauren really had been close to it, and if she had not made it to the burn unit—as she had so presciently demanded when I reached St. Vincent's—her chances of surviving even the first twenty-four hours would have been slim. When she came from St. Vincent's, she was already behind in her fluids; they had done their best to treat her burns, but they didn't know enough about it.

The difference is that burn care is a total effort—not treatment of individual symptoms, but a broad engagement against an entire range of injuries. Neglect of any one danger can lose the whole game. Waiting around can in itself be deadly. If a patient falls behind what is essential in the resuscitation effort, it can be difficult or impossible to catch up. And the resuscitation procedures themselves use the patient's own body as a blunt instrument to fight the causes of death; they tax all the body's systems to the maximum in the effort to keep the patient alive long enough to have a chance to recover.

Youth and strength are key factors; if patients do not have the stamina, they may not be able to sustain the effort long enough to give themselves that chance. Lauren needed to play catch-up, but once she hit her stride, her youth and strength helped her maintain it, so she could stay ahead of the dangers that continued to stalk her like wolves on the trail of an injured deer. One serious stumble, and the wolves might have overwhelmed her. Had she been older, or not as strong, they might have caught her anyway. Nature is without pity, as was proven on September 11 and again last night.

But Lauren is young and she is strong, and that may be why she is lying in her bed now, sleeping peacefully, breathing mostly on her own, and becoming a symbol of hope to an ever-widening group of people.

Of course, that expanding group is elsewhere; in the waiting room we have moved from a crowd to an intimate gathering, as Jennieann's family woke this morning unable to do anything more for her than plan an elegant and loving memorial. But they continue to pray for Lauren; they are wonderful people.

Love,
Greg & Lauren

From: Greg
To: Everyone
Date: Thursday, October 25, 2001 10:52 AM
Subject: Lauren Update for Oct 24 (Wednesday), Late Edition

Lauren remained stable yesterday and through the night in a strangely quiet ward. It is as if the unit has joined the rest of the world in returning to normalcy; the adrenaline rush is gone, the glamour of fighting a life-and-death struggle has subsided, and I have suddenly grasped the reality that these last forty-four days, long as they have been, are only the first steps of a marathon.

That is not my own observation; it was spoken several weeks ago by a friend of mine who cared for her husband through his own serious illness. I told her then that I understood it, but perhaps not as well as I did today. The feeling struck me as I approached the glass partition door to Lauren's room.

I could not put my finger immediately on why things seemed different; then I realized that the cards and banners from children throughout the country had been taken down, and everything suddenly looked neat and crisp and stark—like a hospital. It meant that we were no longer in the throes of a special event, that we were just plain in the unit now, that in fact we had always been. The atmosphere had always been serious, but the hundreds of handmade cards had given a strong sense that many people around the world actively cared, and that brought a slight sense of cheer, a mitigation of the loneliness. (The cards had to be taken down because they were a fire hazard. They were moved to the main corridor outside the Burn Center and newly arranged on a wall there. One of the nurses was snapping a picture of the cards in their new location, "before they're gone," he said.) Now there is a much stronger sense of the long haul.

The Burn Center is still busy compared to its normal level of activity; I believe that there are six critical patients left from September 11, and of course new patients have been admitted since that date. But there is no hiding the fact that three of the September 11 patients have died in the past several weeks, and others have been moved to the step-down portion of the floor. The excitement, if that is the word for it, is over, and we are still here, still facing a very long road.

The atmosphere in the waiting room is also far more subdued now that Jennieann's family is no longer there. It's a reminder that the camaraderie we had developed was a coping mechanism, joined with the hope that we would all be coming to the hospital together for a long time, and that the patients would get to know one another and go through recovery and rehabilitation together. We would talk about how they would support each other, get each other through difficult moments. It was a very optimistic vision, but players in it have been wiped away with each death, and I am left with the impression that I have been strikingly naive.

There will be no routine, no zone that we can fall into to help us cope other than to get our rest at night (something I may have been neglecting) so that we can deal with each fresh challenge. In fact, reading this tells me that some part of me had become complacent, or relieved, that the days were falling into a rhythm, had become a certain set of expectations and disappointments that were almost predictable. The predictability was an illusion.

In fact, I had the proper approach a month ago; take it twelve hours at a time and do not build too many elaborate expectations for the future. There was a point a couple of weeks ago where I started to take things a day at a time, and I think I started to extend that a bit too far. Each day is all we really have.

That was clear last night, when I said good night to one of the other families. There was a safety, or at least comfort, in numbers that has been sharply curtailed.

Partly because of this, when I sat down last night, I wrote the following line: "For the first time since September 11 I don't know what to write." I was at a loss to say something new about what happened yesterday, as if a frenzied contest had paused and I'd looked around to discover that I was playing a completely different game than I thought.

It seemed as if there would be fewer chances for fresh observation, that the stages that are coming will not translate so well to being described because they will be much more powerfully about Lauren's own very real struggle to come to grips with things, not some abstract assessment about what she will need to do.

She is strongly stable. She is still breathing well on her own, her signs are steady, and every day that goes by without trouble is one more of healing. She is doing well, and last night one of the respiratory therapists, just getting off shift, was standing in front of her room, looking at her and telling me that Lauren was doing well, and that she, the therapist, was pulling for her. She is the hope of more and more people, but that makes the potential weight of all these hopes all the greater, and I want to make sure that no such burden is placed on her.

As the days passed and she endured surgeries and post-op recoveries, I developed such a strong sense of her strength that I lost sight of how vulnerable she would be once she was awake and would have to make a conscious effort to find her own courage. I was making assumptions on her behalf. I have referred to her countless times as a fighter, as tough, as resilient, but even if it is all true, none of this will matter to her now as she opens her eyes and looks around.

If this were a movie, now is the time they would go to a dissolve and show a black screen with the words "six months later." But this is not a movie, and the next six months will pass at the same rate as the last forty-four days.

What she really needs is for me to protect her—but not "high concept" protection, some lofty notion that I should be there by her side as she heals. Her needs are very basic—she is hurt and helpless. Last night she was able to look at me, to respond by nodding, but she was also trying to communicate with me, and because she could not speak, I could not understand what she was trying to say. I felt more upset and inadequate than I have since the first days following September 11, yet I was also wildly encouraged.

This is what we will face: difficult moments that will at the same time be wildly encouraging. She is doing great. She will do great. I can tell you this; I have faith in her.

And sometimes the only new thing that ever really needs to be said is that this is, indeed, another day.

Love,
Greg & Lauren

From: Greg
To: Everyone
Date: Friday, October 26, 2001 9:40 AM
Subject: Lauren Update for Oct 25 (Thursday)

Lauren sailed on through another good day, with some encouraging news. The grafts she had last week were 75 percent successful. This is good news because these were permanent grafts, using her own donor skin, and because failure would have wasted that skin, which is a scarce resource. While donor sites heal with almost no trace, each time they are harvested the remaining donor skin is thinner. The tissue used this time was extremely thin; it was difficult to tell until today how successful the grafts had been.

Normally a graft can be assessed after five days, but if the donor skin is very thin, the graft can look almost transparent as the five-day deadline is reached, and another two to three weeks may be needed to make a definitive assessment. What we wouldn't want to see is a longer wait and still a failure to adhere. But a 75 percent success rate constitutes progress. The 25 percent that failed to adhere will have to be redone, but are on her flank, an area that will not require Lauren to lie in a facedown position after the procedure.

So: Lauren's breathing is good (she still has the tracheal tube, but during the day they back off on the settings so she is breathing predominantly on her own; at night she gets an assist so she is not exhausted by the effort), her signs are stable, her blood pressure good. And her grafts continue to heal.

I cannot give much information on her mood yesterday; preparations for Tyler's social schedule kept me so busy that I could not get to the hospital until very late. But I was told she spent much of the day smiling; her night nurse thought that was because she could see the pictures of Tyler on the wall. While I was with her, she was resting after having spent a good part of the evening awake, so I simply sat in the chair near the bed, watching her sleep much as I might watch a child; thinking that even her mere sleeping was a miracle, caring deeply that she be happy again when she woke up.

Tyler is having a birthday, as you know; to usher it in properly we are having not one but two parties for him. The second one, on Saturday, his actual birthday, will be for the family. The first party, today, will be for him and eleven or twelve of his closest friends. I hope I am not overwhelming my apartment, but let's face it, I certainly am. The babies will be here with their nannies and select parents (those who can get off work), so many of them will have double coverage. The menu will be simple: cheese and starch in the form of cheese and crackers or one of four pizzas, some Doritos and salsa to cleanse the palate, topped off by two birthday cakes, one for Tyler and one for his friend Davida, who is also reaching the one-year milestone. Helium balloons will be bouncing off the ceiling, not to mention some of the parents. The television will feature the "Babies": Einstein, Shakespeare, Bach, Doolittle, Mozart, though I think the real entertainment will be the improvised floor show.

The pre-entertainment will be throwing up the streamers and the "Happy 1st Birthday" banners, laying out the vittles, and trying to find a place to hold the party between the piles of nicely wrapped boxes that have been pouring in via various couriers since last week. At least one of these wrapped boxes appears to be identical to another; finger tracings of the toy box beneath the gift wrap reveal no statistically different outlines. This was discovered by the person who brought the second box; he found the fact amusing. Clearly, it was an appropriate gift, having been selected by at least two people (and we do not know yet what tomorrow's party will bring). We will also be scrambling to lay down a rubber alphabet mat featuring interlocking teethed foam squares with removable letters and the numbers 1 to 10, the play floor of choice among Tyler's social set.

Our own decorating project mirrors one that was active at the hospital last night. I mentioned that the get-well cards and banners had been taken down for reasons of fire safety and reinstalled in the corridor outside the unit. In fact, these were only a small portion of the total. As I came and went late last night, four of the staff were busy hanging the rest of them in the area by the patient elevators, a large space that feeds onto a glassed-in balcony above an eight-story atrium, from which you have to turn right to reach the Burn Center.

It was an arts and crafts project they seemed to be enjoying immensely.

The largest banners had already been placed in the center of the balcony wall below the rail. The cards were arrayed around it and on the long glass atrium window above it. There were still piles of cards on the floor; the four women working on the project were kneeling, sorting through them, or standing, tearing off pieces of tape and affixing the cards at a diagonal, as if they were committed high school students decorating the halls before the big prom.

There are others who are just as committed. I still hear from the soldiers prosecuting our war in Afghanistan; they still say they are fighting on behalf of Lauren and so many others. From the perspective of the families of the injured, the war is proper and just, even though war itself remains the worst thing any of us can contemplate.

This war exists because there are people in this world who have dedicated their lives to annihilating those who have in turn dedicated their own lives to the following:

"We hold these truths to be self-evident, that all men are created equal, that they are endowed by their Creator with certain inalienable Rights, that among these are Life, Liberty, and the pursuit of Happiness. That to secure these rights, Governments are instituted among Men, deriving their just powers from the consent of the governed. That whenever any Form of Government becomes destructive of these ends, it is the Right of the People to alter or to abolish it, and to institute new Government, laying its foundation on such principles and organizing its powers in such form, as to them shall seem most likely to effect their Safety and Happiness."

I apologize for the civics lesson and I know it is not a prayer, but to this I say, Amen.

Love,
Greg & Lauren

From: Greg
To: Everyone
Date: Saturday, October 27, 2001 1:21 AM
Subject: Lauren Update for Oct 26 (Friday)

Lauren is still sailing on straight and true. Tomorrow, Saturday, she is supposed to be allowed to sit in "the chair." This is a real milestone; it means she is awake enough and strong enough to do it, even if only for a few minutes. That's progress.

I communicated with her tonight; she seemed less agitated, though she is full of questions and I have to say that try as I might to read her lips, I cannot understand what she wants to say as well as I'd like. In fact, I am terrible at it. But a woman whose husband reached this stage several weeks ago gave me a system to figure out what she is saying; ask what in fact she is asking about—the hospital, her condition, me, Tyler, her family—and then try to narrow it down.

We established that she was too warm, so the nurse removed a couple of pillows that were on her to warm her.

She wanted to know what hospital she was in; I told her the Weill Cornell Burn Unit at New York-Presbyterian, as she had demanded on September 11, and I told her that she had the best doctor in the world, which even if it may not be true—ah, heck, it probably is.

She wanted to know what condition she was in and I told her that we would go jogging together again, would take long walks on the beach with Tyler, would have our old life back. I told her that her body was fine.

I told her to relax, that she is doing great. I caressed her head, I tried to soothe her, and I think I succeeded a bit more than I had in recent days. She closed her eyes and went back to sleep, and as I have said before, it is now a thrill when she relaxes and starts to get the rest she needs.

I told her about Tyler, too, and how he had the first of his two birthday parties today. Though she seemed sad to have missed it, she also appeared to enjoy the news. She will be even more pleased to watch the video when she is up to it.

The party came off today and it was a success on every level. Several of the moms who reached out to me when they heard what happened to Lauren helped the preparations come through almost to the minute.

One mother coordinated the entire inviting process, another, the mother of the daughter who was the co–guest of honor today, got the cakes, the chips, and the pizzas. Lauren's sister shipped the alphabet mat for morning delivery; it provided a very gentle surface for babies to fall on their faces. Everything ran like a well-oiled machine. I think that all I really did was make the executive decision to have a party and to do it at our place, and it took off from there. All I wanted was the entire crowd to give Tyler a big celebration and then film it all for Lauren, and we got a terrific tape.

At one point, I pan the crowd, and there are seven babies sitting together at the center, surrounded by concentric circles of seated nannies and parents, then an outer ring of standing parents. We had about three of the dads and almost all the moms. The babies seemed to have learned something since last week; they looked as if they accepted each other's presence this time; there was less obvious violence and more sharing.

I looked around the apartment and realized we were having this entire party for Lauren but that very few of the people knew what she looked like, so I quickly printed out two excellent scanned pictures of the two of us taken for our wedding story, and taped them to the wall. Then I broke into the party to make an announcement, keeping it short: that these were pictures of Lauren, and she was probably sorry she couldn't be there but she would try to be at the next one—and all of a sudden I got all choked up, and couldn't continue. Not what I wanted to do at a crowded baby party.

I finished off as quickly as I could and then stepped out on the terrace. The sun was brilliant, there was a stiff wind from the west, ushering in a cold front; waves chopped across the river toward me. I leaned on the balcony rail, then back against the gray brick wall between the balcony door and the living room window, and collected myself. I took some deep breaths, looked at the beautiful day, thought of Lauren not being able to be here, and decided again she would be at the next one. There was nothing I could do about it today other than get it all on tape; so I went back in and got most of the people in the room saying hello to Lauren and telling her they could not wait to meet her.

It was a very interesting day. I found that people appreciated the chance to get together. The co–guest of honor's mother was very grateful to be able to have a party for her daughter; their apartment layout was too small, so she was having a family party over the weekend, having given up on a kids' birthday party. Today's gathering permitted her daughter to host a party for her friends, and it was truly a festive occasion. We ended up with two leftover slices of pizza (out of thirty-two), one extra slice of cake (out of two cakes; we froze two slices for Lauren, and gave one to the building doorman, who had let all the strollers in), and half a bottle of diet soda. I now know that this is a Sprite crowd.

I got along with the moms, I got along with the dads, and I reflected on what I'd been told by many people since the first news of Lauren's pregnancy—that we will meet our future friends through our kids. Today, as thirty people from three distinct generations milled about the place, I felt that I had helped both Lauren and me take our first real steps down that path. I can tell you for sure that once all these potential future friends were gathered together (some of whom have already clearly earned that status), I realized that I liked them, that they were interesting people, and they had some incredibly cute kids.

And so I give props (the proper due) to the Nanny Network of the Bleecker Street playground, because they sure pulled a great group of people together. Specifically, this means kudos to Joyce. Thanks, Joyce!!

Standing there, looking at the teeming throngs on the floor, was a new beginning for Lauren and me. There is so much catching up to do. Tonight I read the front-page article on Cantor Fitzgerald in today's *Wall Street Journal* about how the firm is struggling to rebuild. I realized that with so many sudden endings on September 11, the world is filled with new beginnings, and that this is true no matter what the odds against some of them may be. I don't know where this optimism comes from; I can't tell whether it is a belief in the strength of our country and society, and of our industry, or simply a coping mechanism to deal with the scale of horror that we have experienced: as if we suffered a massive blow but are managing, groggily but with resolve, to keep standing because we still think we can win.

I think the kernel of truth in this is that the flicker of hope is growing brighter every day, and that I am able to see three sets of footsteps tracking into the future for us, not just two. I want to believe that it will be a shared road, so I try to make sure that we maintain a seat at the table for the other guest of honor, the one to whom I raise every toast, the one who lies in the Burn Center—until tomorrow, when she will sit up.

We have to learn to walk before we learn to run; two people in my family will be doing that and I will be there with both of them. The road, by the way, is strewn with potholes; but I grew up in New York, and I think we can make it through.

There will be a day when the three of us go running together. That race will be won with the first step. Caleigh, of course, will be the fourth. She will run circles around us.

Love,
Greg & Lauren

From: Greg
To: Everyone
Date: Sunday, October 28, 2001 1:03 AM
Subject: Lauren's Early Edition for Oct 27 (Saturday)

One more time, I am unable to finish tonight; I think Tyler's run of birthday parties has taxed my endurance.

Since many of you look for a word first thing in the morning, let me tell you that Lauren remains stable and her situation is encouraging. Today was another good day.

I will finish writing tomorrow morning, during that extra hour (now if only Tyler understood daylight savings time . . .).

Best,
Greg

From: Greg
To: Everyone
Date: Sunday, October 28, 2001 11:39 AM
Subject: Lauren Update for Oct 27 (Saturday) Really, Really Late Edition

Lauren sat in "the chair" Saturday morning for two hours, the first time she has been upright since September 11. (None of us were there to see this; they put her in the chair at 8 AM for two hours. Her family or I are rarely there before 10 except on days when she has surgery, and on this morning we needed to be elsewhere, as I write about below.) Her nurse said that she was comfortable, looked around, and absorbed that she was sitting rather than lying down.

That single recognition may be the greatest initial benefit of being in the chair. The long-term benefits are, of course, very real; being upright restores Lauren to a more normal position, helps control swelling, rebalances her body and circulatory systems to a more natural equilibrium.

Another significant benefit is psychological. She does not know how sick she was; she is aware only of the past few days. She does not know how much progress she has made in six and a half weeks. But she is aware that she has been bedridden; every time she has opened her eyes in recent days, she has been on her back, except for the five days she spent facedown. The change in perspective from the chair would have demonstrated to her, on a very simple but powerful level, that she has made some progress; and she was able to revel in this discovery for two hours.

When we did see her, she was back in bed; she had recently come out of the tank room, so she was a bit sedated (they "snow" with medication for the tank to control pain and stress). But she did manage to open her eyes, and she did see us, and she smiled more often than she seemed sad. The broadest smile came when I told her that it was Tyler's birthday, that he would be having a big party with birthday cake, and that we would give him a big hug and a kiss for her.

She tried to talk to us, but still could not because of the tracheal tube. We remained terrible lip readers. She raised her head and seemed to be trying to sit up. She moved and raised her arms, and did manage to push her splints away. She appeared frustrated by her limited range of motion; her frustration and seeming agitation would have upset me in the past. But as I've mentioned, it has been explained to me that all of this is to be expected—the movements, the frustration, the confusion—as she passes through the transition from an induced coma to normal awareness. What is important is that she be continually reassured during this stage because it is only temporary.

It is possible that in a couple of weeks her lungs may have recovered enough for her to be extubated, or at least to receive the kind of tracheal tube that would permit her to speak. Then she can finally tell us her thoughts herself.

In many ways the challenges posed by this transition and her subsequent awareness are greater than those posed by the initial, though highly critical, stage of her care. The stress and the pain of the past forty-seven days have often been unbearable, but we family members were otherwise healthy people and there were places we could retreat to when we needed to cope; the waiting room or the normal world (or, as the soldiers said in Vietnam, "the world"). She will have to learn everything that we learned, but truly from the inside; she will learn her injuries, she will learn the world's injuries, but she will have no refuge, initially, other than her own resiliency and the love and support of her family and friends.

I know we all understand the power of that love and support. I firmly believe that it is what has sustained Lauren in this case. But sometimes it is not enough, and in the case of one of the other patients, as you are all aware, the story has simply ended, and we have to deal with its finality.

As Lauren is the embodiment of my hope for the future, Jennieann Maffeo embodied her family's hopes, and they were always at her side, as a military tactician might say, with numbers. A core group of five were at the hospital every day: her parents, her aunt and uncle, and her sister. They came in religiously at 2:00 PM and we had a ritual exchange of information: How's Lauren? How's Jennieann? (And of course, how is each of the other patients?) And there were always other relatives and crowds of friends. I spent considerable time with them; I said a prayer for Jennieann while I was at Ground Zero, and her family prayed (and continues to pray) for Lauren. I was close to Jennieann's struggle for more than five weeks; her room was no more than twenty feet from Lauren's. But of course I never met her, never even saw her; I learned what she looked like from her photograph in last year's Paine Webber annual report.

None of her family ever seemed to lose hope; her sister showed an amazing strength and confidence in Jennieann's destiny. Even when hope flagged, it was quickly rebuilt, and they never gave up, no matter how dire the prognosis. Until last Monday night, she had proven them right by continuing to survive. But she was never able to make the progress that Lauren has made. On Monday, as I've written, Jennieann's broad range of injuries overwhelmed and defeated her, and she lost her brutal forty-one-day struggle to stay alive.

Saturday morning we attended her funeral service.

We headed out early and drove down the Belt Parkway on one of the clearest days of the year. The weather was stunning. The traffic was very light; the air was sharp with the snap that cold weather brings; there was a slight chop on the water and the views of New York Harbor and Rockaway Bay were magnificent. We took the Bay Parkway exit and drove a short distance north, turning right onto 85th Street and a block of well-tended three-story row houses.

Mourners were gathering on the steps of St. Mary Mother of Jesus Church, a modern building in the middle of the block. Others had already gathered inside the glass doors around a tall wooden cross draped with sashes of red fabric, and were waiting for the morning mass to conclude before entering the church itself. Lauren's parents and sister joined the mourners inside and I stood with the crowd outside as the first of several long black limousines arrived, carrying members of Jennieann's family. When they stepped out I approached and gave my condolences to her aunt and uncle, with whom I'd shared numerous jokes about watching my briefcase during "happier" times.

Well over one hundred people took their seats once morning mass ended; and then Jennieann's casket was brought down the aisle, and her mother, father, and sister, always so optimistic, were portraits of grief. Jennie's struggle ended here, in this church; there was no hope left.

The priest said a prayer and the family took their places in the front pew. The priest climbed several steps to a proscenium altar, and stood at a podium beneath an octagon filled with bright light. The decor was simple; the walls of the church were stained-glass windows bright with the sun outside. The service began with prayers and the choir sang, the voice of the female soloist floating gently above it with what seemed a faint Russian accent.

I felt tears in my eyes and realized that this was the first individual funeral I had attended since September 11; I had meant to go to some others but had not been able to. At the time it seemed as if I could not manage the logistics, but now I see that this, too, was a coping mechanism. For me, Jennieann was standing in for everyone who had been lost, many of whom will never be found.

On this Saturday morning, I could not shake how close Lauren had come to this fate. (Or myself; I had originally been scheduled to be at the conference at Windows on the World the morning of September 11, would definitely have been there by 8 AM on the 12th.) Lauren and Jennieann had probably been less than fifty feet apart when the first plane hit. This was the same battle we'd been fighting; this is what happened when the battle was lost.

When the priest spoke about Jennieann, he came down the steps to walk along the front of the pews. He spoke with vigor and reined in his anger; he gave a message of hope and of salvation for Jennie, but he did not hide from the violence that killed her.

He said that violence lasts a short while, that life lasts far longer, that it was up to us to live full lives. He drew strong parallels to the violence of the crucifixion; he pointed to the crucifix bearing the body of Jesus to say that no matter who we are, violence can be inescapable; that sometimes there is no escape, and sometimes there are no answers except a deep faith in the love of God.

But he did this in an interesting way; he was not preaching a sermon. He repeatedly spoke to those of different faiths in his audience; he said that no matter what our beliefs, we were there to recognize that anger and hatred were evil. I do not think he was making a point about war. He was making a point about the slaughter of innocents, noting that Jennieann was the victim of an evil that did not respect life. He said that the evil did not respect any religion; that there was no faith that could possibly endorse this kind of deliberate horror.

Gesturing toward the small crucifix on a narrow pole above the proscenium, he said, "You saw the large cross as you came in. That one does not have a corpse on it. It is there to remind you that the story does not end here."

He said Jennieann was safe now; that she did not need our prayers any longer; that she was with God. He said that we should pray instead that the world we live in be one of peace, without hatred. He said it was up to all of us to live full and complete lives, to dwell not in anger but in love and hope for the future.

Jennieann's sister then approached the podium. She spoke of all the roles Jennieann had filled: sister, aunt, daughter, colleague, friend; the list went on far longer. She talked about how Jennieann was the heart and soul of many groups at work and at home; how she always showed up at every birthday party with balloons. She talked about how hard Jennieann had fought, saying, "We had a miracle for forty-one days," and for a moment could not continue. But she did continue, noting that her family had had time to be with Jennieann and to say their good-byes. I feel strongly, from personal experience, that Jennieann had to have known that they were there, and had to have gained comfort from that.

After the service I spoke to her sister and her mother and father. They gave me deep hugs; and each of them whispered as we hugged that Lauren would make it. Jennieann's sister said, "Lauren is going to make it. Jennieann will be the last one to die. You won't have to go through this."

Among the large crowd were the hospital chaplain and the attending physician who had been Jennieann's doctor. He looked deeply affected. I have written of how I had seen him at the hospital delivering harsh news; I had first seen him just before he informed one family of the death of their daughter five days after September 11; I had seen him meeting with the Maffeos and discussing Jennieann's treatment. He was the one who had struggled to save her despite her prognosis, who had been on call twenty-four hours a day, for just under six weeks, actually fighting the battle against insurmountable odds, and fighting it well. I think only a doctor can possibly imagine just what that involved. He and his colleagues were largely responsible for the miracle of forty-one days, and they were the ones who stood at her bedside, helpless, as they simply ran out of answers and Jennieann passed away.

No matter how scientific medicine may be, people become doctors because they want to apply their scientific knowledge to healing. While doctors must of necessity practice medicine with a certain professional disengagement, there is no question whatsoever that the doctors at the Burn Center have been passionate about saving those patients who were deliberately harmed on September 11.

Saturday morning, this doctor's personal engagement with Jennieann was visible on his face. He spent a long time speaking to each member of Jennieann's immediate family. Afterward, for whatever reason, I felt the need to tell him that I knew how hard he had struggled to save her and how grateful her family was for what he had done. We had never had a conversation at the hospital, but of course he knew who I was.

He said, "I wish I could have done more." So I told him that he had done everything he could, that he needed to hear from the family of a patient that what he and his fellow doctors had been doing at the Burn Center, how hard they had been fighting, was remarkable. Then I corrected myself; I said maybe he didn't need to hear it, but that I had needed to say it. And he graciously thanked me.

From the service, we went to the hospital and heard the good news about Lauren's morning in the chair. Then we headed home and had a family birthday party for Tyler with more presents and more birthday cake. From there, we packed Tyler up and drove to SoHo, parked the car, and pushed his stroller over the cobblestones, up and down over curbs, across metal gratings and narrow, uneven sidewalks, to the Susan Teller Gallery at the corner of Broadway and Prince. We were going to the reception for my friend Kitty's art exhibition; three generations of her family's artwork (hers and the work of her sister, her mother, and her maternal grandparents) were being shown. Kitty is a highly accomplished costume designer; her sister Gwyneth is a highly accomplished artist. (I think they are both sufficiently over their sibling rivalry to be described in this manner.)

When we reached the gallery, Kitty and Gwyneth were there, and Gwyneth's husband and daughter; my friends Bill and Marian and their daughter; and my close friend Scot, Kitty's husband, who has been living in Japan for over a year—it was a pleasant surprise to see him. We drank wine and admired the excellent artwork. Tyler took my hand and had a walkabout to look at the paintings himself.

One of the works was a collection of three of Kitty's costume renderings for *Gross Indecency*, a play that had a long run with a number of global productions. Her designs were stunningly provocative, were noted in the original *New York Times* review, and added as much drama to the play's second act as the script did (and it was an excellent script). Another painting, by Kitty's mother, shows Kitty and Gwyneth as young girls watching the Apollo moon landings on TV; Kitty lounges on a wing chair, Gwyneth is perched on a dining chair, there are craters on the TV screen, and through the window shines a crescent moon. A moment from 1969.

And these are moments from Saturday, October 27, 2001: the interplay of generations: our son's birthday, Lauren's great advance into "the chair," joy felt by parents of all ages in the attainments of their children, and a terrible loss by one family of their own hopes and dreams.

A full day.

Love,
Greg & Lauren

When I entered her room this evening, Lauren was more active than at any time since September 11. She seemed to recognize me immediately. I was surprised to see her waving her arms and mouthing words to me. We are still lip-reading; the nurse told me that she read Lauren saying, "I love you, Greg."

This brought tears to my eyes. I told Lauren the same thing for perhaps the thousandth time since September 11.

Unfortunately, as I have noted over the past few days, increased awareness brings with it increased realization, so she was also quite agitated. While she did not appear to be in pain, she clearly did not want to stay in the bed. She tried to sit up, tried to move her legs; she seemed frustrated. I didn't think my words of reassurance were doing any real good, so I asked her nurse whether I was helping her. She told me, honestly, probably not.

She wanted Lauren to go to sleep, and while I was there, sleep was unlikely; my presence stimulated her and made her agitated. I had the same sense, so I headed home with my father to play with Tyler.

The New York Times ran a story today on the bureaucratic morass that bereaved families must wade through to receive any funds that were donated to relief organizations in the wake of the World Trade Center disaster. The article is accurate.

I was interviewed by a representative from the Red Cross within a week of September 11; I provided all the information I was asked to provide; I mentioned other households I knew about who might need assistance with travel and other out-of-pocket expenses; I was promised a check to help cover our living expenses for a specified period.

The funds have not yet arrived, but I most assuredly am not criticizing the volunteers. Every single one of them has gone out of their way to try to bring closure to the situation, and has conscientiously followed whatever procedures were required to ensure that my file was speedily and accurately processed. Every single one of them has been supportive and listened on a personal level; their very being there means that their highest priority at this time was to devote themselves to helping those in distress. I can only compliment them for being committed to this task. It appears to be the organization itself that has wilted under the stress.

What has happened, I think, is that not only has the amount of money that flowed in been unprecedented, so have been the needs of the bereaved. But the very procedures designed to make help available have seemed to change from one day to the next; you may have satisfied all the criteria on any given day, yet the criteria were changed the next day, and you could no longer tell which extra piece of information you needed to provide in order to complete the file. So you wind up giving the same information over and over, while growing more and more philosophical.

At this point, it does seem as if I am waiting not for a check, but for Godot. I have to say I never saw the play, but I certainly feel as if I am caught in the wings of an absurdist drama, waiting for someone who will never arrive, while endlessly recycling the application process.

I hope that things do get sorted out. There should be a central database, there should be an office created to guide families through the agonizing process of finding the appropriate charities for assistance. The New York State Attorney General is pursuing setting up something along these lines, according to the *Times;* it cannot happen too soon.

This tragedy will reverberate through the generations; it is important to get this aspect of it right, so that families do not spend the coming years not only bereft but bitter at the mismanagement of the outpouring of love and assistance that was directed at us.

From the *Times* story it does appear that some competent people have identified the need to streamline this process. What the government needs now is someone to cut through the Gordian knot of red tape that has held back the distribution of charitable assistance. It is becoming increasingly clear that ensuring that the victims' families are provided for over time will be a huge and demanding job, requiring someone who can shake up entrenched bureaucracies, no matter how well-meaning, to ensure that they perform their intended services.

Love,
Greg & Lauren

From: Greg
To: Everyone
Date: Tuesday, October 30, 2001 12:01 AM
Subject: Lauren Update for Oct 29 (Monday), Capsule Edition

Lauren rested today, so I did not speak to her, but only because she was catching her first real sleep in thirty-six hours. She looked great.

The news continues to be good. We have had it confirmed that the grafts on the difficult area of her back were 75 percent successful. She is now due for her next surgery on Friday; the remainder of the back grafts will be redone, some open spots will be closed, and she will have additional work done on her hands.

For the moment, she is not on any antibiotics, and considering the infections that she was fighting only two weeks ago, this is a remarkable performance.

She is still hanging in there, and so are we. I feel thankful for a day where there is not much to report.

Love,
Greg & Lauren

From: Greg
To: Everyone
Date: Wednesday, October 31, 2001 3:16 AM
Subject: Lauren Update for Oct 30 (Tuesday)

Lauren had her eyes closed when I entered her room, but I'd heard from her parents that she was awake and alert most of the day. Her nurse called her name out and she opened her eyes. As I had so many times in the last seven weeks, I said, Honey, hi, it's Greg.

This time she looked me right in the eye and smiled.

There she was: still hurt, still vulnerable, still critical, but fully alert and expressive. She still cannot speak, but she clearly understands and clearly answers, to the best of her capability.

So I told her I loved her, and then I asked her if she remembered how sometimes she would ask me how much I loved her, and I would have to show her by holding my hands apart and saying, This much; so tonight I told her that I couldn't hold my arms far enough apart to say how much I love you.

The nurse told me that I did not need to wear a surgical mask anymore. So I took off the mask and was able to smile at her; before, my smiles were hidden by the mask and she would have had to guess at my facial expression.

I asked her if she wanted to see the video of Tyler's birthday party and she immediately nodded yes. I had brought our camcorder with me to play it back; it is a digital Sony and has a playback LED screen with sound. I held it in front of her and played back the video, and I watched her smiling as she looked at Tyler crawling around or walking while holding someone's hand. She got to see the baby convention we had in the apartment, including the shot of the five babies, Tyler among them, standing around our coffee table and supporting themselves with their hands on the glass top.

Her mood was, frankly, a lot more positive than I had feared it would be, but I guess she is simply glad to be alive. She smiled when I called her the Princess of Perry Street. She cried when I told her I was so happy, I was going to cry; so instead I smiled and she smiled again with me. She was clear, and she was present, and she was trying to be strong.

She wanted to hold my hand; at one point, she waved both arms at me and seemed to need something, and I asked if she wanted a hug and she nodded yes. So I got as close to her as I could and put my right arm around her left shoulder, and held her for a few minutes as she relaxed with her eyes closed.

But she is still very ill; there is still a long road ahead. She is aware that she is hurt; when she was in the tank, she saw her left hand and wanted to know what would happen—what the surgical course will be. She experiences discomfort now that she is awake; she may need to be moved because her back hurts, she may need sips of water because she is parched. She does not like the feeding tube, but she needs it to continue receiving the high protein diet that permits her to heal so well.

The nurses have all said that once patients are awake, having to lie in an ICU bed will drive them crazy. The lines and the tubes are foreign bodies and can be very scary; I could see all this in Lauren's face as well, but I knew immediately that my faith in her was well placed. When I saw her being sad, I told her that I would take care of her and we would have our life back, and that it would be better once she was back on her feet.

It is so different being able to communicate with her. For close to seven weeks she was absent from her own body; I could speak to her but I could not even be sure if she heard me. The first few times she opened her eyes she struggled to give a hint of a smile, but clear communication was impossible. She might get upset; she might take a long time to answer; she might not answer at all. This is so different; this is my wife again, this is Tyler's mother, this is someone able to experience joy, and unfortunately also pain, but also able to be present and have a personality.

That's the difference; she was there, in the bed, but her personality was on some sort of extended leave. Now it is back.

The best example of her restored communication skills came around 6:30 PM, when her nurse mentioned that this was a big sports night in New York, with Michael Jordan returning at Madison Square Garden and the Yankees playing in the World Series. I said, Guess who has a ticket—I do! The nurse asked if I was going to the game; I said, It's up to her, pointing to Lauren. And Lauren's response was to mouth the word "Go" clearly enough that I could read it, and to wave her right arm simultaneously, waving me off to go have fun. So I went, after kissing her good night.

I scrambled to Mitch's place and got there just as they were loading into their car. We headed off to Yankee Stadium. We were all actually guests of Mitch's lawyer, a man I came to know well during the course of the evening. The driver took local roads through the Bronx and we got to the stadium fairly quickly—but it was slow from then on.

The entrance areas at Yankee Stadium were thronged with crowds twenty deep. We headed down to our entry gate and got into the slowest-moving line I have ever stood in. From 7:45 to 9:00 PM, we moved about twenty feet. The guy behind us asked for permission to smoke, saying we were standing so close we were family. We saw President Bush's helicopter approach the stadium for the landing, and we heard over our cell phones that he threw the ceremonial first pitch for a strike. We followed the game through the first two innings, and still we stood stranded outside.

At one point everyone started chanting "Let us in, let us in," and almost at the same moment, two fighter jets swooped over us at less than five hundred feet. I could not stop myself from thinking: this is what the jets sounded like at the World Trade Center, traveling low with engines rumbling just before they hit. It may sound melodramatic but it was also natural, they were so low above us. I think everyone in the crowd was a little spooked; we started chanting, "We're sorry, we're sorry!"

Finally we made it into the stadium, first passing through a metal detector, and passing our cell phones, pagers, wallets, and keys around it. We found our way to our seats, on the main level diagonally back from home plate on the first-base side, just as the pitcher dealt to the plate and Jorge Posada hit it out, for the first of the Yankees' two runs in this game.

Mitch and I stood up to get the requisite hot dogs; we ordered a total of four, plus four hot sausages for our little group of four. The counter girl who packed up and wrapped each dog was an artist, taking the time necessary to do the job right, being careful with the foil wrappings and neatly arranging the food on two trays, while the people behind us in line stewed good-naturedly. We also got two waters. Later it was time for soft ice cream; then for baked goods, chocolate-covered almonds, and hot chocolate.

I bought a Yankees World Series 2001 cap, and then a gray thermal T-shirt because I was feeling cold; later I borrowed a pair of gloves from Harvey. Afterward, we discussed the two reasons people probably come to Yankee games: the food and the fashions.

Or maybe it's the baseball. We saw Posada's home run. We saw an inning with two errors, giving the Yankees five outs but unable to score. We saw Roger Clemens strike out the side in the seventh inning; we saw Mariano Rivera dominate the last two innings. And the Yankees won.

So three major things happened today: the Yankees finally won a game in this series, Tyler took his first four independent steps, and Lauren returned fully.

Love,
Greg & Lauren

From: Greg
To: Everyone
Date: Wednesday, October 31, 2001 8:39 AM
Subject: Lauren Update for Oct 30 (Tuesday) Morning-After Edits

A couple of notes.

Tyler's first four steps kind of sneaked in there at the end. Actually, he had a play date with two of his girlfriends, one his age, the other eight months. We could tell that they were aware of each other's existence because they started fighting over the toys. One in particular, a grumble rumble dump truck or something to that effect, caused such tension that it had to be removed from the play arena. At one point Joyce was holding Tyler and he just walked away from her, taking four steps, or two strides with each foot, before sitting down.

We tried to get him to repeat the performance on video, but he was wise to our game and instead gave us the serene, unflappable stare of someone above such petty pursuits.

And I said I kissed Lauren. I have kissed her on the forehead, or on the hand, through my surgical mask, many times; this time I bent down and deposited a very, very light peck on her lips. This tiny act of intimacy may have been the biggest milestone of all.

Love,
Greg & Lauren

From: Greg
To: Everyone
Date: Thursday, November 1, 2001 1:57 AM
Subject: Lauren Update for Oct 31 (Wednesday)

Lauren does well on days when the Yankees win, and she does well on days when the Yankees lose; but it's nicer when she does well on days the Yankees win. This was one of those days, though I did not know it at about 7:15, when she told me to go home and watch the game. Spectacular baseball—come from behind, when no one thinks they have a chance. In a very small way, that is an analogy of what Lauren has done; now, in hindsight, it seems inevitable.

Of course, their fates are not really linked; and neither of them is out of the woods yet. They're just doing what they need to do to get the job done.

Lauren is so much happier than I expected, though the reason is pretty simple. She is glad to be alive. I thought she would awaken with anger and bitterness, and some of that is coming, no doubt about it; but her first choice has been joy. That alone tells me she meant what she said in her hospital bed in the very early going, that she wanted to live for Tyler and for me.

I wrote an uneven poem (and no, I have no intention of repeating it here) about two weeks after September 11, struggling to give some voice to the thoughts that were racing through my mind—the sadness over Lauren's injury, the despair over her suffering, the guilt that our last couple of days before this disaster had not been ideal, the ability a poem has to encapsulate deep emotion in a brief string of words and render it powerfully—but the last few lines did get it right:

> *Your life throbs deep, but rising,*
> *Of unmeasured strength, no power*
> *As great to link two souls*
> *As love*
> *Perfectly spoken.*

So now I have a son at home who smiles all the time, who gets excited and takes off across the floor to examine whatever strikes his fancy; and I have a wife at NY-Weill Cornell who smiles at me and whose eyes pop at stories of Tyler and Caleigh.

There were so many things I was able to tell Lauren tonight that made her happy. I told her about Tyler, of course, and how I intended to enroll him in a Gymboree class and in a music class; she agreed those were good ideas. I told her about his play date, how the fights had started over the toys and how Joyce had said, "He acted like a boy yesterday."

I also talked about our dog, Caleigh. I told Lauren that she was staying with friends a block away from us, and would be staying with other friends for the month of November (friends who have a one-acre landscaped backyard and two dogs of their own), but then would come back to the 'hood. That our friends a block away had fallen in love with Caleigh and liked having her around, so would be pleased to keep her indefinitely, so that Caleigh would be living just around the corner, and when Lauren came home, even if she couldn't handle Caleigh immediately, her dog would be close by.

These same friends had given me a picture of Tyler and Caleigh together that I showed Lauren; the picture drew a very big smile and wide eyes, and she asked that I hang it on the wall; so it joined the gallery.

It is impossible to describe the way the experience of the Burn Center has been altered in just a few days. There is no more uncertainty over how Lauren will react to being truly awake; we have the best possible answer.

But there is also discomfort, of course. Now that she is fully conscious, Lauren is aware of itching. This is one of the most difficult aspects of burn recovery. It is an excellent sign; it is one of the questions answered in the Burn Center brochure, in what is really an FAQ for patients: itching means the burn is healing. That doesn't make it any easier not to scratch it.

Her greatest difficulty this evening came when she asked me to scratch her thigh where it itched. This is something I cannot do. She was using her splints to try to scratch it. The nurses ordered Benadryl and a special cream to help stop it; we will see a lot more of both. And then, as they were administering them, for the second night in a row she told me to go and watch baseball. I said OK, I would go over to the friends who were watching Caleigh and spend some more time with her; that brought more big smiles. So then I had to call my friends and actually arrange it; I went there, we had Chinese food, watched the game, and I watched their very young son leap from sofa to hassock and back with a level of energy that was simply remarkable. I decided that Caleigh alone had the energy to match it, until she decided to spend the final hour curled up at my feet.

When I'd first walked through the door, Caleigh clearly had remembered who I was; she'd gone practically insane jumping on me with what is called the "wheaten greetin'." I had a good time hanging out with her; it gave me material to make Lauren smile.

Lauren is making such an effort to be normal, and such an effort not to burden me. I wish I could do more for her. It is frustrating because I remain a lousy lip-reader and am completely inept at figuring out what she is trying to say. I asked the nurse to come over when she kept repeating something; only when the nurse got there did I realize she was mouthing, to me, "I love you."

Again, I sat and told her how much I loved her, and that I would care for her, and that she had given me a perfect son. I told her about the Burn Center. I told her she was at the best unit in the world, and had one of the best doctors in the world. (I had told her this a few days ago, but not when she was in any condition to remember it.) She asked me who her doctor was; I told her his name, then added something else. Two years earlier, I had been diagnosed with an acoustic neuroma, a benign tumor of the auditory nerve that starts in the ear canal and grows into the brain cavity. From the available treatments, I chose microsurgical removal over radiation. Lauren came with me to each consultation, and I still recall the serenity that came over us when we first met the neurosurgeon and neuro-otosurgeon whom we chose to perform the procedure. I felt instantly that we had met the people who could help me, and I told Lauren that her doctor had given me that same immediate feeling of confidence. Hearing this meant a lot to her.

I also told her that I liked her nurse that evening, and that the nurses on the unit worked very hard. I told her that very many people prayed for her and were rooting for her, and that the nurses themselves had taken a great liking to her, and written "We Love You Lauren" with red Magic Marker on the whiteboard in her room. This, too, turned up the smile wattage; she looked at the message written there, and I said, That's not from us, that's from the staff.

I also discovered that there had been a discussion of Tyler coming to visit. I had thought this would be further in the future, but what did I know? Or maybe I can't tell that we already are further in the future; it has been seven weeks and one day since the attacks. I would love to bring Tyler to see Lauren as soon as possible. I will find out more about the logistics of this tomorrow. (It involves seating Lauren in a chair in another room, one that is more innocuous and not filled with so many beeping machines.)

But I am also stunned by that figure: seven weeks. Yesterday was the first day that Lauren's personality was back to itself. Even now she may have a hard time remembering the day-to-day; but the period from September 11 to October 30 is almost certainly a blank. Lauren was simply unaware of almost two whole months spanning the most hazardous period of her life. I try to imagine what it would feel like to lose that much time, but I can't; no one can who hasn't gone through something similar.

I am overwhelmed with positive energy tonight. I have had two days of Lauren's return; the Yankees have won two games in a row to tie the series; I spent a couple of hours with Caleigh, and, of course, I hugged and held Tyler today. But I am never without a reality check; harsh truths lurk everywhere along this new road that Lauren and I, and New York, and all Americans, are traveling.

Yesterday evening, before I left for Yankee Stadium and at the height of my joy over Lauren's wonderful first day of wakefulness, I learned that the patient in the room next door to her had died earlier that evening. I had seen her sister in the waiting room many times; she had always been positive, easygoing; we had exchanged the usual questions about our loved one's condition whenever she had come into the waiting room, usually in the evenings.

I hadn't grown as close to her as I had to other members of "the group." But there were always smiles.

The death of her sister had come as a surprise; she had been doing OK, and then she took a turn for the worse and they couldn't stop the decline.

I found out about this because I'd seen the chaplain in her office and gotten into a conversation; then she told me of the patient's death, and that the family was taking it hard.

I became very subdued; most of my thoughts were on how hard this had to be, not only on the family, but also on the entire staff, from the doctors to the nurses to housekeeping. Jennieann's family had prayed that Jennieann would be the last. She was not.

I have often seen the critical patients as a cadre escaping across miles of enemy turf, with a cruel and deadly predator stalking them from behind and picking them off one by one. That is why it has seemed so important to establish forward momentum; there are places in space and time where you simply do not want to spend even one moment longer than you must. But even if you are moving, people can still fall behind or away; it is never a good thing when another member of the cadre falls.

And so the crowd in the waiting room dwindles yet again. Ours is becoming a very intimate game of survival.

I like that Lauren made the transition to awareness so strongly; I like that she continues to consolidate her strength. But we can take nothing, nothing, for granted. And I will close tonight with several more lines from the poem I wrote on September 30, finishing it at a table at the Beach Café:

Your strength returns in tiny drops—
As rivers feed the oceans,
Let it rise.

Love,
Greg & Lauren

P.S. Tonight, as the Yankees were winning and I was watching alone at home, Mitch and I maintained an exchange on our BlackBerries between my apartment and his hotel room in Philadelphia. At one point we were speaking on the phone, but the Yankees hadn't scored the winning run, so he decided we were having better rally luck on our BlackBerries. He was obviously correct.

From: Greg
To: Everyone
Date: Friday, November 2, 2001 3:18 AM
Subject: Lauren Update for Nov 1 (Thursday), Yankee Sports Extra

I will give you all a very brief note due to the lateness of the hour. Lauren did fine again Thursday; she is scheduled for surgery Friday at 10 AM, to receive additional skin grafts.

Quite a lot to tell, but I will finish it tomorrow.

For now, with apologies to Mets fans (you know who you are, Dan & Mike), Go Yankees!!!

Love,
Greg & Lauren

I spent a lot of time with Lauren today, talking to her and failing, mostly, to lip-read and thus decipher what she was saying to me. She still smiles a lot and she is patient with me and my failure to understand her, though she does get frustrated.

Of what I did understand, she was mostly interested in what is up with her family, my family, Tyler, Caleigh, her office, my office. I have told her about everyone who is fine, not about anyone who isn't. I tell her about all the old, some very old, friends who have reached out to us, especially to her; and she smiles, and then she becomes a little more emotional, and cries a bit. I tell her it's OK to cry; but that I wanted to tell her that all these people love her and are rooting for her, and if she wants me to stop telling her, I will; but she doesn't ask me to stop.

When I notice that something is having this effect, I try to steer away from it, but there are some unavoidable facts that she will simply find to be very sad, and there will be no dodging them. It will be far better for her to find out important details about this new world we live in from me and her family than from some other party.

I have asked her doctor about this, and he said, If she asks questions, answer them, but let her bring it up. Don't necessarily volunteer anything, at least not in this early stage.

Lauren met her doctor for the first time today, really met him, the same man who has been caring for her for just over seven weeks. I have had many conversations with him and signed many surgical consents; but when we talked today, we did it at Lauren's bed, and she was a full participant.

He told her about the surgery she is scheduled for tomorrow, where the grafts will be done, where the donor skin will be harvested from, what will be involved in the recovery. For example, her left arm will be kept in a fixed position for five full days to permit proper healing of a graft at her shoulder, five days being the period required for a skin graft to adhere.

He explained to her why both her ankles were placed in casts two days ago—she has not walked in seven weeks, and her toes, if left unsupported, will start to point like a ballerina's. The casts immobilize her ankles and preserve functional position.

He explained that following the grafts tomorrow, she might need one more operation—and she nodded that she understood this—and then, when the healing has progressed, the goal will be to get her up and walking. That we are talking to her about this, and she is listening, is remarkable. He did tell her that she has made great progress, that she has had other operations and she has done well after those.

I liked the experience of seeing him talking to her about her; the personal pronoun "she" has now been switched to "you." And I so loved seeing her nod with understanding. It was as if she were totally relaxed about what she faces. I know that part of this is the drugs she is taking to help her with pain and anxiety; but part of it is also her strength, the same strength that has made her terrific smile her calling card now that she has snapped to and joined us.

Following the conversation at Lauren's bedside, I did ask her doctor in the hallway for a more detailed discussion—nothing that would be hidden from her; I just wanted more medical detail than she may be ready for yet, to get a gauge as to where she stands in her overall prognosis.

Her burn area has been reduced from 82.5 percent (her admitting sheet on the wall behind her bed says 85 percent) to 8 or 9 percent. Yes, that's just 8 or 9 percent. I feel like repeating that one hundred times, slowly. This is a credit to luck, fate, destiny, health, genetics, surgical skill, prayer; it is where we need to be, with the percentage falling into single digits. On its face, this seems like fabulous news.

Still, it is very important to keep it in context. Her injury is being controlled, but that doesn't mean that once the burn area is closed she will then be fine. She will have to rebuild her strength, with many physical compromises, for some time to come; her grafts will continue healing for at least another year. She is in the very early stages of a full recovery. Her systems, functional though they are, have been under tremendous stress. For all that she is awake and communicative, she is still in the woods. At best, we can say that she is now at the edge, looking out of the forest.

But she has moved along the path very steadily since her arrival. She has tolerated numerous operations. She has been a quick healer. She has been lucky. She came back to alertness in a rush; most people come back more slowly, her doctor said, though some do come back overnight, as Lauren has.

On the other hand, she is up against a very tough injury, one that has continued to punish other patients and patient families.

The patients who died before this week had all had belly surgery, an operation where the abdomen is opened up to relieve burn-related tightening on the trunk or torso. There is a phenomenon known as circumferential swelling; since the skin forms an outward boundary of the body, swelling around the entire circumference, whether a wrist or a torso, will necessarily head inward, constricting the flow of fluids. Where the abdomen is badly burned, large amounts of fluids can build up inside the torso and threaten the internal organs or ability to breathe. Belly surgery is performed on those patients who could not otherwise be resuscitated. Lauren did not need this particular surgery; that was one more "tangible" in her favor. But the belly surgery was only one distinguishing factor to this point.

The patient who died two days ago had not done as well as Lauren, but her family had still seemed optimistic. Another critical patient, who had been doing pretty well, had a seizure and the doctors are not sure why, though the most likely reason is the most discouraging one: that the original injury may have been more serious, and had a greater impact, than they were originally able to assess.

Lauren's doctor explained that this is what made it so hard to make a single assessment of a seriously injured patient's long-term prognosis. The family may get hyped up—the doctors get hyped up too—but then the patient can suddenly decline because of some unknown or unseen factor, or sometimes because, quite simply, all these patients are very sick, and their baby steps are really only that in the very lengthy struggle against a total systemic bodily assault.

This is why I am so careful to balance my expectations for Lauren. Right now we are in the stage of guarded optimism, but it is too soon to embrace it fully. The danger of infection is still present, as is the danger of the body simply being overwhelmed by the total effect of the burn. That is why I tell Lauren to relax and let the doctors and nurses take care of her.

I see her strength; I measure every step with her; I look to all sorts of external factors—faith, coincidence, superstition, the Yankees—for some sort of reassurance, but there really isn't any, other than her smile, though that is a remarkable source of inspiration.

I will say that when Lauren is in the hospital, amazingly good things happen to the Yankees. I know for sure they are not linked, but I do think the Yankees, through their games the last few days (including the minor miracle of Tuesday night and the historic victories of the past two days), have given me a place where I can rejoice without restraint, and channel any joy I have without feeling the least need to moderate my feelings. And I'm not the only one. A friend of Lauren's has written: "At the pace of these most recent Yankee victories, most of us expect Lauren to be ready to come home to her family by Sunday at the latest."

I would feel that way about the Yankees anyway because I have been a Yankee fan for decades, but it sure is a help to have an avenue where I can celebrate like a high school student.

Speaking of high school, I have written how, in the vacuum left by the destruction to our present lives, our past has rushed in, our entire past, almost to our birth. Or at least to the birth of our true eccentricities, namely, high school. This has happened in waves: first college friends, and now high school friends, are reaching out from across the country.

In my case, I have recently started to hear from a lot of kids I knew in high school. We were all fifteen, sixteen, seventeen, and many of them have stayed that age in my imagination; when they write to me now they are forty-four years old. And they are a lot more mature than they were at seventeen; the messages are all heartfelt, giving accounts of children, careers, strong feelings, and bonds that never went away.

I got the message "Do you still listen to Led Zeppelin?" from a friend who is now a judge!! If he spends too much time recalling our high school days, he may have to perform a citizen's arrest on himself, though the statute of limitations on most of our misdeeds has probably long since expired.

I have written of how this event has stripped away all the pretense of our contemporary world, all the little barriers we had built up or distance we had allowed to grow. We are all speaking about a lot of very painful things without thinking about what we are saying; the protections we have built up to guard our emotions have been blown away and we are suddenly much more honest about how much we really love others and our country.

The reason we as a nation have banded together so powerfully is that, for hundreds of millions of us, these friendships, these scraps of love that had been buried under the flimsy shield of a thousand petty concerns, have been exposed to the air and started to grow and re-form. It happened between families, between friends, between communities, between cities and states, and eventually had nowhere to go but throughout the entire country.

I had lunch outdoors on Thursday at Philip Marie, the restaurant where Lauren and I were engaged, where I first told her I loved her, where we've had countless family brunches, where we would sit at an outside table as people stopped by to comment either on our dog or our baby or on both (we had a 50-50 ratio of dog stops to baby stops). As I was leaving this time, the couple at the table beside me asked the waiter to take their picture.

I asked them if they were visiting; they said yes, from Minneapolis. I told them I'd been helped a lot recently by Red Cross volunteers from Minneapolis. They knew one such volunteer; I don't believe I'd met her, but I told them there are probably a thousand of you here. So I said Welcome to New York, enjoy your stay, and thanks.

(By the way, we have received the promised assistance from the Red Cross.)

What is it about Minnesotans? They elect Jesse Ventura, they volunteer for the Red Cross, they come and visit our city at the urging of our mayor. Here's to the Land of a Thousand Lakes.

And while we're at it, here's to Lauren.

Love,
Greg & Lauren

From: Greg
To: Everyone
Date: Saturday, November 3, 2001 1:14 AM
Subject: Lauren Update for Nov 2 (Friday)

I arrived at the hospital early today to see Lauren before her surgery. She was surrounded by five physical therapists who were removing fiberglass casts from her lower legs. They were using a handheld saw with a round circular blade to cut neat lines in both sides of each cast. They paused when Lauren said it got too hot; then they resumed.

It seemed to me that there were quite a few of them working on a simple project, but they were taking great care. It became clear why an hour later, when one of the physical therapists returned with the newly engineered casts; the cut edges of each half had been lined with foam, and Velcro strips mounted. This would permit the casts to be easily placed back on, and just as easily removed. While the casts are on, the ankles are immobilized; but they can be removed without difficulty to check on the condition of the grafts beneath.

Lauren was scheduled for surgery at 10 AM but did not go down until 12:40. (The only case that is sure to start on time is the first case of the day, which goes in at 7:30.) She did fine; more about that later.

Before she went down, I spent a lot of time with her, smiling with her, joking about the Yankee game. I asked her if she had watched it—in fact, she had watched the whole thing, in her room, all the way through to the second miracle comeback in two nights. (I had gone to a gig where the band, at seven members, outnumbered the audience, at four members. We played too long, wound up doing a couple of Cream covers, and so missed any chance of seeing the miracle comeback live.) I said, Some game, huh; and she answered the way she has been doing since she became alert, with her eyes widening and a big smile, meaning Yes with an exclamation point.

Within the limited tools she now has to communicate (she will be able to speak again soon), her eyes have become very expressive. She grins and her eyes widen when she thinks something is fun. I have also become aware of how expressive hand gesticulations are; with her hands now in splints that are wrapped to her arms with gauze, she has a very limited vocabulary of gestures, so the same gesture can mean many things.

Last night, when she was asking me about something, she held her left hand up, then used her right hand to rhythmically bob up and down, and I realized she was miming playing the bass. I told her about the ill-fated gig that caused me to miss one of the greatest World Series games of all time. Frankly, I was amazed that she was able to get her point across. I am still amazed.

(Of course, far more pedestrian points are harder to make, and that is where the frustration comes in. There is something called an alphabet board, which permits patients to spell out what they want; one side has the alphabet on it, the other a series of captioned boxes—hot, cold, nurse, doctor, turn, pain, sleep, etc.—to more easily convey the message. Lauren has used the alphabet board sometimes, but it is very hard for her to point just now, so when I tried to use it with her, the results were disappointing.)

At one point this morning, her doctor, who would shortly be performing the surgery, walked past Lauren's room. He stood in the doorway, and so I told Lauren, Look, it's your doctor; she looked over at him, the subject of the game came up, he asked if she'd watched it, and once again she had the wide eyes and the playful grin, nodding yes. He said she should have slept more. (I think he was joking; maybe he was reprimanding the overnight nurse!)

I spent a fair amount of time before her surgery telling her that she had been through many surgeries already, and done well every time. She had healed quickly because her blood oxygen and protein intake were so good. I made sure she acknowledged that she heard this and understood it. I wanted her to realize today's surgery was not something new, but rather something routine, something she had already shown a persuasive ability to handle.

I can't imagine what it is like for her, in her state, to have to understand this and to go through it yet again; but she appeared to be resolute, and she wasn't on any medication at that point to manage anxiety.

When her doctor reappeared in the waiting room at 4, he said, "We were having so much fun, we ran long."

What actually happened was this: he did the graft to her left flank and to her left hand, and also grafted some small open spots on her leg and her buttocks. This took a little longer, but five days from now, if we learn that these grafts adhered, her burn area will have been reduced to 1 or 1.5 percent.

I have to pause at that remarkable statistic.

It is not as conclusive as it sounds; the remaining 1 to 1.5 percent involve her hands, which will be her most difficult and painstaking rehabilitation. But the statistic is meaningful as to her recovery; as her doctor explained, if you or I had a 1 to 1.5 percent burn, we would be treated at home with medication; we wouldn't be in the hospital. It means that two to three weeks from now, she will have significantly improved her resistance to infection; what I think he described as her immunosuppression will have been reduced by 50 percent. And a month after that, the hypermetabolic state that she is in—an elevated heart rate that is the result of all the healing that she is doing—should also subside.

It seems like a long time, but it is less time than has elapsed since September 11. We are already more than halfway there.

If all goes well—and that IF is constantly present—there is a checklist of good news that we should experience in the coming weeks. The removal of the tracheal tube so that Lauren can resume talking; the healing of the major grafts in two to three weeks so she can resume walking; and in two or so weeks, a first, very brief visit from Tyler.

The longest days in that span are the next five because they are the fulcrum for everything that will follow; if the grafts don't take, the celebrations will be postponed. And for this five-day period, she is wearing splints that will immobilize her left arm and severely restrict the range of motion of her left hip and flank. She will receive plenty of pain medication, and should also receive sedatives to help her relax. But she will have to stay still.

It is hard to believe that it is only a couple of weeks since she was facedown for five days while in the induced coma. That was a harder position, but there was almost no emotional component; now her mood will need to be managed as much as her wound care.

And that mood is a precious thing. I have written for the last several days about how unexpectedly happy she is. It is clearly not over where she is, or the condition she is in. But she has such a winning attitude, she is so earnest and willing, she has affected the staff of the unit.

I think I can read it in her doctor's mood; when he said yesterday that the staff also gets hyped up about patients who are doing well, I think he was very much referring to Lauren. There was the note of caution when he spoke of the recovering patient who had a seizure that had come as a total surprise; but there was also the enthusiasm for a patient who has made this much progress. When he came up from the surgery and said they had been having fun, maybe he was just joking, or maybe he was jubilant because he has actually reached the 1 to 1.5 percent mark with this patient after starting at 82.5 percent.

The nurses comment on how strong Lauren is, and how rare. Her strength, like a fine athlete's, is as much mental as physical.

Her day nurse for much of the past two weeks said today that it is very unusual that a patient will jump from the fugue state that Lauren was in to complete alertness; it was a sharp, dramatic return. One moment she is showing traces of a smile; the next she is hearing complex statements and giving immediate responses, a nod of her head, a smile, a frown.

She seems to be an inspiration to many. One of the physical therapists came out today and sat next to me in the waiting room and said, You probably know this, but I just want to tell you what an amazing woman your wife is. The therapist went on to say that she was running the NYC Marathon this weekend and that she would be doing it in honor of Lauren. It's the same for this woman as it is for so many others, including me.

But the tough part comes when the drama of all this respect gives way to reality, and Lauren is left, still in the bed, still having to heal, still having to confront as yet undefined limitations. When she came out of her surgery today, she was back to being very tired, very subdued; I was overjoyed that she had again sailed through, but I was also aware of just how slowly minutes and seconds can pass during a time of physical and mental ordeal.

I am pleased to have good news, but I still am aware that this isn't a movie, and there will be no dissolve to "six months later." We have to get there from here, one step at a time.

Love,
Greg & Lauren

From: Greg
To: Everyone
Date: Sunday, November 4, 2001 3:09 AM
Subject: Lauren Update for Nov 3 (Saturday)

One day following her most recent surgery, Lauren was back to being alert, decisive, in charge. She is on a cocktail of painkillers and mood mellowers I thought might have kept her subdued—but there she was, already getting in the middle of things, exerting her sheer force of personality from what is an immobilized horizontal position with a maximum of 20 degrees upward torso elevation.

For the next four days (up to five post-op), her hip will be splinted to immobilize her flank; her left arm splinted to protect a graft at her left shoulder; she has "bio-brane," a healing covering, on her donor sites—and she is trying to match people up together.

Specifically, she is trying to fix up two people who number among the recipients of this e-mail. (This was one thing I actually guessed at without having to go through a lengthy pantomime; I saw the first two letters she spelled out using the alphabet board and the only word

I could think of was a man's name, so I guessed that this was a match-making attempt. She said she would help create the appropriate venue for an auspicious encounter.)

She has also continued her interest in the Yankees, and was disappointed at their meltdown in tonight's game, when they must have remained on Eastern Standard Time and thought they were pitching batting practice. (Stop gloating, you Mets/Red Sox/Diamondbacks fans.)

If anything can prove the fact that Lauren's fate is not linked with that of the Yankees, it was the fact that she did well today while the Yankees approached all-time World Series records for defensive futility. Her doctor had already reprimanded her for not sleeping enough Thursday night; she did not get very much sleep Friday night either. By ending this Saturday night game before the third inning, the Yankees permitted Lauren to slip off into sleep early for some much-needed rest.

So maybe her fate is linked to them after all; maybe they are really a drug that is perfectly designed to improve her health, whatever the circumstances. The Yankees gave Lauren a miracle game to occupy her mind until well past midnight the night before her surgery; on the first day post-op, they were so inept, they permitted her to go to sleep at least three hours earlier than a competitive game would have allowed.

Lauren's Yankee spirit actually took us by surprise earlier today; we were using the alphabet board to clarify what she wanted, and we had arrived at "why an" instead of "Y-A-N," when someone guessed the Yankees and she rolled her eyes and nodded. She wanted to know if they were playing and at what time.

I should probably have added "Yankees" to the list I made of the things she has asked for urgently but have taken us the longest time to figure out: suction (to clear her breathing passages), itch (so that they can give her Benadryl to control it), pain (this is actually on the alphabet board, but it was still useful to have it on the important items list), and nap (so she doesn't have to spend ten minutes telling people she wants to sleep).

Given all her energy and enthusiasm and firm opinions, it is possible to forget for a moment that she has been returned to full alertness only for three days.

This is her take-charge nature. It is in play almost from the moment she awakens, whether from a night's sleep or from seven weeks of unconsciousness. I had thought that the medications she was receiving would keep her tranquilized so that she could better tolerate being in a virtually fixed position. Instead, far from a passive, resting behavior, she was focused on planning other people's futures. And she had other instructions for us too—we are all to get our regular exercise, and I was to get her flowers to match the balloons that her sister had brought. (I had to explain that flowers were not permitted.)

She is reengaging in her life, and she is doing it quickly. Her voice is ready to make its debut, first as a whisper, translated painstakingly one word at a time, but soon enough in the coming weeks as a complex and compelling presence. The signs are that she will be just as strong-willed as she was before, with maybe a heightened interest in baseball.

For the first seven weeks after September 11, I spoke for her; I guessed at what she thought, and reported on her medical progress as she struggled to merely survive; I wrote about how the families of the burn patients were all trapped at Time Zero, in a prolonged uncertainty whether our loved ones would pull through. The answer to this is still not known, but I feel as if we have slipped the moorings of that horrible moment and are starting, slowly, to pull away.

I feel compelled to say again that I know this is far from over or even decided; the data yesterday said we were still about three weeks from being able to say Lauren was out of the woods, and three weeks have not passed in twenty-four hours. Still, when I see her trying to fix people up, when I see her excited about the Yankees, when she is telling me enough already with the "I love you" stuff, I get reassured about my faith in her and her underlying strength.

One more sign she is really with us—she has complained about the poster on the wall in her room.

It is a drab landscape poster, a blue and gray painting of a lakeside on a rainy day. It seems as if everyone who has ever painted a landscape has painted that scene; it is as if the artist's name were stenciled beneath a generic drawing. There is a lake near our country house in Pine Plains, in Dutchess County, called Stissing Lake, in the lee of Stissing Mountain. The winters there are cold, steel-gray times; I could describe the painting as Stissing Lake in February. I hadn't especially liked the poster, but who really takes steps to improve hospital art?

Lauren, for one; she was fairly decisive about not wanting it on her wall.

It so happens that two weeks ago, an artist sent us two signed posters, specifically to brighten Lauren's hospital room once she was awake; just another example of how the web of reality has elements of destiny that time keeps teasing out. She knew one of the posters, a very well known watercolor of a Nantucket lighthouse. Tomorrow I am having the Nantucket poster framed, and it will soon be hanging on the wall opposite the foot of her bed. The old poster is an island of impersonal, institutional decor amid Lauren's gallery of highly personal photographs and get-well cards. The Nantucket poster will blend with them more fittingly—an expression of beauty and love by the artist for Lauren herself.

I don't want to give the impression that she is strong and decisive at every moment; she is badly hurt and she understands that; she experiences pain and discomfort and needs help; she has tears of sadness over her injuries, and tears of joy over the prayers and gestures of support. One of these is particularly noteworthy.

You know about the physical therapist running the New York City Marathon tomorrow in Lauren's honor; there is another runner with a message just as inspiring.

After the article about Lauren ran in *The New York Times,* I heard from a woman whose brother had been badly burned when he was nine years old. She was seven and watched it all happen. This was more than twenty-five years ago. She wrote me of his resolve in overcoming his injuries and building a life for himself and included a news story about him. And today she wrote me that she and her brother have been chosen to be torchbearers in the torch relay for the 2002 Winter Olympic Games in Salt Lake City, and that they wanted to run in honor of Lauren (and of me). She asked for my blessing, saying that the theme of this year's relay is "the flame within." I wrote back to her saying that we would be honored, that they have my blessing, and that Lauren would be thrilled to hear about it.

You know what? She was.

Love,
Greg & Lauren

Lauren has continued to do well, and for the second night in a row we watched the Yankees, unfortunately, lose.

I spent a long time with her, and she is doing fine today.

More later—

Best,
Greg

The Yankees lost, and it meant nothing, really, but a little disappointment at the end of the evening. Lauren had grown pretty enthusiastic about the games and they served as a terrific distraction for her. (The patient next door to her had also become a big fan.) In neighboring rooms, there were two critically injured women, recovering from grave injuries, watching Fox Sports with the volume cranked on full.

Lauren had a lot of needs during the game. Itching is a real problem; it's what happens when burns heal, and Lauren has it all over her body, in spots that can be reached and some that can't. Of course, we can't scratch; we have to tap our fingertips on the area, and following her surgery, some of these areas are under thick dressings. It is a situation that would drive me nuts, but all in all, she is handling it OK.

When I got there at 4 PM, I sat at her bedside for about half an hour as she slept, and then stepped out of her room so she could rest undisturbed. When I returned, she waved wildly with her splinted right hand. She'd woken up very hot and been unable to call the nurse. We wiped her brow, and she was suctioned.

She also asked who was pitching for the Yankees; I told her Clemens, and she was satisfied. We did little deals; I would help her, and she would agree to rest for five minutes at a time. There was discomfort, but what we were really dealing with were anxiety and fear.

We know so much about her condition, I think we keep forgetting that she does not. She needs the information; it removes the unknown. She is in a phase where she is very anxious, and also fearful of certain procedures; in part this is the drugs, and partly it is the very stark reality (more than partly). When she wakes up after nodding off, due to the drugs she is taking (the painkillers and the Benadryl have sedative effects, and she is also receiving Valium to help her relax), she can be very alarmed, feeling that she is alone, and agitated, thinking about her injuries.

What she needs to hear repeatedly is that she has done really well; that this is nothing new; that she has handled much tougher operations and recoveries since her injury. Of course, she wasn't aware of those, so this is very different; but if she can be made to understand that she rallied through much tougher circumstances with resolve, she can reestablish that resolve for the current situation. Once she has the information and is reminded that she needs to relax, she does, quite purposefully; she makes clear that she understands, she says she will be OK, and she takes her deep breaths and tries to manage her discomfort.

Still, she is under very bulky dressings that immobilize her entire left side, and an Ace bandage wrapped around her torso to promote healing of the donor sites on her abdomen. To think of what she has to handle now, upon waking, is tough; when I left the hospital Sunday night, I was very emotional. As tough as the period since September 11 has been for us, this is a new order of magnitude; because while Lauren was sleeping, the nurses could tell us that she was OK for the moment and we would relax. We could see the progress she was making and be reassured. But now that she has joined the journey midway, that reassurance is harder to come by—she has an enormous amount to absorb. The most important thing is to project a positive attitude to her (and we do feel positive; she is one phenomenal woman), so that our presence helps her. She is frustrated enough as is, and of course we have to add to this her inability to talk and her occasional eye-rolling impatience with us when we can't figure out what she is trying to say.

I have to say it was an odd day. I am feeling the effects of the last almost eight weeks, the last two months. I haven't been living a very normal life. None of that is surprising; brutal tragedy changes everything, and we were knocked countless miles from our comfortable routine. I coped; but I think the 3 AM updates are a thing of the past.

Lauren needs me, but now on a different schedule. For example, she wanted me to be there Monday before her dressings were taken down. I have always been there before her surgeries to give just such reassurance, even though she could absorb little more than the sound of my voice. Now this support means more than ever. It is my new job to adjust to her new routine so that I can do this for her; the past eight weeks have been little more than training for me to take on my share of the heavy lifting, which starts now and will continue for a long, long time.

Sunday's World Series game seven was played on the night following the running of the New York City Marathon. Even though the marathon is a globally televised event and draws on the civic spirit of New Yorkers in all five boroughs, I have rarely gone to see it, mostly because I live in Greenwich Village—it is an East Side/West Side thing. The thought of traveling into all those crowds was a bit much. But this time, there were the two women running for the burn unit: the physical therapist who was running in honor of Lauren, and Christine, the singer-songwriter (and self-described karaoke queen after I wrote about her performance in the staff room), who was running on behalf of the entire Burn Center.

Four days earlier Christine had tried to gather a group from among the medical staff, patient families, and discharged patients to sit in the grandstand as she crossed the finish line. I figured I'd give it a try; I watched the start of the marathon on television while doing stuff around the house, and then hopped on the subway to West 72nd Street.

I emerged onto a closed Central Park West streaming with crowds of people flowing north and south and milling about at the 72nd Street entrance to the park. Family reunion trailers, where runners who had finished the race went to meet their families, formed a long line north; they were organized by the first letter of the runner's last name. There were mothers wheeling strollers, young men wheeling bikes. Runners who'd completed the marathon walked in their midst with a deliberate gravity, draped in Mylar shields to preserve heat and moisture.

When I got to the park entrance, I noticed that police were manning barricades and turning people back. The park was closed for security reasons. To get inside, you needed a pass. I asked where I could get across the park to the East Side, and a tall, stout man in a Parks Department uniform and trooper hat bit off "96th Street" as he pointed north with his right arm. I found a friendlier-looking cop and mentioned the grandstand, and he sent me to the 69th Street entrance, where there is a ramp wide enough for a single vehicle to pass through. But security there was even tighter; I saw one person show a pass that said "Celebrity Family Reunion."

It was clear that I needed prior security clearance to enter the park. A pleasant cop in a light blue windbreaker said there was nothing he could do to help me. I told him I didn't know about the park closing; he said a lot of people didn't. I wasn't about to walk north to 96th Street and didn't like the idea of having to walk to 59th Street to cross east, so I asked if there was another way through, and he said maybe the 66th Street transverse road. I walked south three blocks and there it was: a sunken swath cutting directly across Central Park, passing under several tunnels and framed by black stone retaining walls eight feet high. Normally the transverse is the province of buses, taxicabs, and speeding cars, but today it was an asphalt conduit for people.

It was quiet. Walkers followed the traffic pattern, eastbound to the right, westbound to the left. The tunnels were higher and longer than the pedestrian tunnels inside the park itself, their arches far grander, their innermost reaches darker.

There are some wonderful old trees that have been silently growing above the transverse for ages. They meet high above the road, like the description I'd heard of trees joining above the raised hedgerows crisscrossing Normandy. There were beautiful fall colors: gold, red, yellow. Though it's November, leaves have remained on the trees because of our warm September and October. The weather has barely changed; we still have highs of 70 degrees. The Yankees, normally reigning in October, gave up their crown four days after Halloween. It was as if autumn had slowed itself down for Lauren, as if the seasons themselves hadn't progressed in New York because the entire city remained locked in a moment of tragedy.

But the moment is releasing us. I spoke yesterday of slipping Time Zero's moorings and starting to drift away; we may be only feet from shore, but we are embarking across the ocean.

And despite the unexpected beauties of the passage, now that I have moved from Time Zero, I can tell that the journey may be ugly. The world has long since moved on, to bioterrorism and war. Outside the cocoon of the waiting room or the family center or my own gigs, I don't have a special badge of sincerity that could get me past security. Nor should I.

People have dealt with it. The slightly flat note is that people are dealing with preserving memory, or heroism, or reassembling their lives, as able-bodied survivors. There are very few who have maintained a life-and-death struggle continually since September 11.

I crossed the marathon course at First Avenue and 67th Street. The course was empty, strewn with cups and papers. Most of the runners had already passed. Instead, the mop-up street cleaners were there. That was the sensation; left behind while the majority experience is elsewhere. But there were occasional outbursts of cheering when a straggler appeared; pockets of rooters would give a whoop for them: the ones who weren't in good shape were far behind and walking now but still wearing their numbers and smiles on their faces.

That sounds like us. For now we're the stragglers, but we have to remember we haven't been abandoned.

So thank you, everyone, for all of your continued support; it means a lot, so very much, to Lauren.

Love,
Greg & Lauren

From: Greg
To: Everyone
Date: Tuesday, November 6, 2001 1:46 AM
Subject: Lauren Update for Nov 5 (Monday)

I have an Upper East Side Blockbuster card now, because Lauren wanted to watch movies on her TV to take her mind off her situation. She is very bored; she needs a bit of stimulation, and she is very limited in what she can do independently.

For the moment, her hands are bandaged and in splints, so she cannot point to things, pick up and read a book; she is pretty much limited to music and watching TV, but music does not involve her on enough levels. Television draws in your mind—so I need to pop on good movies for her.

And we are not talking *Braveheart;* we are talking good comedies. There are not that many. I went to the Blockbuster a block from the hospital to rent *My Cousin Vinny* and/or *The Producers.* Both were out. Instead, I got *A Fish Called Wanda, Dumb and Dumber, The American President,* and Eddie Murphy's 1996 *The Nutty Professor,* all for a five-day rental.

We popped in *Wanda* and it played on the TV. Lauren mostly slept through it, but at least when she was awake there was something to think about other than her own condition. (The night before we'd asked her nurse to check on the videos in their library; from this, Lauren selected *The Odd Couple,* but the tape inside the box turned out to be the Power Rangers.)

This was the third day following Lauren's most recent surgery, and the early reports say her new grafts look good; her flank seems to have mostly adhered, and that is the one that mattered. This is only an early report; the real test comes after five days and possibly longer, but good news is still encouraging; it beats bad news.

The evaluation was made during her visit to the tank. By the way, the tank is not really a tank. It is a room just off the main corridor of the ICU where burn patients are taken to have their wounds cleaned and debrided, using water jets. The patients are given medication for pain and to relax them; then a team of nurses gently places them in a metal tub about twelve inches deep and raised about thirty inches off the floor. This is where the burn patients take a shower, where they get shampoos, a pedicure; Elizabeth Arden with a little something extra.

It is also where the doctors can assess the status of a patient's healing. Since this is where the dressings and bandages come off, it is the best place for the surgeon to check surgical progress. The patient receives new bandages and dressings and is returned to his or her room, preferably to watch an excellent comedy!

Just before lunch today, Lauren met the nurse who cared for her the first few days following September 11, and to whom I feel so indebted for the job he did helping Lauren (as I also do to the two night nurses who worked with her those first few days). Remember that I said he seemed like a crazed monomaniac at that time? He now seems like the most relaxed, well-adjusted, and easygoing person imaginable.

He was at the nurses' station and saw me and said hello. He came over to the door of Lauren's room and I asked him, "Have you met Lauren?" He grabbed a gown and came into the room, and I told her, "This is the man who was your nurse the first few days you were here." He said, "Hi, Lauren, you probably don't remember me." And she scrunched her face and mouthed, "Not really."

If she does remember him, it will only be traces; although he spent four to five days caring for her twelve hours a day, she was heavily sedated and medicated throughout. Yet his voice is probably familiar to her; he spoke to her every time he did something, and always by name. "Lauren, I'm just going to move your left arm." "Lauren, I'm just taking your temperature." "Lauren, I'm moving your leg for a moment." If she heard my voice during that time, then she also heard his.

I told her that he had taken really good care of her those first days. She mouthed, "Thank you." He told her that she had done really well; she was the pride of the unit; she had impressed a lot of people with her strength and resilience. She smiled and thanked him again. He told her, Keep doing well. And then he stepped away.

I was glad he had told her those things; I was able to reinforce them, to say, "You heard what he said, you have been healing really well. You've already been through tougher times; you will make it through this. You should be confident."

This encounter took place before the visit to the tank; afterward, Lauren was in some pain and discomfort. It is hard on her, and it leaves me feeling helpless. I understand the reasons for her pain and the treatment plan to deal with it. She is being weaned off the heavy-duty medications she received for almost seven full weeks; restoring them would undermine the work they have done to get her away from feeling a need for them. They want her awake and alert, not groggy or "zoned," because they want her to regain her strength. They want her vertical again. They want her to be moving her body. That is the path to recovery; going back on serious narcotics would only postpone that date.

I want her to be moving her body as well; I wish I could pick her up and carry her out of there. I get caught up in the daily routines of recovery and I don't think about how terrible all this is, but then I think of why she is there and who put her there, and I recognize feelings that will forever be stored in my own reservoir of sadness.

I don't want my wife to be in that place.

Thank God she is doing so well.

Today the splint was removed from her right hand; her middle and ring fingers had rings of foam on them to protect them, but for the first time since September 11, she has the opportunity to articulate her right hand. The graft looks excellent. The nurses all say that she has done phenomenally, that she is ahead of schedule for her wounds. They repeatedly comment on how unusual it is for someone to emerge from even an induced coma and suddenly be present and lucid. She may have been a bit ahead of time on that. And I know her right arm is coming along, because today, as I leaned in to try to understand one particularly passionate statement, she smacked me with it.

Good for her.

I get e-mails all the time from people who pray for Lauren, and cards from those who support her, messages that start, "You don't know me, but . . ." She gets tape compilations from her friends, songs from her college days, burned CD copies of albums her friends think she might like. Today she received a stuffed animal from her summer intern, a University of Michigan teddy bear in a Michigan T-shirt, accompanied by a beautiful handwritten card. I tell her again about the huge outpouring of love for her, the churches and synagogues around the world praying for her.

And then I think of her as I write this, hopefully sleeping or watching a movie; please, let her be relaxing and putting her mind at ease. Let her believe in herself. Let her make it back.

Love,
Greg & Lauren

From: Greg
To: Everyone
Date: Wednesday, November 7, 2001 1:21 AM
Subject: Lauren Update for Nov 6 (Tuesday), Condensed Version

Lauren did well today; for most of the day, she was on a "trache" collar, which permits the patient to breathe on her own while also permitting the nurse to easily restore ventilator support should the need arise.

She was breathing on her own for most of the day! In the evening, she asked to have ventilator support again, so she could rest overnight.

I will, as ever, send out a longer piece, but want to make sure that I have at least told everyone how Lauren is doing: just fine.

Best—
Greg

From: Greg
To: Everyone
Date: Wednesday, November 7, 2001 10:38 AM
Subject: Lauren Update for Nov 6 (Tuesday), Late City Final

Lauren hurdled a major milestone Tuesday, but we were also reminded of how difficult the road in front of her remains.

First the milestone: as I wrote earlier, she was placed on a trache collar. This is a plastic crescent that fits under her chin and covers the tracheal tube through which she is breathing. The volume inside the collar is filled with oxygen tapped from a valve on the wall. With the trache collar on, she is off the ventilator. For the first time since September 11, she is breathing on her own.

This happened in the morning; I heard about it when I reached the hospital. By the time I saw her at 5:30 PM, she had been breathing on her own since at least 10 AM. She asked for the ventilator back at about 8 PM because she was tired from the effort, but the day was a major achievement.

But we also learned that she had a bad moment the day before; one of the drugs she was given for pain can, as a side effect, cause hallucinations, and apparently that is what happened in the tank and was why she was so agitated afterward. Her day nurse was patient enough to interpret the complex account from Lauren, so she will not have to go through it again.

It must have been so difficult, to experience something like that and not be able to tell anyone or even indicate it, to simply have to outlast it and to be afraid that it will happen again.

This is why she was anxious about tomorrow (Wednesday), the fifth day following her surgery, when all the dressings will be removed, once again, in the tank room. She will not be given the bad drug again, and before his shift ended Tuesday evening, her day nurse (who Lauren learned had attended the University of Pennsylvania School of Nursing) was standing at her side, stroking her right hand and telling her that everything would be fine tomorrow.

Every day her situation is filled with more hope, though for now this is matched by her greater awareness of pain and discomfort. The bed can be uncomfortable, the bedding can be lumpy, she may want her head raised or lowered; her skin itches; the ceiling vent is providing too strong a breeze; or there is pain for which she needs more, or more effective, medication. It is such a hard situation, and I have moments where I think I cannot deal with it; but they are only moments, and they are the result only of my own seeming powerlessness.

She chose to live, and we are honoring that decision, with all the hardship it brings. This is the part we have known was coming. This was all expected, all patients go through it; and parts of it—the pain and discomfort, if not the disorientation, anxiety, and inability to communicate—are going to last a long, long time. This is where the true challenges lie. I have written many words of tribute to Lauren's struggle and about my support role, but those words were like war poetry, lyrics written to foster emotional commitment to a higher cause. At the front lines, in the trenches themselves, there is a much grimmer reality.

Lauren's battle, the battle of all the September 11 patients in the Burn Center, is so much more literal, and with a much longer arc. The scars they bear are not just inside, but also external, and they are, she is, becoming aware of them. These patients are still on the battlefield, where there will be no surprising arrival of normalcy; in fact, there is only the question of whether it can ever be attained and what form it will take. We do not yet know the compromises we will have to make, nor do we know which ones we will refuse to accept and will thus, by rejecting them, triumph over. We know only that whatever heartless fate awaits us, there is no avoiding it.

We have to believe that we have sufficient courage to conquer the challenges ahead, and in that, we probably are not that much different from soldiers. We know that attacks are imminent, we know we must fight to survive, and no one can offer protection. Yet what will save us is how we have learned to respond, rather than surrender. And it is not just one grand contest; there will be skirmish after skirmish, and there are no exemptions for the wounded until we can make it off the battlefield.

I try to learn from the nurses what is expected and typical, and how I need to react to things; specifically, if I am there when Lauren is upset, what I can do to help her. The precise way to help is not always clear; for example, she wanted me to remove the splint on her right hand, and she was impatient when I asked the nurses whether I could do that. They said yes, I did, and she felt better. She then asked me to remove the Ace bandage wrapping the surgical dressings on her left arm; she was just as fervent in that request. I told her I couldn't but she didn't want to accept that answer from me. So I had to bring in the nurse, who said in the identical words, "I can't do that." And from the nurse, she accepted the statement.

We just have to cope with each particular problem. If we can manage whatever it is, and string together a day's worth, then a week's worth, then a year's worth of such moments, a day will come when the challenges recede, and we will know a relief that is unknowable to anyone who has not experienced a similar trial by fire.

I hope that there is that kind of payoff down the road for Lauren, and not too far either; I hope that there is that kind of rejoicing for reengaging with the world, for returning to a daily existence, even with memories like these. I understand those kisses between sailors and damsels following World War II, and even if they were posed, it doesn't matter; we all understand the image, and that there will be a kiss like that at the end of this road.

Until we get there, I can always offer the most basic form of reassurance; at one point Tuesday, I did lean down and hug her, and speak softly into her ear that everything will be all right, that she has been fine, that she will be fine, and our lives will be normal again. I looked right into her eyes and told her I was telling her the truth; sometimes you have to state your beliefs with conviction to make them come true.

Lest people become too discouraged, there were also high points Tuesday.

One of the mothers at Tyler's baby madhouse birthday party took about fifty pictures of him and made them into an album, which we brought to Lauren yesterday. She spent a lot of time looking through it, and got a lot of joy from that. She certainly knows who and what she is living for.

Tyler himself did a fair amount of roadwork, and I am cheating by reporting something that happened Wednesday morning but it's worth it: he walked to the elevator, and back, using his little white pushcart.

Our apartment building has a diagonal carpeted hallway that stretches over 125 feet, with two forty-five-degree turns. The building was built short and long, combining two lots that face Perry Street and West Street but not the corner lot at Perry and West; our elevators are at the rear corner of that corner lot, so the hallway stretches into the two wings of the building.

Tyler walked, leaning on the cart, about thirty feet, from our door to the elevator. And then he came back, turned the corner of the hallway and walked another thirty feet to the fire stairs at the end. At first, he would veer into the wall and come to a stop; Joyce and I taught him to use his arms to steer the cart, and by the end of the exercise, he was steering to stay in the middle of the hallway as he walked between us. He did this circuit a number of times, laughing with great satisfaction as he reached the end of each leg.

Without seeking it, of course, that's a better analogy for what Lauren is going to do; at some point, she will gain control over her own journey, and there will be some significant satisfaction as she completes each crucial leg, and laughter as this becomes routine.

Good-bye until later—

Love,
Greg & Lauren

From: Greg
To: Everyone
Date: Thursday, November 8, 2001 9:51 AM
Subject: Lauren Update for Nov 7 (Wednesday), First Quarto

This being the fifth day following Lauren's most recent surgery, we found out how the grafts did, and the news was excellent: 95 percent take on her left flank, good performance on her left leg and left arm. These latter sites may require a few more days to be sure of the results, since the grafts are very thin. But she has a good track record; her previous grafts that were too thin to assess after five days turned out to have adhered 75 percent after an additional week.

All of these were autografts, with Lauren's own skin, so once they have taken, they are permanent.

The assessment was made in the tank room when her surgical dressings were removed. The visit to the tank went better than Monday's, since she did not receive the drug with the psychotropic side effect. When I got there in the afternoon, she had just returned from the tank, and was sleeping peacefully. It really was like watching a child who has been restless finally falling asleep and resting like an angel.

She had been on the trache collar again for several hours; but following the tank visit she went back on the ventilator to conserve her energy. Breathing with the collar is more difficult than breathing on her own would be without a tracheostomy, so it is an especially effective means to exercise her lungs; but this is also why she can do it for only a few hours, and is returned to the ventilator to rest.

Three to four days from now, they plan to reduce the trache tube to a size that would permit Lauren to send air past her vocal cords so that she can talk (it would remove a significant cause of her frustration), while still giving her doctors access to a tracheal tube just in case she again needs ventilator support. (Maintaining this access is far easier on her than being reintubated through her mouth would be.) At one point today, one of her doctors actually tried to inflate a balloon in her existing tracheostomy tube to enable her to speak briefly, but the tube itself was too big for the balloon to truly rechannel the air, so this attempt failed.

Lauren slept for about two hours and woke up around 6, and her nurse fetched me from the waiting room. When I returned to her room, she gave me a big smile. Soon afterward, she started to complain that she was very hot. When the nurse told her she had a fever, Lauren asked why, and asked to see a doctor.

Twice a day the doctors do rounds; wheeling a cart carrying patient charts, they stop in front of each room to review the patient's treatment plan and lab results, and to discuss any changes that need to be made. The nurse also comes out to give an account of how the patient is doing: any major events that day, and a general assessment of the patient's condition and mood, whether agitated, passive, subdued.

The medical hierarchy, with increasing seniority, is intern, resident, fellow, then attending. (There are two fellows, I believe, who do alternate weeks running the ICU or assisting in surgery. It is always the attending who performs the surgeries.) As I've noted, Lauren's doctor is the associate medical director and one of the three attending physicians on the unit.

The rounds team includes one of the three attendings, one fellow, the resident on call, plus an intern, and today (and frequently) a medical student. The resident on call presents the case, which is then discussed. As all the doctors rotate days on call, this system ensures that the entire team is acquainted with each patient's condition and involved in making treatment decisions.

Lauren made her request to see the doctor just after rounds concluded. The first to come in was the fellow, who had assisted with about half her surgeries to date. He was very gentle and soft-spoken; I had not had a chance to see his bedside manner before. He helped Lauren identify the exact location of the pain in her right foot and removed the splint from the foot to relieve a pressure point. He also checked the grafts on the front of her right foot and explained to me what I was seeing, why they were healing well.

On checking her computer-based chart, he noted that her temperature was indeed spiking and sought to take a blood sample to determine whether an infection was present. She is not currently on any antibiotics.

The fellow told her that spiking a fever was a typical event, that this was not her first fever, and that a new case of pneumonia would not be her first either, that she already had a track record in shaking these things off. He explained to her how antibiotics would be used in the case of a positive bacterial culture; he also reviewed, and agreed to slightly increase, her pain medication.

He explained that infections might take one of three forms: a skin infection, a blood infection, or a lung infection. He explained how a widespread burn created more entry points for infectious bacteria (something we all know but she is just learning). He also explained how the fever spike could merely be a result of the hypermetabolic state that she is in as she heals. But fundamentally he told her that she had faced infections before, had, in his words, "been there, done that already." This was important because it would give her confidence that she would get through this episode too.

It was a little tough when he tried to take a separate blood sample from another location on her body rather than from an existing IV line. The advantage of a "fresh stick" would be to test whether the infection was present at a site removed from the IV line; if it is not, then changing the line would be a first and immediate step to counter the infection. Unfortunately, as can happen, he was not able to find a good vein in her right arm; and when he suggested trying another site, she asked strongly that he not do it; the failed attempt had been too painful. So for the moment they tested a blood sample from the existing IV line, and will wait to see if she continues to spike a fever.

(Overnight she slept for another few hours, the fever subsided, and her temperature returned to normal.)

She also asked why she was agitated and he gave a good answer; it was the effort of being in the tank and having her dressings taken down and staples removed, and simply the nature of her extensive injuries. But he did review her anti-anxiety medications with the nurse.

At one point, as he was talking to Lauren, he mentioned in passing that his own father had been a burn survivor too.

Lauren's doctor came into the room then, and she asked him about the outcome of her surgery; he was strongly positive, citing the 95 percent success rate on her left flank. He also discussed the plans for the ventilator over the coming week, as described above, and gave her some general information about her surgical and treatment schedule.

Rather than go in for another surgery on her left hand next week, he said, the focus would be on rehab: sitting up and then "getting you on your feet."

Right now her legs are atrophied from lack of use; she will have to walk, and do a lot of therapy, to regain joint flexibility, and to literally get comfortable in her own skin. She will have very unfamiliar sensations because of the pressures in her legs; a physical therapist told me that the grafted skin, being newer and thinner, gives a far different feeling during standing and walking. But over time, and especially with active rehabilitation, this resolves.

Shortly afterward, her doctor gave me a more complete picture of her long-term plan. Without providing any definitive timetable, he said she was likely to spend two to three more weeks in the ICU (leaving the ICU will be a major cause for celebration), followed by one to two months at a rehabilitation facility. This implies that she may not be coming home before March.

I asked him whether Lauren would require any special facilities on returning home (a physician friend suggested I start exploring such things in an e-mail). He recommended that I speak to the social worker on the unit, who would also be able to help with insurance claims, coordination of other support services, and researching available rehab facilities. As part of her duties the social worker attends the morning meetings where each patient's status is discussed. But he did point out that patients are typically released from rehab facilities once they are capable of handling "ADL," the tasks involved with activities of daily living. His preliminary assessment was that Lauren wouldn't need anything special to be built at home.

During Lauren's late afternoon nap, a man in a black skullcap and leather jacket came into the waiting room, sat down, and said my name; I looked up and recognized the stock trader who had been discharged several weeks ago after treatment for burns that covered 34 percent of his body. Under the arms of his jacket he was wearing black pressure sleeves that extended above his biceps, where they were anchored with two rings of circumferential rubberized elastic. Only his fingertips protruded; it was as if he were wearing some cool new variety of glove.

When he was discharged he held a news conference at the hospital. He was all over the media and he said that it helped enormously with his healing. Instead of avoiding him, people have been coming up to him and asking to touch him, to shake his hand, to hug him. Everyone he meets on the street knows who he is and knows his story. Maybe they won't remember two months from now, he said, but when he needed the help with returning to the everyday world, the fact that his story was known to everyone he met, and he didn't have to explain it, was immensely beneficial.

He said he had been vain before this, very focused on his appearance; he had gone to fashion school and was very style-conscious. Now, he said, he doesn't care about any of that. He talked about the grafts he had received on his arms and back, mesh grafts similar to Lauren's. I asked if I could see how his fingers looked; that's when he offered to show me both his arms. I have to say I was very grateful to him for suggesting it—I would never have asked.

He took off the pressure sleeves and told me he was happier with his right arm than his left. The left arm was grafted shortly after September 11, so it was two months old; the right arm graft was only a month old but almost looked like normal skin (it did not appear that this graft had been as deep). You could tell that he had been grafted, but the texture was even, the arm contours normal, the scarring much less than I would have imagined.

We exchanged e-mail information to keep in touch; then I went in to see Lauren, and that is when I spoke with the doctors and discussed her grafts and treatment schedule. The episode with the right-foot splint and the attempt to take blood had been stressful and she fell asleep again, so I returned to the waiting room.

I am frequently at the hospital after visiting hours, which technically are from 11 AM to 8 PM. There are two color TV sets mounted near the ceiling at opposite ends of the waiting room; the remote controls for these units are mounted on the wall. We used these televisions to watch the news in the weeks following September 11, though with the crowds in the waiting room at that time, the news was more wallpaper than anything else (although you could read the headlines scrolling across the bottom of the screen). The September 11 families often stayed until 11 PM.

More recently, a smaller group watched the Yankees storm through the playoffs and lose the seventh game of a dramatic World Series.

Now that the crowds have ebbed, I've noticed that as of 8 PM, the waiting room becomes a staff TV and break room. Last night, there was a doctor eating a hero sandwich and a very large bag of potato chips; then he moved to the south end of the waiting room and turned on the Knicks game. Another man came in and turned the other TV to the hockey game. With both winter sports on televisions to either side of me, I sat at the center of the room and wrote an e-mail on my BlackBerry.

The nurse came and fetched me when Lauren woke up; they were about to do burn care, so I said good night and wished her well. And the nurse said, Don't worry, she'll have a good night; and she kept her word (I spoke to her this morning to hear that all was well).

Let me also briefly tell you about the Kramer incident. My next-door neighbor, my Costco pal but also my baseball playoffs pal, the woman whose house we shared last July in Bridgehampton, and who every weekend offers her apartment to any guests we may have staying with us, works from her apartment. I have a key to it; when I go over there (after calling first), I open the door slightly and say, "Breaking and entering!" Following our last visit to Costco, I actually needed to store some food in her freezer (that was a real Kramer moment right there, but it gets worse).

Yesterday around lunchtime I went to knock at her door to get something from her freezer. The deadbolt was extended to prop open the door. I pushed the door, said her name, heard her say yes, and entered to see a group of people in business attire sitting around her coffee table. I was wearing jeans and a T-shirt.

I asked if she was having a meeting; she said yes; I said, I just have to grab something, and stepped in and went to her refrigerator even as I heard her tell her guests, "He's my Kramer." And of course I went directly to her freezer, took something out, and went right back out the door to the sound of uproarious laughter.

I will close on a more serious note: there is an amazing photo montage on the Net about September 11. I have received the link from two people now: it is www.politicsandprotest.com. You should watch it with the sound on; it is immensely more powerful with the musical sound track. (It is a 7-meg file; a message asks you to be patient while it loads.)

Make sure you are prepared to be emotional; the photos are very carefully selected, you have seen many, if not most of them, before. But in the same way that music is the tension created by each particular note following the note that came before it, and films take their drama from the way the sequence and timing of the images and sound are projected, so does this montage take its special power from the way the individual photographs appear, are grouped and timed, and juxtaposed with music (really a single looped song, but well chosen).

You will see the faces of the people who died on each of the hijacked jets; the intense smile of one of them, a plain-looking man with glasses who appears on the right-hand middle of the screen, is heartbreaking. You will also see the destruction, and the occasional question posed (Why?); you will see faces of five men, then the words "Let's roll," and realize you are looking at the heroes of the flight that crashed in Pennsylvania.

I don't know how this man did it, but he appears to have chosen, perfectly, the most affecting photographs, and to have put them in exactly the right order; his written message, at the end (you have to click the arrows to follow it through), mentions everyone it needs to mention and is both shattering and inspiring.

There is nothing extraordinary at work here other than the rightness and skill with which this was assembled and the raw emotion that seems to have guided every single correct decision. I wrote to the man who did the site, thanking him; he wrote back, thanking me, saying that he had been nervous that he might offend the families of September 11 victims (and patients), and that my approval meant something to him.

It turns out he was a friend of one of the people I knew at Euro Brokers, and who I'd discovered had died when I saw his framed picture at the Euro Brokers memorial service. Of him, he said, "He was one of the good guys."

So is this artist; there are so many who have emerged since September 11.

Love,
Greg & Lauren

From: Greg
To: Everyone
Date: Friday, November 9, 2001 1:23 AM
Subject: Lauren Update for Nov 8 (Thursday)

Lauren spent a long time in "the chair" today. As I've mentioned, the chair is a hospital-class power recliner, where she can be put into a sitting position, which helps her recovery by getting her off her back.

When I arrived, the occupational and physical therapists were working with her, redoing the splints for her ankles and taking special care to fix the pressure point in the right ankle splint that she had identified the night before.

I have discussed these splints frequently; they are white plastic that is malleable when it is brought to Lauren, and is then shaped around her forearm, hand, and wrist, or her lower leg and ankle, and held in that position until it hardens. To avoid pressure points, foam is placed at the key places where the splint material might press and cause pain, and these foam pieces are integrated into the splint. The splints are then applied in a rotation throughout the day; they are fastened with Velcro straps, sometimes also with gauze bandages.

The purpose of each splint is to support Lauren's extremities in functional position, so that they do not lapse into nonfunctional alignments that may be harder, or impossible, to reverse during rehabilitation.

The process can be painful and exhausting; she needed to take several breaks during the session. She seems demoralized by her physical limitations, again because she does not realize how far she has traveled in the past eight weeks.

The occupational therapist told Lauren that she was an inspiration to them because she always does so well; Lauren shook her head, as if disagreeing. The therapist insisted she was serious, and said to her, this is why they spend so much time with her; because she is so motivated, and does so well, that they can't wait to come back and torture her again.

But that is what will get Lauren on her feet and out of there faster.

And she is trying very hard.

Her key complaint during and after the therapy session I joined was that she was hot. She had a high fever at one point, and she was being fanned, using the laminated alphabet board. I took over the fanning and did it for at least another hour; I offered to feed her a grape, but she didn't laugh.

Once the splint-fitting session had ended, we had another problem; she had lost her bed to an incoming admission elsewhere in the hospital and they couldn't find another one for her, so she was suddenly trapped in the chair.

She was very uncomfortable and wanted to lie down, but there was nowhere for her to go.

This was the first time I became angry at the hospital. They brought up two broken beds that would do her no good (one had a ripped mattress, the other was stuck in its lowest position, eighteen inches above the floor). As her discomfort grew, I became more frustrated; but then I ran into one of the support staff, a woman who has been asking me about Tyler ever since she heard me telling Lauren tales about him in the early days of her injury.

Though we had been on a bed hunt for close to an hour, she said it was the first she was hearing of it, that she would take care of it. I asked her if I needed to lose my temper with anyone in order to get the bed faster; she said no, had she known sooner she would have taken care of it for Lauren. And she did, within ten minutes.

Lauren received two gifts today, from strangers. One was a beautiful quilt from a group of eleven- and twelve-year-old cross-country runners at an Ohio middle school. The other was a signed football jersey. This had been sent by the owner of an NFL team, who wrote that after reading the newspaper article about her, he wanted to send Lauren a jersey from "another Manning who likes to win."

She got a huge kick out of both gifts, but then she wanted to know, What newspaper story?

So I told her that there had been a story about her, and that it had appeared, along with a picture of the two of us, on the front page of

The New York Times. At this, she became emotional, so I asked her if she was upset that the story had run, and she said no. She seemed glad that someone had taken note of the horror that had been done to her.

I told her more about the story; that I had been bothered that her condition had been reported on but not her name or anything about her; she had been a statistic, a body, and I wanted to give her back her dignity.

I told her, "You did something heroic, Lauren, and I thought the world should know about it." I told her how much I admired her, that she had no idea how intensely I felt that emotion; that she had carried herself out of there and decided to live, that I thought it was the bravest thing I had ever seen. I told her I wanted her to have a record, and for Tyler to know what his mother had done. I told her again that people around the world were praying for her, churches and synagogues on every continent (except Africa?). I told her that there was a woman who had placed her name on prayer lists at a number of churches on Nantucket, and always sent me a description of the church and the priest.

I told her who among her friends had been interviewed and quoted in the newspaper, and I told her the last thing I was quoted as saying, that I wanted her to be happy again, that I didn't know what form that would take other than that good things would happen to her and she would deserve every one.

I could see her becoming emotional again, but she told me that she was glad the story had been written. I told her she was very important to a lot of people, and that this wasn't a burden; they were supporting her, and that she should know there was an amazing amount of love being aimed in her direction.

I told her that she had a place in history.

It felt wonderful to be able to tell her what I thought of her and have her lucid enough to comprehend what I was saying.

I was on Tyler watch Thursday night, so I left the hospital a little early and went home to our son. Soon after I got down on the floor to play with him, it seemed as though he had made a decision about what he wanted to do, because he matter-of-factly stood up behind his pushing toy (more of a lawn mower shape). I opened the door from our apartment to the building's endless hallway, and off he went.

We taught him to steer the contraption two days ago. Forty-eight hours later he was steering like a pro, making frequent adjustments and laughing all the way to the end of the hall and back.

Meanwhile, Tyler's mother will also be learning to walk again. She will not be laughing at first, or even close to it. She will be concentrating intensely; she will be struggling to maintain her balance and to find her rhythm. But once she does, she'll be smiling too.

Love,
Greg & Lauren

From: Greg
To: Everyone
Date: Saturday, November 10, 2001 1:38 AM
Subject: Lauren Update for Nov 9 (Friday)

We are in an area of tiny steps; it may not always seem that things are very different from day to day, but the cumulative strides that Lauren has taken over the past two months are truly remarkable.

She is still very much in the early stages of a lengthy recovery. Yet her determination and will, present but so sublimated during the period of her induced coma, are now palpable. She does arm range-of-motion exercises, lifting both arms in coordinated fashion and matching the movements of each as she raises her forearms, brings her hands together, brings her elbows back to articulate her shoulders, then lowers her arms again.

The occupational therapists have told her that exaggerated facial expressions are good for rehab and scar control; today she winked at me and I wondered why, but then she winked the other eye, opened her mouth, puffed her cheeks, then made a big smile, then relaxed, raised her eyebrows, curled her face from side to side—giving all those muscles a workout.

She also works her legs, all this while lying in a critical-care bed.

She is working out, in her limited way, to get the jump on her physical rehabilitation.

I had missed the physical highlight of her day; she was placed in a seated position on her bed, not in "the chair," and had her legs dangling over the side, and having done well in that position, the next step, in coming days, is literally the first step, when she will get back on her feet for the first time in close to nine weeks.

She is capable of greater precision in her arm movements. Until the last couple of days, she had seemed to be unable to spell letters clearly on the alphabet board; she always seemed to be pointing out nonsense letters.

It occurred to me today that maybe this was because she was trying to point out letters with her index finger, which is about two inches to the left of the tip of the splint. Once I pointed out the exact spot on the tip of the splint to point with, she was able to spell words out more quickly. And suddenly, with just a couple of letters, it became much easier to anticipate words and understand complete statements.

This is all encouraging. We hope it signifies that we are in the final days of Lauren's critical-care period.

Because she is not done yet. She is still critical but stable; her wounds are not completely closed, and the remaining open areas still leave her vulnerable to infection. A mask is no longer required in her room, but gowns, gloves, and caps still are. She still needs ventilator support to rest properly overnight. With all this she is still on schedule to reach closure, which in her case is a very literal term, within the expected ninety days since she was admitted.

To understand how much of a triumph this has been for her, you just have to realize that Lauren is one of only two patients with more than a 50 percent burn still on the unit; the others did not make it this far.

I spoke briefly today with the associate director of the Burn Center and asked about her long-term recovery; for example, whether she would be able to jog. I found out that the problem with jogging would not necessarily be agility (not for someone as determined as Lauren) but heat control. She has been grafted over large areas of her body; she will not have sweat glands in those locations so she will not be able to shed heat as efficiently as she used to. The doctor said that for this reason, she might enjoy swimming more than running.

Earlier today there was another medical event a little farther downtown. Tyler had his one-year checkup. You will be pleased to know that he now weighs 19 lbs., 2 oz., and is 29½ inches tall. Or, as I explained it to Lauren, he is nearing the end of his twenties and is about to begin his thirties. Once again he was totally relaxed as the pediatrician examined him; while he was checking him and placing the stethoscope on his chest, Tyler was playing with the looped cords of the instruments and smiling. The doctor said that only 2 to 3 percent of babies are calm like that; most babies are crying hysterically throughout the examination.

Tyler started to do that after he got his injection; all of a sudden he morphed into typical baby behavior, tears streaming down his face. I was able to get him to stop, though, by taking his hand and walking him from the examination room back to the doctor's office. Once he was focused on walking, he lost interest in crying.

At the start of the exam, I explained to the pediatrician why Lauren was not there with Tyler instead of me (she had gone to most of his previous appointments). Upon hearing her story he was shocked; he remembered her vividly and felt that they had "clicked." When I finished telling him about her injuries, he told me that one of the young men in their twenties who had died at the World Trade Center had been a pediatric patient of his. He also told me that the baby who had caught anthrax was a patient too; and that the initial diagnosis of the anthrax had been a spider bite.

This last news brought the anthrax story close to home, yet another reminder that Lauren, Tyler, and I, and all New Yorkers, are living our lives amid the stuff of headlines. We know so many people who have been on news programs; and, of course, our own story was on the front page of the *Times*. We are sampling our fifteen minutes of fame in thirty-second bursts.

We have all seen historic front pages; I have *The New York Times* front page from the day I was born. When I see framed front pages from the era of World War II, I think of my parents having lived through those events; my mother was a Holocaust survivor, my father was at Normandy. We know how that war turned out, so we always see the hope in the stories of that era rather than the threats of global tyranny and genocide that then were so real.

Tyler will look at other front pages many years from now and he will have a similar experience. He will know how the war turned out. He won't even have to make an effort to think of his parents having lived through those times; he will have a front page, not from his birthday, but close enough, showing his parents doing exactly that.

The more time that goes by, the more I realize that we will never be truly free of the changes of September 11, so I hope that we, too, will someday come to see not the uncertainty and danger of this era, but the hopes, and how they were fulfilled.

Love,
Greg & Lauren

From: Greg
To: Everyone
Date: Sunday, November 11, 2001 12:59 PM
Subject: Lauren Update for Nov 10 (Saturday), Extended Play

I joined Lauren today as she was in the chair having physical therapy. She was doing an exercise to reverse the pigeon-toed position that her feet have assumed after almost nine weeks of inactivity. She was practicing rotating her feet outward while her heels remained stationary. This is something that you, or I, or Lauren on September 10, could do with ease, but Lauren on November 10 needed to work at it, and she did, with resolve. She was also doing exercises with her toes, curling and then raising them.

It is amazing, the range of motion that can be lost after two months of complete inactivity. We never realize how much our bodies are really the consequence of every action we take every minute of our lives.

Those of us who are healthy have a much longer term view of this. We are told of the benefits of exercise and of eating right, and we come to view any deterioration as taking place over the years, and catching up to us via heart disease or another chronic condition. But deterioration is ready to begin every moment of every day. Even those of us who live sedentary lives do not realize we are always staving it off to a certain extent just by getting out of bed and moving from place to place, meal to high-calorie meal, accumulating enough exercise and enough nutrition to maintain locomotion and perform what the rehabilitation field calls ADL. As a family member of a burn patient, you discover that without daily activity, the deterioration takes complete control; and further, that the burn injuries aggravate it. The toughest part of the recovery is returning to what had been taken for granted: the simple ability to function.

Lauren is completely resolute as she performs her exercises, though it is a struggle to maintain morale; the figurative steps she can take now are so tiny that they seem barely perceptible. But they are measurable, and they will lead to real steps. Another critical patient on the ward walked about sixty feet with the assistance of a walker and had everyone talking; Lauren wanted to know when she would walk. Actually, she wanted to know if.

The physical therapist explained to her that the other patient had not suffered severe injuries to his legs, as she had. So she was not behind; in fact, the therapist assured Lauren that she was doing great and that she was her inspiration. As she has done before, Lauren shook her head as if to deny it, but the therapist insisted she was serious.

The mantra is to remind Lauren that she has come an enormous distance already, that the distance from here to her walking is much shorter than the road she has already traveled, and with fewer bridges out.

To understand why this is so, we only need move a few doors down to another patient on the ward, also from September 11, who is suffering from severe infections and hasn't healed as well as Lauren has; that patient's family heard that their loved one's status with respect to an active infection was worse than it had been six weeks earlier. (Lauren endured a similar crisis several weeks ago.) And as that family member said, six weeks earlier they had not exactly been celebrating.

We have all had to withstand such shocks. The difference for the cadre of burn patient families is that the shocks keep coming, are fresh ones. There is no way to anticipate them; our only option is to steel ourselves to face them. Still, they invariably take our breath away.

Not that the lingering shocks from September 11 do not do the same. I went to a birthday party last night in a SoHo art gallery lined from floor to sixteen-foot ceiling with the works of Peter Beard.

I forgot to ask the pros last night to define the genre, so I will call it African naturalist action painting; single or series photographs of African people or game, including giraffes, lions, cheetahs, elephants, and rhinoceros, living or dead, lined with smaller drawings and quotations (many from Karen Blixen/Isak Dinesen, who, as an old woman, is prominently featured in several works), all bordered or overlapped by bold strokes of paint or blood.

Some of the works are ten feet high or eight feet wide. There is a life-size photo of a rhinoceros at the end of the gallery. Another work features a series of eight photographs of a slightly out-of-focus lion charging, framed as one. And of course beautiful women creep into these works, either as participants in the primary photograph (in one nighttime flash photograph, a naked woman, whose pose and extension speak of her grace as a dancer, holds out a gourd to a giraffe whose neck is bent down to drink) or as decoration and contrast with the subject matter. There are also photographs of large animals killed by hunters, including an eighteen-foot crocodile being held and skinned by a dozen tribesmen, and a bull elephant with legs extended. Trophy hunters are climbing on it, preparing to harvest its tusks, their bodies dwarfed by the elephant's forehead.

Amid these striking works of primeval nature and bloody struggle, a large crowd of young people gathered to drink champagne and toast our hosts' birthdays. This was not strictly a Wall Street crowd, but there were many Street people there, including some I knew from Euro Brokers (though none who were still working there on September 11). When I was introduced to friends of the hostess, I learned that many people I had not met, or had met only briefly, wanted to know how Lauren was doing. One woman introduced herself, saying, I'm praying for your wife. So were others whom I had known for several years. I told them about how hard she is fighting, how far she has come, how long and hard her road remains.

I learned more about what had happened to some of the people at Euro Brokers who'd been trapped on the 84th floor on September 11. Two of them had tried to escape but had been unable to get down the stairs; they had returned to their desks, probably despairing. There was one phone call at 9:54 AM from one of them who understood what was about to happen (but not how), and he was emotional; he did not want to die there.

They were colleagues I respected and I had probably been to their desks a couple of hundred times over four years; I can still see it vividly now, with its view to the north of the Empire State Building and 1 World Trade Center just to the left. At midday the sun would reflect off the skyscrapers in Midtown and the Empire State Building's windows would shine with thousands of diamonds; but of course the view had long since become wallpaper.

September 11 was a particularly clear and beautiful day, and the uptown diamonds were probably just beginning to glitter as the black smoke and fire obscured them, and as the ceiling of the trading floor caved in just four minutes later, at 9:58.

People told me about the moving and difficult memorial for one of them, and his father who had been able to say only, "I've lost everything."

I had to sit down after hearing this; I remembered pausing at the main entrance to the hospital, a couple of days after September 11, to touch my fingertips against the smiling faces on the missing posters for each of these men, to be silent just for a moment as tribute, and to whisper, I'm so sorry.

One of these two men had a baby less than a year old; the wives of two others who died were expecting, and the son of one colleague I knew and liked was born on October 2.

Many of those who died were members of the same crowd that filled this party; young and beautiful enough, hard-working and ambitious, serious about their careers and building their families, with no more expectation of tragedy than anyone to whom I spoke last night. Enough of them had probably been out on September 10, having just as good a time, and taking for granted the decades in front of them.

The beauty and blessing of the hard road that Lauren and I are traveling is that with all the rough places and roadblocks and mountain passes ahead, it can still thread its way to those future decades.

On Saturday, Lauren and I had the best day communicating that we've had on our new journey. I saw less frustration, more connection. She was able to spell things out rapidly on the alphabet board; at one point she spelled out that she was really glad I was there. I told her, of course, that there was no place else I would want to be.

It filled me with such satisfaction that my presence reassured her. Try as I might, my own energy is flagging. Her frustration and anger, no matter how fully I understand them, can be exhausting; it is hard for her to express subtle thoughts through mouthing words or spelling them. She can thank her nurses, therapists, and doctors easily enough; but her positive emotions for me may require more complex expression. So it meant a tremendous amount for us to finally find a groove.

And that is what we found yesterday; the first outlines of a groove that we may fit into and that I, as a bass player, can understand. (The bass player lays down the foundation for the music so that the lead play-ers can stand on it, and the groove Lauren and I need to find is not much different.) For a while, we danced together (there was actually an old Parliament funk tune, "Flashlight" on FM 105). The therapists have told Lauren to dance with her face and her head, to do the exaggerated facial expressions to music, so that these stay interesting, and so that she can structure it rhythmically to make repetition easier. So I stood there and danced with my face, but also my body, as she did, moving her head and neck and matching the beat. And she was smiling.

I was much more active on Lauren's behalf, helping her with mois-turizer, blankets, and pillows. I can tell when I rub on the moisturizer that there is some scar tissue even where she has healed beautifully; the skin may look pink and normal but it is harder to the touch. Hence the dancing, the movements.

Our day stayed good. She was uncomfortable in the chair but she needed to remain in it for another two hours after I got there, so we popped in a video to take her mind off her discomfort. We watched *Liar, Liar,* a moderately funny movie in which Jim Carrey does some amazing overacting.

Next we watched *Blazing Saddles,* which, incredibly, Lauren had never seen. It works just as well today—maybe better; some of the bad guys in that infamous queue of outlaws could be right from Al Qaeda. It was nice to see the humor in her eyes when a truly funny movie was on. Before I left late in the evening for the party, I popped in *The Odd Couple,* the 1968 movie with Walter Matthau and Jack Lemmon.

I think she and I finally have a strategy for getting through this; she has things to do, I have things I can do for her, and we can begin to es-tablish our new and quirky routine. We may not fill the roles, but we fit the description; compared to our former selves we are now The Odd Couple, and we should only wish for a lot more laughs.

Love,
Greg & Lauren

P.S. Our dog, Caleigh, returned to Perry Street for twenty-four hours before being whisked off to Sands Point, her country home for the next month. As she entered our building, I was told she be-came excited, went crazy coming down the hall, and stopped right in front of our door. When I opened it she came running in, bark-ing, spending 50 percent of her time in midair. She was whining, looking for Lauren, until we let her search the entire apartment. She was incredibly happy to be home. I'd been concerned about her reestablishing her truce with the cats, but she just sniffed noses with them and lay down. Tyler crawled up and touched her, crawled away, then crawled back, laughing, and started to pet her. She didn't move. An online breed guide said wheatens are supposed to be baby-sitters; Caleigh is.

For a day, Caleigh stayed glued to my side or curled up at my feet, exhibiting a newfound serenity. She will be a great comfort to Lauren when she comes home. With this new level of calm, we may not need to keep her in foster care for as long as I'd thought. At this writing she is chasing two puppies madly around a fenced one-acre yard, so she is getting her exercise.

From: Greg
To: Everyone
Date: Monday, November 12, 2001 12:02 PM
Subject: Lauren Update for Nov 11 (Sunday), Monday Morning News

When I entered her room, Lauren said, "Hi, Greg."

It was the softest whisper and I wasn't even sure that I had heard it; it took a second to register that the rush of air had been my name. But in truth there was no mistaking it.

I said, "Are you talking?" and her eyes smiled as she whispered, "Yes."

I looked at her and I said, "God, that's wonderful. I am so—" and then my voice trailed off, and my eyes misted, and the lump in my throat stopped me for a moment. I took off my glasses, dried my eyes, and told her the word I had meant to say: "happy."

She could talk because she had received a smaller tracheal tube, which could be capped so that she can talk. The cap is about a half inch (maybe a little more) in diameter. The top of it is divided into four equal quadrants, or pie slices. Each quadrant features a flange that permits air to be inhaled, but closes when air is exhaled, forcing the air upward past her larynx, where she can vibrate her vocal cords and attempt to speak.

I was able to lean close to her and understand her perfectly. Even though she speaks only with a windy whisper, she sounds like herself, so she has made another enormous leap to reclaim who she is. During her sedated period, she was merely surviving, her eyes shut, not moving or aware of her surroundings. Initially when she opened her eyes, she was capable only of the slightest, most delicate facial movements, and could barely nod. She progressed rapidly to full alertness and was aware, and responsive, but she could communicate only by spelling words or waiting to have her lips read. Within days she became capable of animated facial expressions and bobbing her head to the rhythms of dance music. And yesterday, for the first time, she spoke in a whisper; I can't tell you how wonderful it was.

I was impatient to hear her voice. Saturday night, on the way home from the birthday party in SoHo, I had dialed her cell phone maybe ten times, just to hear her speak on the voice mail announcement. Our vocabulary had shrunk to gestures and hospital problems and the ponderous deciphering of her questions about family and friends. Suddenly, within moments, we regained full use of the well-evolved English language.

I spoke about how many people cared about her and loved her.

We spoke about Tyler; she told me she loved the tape of his birthday party, which was one of the first things I had shown her after she truly woke up. We talked about many things, but especially about how wonderful it was just to be able to communicate; we got a chunk of our relationship back right then.

Of course, the hospital complaints were far from over. Now that she was able to be very specific about any discomfort she felt and to express her anxiety, those feelings jumped forward and reached a peak; she was worried about potential infection, and very concerned about how isolated she felt lying in the bed without the nurse in the room. She is unable to call the nurse because the forearm and hand splints she is wearing make it impossible to reach the call buttons on the side of her bed; similarly, the splint makes it difficult to press the buttons on the television remote. So when she is alone in there, unless someone looks in on her, she is cut off.

We tried to secure an overnight companion or nurse so there would always be someone in with her. But there was no one available from the hospital's on-call lists. We then made plans for me to spend the night with Lauren, until it was explained to us that I am not allowed to stay in the room with her overnight. So the goal became to set up the night shift so that she could at least be comfortable, and her nurse be alerted to the need to check her frequently.

We were able to work things out; I helped Lauren relax, and once the night nurse came and it was someone with whom she felt comfortable, she told me it would be OK for me to leave, as long as I made sure that she had received medication to help her with anxiety and to sleep.

We then watched the movie *Overboard,* with Goldie Hawn and Kurt Russell—a cute one with an especially pleasing payoff. That got us into the late evening; Lauren got her medication and concentrated on relaxing, and by the time I left, it seemed that she would be OK for the night.

Overnight she is still placed on the ventilator so she can rest, and also so her respiration can be monitored while she is alone and sleeping. Once that was done, we no longer had the trache cap and were back to lip-reading; the frustration and limitations of that were immediate, extreme by contrast even with the very short time she had been able to speak.

Still, there can be no feeling like that rush of air that spoke my name.

Love,
Greg & Lauren

From: Greg
To: Everyone
Date: Tuesday, November 13, 2001 3:07 AM
Subject: Lauren Update for Nov 12 (Monday)

I arrive, typically, about three seconds after each major milestone. For example, I reached the hospital at a little after two in the afternoon, and discovered that about twenty minutes earlier, Lauren had taken her first steps.

These were not strides, except with respect to recovery; in actual linear measurement they were mere shuffles, but the facts are that she was helped into a sitting position, maintained it, placed her feet on the floor (I assume with some assistance), and shuffled a couple of feet to sit down in the regular lounge chair in the corner of her room.

This was not the rehab "chair" with the pink mat and special seat belts that she's been placed into over the past week; this was a regular four-legged hospital seat with slate-gray vinyl upholstery, a high back, and black metal armrests.

When I entered her room, Lauren was seated in the chair surrounded by her court of occupational and physical therapists and attendant family members. The window curtain was up, and on another impossibly sunny New York autumn afternoon, the room glowed with the happiness of all within. Lauren's accomplishments were described to me. The therapists resembled ladies-in-waiting as they knelt beside her, wearing uniforms of yellow hospital gowns, blue bouffant caps, and gray scrubs, and attended to her leg splints or debated the proper material for pressure sleeves to wrap her left arm. They had already placed a cast on her right forearm and hand to help realign the fingers in a more functional position.

In the center of all this activity Lauren sat with an impassive face, wearing a blue patient gown draped with white blankets and sheets that could have resembled the royal garments of the Princess of Perry Street. Then she saw me, and gave her best sovereign smile.

As if on cue in Shakespeare's version of Lauren's tale, another of the physical therapists literally bounded in, her face all smiles, to tell her that she had indeed run the New York City Marathon with a message on her back saying "In Honor of Lauren Manning, WTC Survivor." She said she had felt Lauren behind her, giving her wings all the way through. I asked her if she was trying to make me cry in front of my wife, uh, the Princess.

Soon afterward I passed the reception desk and noticed two letters addressed to Lauren. One was a card from a woman in Virginia, who wrote, "I admire the strength and courage you have summoned in this mighty fight for your life. May God bless you and carry you in His arms as you continue your struggle to recover." The other envelope bore a Baltimore postmark and a U.S. Senate return address. Hillary Clinton had sent Lauren a beautifully worded note, including the sentence, "You are brave and courageous and a hero to all of us."

This all means so much to her, because after the spiritual glow subsides, and the therapists leave, and she is placed back in her bed, her arms and legs in splints and a trache tube in her neck, she remains inside the body that has been gravely injured, and whose strength depends on the conviction in her soul to reshape and heal herself.

While she serves as the inspiration for so many, she herself needs to be inspired to fight on. The key inspiration is Tyler but every bit helps, and today I reminded her again that she is the object of prayers of thousands around the world (including, I have been quite clearly informed, Africa).

She started to ask about what happened on September 11. Her first question, with heartbreaking vulnerability: "Was it an act of terror?"

I told her yes. Anger and anguish flooded her face; she began to cry and screamed softly, "I'm going to get those bastards," and beat her right forearm, in its cast, into the bed, as if pounding her attackers.

I got her attention by saying firmly, Lauren, listen to me: you don't have to do it, the United States of America went to war. George W. Bush declared war on the terrorists and any country that harbors them. A month ago we launched our response. The United States has gone to war to get the people who did this to you. And this is not a figurative statement; there are units over there who are fighting in honor of you.

I then told her about the guys from the Hamptons (Westhampton Beach, that is, the 106th Air Rescue Wing) who wrote that they were fighting "in honor of Lauren."

All of this made her cry, but in a different way, the way you feel when there's a battle you are too weak to fight, but someone else has taken it up on your behalf, someone far stronger than you, whose job it is to protect you. I told her I, too, had cried when I read the note. I asked her if it made her feel better and, amid her tears, she nodded yes.

She went on; she remembered that the World Trade Center looked as if it would fall (she does not remember me telling her in St. Vincent's on September 11 that both towers fell). She asked, "Was anyone hurt at Cantor?" Yes. "Did people die?" Yes. "Anyone I know?"

Please forgive me, but right there I lied to her; I told her, I'm not sure. I didn't think she needed the entire load dropped on her this evening; that her boss, and 657 other Cantor employees, had died without hope of rescue. I told her, Let's talk about that tomorrow, I have to check the list. She agreed to wait.

I did tell her that she had become the focus of hope for many of the families of Cantor Fitzgerald victims. I told her this was not a burden but support; that there were that many people praying for her, every day. That she was important to a lot of people. That's when I read the note from Senator Clinton; that's when I reminded her that on the day of the *Times* article, millions had probably prayed for her. And she said, "I'm so glad you did that."

We talked about other things; I told her again that she was my girl, and that no matter the pain or discomfort, I would be there by her side and she would get through this. That I would take care of her and of our son. And she nodded and mouthed, Thank you.

I also remarked how odd it was that each of us had had to relearn how to walk (I because of equilibrium problems following my operation in August 1999). She saw the strange humor in that.

A little later, one of the patient care technicians on the ward who help nurses with bedding changes, bathing, and burn care came in and asked Lauren how she was, then asked me how I was, and I pointed to Lauren's broad smile and said, Anytime I'm in here and you want to know how I feel, just look over there. Whatever expression is on Lauren's face, that's my mood.

Shortly after this I spoke to the social worker on the unit. I started to discuss Lauren's future care and return home; but the social worker said that the best way to begin that discussion would be to gather the entire family team for an initial meeting, where we would start to identify all the issues with respect to her future care. There are so many questions: where the rehab facility will be, what levels of care are covered by insurance. Briefly, the social worker said, we should know that Lauren is an important patient for the unit. To come in with her level of injury and to make it this far was simply remarkable. She is motivated, energetic, her desire to heal substantial. But mostly, she is an amazing fighter. Her occupational therapist agreed, calling her a miracle woman.

With all that fighting spirit, however, she still feels isolated overnight. The last two nights were a problem; as I've noted, she cannot signal the nurse because she is incapable of pressing any of the call buttons, or of making a sound to get attention. Plus, she is returned to the ventilator. It is all so hard for her that we decided to do something to make her night easier.

So we hired a companion to be in the room with her. Lauren's greatest anxiety comes when she feels she is being ignored, but tonight she had a wonderful woman from Jamaica to stay with her, spin her CDs, play the video movies, or simply watch her sleep and be there in case she wakes with a fright and needs help to relax. The moment Kareen walked in, Lauren's fear and sense of isolation evaporated.

Lauren liked her so much that she rehired her for a second night before she had been on the job even five minutes. It was clear that, for this night anyway, the companion would be the source of Lauren's peace of mind.

And of mine.

Love,
Greg & Lauren.

From: Greg
To: Everyone
Date: Wednesday, November 14, 2001 1:14 AM
Subject: Lauren News

Today was another good Lauren day; she ate applesauce, Jell-O, and yogurt. She had a smile on her face when I got there and a smile on her face when I left. She took some more steps.

It is all so remarkable.

As ever, I will write more (a LOT more) in the morning. Until then:

Love,
Greg & Lauren

From: Greg
To: Everyone
Date: Wednesday, November 14, 2001 2:39 PM
Subject: Lauren Update for Nov 13 (Wednesday), Weekly Magazine Edition

The experiment with the companion was a great success. Lauren told me that Kareen was a godsend. She changed her bedding, kept her comfortable, ministered to her needs, and got the nurse when necessary. Most important of all, she was simply there, and she was there again the next night.

Monday night, that meant no feelings of isolation, no helpless waving toward someone passing by in the hallway. Instead, Lauren had the confidence that she would not be neglected, and with that confidence came a measure of relaxation and serenity.

I want to stress that the nurses are not actually neglecting her; she is getting the necessary care, they are checking her at least once an hour, as required, and if she were able to stay comfortable, that would be more than enough. But she gets very uncomfortable, and it is a problem when there is no immediate assistance. Also, she has only recently awakened into this, her mind is racing, and there is very little reassurance in the here and now. ICUs will drive anyone crazy, and the only thing worse than the nurses constantly messing with you, fiddling with your IV lines, and performing countless other ministrations, is when they stop. Then come the feelings of helplessness and isolation.

I spent twenty-four hours in a neurosurgical ICU in 1999, and I remember those very feelings of isolation and neglect, so I am all too able to imagine how Lauren feels. But even so, I could speak and I could press the call button; she cannot even do that. I was out of the ICU and into a private room within twenty-four hours. On a friend's advice, I hired a private-duty nurse, a devout Jamaican woman. I still remember the absolute joy I experienced when every time I needed to shift position, she came running with sheets and towels to prop me up and support my weight. She sat there the entire night reading the Bible; when I couldn't tell if I slept, I would ask her and she would tell me with a lilt, "You slept beautifully, for forty-five minutes."

Since Lauren is still in the ICU, she does not need an extra full-time nurse (she shares her nurse with only one other patient). But she benefits greatly by having someone there to make sure of her comfort throughout the night. Kareen is a certified nurse's assistant (CNA) who usually works in an old-age home. She was gentle and patient, standing by Lauren and feeding her ice chips, learning which CDs Lauren enjoyed listening to. She was also strong, able to lift Lauren to reposition her in the bed. What she is not permitted to do is perform a "supervised medical need," such as giving medication or taking blood; these remain the nurse's responsibility.

On Tuesday, Lauren hit a few more milestones, but her favorite was that she ate actual food. She has been receiving a 6,000-calorie-a-day diet through a feeding tube; she has tolerated this well and it has been one of the major engines of her healing. But it goes straight to her stomach through a tube in her nose and she doesn't taste anything. For someone who likes fine dining (even someone who likes Wendy's), this is difficult. The only things she has tasted since September 11 are ice chips. So Tuesday, as I mentioned, she was absolutely thrilled when she was able to eat applesauce, yogurt, and Jell-O; she said, "It was heaven." This was certainly a milestone.

She still needs the tube feedings, but there is nothing that says she can't supplement them with soft things she can taste.

Later Tuesday, while I was standing with her, her doctor came in and we discussed Lauren's surgical schedule. The plan remains to concentrate on rehab this week, saving surgery to her left hand for a week from this Friday. Any surgery will require her to be fairly inactive for about five days and restricted to her bed. The surgery is not a limiting factor in her rehab, which she can begin now, but delaying it will give her additional time to recondition and to heal.

Lauren mentioned how she had slept the previous night without support from the ventilator, something her doctor confirmed had been a good thing.

Another doctor whom Lauren had seen prior to her burn injury came in to consult on a digestive problem she was having. After determining that the old problem was not behind her current discomfort, the doctor spent the rest of her visit simply and gently reassuring Lauren that she had a lot to live for, in Tyler (drawing a smile), and in me; she should not rein in the powerful emotions she felt but express them, and have faith that she would recover. At one point the doctor said very quietly, "Lauren, you have experienced a lot. All of this is a lot to deal with."

Tears built as Lauren responded, "When I was running out of the building, onto the street, I had one thought, God, please let me live for Tyler, let me see my son, I want to see him, I have to see him grow." And she finished with great sadness, "It was terrible."

The doctor stroked her arm as she said this and kept reassuring her until she left.

Lauren is not yet ready to see visitors beyond her immediate family. In addition to the infection risk, which is still present, I don't think she feels she has the energy. She can speak in a whisper, but only if someone places a gloved finger over her tracheal opening and seals it so she can send air across her vocal cords. I think she wants to be stronger before she starts to receive guests, but that time is not that far away.

She stood yesterday, and took about ten steps. She remains determined and highly motivated. She does her facial exercises, her arm and leg exercises. She bobs her head and we dance together. She is more helpless now than she will ever be; it is sometimes hard, but her degree of motivation strongly implies that she will move her rehabilitation along as quickly as she can. We all have to keep in mind where she is headed, not where she is.

That "where" is someplace new. She is becoming a short-timer in the ICU. Within weeks she will move to the next stage in her care, a rehab facility, and then it will be time to return home, to our future.

Lauren's mother and father are with her at the hospital during the day, returning home to be with Tyler in the evenings and put him to bed. I wake up with Tyler, do errands, and try to take care of administrative stuff, then go to the hospital in the afternoon and stay as late as I can (most nights 8 or 9 PM, sometimes midnight). I spend time writing these e-mails and answering other e-mails, whether late at night or early in the morning. We go to and from the hospital, knowing the distances and times of what is our regular commute. But this is just an outpost on a very long trip, and even though the greatest single change has already occurred—from our life at 8:47 AM September 11 to our life following 8:49 that same day—the cumulative changes of the future will be far greater.

First there will be a new facility; there will be a series of "knowns" replacing the present unknowns: the full extent of injury and rehabilitation versus what is now anticipated as we complete the cycle of post-trauma surgeries. There will be a new routine at home, with a growing child learning about the new structure of his home life. We will find out what is expected of us day to day without the rank and file of nurses and techs and companions there to assist with the simplest of tasks. We will find out how much energy and strength we have to handle the Activities of Daily Living; we know we will handle them but we don't know how tired we'll be.

Of course, the last two months prove that anything, even daily trips to the refuge from hell, can become routine. We can learn to tolerate anything if we can change it enough to make it survivable. And in the chinks of those changes, joy will seep through.

There will be a day, not that far in the future, where we will laugh in a private moment. That will be the happiness we own again, and will not need others to structure or provide.

We will all adapt. I am changed, but only inside; outside, I look the same, maybe with bags under my eyes. Lauren and Tyler, however, are both growing into their new lives.

There are so many parallels—learning to walk, to speak (Tyler to form words, Lauren to reverse the deconditioning and trauma to her larynx), to handle new activities, to overcome one day's limitations so they become the next day's accomplishments. And they will have to get to know each other again.

That will start on Friday, when Tyler visits the hospital between noon and 2 PM. They may still be in separate rooms but Lauren will see him, live, for the first time since September 11, and she will be thrilled at the way he has grown and the way he has coped with the whole situation. Because he has stayed the same child; whatever he may have sensed about that situation, he has continued to be warm and happy and confident and playful, and he will present all those aspects to her. I was lying in bed last night, realizing that the energy jolt this visit will provide—gleaming through the rain of tears—will be the single most valuable boost she needs to get through all the stages to come.

I also notice much more mundane habits that are finding their way into my daily life. I have one friend who seems to be giving me a lift from one point in Manhattan to another whenever I see him; I have another friend who has encouraged me to call him at night, at late hours, because he is "nocturnal," and I have begun to do this so often, I call him my cab buddy or my car buddy, the person I speak to late at night as I head home. I have friends who are doctors, who help me integrate what is going on every day; I have friends who are rock and rollers, who help me get away from it all for a couple of hours. I am still catching lunches and dinners at the Beach Café, where the managers instantly adopted me and have continued to welcome me and my friends. All of them help me through the hours outside the hospital, what some would call my life; but they are all proxies for the woman who will come back to fill it.

Love,
Greg & Lauren

P.S. Some housekeeping.
Monday Poetry Marathon—So much happened Monday that I faded before I had a chance to recount it all, literally becoming so tired that I could not keep a full sentence in my head. I forgot to tell you

that I stood by Lauren's bed and recited the Robert Burns poem, "My Love Is Like a Red, Red Rose," from memory, as I had so often while she was in her drug-induced sleep. Once she awakened from this, I hadn't thought she would be into poetry, but she watched me with sweet eyes and mouthed, "That was beautiful," when I finished. So I read another: Ben Jonson's "Song to Celia"—"Drink to me, only, with thine eyes."

Cantor—There was a reason she asked me, with the most delicate and vulnerable dignity, whether September 11 was an act of terror. Someone, I don't know who, had told her that Howard Lutnick had been emotional during a televised interview. After I confirmed that people had died at Cantor, she said, "That's why Howard was crying."

From: Greg
To: Everyone
Date: Thursday, November 15, 2001 2:35 PM
Subject: Lauren Update for Nov 14 (Wednesday)

Lauren had her tracheal tube removed Wednesday, so when I walked into her room, for the first time since September 11 she didn't have a blue hose running from her mouth or her neck to a ventilator or to a gas connection in the wall. Instead, she had foam dressings covering the healing tracheostomy.

I said, No trache, you must be talking. She said yes.

Her voice sounded hoarse and congested, as if she had a bad cold, but it was her voice, not a whisper with a faint facsimile of her normal tone. Occasionally air would leak out below the dressings, so we would still have to press down on them to permit her to speak without interruption (her voice would go on and off, like a bad cell phone connection), but it is hard to assess the joy of seeing her freed of these devices, because it means that her lungs are strong enough to breathe on their own, just about two months after suffering an 82.5 percent burn.

I told her it was great to hear her really sounding like herself; I told her that I had never suspended her cell phone, paying the bill just so I could still hear her regular voice on her message announcement. She told me, in largely her regular voice, that I was nuts.

Before I went to the hospital, I bought three pairs of shoes for Lauren; she needs high-top sneakers with good ankle support to walk around in. I bought one pair each of New Balance, Asics, and Nike, and lined them up for her to see. With the therapist, she will choose one pair to keep.

The New Balance were waterproof, olive-drab walkers; the Asics were tall versions of their normal design, with a black pattern on white leather; the Nikes were high-tech, shiny white and royal blue women's basketball shoes with four Frankenstein-neck-looking, ribbed cylindrical pillars supporting the heel. These were the hippest, baddest-looking ones (with a snap-down blue-ribbed white fabric strip covering the laces), but they were also the highest, with the strongest lateral ankle support. My money's on the Asics (actually, it's on all three, but I can return two for a full refund).

Before going into Lauren's room I spoke with the Burn Center's staff psychologist. Lauren is starting to ask questions about what happened, and to learn more; she knows that she was burned as a result of an act of terrorism, that people died at Cantor, but she does not know the extent of the carnage. The psychologist wanted to discuss the way she is given information, to slow things down if possible, to help her cope.

Much of what she said coincides with what I have written here; that in addition to learning about her injuries, Lauren also must catch up with our knowledge of how the world has changed. For her, the facts of the attacks and their aftermath will provide shocks as powerful as those all of us felt on September 11—this on top of brutal knowledge of how she herself was hurt. The key concept the psychologist conveyed was to manage the sharing of information through timing and dosage: to try to space it out, and to limit the size of any one chunk. Lauren is likely to learn everything over the next five days, she explained, but it would be best to give her the information in a way that does not make her agitated. She added that Lauren is not likely to ask questions to which she does not want to know the answers.

Rule number one is not to lie to her; if she asks a question, answer it. Rule number two is to tell her information early in the day. This way, she can absorb it with family around rather than in the loneliness of her room at night (though this loneliness is ameliorated by the presence of her companion). I had followed rule number one with respect to the newspaper article, which she learned of when she was read the note that accompanied Peyton Manning's jersey; and with telling her

September 11 was an act of terror when she was trying to learn why Howard Lutnick would cry in an interview. Unfortunately, rule number one supersedes rule number two, which I was forced to break Wednesday. I had previously deflected the question of whether she knew anyone who died at Cantor Fitzgerald; I did not tell her that almost 700 were lost. But it was only a matter of time before she asked me about her boss, Doug Gardner, who did not survive. That question came tonight.

At first I said I wasn't sure; then I said no, I'll answer that one; he did not make it.

She looked emotional; I asked if she was OK. She said she was. "I expected it. He was always at his desk by seven."

I told her I'd hoped she would ask that question tomorrow.

She then asked about the COO of eSpeed, who also died; this time I told her I wasn't sure, and she accepted that, though I doubt she believed me. I thought one fact like that was enough for the evening, and of course I had done exactly what I hadn't wanted to do. But Kareen would be there with her, so maybe she wouldn't feel so alone, and would be comfortable enough to simply rest, and grieve without her grief spinning out of control.

During the course of the evening, Lauren asked me several other questions, to which I gave "answers lite." At one point she asked me, "How do the buildings look? Have they been dismantled?" I told her crews were working on them. My goal was not to deceive, but to pace.

"They got us," she said. "They got us, they kept trying and they finally got us. The icons."

I told her, That may be true, but now we're getting them. I told her that the Taliban were running like cowards from a real army (I didn't tell her they were running from a bunch of infantry and guys on horseback, with U.S. air support).

Lauren has learned some other hard news; it is likely that she will lose the tips of several fingers on her left hand (but not of her thumb); she knows that is what her next surgery will be about. She asked me if I knew that; I said I did. She also knows that her left ear may need some cosmetic work. She appears to have handled this news, so far, with equanimity. About her left hand, she said, "I can always wear long nail tips!"

The strongest feelings she expressed to me Wednesday night were that she loved that her parents were here with her, that it has been "wonderful," and that she did not want them to leave (the plan is that they would leave in mid-December, then come back). But I told her that they can't stay here all the time and they will be back, and that this was still a month away.

Shortly after entering her room and noticing her trache was gone, I fed her her dinner, at her request. It resembled the dinner you would see in a '60s film about deep space; three colors of gruel in different triangular sections of the hospital plate. However, it was a crowning achievement of hospital cuisine—pureed everything, the only way Lauren could eat it: chicken, mashed potatoes, and a vegetable that looked like something from (the movie) 2001, but apparently tasted good.

Throughout the evening, she was tired but otherwise in good spirits. She was spoon-fed hot tea; I read her many of the get-well cards she has received, as well as a number of e-mail messages. I know she is looking forward to seeing Tyler on Friday. One thing the psychologist told Lauren about this coming meeting was to be prepared; it is likely to be very difficult, and Tyler is likely to be frightened. I think Lauren will be ready; one thing she wants to do is to give Tyler a toy, from her, during his visit. Buying that toy is my key task for Thursday.

Kareen remains a godsend. She is warm and energetic; when she arrived today, Lauren's face glowed. She herself seems quite taken with Lauren; it doesn't seem to take long in Lauren's presence for anyone to be inspired, despite the extent of her injuries. At one point, Kareen told me, when Lauren could not hear, of how she had gone home and cried on Tuesday morning, not over Lauren, but over the entire tragedy; and she told of how Lauren was giving her an opportunity to help.

With Kareen there, I was able to leave by 9 PM. I headed for a band rehearsal, and had to figure out the best way to get downtown from the East Side to the rehearsal studio (The Off Wall Street Jam) on Murray Street, three blocks north of Ground Zero.

In the end I took a cab to the West Side, then went into the subway and boarded the number 2 express, which ran local to Chambers Street. There was a scent of smoke all through the station; when I emerged, the visual sensation was again striking. I looked up and I saw nothing; not Tower Two (the South Tower, my building), not World Trade Seven, just an unbroken indigo sky. In a slot between the buildings of West Broadway and the remnants of 5 World Trade, a single white X-frame crane boom reached upward through floodlit haze.

From that same vantage, the World Trade Center used to loom with such mass, it had been claustrophobic. West Broadway terminates on the north border of the World Trade Center Plaza; even though it was a two-lane southbound avenue, it had always seemed like a dead end. The truck entrance to the complex had been just off West Broadway, a full block north of the pedestrian entry to 5 World Trade. In the morning, trucks would be lined up for several blocks, passing through the extremely tight security designed to prevent any bombs from finding their way underneath the structure.

Now unauthorized automobile traffic is turned east or west at Chambers Street, five blocks north of the Trade Center; there was already a sign posted high on a lamppost reading "Authorized Pedestrian Traffic Only." Concrete dividers lined both sides of the street where the metered parking used to be. Most of the parked cars display "Emergency" placards on the dashboard.

I went up to the Jam and we had our rehearsal; we auditioned a new sax player; we told him he sounded great after just one song. It was obvious—and later confirmed—that he was a ringer. If he sticks with the band, we'll be that much better.

My friend Billy Bennett runs the Jam and is the leader of the Rolling Bones. He bought the Jam from its founders about four years ago and has lived it since, sometimes literally lived in it; the Jam occupies the second and fifth floors of a five-story building, and he would sleep on his office sofa bed and use the kitchen and bathroom at the back of the second floor. Before buying the business, he had sold stock photography to periodicals and media worldwide.

On September 11, he stayed in the studio at 47 Murray Street as the towers fell three blocks away, leaving only when 7 World Trade came down. He feared he would lose his business; he reopened temporarily in the Music Building at 250 West 30th Street as quickly as he could, but reopened the downtown location about two weeks ago. He's posted leaflets in the area welcoming musicians from fire department and construction crews.

In the middle of rehearsal, we took a break, and Billy and I headed down to the kitchen, where he made peanut butter and jelly sandwiches with oval crackers and crunchy Skippy. "Dinner?" I asked.

"Snack," he responded. I asked him about reopening, whether business was bad; in fact, he'd had a full house most nights. That may be because his place is now more of a refuge than it ever was from the hard knocks of Wall Street.

We spoke about Lauren, and about whether *The New York Times* might like to cover his story, that of a small businessman struggling to maintain operations in a shattered neighborhood without the benefit of business-interruption insurance or a substantial cash cushion. I said, Make me another PBJ and I'll get you in the *Times* (I don't really have this power); he said, Make it yourself and I'll take the *Enquirer*.

I told him a friend of mine was an investor in a fund that may control the publisher of the *Enquirer*. He told me he knew that editor, the one who died. I said which editor; he said Bob Stevens, the photo editor who was the first American to die of anthrax. Billy had sold him stock photography.

It turns out that it's time to go back to work; and as I finish this Thursday, I have received a call from Gil Scharf inviting me back part-time, not just to work, but to reconnect to colleagues and friends and get on with resuming my career. So Monday morning, I'm back at the office.

It is time; Lauren is getting on with things, so should I.

Love,
Greg & Lauren

Today, sixty-six days after September 11, Lauren took a walk: from her room, past the room next door, and around the corner to the reception desk, a distance of thirty or forty feet. Again, I was not a direct witness, but I heard testimony.

I heard that the physical therapists had gone running out to the waiting room to fetch Lauren's parents, telling them to run, they had to see this; and they had gone through the wide electronic swinging doors of the Burn Center to find Lauren standing by the reception desk, a long distance from her room.

Her day nurse told me, when I arrived there later, that she had people crying on the ward; they had not expected her to walk so far, so fast, so soon. But she had.

The miracle continues each day.

As I expected, she and the therapists had chosen the high-top Asics basketball shoes, the ones with the simple logo pattern on white leather. But once they were on Lauren's feet, they were transformed to the winged sandals of Mercury (in Lauren's case, more probably Hermes), at least for a moment.

It is hard to believe that twenty-eight days ago, she was lying in a prone position, facedown, heavily sedated, only occasionally moving her head, while we waited to see whether autografts that she had received on her buttocks were going to adhere.

On that day, we could only wonder what thoughts were on her mind; we could not imagine her doing much more then than slightly opening her eyes, to show us their color. Just four days earlier, she had almost imperceptibly moved the muscles of her face to form a smile; we were reaching for the smallest of actions as proof that she was somehow aware of our presence, in some way actively engaged in her own fight for survival.

Now, just four weeks later, she is talking (mostly), and she has put on her shoes and taken a walk.

The effort that was required to do this was apparent; she spent much of the evening exhausted, and at 8:30 PM, as I was about to leave, had already fallen asleep.

But she is with us, and when we say she is a fighter, we are not just saying it because she has managed to survive a highly critical period, when every waking moment required extraordinary measures just to keep her breathing until the next moment. Now we say she is a fighter because she lies in bed and does her rehab exercises with her face and her arms, and when given the opportunity, runs her forty-foot analogue to the New York City Marathon on legs that have been used just twice in ten weeks. Her accomplishments every day are enough to make grown people weep; and it happens over and over.

The road in front of us is still so much longer than the road we have traveled. Still, you want to hit the ground running, and you could say that is literally what Lauren did today.

Another gauge of how fast she is moving is that we were told tonight that she may well leave the hospital—not the ICU, but the hospital—for a rehab facility in two to three weeks! We used to wonder when she would move a finger or a limb; now we wonder when she will move to a new home, and where that will be.

Tonight instead of feeding her pureed everything, I fed her meat loaf, mashed potatoes and carrots, applesauce and vanilla pudding. I actually took her alphabet board, such a vital tool only a week ago, and slipped it into the bag that holds her videotapes so that we would have it as a souvenir. I noticed that she has gone from a body lying in a room among tubes and beeping pumps to someone with a CD collection, a video collection, and a shoe collection, not to mention a library of poetry and literary humor. And a desire to reach out to others.

Tonight Lauren was again asking me to give people messages, and I said to her, why not let me type e-mails on my BlackBerry at her bedside and send them directly to her friends over her signature? So we did just that; we sent messages to three people; instead of a note from me on Lauren's behalf, they got her own heartfelt and emotional words, and the messages were not signed "Greg & Lauren" but only "Lauren."

Think about the statement that makes about survival.

I do not doubt that the messages were a profound experience for the three friends who received them; waiting for the chance to see her in person, they've instead heard from her at their desks, or on the road, or simply on their own BlackBerries, walking down the street. She got a big kick out of sending them.

Not all the milestones today were joyful ones. Tonight Lauren learned how many people died at Cantor Fitzgerald.

We had been approaching this for several days. She had learned that the attacks of September 11 were terrorism, that her direct boss had died; but I had convinced her to wait a little longer, until I could check the names of her colleagues against the list of those who survived. I brought that list to the hospital today. And she started to ask me about it.

I told her to take it slow, but name after name was someone who died. She asked about the two men who had been her direct managers before Doug Gardner; both had died. She asked about one of their assistants; she didn't make it; she'd been pregnant. She named programmers and salespeople, also lost. She asked about the head of eSpeed, the head of the Agency desk, and the head of taxable fixed income—all gone.

Finally she looked at me, and asked me how many had died. I asked her if she really wanted to know; she said she did, and I said almost 700. She blinked her eyes.

And suddenly she raised her right hand, and waved it in its cast and said through tears, and raising her voice as loudly as possible, "I will avenge them."

And I had to tell her again that she didn't have to, that the United States had gone to war to avenge what had been done to Cantor. I said that she could not take on that burden, but instead should understand that she was the focus of many families' hope, because they had no other. That she had avenged the lost just by making it out.

I told her that she had been the subject of the quote of the day in *The New York Times* the day the article about her had been published: " 'She's got to pull through, because she's got 700 families' worth of love. It's not fair, but she's part of their hope.' Howard W. Lutnick, of Cantor Fitzgerald, on Lauren Manning, a burn victim in the Sept. 11 attack."

She asked me about the firm-wide Cantor memorial, so I described the speeches by Howard and Rudy Giuliani, the blessings by the priests and a rabbi, the singing of the Harlem Boys Choir and of Judy Collins, the speeches by wives of lost Cantor executives, the very men she'd asked about just moments earlier.

I told her that the only battle that she had to fight—ever—was her own battle to survive.

She doesn't need to be an avenging angel, just an angel of hope.

Love,
Greg & Lauren

From: Greg
To: Everyone
Date: Saturday, November 17, 2001 2:49 AM
Subject: Lauren Update for Nov 16 (Friday)

Tyler Jacob Manning, at the age of one year two weeks, delivered a performance today that was exceeded in its beauty only by that of his mother. The encounter between the two of them was, quite simply, the most beautiful thing I have ever seen. And I love them both, so for me, well, I am crying as I write this, and I will probably keep crying until I finish.

Lauren prepared for this meeting like for nothing else in her life; she had her hair blow-dried; she wore lipstick; her father searched nearby stores to buy her Vanilla Fields perfume, which she wore on a towel draped across her shoulders so that Tyler would be more familiar with her scent. She made sure she had a gift to give him; she wanted a noisemaking toy, something with buttons and flashing lights, that he would play with; she asked us to bring his lawn-mower-style push toy, which he uses on his hallway constitutionals. She asked for a baseball cap so she would look "more normal."

I entered her room before the meeting to make sure she was ready, and she was seated in a rolling chair (not a wheelchair, but a lounge chair with wheels), in her blue patient gown, with sheets across her lap and the scented towel across her shoulders. Her smiling face peeked at me from beneath the brim of a white Cantor Fitzgerald baseball cap. Because her forearms and hands are still in splints and casts, Tyler's gift sat in a colorful, beribboned, tissue-paper-stuffed shopping bag on her lap.

At the time, I think I was more concerned with finding the video camera to film the encounter, but as I remember it, the dignity amid suffering that she presented at that moment, the love and the longing and desire to resume her life, were overwhelming. This is what she lived for, to see her son, and she was about to live the thing that had carried her across a field of flame to her rescue. If there are angels' wings in this story, they enfolded her at that moment, and at this one.

Back out in the waiting room, Joyce, our nanny, waited with Tyler. I returned to find Tyler at the center of a crowd of nurses and therapists, all dressed in gray scrubs and all waving and smiling at him as he looked at them with contemplative assessment. I took out my new digital Elph camera to snap the first of many pictures, and got a beautiful one of six women staring intently at whoever sat in the McLaren Techno stroller of which I could see only the back canopy; and the computer displayed the warning, "Flash Card Full."

There are two types of people on this earth: those who read the instruction manual and those who don't, and I was always a member of the former group, but let myself, just this once, fall into the latter group and paid the price. For the second year in a row, I was without a photo camera at a once-in-a lifetime event.

Anyway, I did have the video camera, and for the first time since September 11, Lauren was photographed, this time saying that she was about to see Tyler for the first time following her injury. And I filmed her mother wheeling her, using my vast knowledge from my long-ago New School film workshops to track her as she exited her room, turned the corner of the Burn Center, and came through the power-assisted double doors to the corridor by the waiting room.

Uncinematically and unexpectedly, Tyler was then turned loose about thirty feet behind me and allowed to walk up the corridor pushing his lawn mower, so I had to choose between getting him coming toward us or getting her reaction. I think I tracked him, then shot her, then stepped away to get them both, and wound up filming this incredibly emotional and private moment in a public hallway as strangers wandered by.

The rules were that Lauren could not touch Tyler because of the risk of infection, and he could not touch her. So, instead of placing him on her lap, Tyler was picked up and held near his mother, who said hello to him through her tears. She was overwhelmed by happiness, but also by the totality of the loss she had experienced on September 11, and by the vast gulf between the shape she was in the last time she saw Tyler and now. I am reading her mind here, but I felt the same feelings, and I have seen him every day.

I was just so, so happy—I can't possibly describe it; it was equal parts elation, grief, joy, empathy, wonder, an impossible yearning for what could never be—the past—coupled with the infinite promise of what we are immeasurably lucky we still have—the future.

As Tyler was held near her, he showed some fear at first; the psychologist had warned that he would probably not recognize his mother and might be quite frightened. But he cried twice and then was past it; as more people walked by, I suggested we retire to the Quiet Room, the private waiting room reserved for firefighters, which had been opened for us for this special occasion.

Once there, we again held Tyler near Lauren; she said, The gift, the gift, flicking it with her right hand so someone would give it to him. She was so full of joy that she could give her little boy a present. We set him on the floor beside the keyboard toy with the requisite tones and flashing lights, but he did not show much interest in it; instead, he wanted to push his lawn mower.

And Tyler knew her. Whether it was the perfume, or her voice, or her face, which looks much the same; whether it was her smile beneath the brim of the baseball hat, or whether he recognized her from the photos we have shown him (that's Mommy!), he knew her. We play a game with him; we'll say, Where's Joyce? and he'll look at Joyce. We'll say, Where's Daddy? and he'll look at me. We said, Where's Mommy? and he looked at Lauren.

Tyler is a miracle; yes, I'm his dad, but we hear how beautiful he is, how easy, how much fun, how smart, all the time. Today, just shy of thirteen months, he showed poise. He pushed his lawn mower back and forth across the floor of the Quiet Room, toward his mother and toward the door; and Lauren got to see exactly what she lived for. She kept looking at me and saying, "He's gorgeous."

There was a song she used to sing to Tyler; I tried to sing it to him on her behalf but I couldn't make it through the first line before choking up.

So Lauren sang it, even though she has had her regular voice back for only a few days and still needs someone to press the dressings over her healing tracheostomy so that she can speak without air hissing out of her chest. With Joyce's hand pressing down on the base of her neck, Lauren sang:

I love you in the morning and in the afternoon,
I love you in the evening and underneath the moon,
I love you, I love you, oh yes I really do,
I love you oh my darling through and through.

She made it all the way through (she actually sang it once before I could film it, but I asked her to do it a second time, and she made it through again). And he started to dance. Kneeling, he shook his body to the music. Tyler came to see her; Lauren sang to him and she made him dance.

So the Princess and the Angel of Perry Street met again, and it was wonderful. They had a receiving line of physical and occupational therapists, Lauren's nurse for the day, Andrew (a tall, slightly wild-looking man in gray scrubs who was the first person I'd seen on the burn unit on September 11, who cried "Next!" in a loud voice as Lauren was brought in, and whose manner and heart have proven incredibly gentle), the social worker who sees Lauren as a singular patient in her twenty-five years of experience on the unit, and Lauren's doctor.

He said he had come to meet Tyler, and Tyler walked toward him, pushing the lawn mower, and stopped, sizing him up; I said, Tyler, this is one of the good guys. The doctor spent some minutes with us; we discussed that Lauren's next surgery would probably be Wednesday.

I can't remember much else about the conversations. I know, simply, that there are no affirmations of the soul more powerful than what I witnessed today.

The visit with Tyler lasted, I think, an hour, though I can't say I had any idea how much time had passed. Lauren grew tired and Tyler needed to go home, so I wheeled her back to her room and left her in the company of her mother and father for the rest of the afternoon; I would be coming back at 4:30. Joyce and I packed Tyler back into his stroller, and I told him, Tyler, today you made your mother as happy as you may ever make anyone.

A year ago, the battery on our Advantix Elph failed minutes before Lauren was to deliver Tyler. I ended up videotaping his birth from a tasteful position behind Lauren's shoulder. Today, in an almost eerie coincidence, I was forced to film, rather than photograph, another life event. It is possible that a fleck of destiny required me to film both moments, the movements and speech of the participants, as well as their faces. Each tape is now infinitely powerful because of the other's existence. One is a birth, the other a soul's rebirth. In one, Tyler will see himself as he was born; in the other, he will see the day he helped his mother be reborn. Lauren will see herself giving life to her son; and then she will see her son giving life to her.

What a day; and it didn't stop there. At 4:30 the Burn Center was holding its traditional pre-Thanksgiving meal for patients and their families. Lauren was planning to attend the dinner, looking forward to eating normal food; food cooked not for a patient, as her hospital meals were, but for people who had the ability to go off to a restaurant, and who were thus in a position to be more demanding.

When I returned to the hospital she was in her bed, not in the rolling chair. It turned out that the psychologist had urged her to rest after a very strenuous day, and she was taking the advice. But she was still looking forward to a real turkey dinner, and she sent me on a mission to get her a full plate.

In the Burn Center's conference room, the large conference table— around which Lauren's parents and I and my friend Mitch sat with one of the doctors the day after she was injured so that her parents could be prepared for what they would see when they entered her room—was covered with food: two turkeys, stuffing, gravy, sweet potatoes, broccoli and carrots, spinach, two types of cranberry sauce, rice dishes, zucchini casserole, beans, and biscuits.

There were patient families and patients: babies, teenagers, grown-ups. The babies sat on their mothers' laps. One teenager, who'd been treated at another burn unit but who hadn't been taken through range-of-motion therapy while he was healing, had come to the Burn Center to treat the excessive tightness of his skin. I had seen him screaming in the hallway as they cajoled him into walking the lap around the unit. Today he sat in the corner of the room, smiling from ear to ear, bright-eyed, laughing, his hands crossed on the handle of his four-footed walking cane. One adult man was bald from his burns; his head showed grafting to his face and scalp; he was smiling.

The food was blessed, and it was time to help ourselves; I wound up carving one of the turkeys, then I brought Lauren a plate of normal food. I fed her a bite of turkey with gravy, then she would ask for some cranberry sauce; then the zucchini casserole; then a carrot, some stuffing, and back to the turkey. Many bites featured appropriate combinations of the above. It would be a gross understatement to say that she enjoyed this meal. I fed her as carefully as I've fed Tyler, and with as much love.

I went back to the conference room to get a plate for myself, and ran into another adult male patient, Harry Waizer, seated in a rolling chair similar to the one we'd used to wheel Lauren to the Quiet Room. He's also from Cantor; his wife, Karen, is one of the family members I have spent the most time with since September 11. I had followed his individual struggles, but though his room was next to Lauren's, I had never seen him, and then suddenly, there he was. He wore pressure garments on his arms and hands. I didn't have time to talk because I needed to get back to Lauren, but I introduced myself, and told him I was glad he was doing so well.

Later, as she was leaving, I saw Karen in the hallway and said I'd met Harry; she told me she'd met Lauren earlier in the day. We had followed each other's stories closely, including intimate details regarding the injury and treatment of our spouses; for a moment it was possible to wonder why it had taken us so long to meet them. But of course the reason is that for the first few weeks, we were standing a vigil over comatose or deeply sedated patients; we spent as much time in the waiting room as we did in the patient's room because there was little to do in the room but watch the nurse. Only now are we able, for the first time, really, in two months, to interact with our spouses. Only now have they awakened; only now are they able to respond and to be gracious about meeting.

Lauren had a gracious moment herself when one of the medical students came by to say good-bye since she was ending her one-month surgical rotation at the burn unit. The student told Lauren how happy she was to see her improvement over the four weeks. Lauren asked her what her specialty would be; she said general surgery. Lauren talked to her about what it was like to be an attractive woman in a profession, that sometimes, because you're attractive, you can get what you want early in your career, and it takes years to discover that discrimination still is present. We learned that New York-Cornell is considered a gentleman's hospital, not as bad as some others, maybe a good amount better, on this issue. Lauren wished the student well and good luck; she told her she would miss her, the student said she would miss Lauren, and suddenly we were all in tears.

Tonight Lauren was still working through the list of Cantor Fitzgerald survivors, and still learning that most of the people she asked about did not make it. Twice someone she named had survived and her face lit up; but far more often, the answer was negative.

We talked about many things, but mostly we talked about how wonderful it had been for her to see Tyler. I told her this was why she had survived; this was why she decided to live. I told her that he had known her, that he was marvelous, that someday he would understand what his mother had done for him. And I told her she had done it for me too. I looked at her and told her I was so in love with her. I told her we were meant to be; we'd always been; she told me that she'd always said that to me, and I told her I knew that. She told me I was her soulmate. And I said she was mine.

I came so close to losing her, and the game is still not over; one of the patients from September 11 is doing badly with serious pneumonia. I look at Lauren now, and I am filled with such longing; the border is close, the edge of the woods, and I want us to make it out.

We're running now.

Love,
Greg & Lauren

From: Greg
To: Everyone
Date: Monday, November 19, 2001 12:12 AM
Subject: Lauren Update for Nov 17 (Saturday), Day-Late Edition

"Day-Late Edition" means that this should have come out at this time yesterday but didn't. I got tired, then busy; tonight I will catch up. In this particular entry, the words "Saturday" and "tonight" all refer to Saturday, November 17. Also, I think I rambled; but I guess I can do that a couple of times. So this refers to SATURDAY.

Lauren took her first field trip Saturday, visiting Harry Waizer and perambulating all the way down the hallway of the Burn Center, a distance of perhaps eighty to one hundred feet. During the stroll, various levels of support were withdrawn, and she took her first unassisted steps.

First, the therapists removed the walker, and she was supported by a nurse and a therapist as she walked. Then the nurse let go of her, then the therapist (both staying beside her, of course), and she took a step on her own. Again I did not see it (but that is ending today—I am going to the hospital to see, and to videotape, her walking), but I heard about it. She was so proud.

(Without belaboring the parallels to Tyler, he is about to do the same thing; and I think he will be as proud of himself as she was of herself.)

The other big event was the arrival of my sister, with her daughter, our niece, who will be two years old in January, her husband, and his aunt (who was conscripted to do some baby-sitting last night). They drove up from Florida on Thursday and Friday, reaching New York

Friday evening. Late yesterday afternoon they came by to visit Lauren at the hospital.

The first thing Lauren said to my sister was "I'm happy to see you."

It was a beautiful visit; my sister was upbeat, positive, and conversational, as if Lauren were just hanging out in a day bed and nothing much had happened. That was the tone; the substance of the conversation was very direct. My sister talked about how strong Lauren had been to run across the street and escape the fire; she talked about how quickly we all became patriotic, and how there was a shortage of flags in the country, and how flags started to appear on homes throughout Lake Worth, where she lives in Florida, on the border of Boynton Beach, in the days following September 11.

Lauren asked to see our niece, so I went out to the waiting room and picked up this little twenty-month-old girl, who relaxed in my arms, laid her head on my shoulder, and let me walk her into the Burn Center and to the door of Lauren's room, where Lauren called out hi, and waved as my sister sat next to her. It was the second day in a row that a small child had entered this place and been completely unfazed by the strange sights, smells, and sounds. Of course, that is probably a product of innocence; they can have no idea of where they really are; but it still made for such pleasurable visits with Lauren.

(My sister came out and told me the lingering image from her visit was how Lauren's eyes had danced. She went on to say that Lauren was special, that from the first time she'd met her, she sensed her power, but she'd had no idea.)

The nurse today was speaking to Lauren, at one point, about her destiny, that she had been saved for a reason. He told Lauren: "I told Greg, when you got here, that you would pull through." I don't remember that, but I do remember, several weeks later, that he was the first nurse or doctor to come out and say he had just such a feeling about Lauren, that she would make it. (He said this before it was in any way certain—of course it is not wholly certain even now.)

While Lauren sat with my sister, the nurse pulled me out of the room and said, This is good; the more visitors, the more engaged she is in a life outside of this room, the better for her recovery, the faster she will get out of here. He said Lauren had dipped in the days immediately following September 11 but had rallied soon after and was climbing almost vertically since; that she was well ahead of anywhere they could have projected. I am certain that this is true, but it is also true that her strength masks such difficulty.

She has to maneuver on and off bedpans; she is in frequent discomfort, trying to find a comfortable position while the grafts on her buttocks conclude their healing cycle; she still has a feeding tube running into one nostril, held in place by tape on the tip of her nose, and constantly itching; electrodes on her torso give twenty-four-hour readings of her heart rate, and she wears a blood pressure cuff on her upper right arm for hourly readings. (For weeks, while she was sedated, an arterial line measured her blood pressure moment to moment, and during one particularly difficult period for her, a valve was floated through her veins into her heart to measure her pulmonary blood pressure, as the ultimate early warning system.) The ventilator still stands by the bed in case it is needed.

A single IV tree stands by her bed, from which she still receives 6,000 calories a day of liquid protein; earlier, there had been two IV trees by her bed at all times, with sedatives, painkillers, antibiotics, and fluids, in addition to the liquid protein (what they call her "feeds").

She has been through three different types of beds: a percussion air bed that vibrated her lungs to loosen any discharges, the liquefied air bed that aided the first five days of her recovery from the grafts to her buttocks, and the regular hospital bed on which she fidgets now.

She is incredibly strong and motivated, but there is so much pain and discomfort that the tears, and the fear, are never far from the surface. If she is mentioning a problem, she will sometimes finish a sentence in tears, her face, with its healing skin, going beet-red; when she saw the gastroenterologist to complain about not being able to control her bowels, and needing to wait for someone to come clean her—sometimes for a longer time than you would expect—she said, "I can't go on like this." (This problem was cleared up that night and hasn't returned.)

I am presenting Lauren with dignity, because that is how she presents herself 99 percent of the time. But it is with her equanimity during the other 1 percent of the time that she is truly proving her resilience and strength, because it would be so easy to surrender to tragedy; there are patients who become slugs, completely passive; who fight their treatment; who, in the words of one nurse, simply "do not like being an injured person," and who may not make it because they decide that the life that has been saved is not worth living.

It seems that all burn patients start down that road, and that for some, there is a light that flashes on—an image, a face, an idea; in Lauren's case her son (and, according to her, her husband)—that gives them the strength to fight just hard enough to have a chance to make it.

That single fact may also have given her the strength to maintain an even keel through what is, essentially, a horror film viewed from the inside. Her conduct now, her strength and resolve, certainly confirm that she knew what she faced almost from the beginning, and she meant to beat it.

She has had some very significant help, of course. Her mother and father have been marvelous, so much so that Lauren cried, briefly, when they left for the day at 4 PM on Saturday, and then wondered aloud why she had been so emotional. But it was not hard to understand. These days, her parents bring her the same feelings of comfort and safety that they brought to her as a child. Parents are the people you can still be a child with, and when you are dropped this low by injury, to have that ability is a blessing; to have someone around who doesn't need you to be a grown-up, but to be their little girl, is a significant form of release.

Before the reunion with Tyler, it was Lauren's mother who washed and blow-dried her hair and put on her lipstick while her father shopped for her perfume. They spend each day in the room with her, with the physical and occupational therapists, helping her perform basic range-of-motion exercises. When she thanks them, they speak to her of what an inspiration she is to them.

I have not written about Lauren's mom and dad much, nor will I, because they are private people, and may not want their private moments shared with concentric circles of hundreds or thousands; but they are just as involved in her care as I am, maybe more so, and their clockwork dependability and indefatigable energy have freed me to be with Lauren and to write these e-mails so that her large group of friends can follow her day to day.

Six nights a week, they are home to take care of Tyler; to play with him on the floor, to feed him dinner, to help him walk, to put him to bed. They keep him to his schedule; he gets his dinner and his bottle, and is put to sleep with military precision, but always with love.

When people say, How is Tyler? I can answer confidently that Tyler is fine because he is cared for twenty-four hours a day by people who love him dearly.

When Tyler came to visit on Friday, Joyce saw Lauren for the first time since September 11. She normally works five days a week, but she stayed with him the first two nights after September 11, before Lauren's mom and dad reached New York from Georgia, and she worked a number of Saturdays during the following weeks. She is wonderful with Tyler, and she also has an excellent relationship with Lauren. She is deeply religious and is praying for Lauren, and she had wanted to see her as soon as she was ready.

During the reunion, she stood for a long time with her gloved hand pressing down on Lauren's healing trache wound so that Lauren could speak clearly and could sing. And of course, she told Lauren how glad she was to see her, and Lauren said she was glad to see Joyce; and Lauren asked her if I'd been making sure to leave money in our junk drawer every day so that Joyce could buy supplies for Tyler; and Joyce laughed, because it has been ten weeks and of course we've worked that out.

Lauren's mind is eased because she knows Joyce is with Tyler.

Following the reunion with Tyler, I found myself becoming sad. I think I understand why: this is my family, the new one of limitation. I have been free to experience a certain form of denial for several weeks; I am healthy, Tyler is healthy, Lauren was fighting her way back, her parents were helping enormously with running our household; the future was still in my imagination. But now it is here, and we are learning how much pain she has to endure, how much fear she must conquer, and just how hard the road is that she must travel.

For all her joy and all her love, when she saw Tyler she could not touch him; we had to protect the two of them from each other, and the true reunion—the one where he nuzzles up against her cheek, where she can pick him up and hold him to her—is still so far away. It will be miraculous enough when it comes, but until then Lauren will have to be patient, and to recognize the cumulative grandeur of the thousands of baby steps to that date.

And until then, the limitations will be with us, and she is becoming aware of them. She is thinking about her appearance; she said to her doctor, "I want my body to be a work of art," and the tears came at the end of that. But that will be the cosmetic stage; for now we are completing the survival stage and entering the functional stage.

The surgery next week will define the condition of Lauren's left hand. While she has had several grafts there, the most recent a largely successful autograft to the back of it, the fact is that her left hand was the worst burned place on her body. Burn patients tend to be burned worst on their dominant side. Lauren is left-handed, or left-side dominant, so she would have used her left arm to try to escape. This may explain why this arm had to be completely grafted, while her right arm healed largely on its own.

Her doctor has been waiting as long as possible to let the hand define itself, meaning that those areas with surviving tissue and sufficient circulation would have the opportunity to heal as much as possible before being operated on. Next Wednesday we will learn the final extent of this healing, and so whether she will lose more than the tips of her left index and middle fingers. That prognosis itself is better than it was four weeks ago, when it was felt she might lose the tips of all four fingers on her left hand, though keeping the thumb intact. Beyond this is the question of function; whether even physiologically intact digits will retain full flexibility and gripping strength. It is a lot to carry in her mind.

Thanksgiving will be hard, no matter what; but it may yet earn its name.

Lauren is not bowed. She is fighting. What was physiologically true is also behaviorally true. Despite her vulnerability and trauma, she is still considerate, still thinking, still resourceful, still loving.

We had a beautiful moment Saturday; I think I've mentioned that there was a Dwight Yoakam song, "I Got You," from the CD "Just Lookin' for a Hit," that we used to sing to each other. One night she'd called me from the car and played it to me over her cell phone while she sang along.

This evening we were picking something from her CD collection; the choice was between Willie Nelson and Dwight Yoakam and Lauren said, "Try Dwight." So we put on the CD, and soon enough, "I Got You" was playing.

I started to sing it to her, and at the same moment she started to sing it to me. I put my hand on her neck so her voice wouldn't go in and out, and we sang the whole song to each other. A typical chorus goes like this:

> Well, I know I might seem near dead,
> But, honey, I think I might just get well—

'Cause I got you, to see me through,
Honey, I got you, chase my blues,
I got you,
To ease my pain,
Oh, I got you, to keep me sane
So, let 'em do what they wanna do,
It don't matter as long as I got you.

We kept it up for the whole song; her singing to me while wearing her FDNY baseball cap, moving her head from side to side, belting it out, while only a week ago all she could manage was a rush of air. The whole song was a picture of fun, and if I hadn't had to maintain my hand on her healing trache, I could have imagined it was four years ago and we were on the road to the country, not a care in the world. I think she felt the same way; she was smiling.

Love,
Greg & Lauren

From: Greg
To: Everyone
Date: Monday, November 19, 2001 7:33 PM
Subject: Lauren Update for Nov 18 (Sunday), Catching-up Edition

On Saturday I promised Lauren that I would be at the hospital to see her walk, so I ran there today at noon (this is the reason the Saturday update went out a day late, showing all the strains of being written under deadline pressure, I hope it was coherent!). I got there fifteen minutes late, but it turned out that another milestone was coming before the walk—her first shower.

This was a big change from the tank, and much more benign; instead of having her wounds cleaned and debrided by a team of nurses, Lauren was simply bathed. Plastic wrap protected the cast on her right arm and the wound dressings on her left. Both the shower and the tank sent her back to her room freezing and exhausted, but this was clearly easier and less painful.

After a fifteen-minute break, she was ready to take her walk, and after helping her get ready, I stood by with a video camera. (This turned out to be contraband; I was not permitted to bring it back into the hospital later that afternoon, when I took it out to a party; but I got the footage I needed.)

Before standing, she needed to have her legs wrapped in Ace bandages to control the blood pressure in her legs. Then with great and determined effort, she sat up in bed, maneuvered her legs over the side, and waited to have her new high-top Asics sneakers placed on her feet. We also draped a yellow hospital gown over her back where her blue patient gown was open. When this was done, and again with help, she stood up slowly, and was on her feet.

The walker that she uses is nothing like the walkers you are probably envisioning. It is designed strictly for rehabilitation. It has wheels, with brakes. Instead of a bar that can be grasped at waist level, it has two blue cushioned armrests that form a square-sided U in front of the walker, so that the patient can use her forearms to support her weight.

With her sister on one side and the physical therapist on the other, Lauren began to walk out of her room, into the hall, and turn right. I asked her to give a smile, and for a second she shot a smile, but mostly her face was deep in concentration. I taped her as she walked slowly down the corridor, a hundred feet to the end, and stopped in front of Harry Waizer's room.

She said, "Hey, how are you? I hear you're checking out of this hotel. Good luck with rehab, take care." He waved back at her (he is leaving the hospital for rehab tomorrow morning, a great milestone).

As she spoke, she turned around, and headed back down the hall toward her room. But this time she was going to do it without the walker. As had happened the day before, with gentle support from her sister and the physical therapist, they pushed the walker away and she began to walk down the hall under her own power. Again, I have it all on tape; the steady step, the steady progress, the determined face, the encouragement and cheers from family and staff.

This was a woman who had been burned over 82.5 percent of her body just sixty-eight days earlier, had received grafts on her back from the base of her neck to her Achilles tendon, and had lain on her back for just about two months; and here she was walking, using her legs, getting them back in shape after this horrible disaster.

As she approached her room, she started to get cheers and applause from her mom and dad, from the charge nurse, and from me. At a steady pace, she reached her room and turned left through the door. She had to wait a moment before she could sit back down on the bed, so I helped support her. We were supporting her at her elbows because she cannot grasp anything with her hands; she was supporting her weight, but she did not have tremendous control over her balance; she would not have been able to compensate and stay standing if the support had been removed. But she was solid; I could feel her muscles, her strength, waiting to be rebuilt.

We sat her down, removed her sneakers, cut the hospital gown off her (we'd had to trim the arms to fit them over her casts and dressings), and helped her lie back down. I told her how incredibly proud I was of her.

She saw a few visitors during this time: my sister, and my mother, who stopped in to see Lauren for the first time since September 11. My mother had come up from Florida, where she lives. She was particularly warm and comforting, sharing some kind words and a discussion of her granddaughter, our niece, with Lauren. My mother is the Holocaust survivor who said, days after September 11, that she had been in many terrible places, but that this tragedy was the worst thing she'd seen.

Also in attendance was my stepsister, who has not been featured recently in these e-mails, but who spent an enormous amount of time at the hospital during the very early period after September 11, when I was not yet writing updates but when the stresses, and the odds against survival, were the greatest. She also has a background in rehabilitation; she has corrected me when I've made mistakes in my discussion of such matters; and I will never forget how she showed up at the hospital in those first difficult days and spent hours by my side and Lauren's.

Lauren's walk ended about the time a friend of ours was set to begin celebrating a milestone birthday a block away from the hospital, at Evergreen, a Chinese restaurant at 69th Street and First Avenue. Her husband was throwing a surprise party for her; she thought she was meeting a few friends for brunch; instead, she met ten times as many.

Her husband is one of those people whom I can describe only as "one of the kindest people you will ever meet." This is a generic description. We all know a couple of people like this: uncomplicated (but complex), hardworking, capable, considerate, indefatigable in their hospitality. He had suffered severe second-degree burns when sparks lit fuel in his workshop (his business is to install bulletproof store-fronts), and he was a patient at the same Burn Center. He was one of the first to say that it was the best burn unit in the world (he had an excellent outcome). He is also a wonderful friend, and has come by the hospital many times.

Having worked with his wife at two companies for the first thir-teen years of my career, many of their friends were our friends; so I went over and videotaped a lot of hellos to Lauren. Then, with ten minutes of fond wishes in the can, I returned to the hospital, where I told the guard, as he was about to pass my camera bag by without in-specting it, that it was a video camera; I was instantly informed of the hospital's zero tolerance policy regarding cameras on their premises, and that was that for the tape that night (I would have to make a VHS copy).

But while Lauren did not see the faces of her friends, I saw some-thing new in her face. It looked like her face of old. The skin tone seemed the same; the facial expression the same. She had regained mobility and recovered the muscle function, the suppleness, that had been lost. What was so striking about it was that this was her smile, the one that always reassured me; the one that I had always loved; and it was back. Her face is not exactly the same, but it is so, so close.

These are surprises I don't even know to look for: the struggles to talk and to walk were one thing, but recovering the subtlety of her face, the loving expressions of a more innocent time, may be just as remarkable.

Love,
Greg & Lauren

P.S. As you may remember, I have dedicated "Wild Horses" to Lau-ren in the past, the first time on September 27; but did not dedicate the lines "Graceless lady" or "Let's do some living/After we die." I usually do the dedication. On Saturday, our lead singer called me to the front of the stage and dedicated the song to her himself; he forgot to tell people where or why, but he sang it "GraceFUL lady" and pointed at me.

Also, my sister was there; believe it or not, this was the first time anyone with whom I share DNA has seen me play. At one point I looked out on the dance floor and saw someone waving wildly; and then I recognized her. Not being a true Stones fan, she told me later, "I like the Bones more than the Stones." My sister was widowed in 1995, and completely shattered by the loss of her husband, thinking she could never cope. But she found true love several years later, and her second husband, my brother-in-law, was there with her last night.

My sister was not the only current or former widow in the audience. I ran into a woman I'd spoken with at the Euro Brokers memorial in October, a former options broker there who'd married another broker at the company and had two children with him. On September 11 she lost him and was widowed, one of her children a son almost exactly the same age as Tyler. I was disoriented to see her, until I realized she was really there to see another musician at the Jam, a Euro Brokers swaps broker who plays the drums in another band. There was a whole crew of Euro and ex-Euro people.

I have corresponded with her since the memorial; it was good to see her out and about. Her friends drag her out at least once a week. They are trying to keep her busy, keep her mind active, and help her cope. For the evening, it seemed to be working.

At one point in the middle of our set, I looked over and I saw the new widow with her friends, dancing to crunchingly loud Stones tunes, while right behind her, another young former widow stood waving at me, smiling, beside her new husband.

It is true that in any crowd of people, there are threads of tragedy interspersed with threads of joy; we all cope, and sometimes people stand right beside others who may indicate that their destinies, however sad they may appear, can still be redeemed, that the sorrow they feel can be integrated into a joyful future, that lives can be rebuilt. The dead must be remembered, but honored with our own survival.

Monday I got to the hospital late, and Lauren was justifiably upset with me. I can't tell you how terrible I felt. She had been moved to a new room, and was waiting for me, feeling abandoned. I promised her to never, ever put her in that position again.

She had a right to be angry, though she shouldn't have had the need. But we managed to get along again; she is entitled to any and all emotions she has and then some and my job is not even to say ouch. It's really just to make sure that I spend more time with her.

She had a difficult day. The itching is severe and everywhere. She receives antihistamines to deal with it, though they can make her drowsy. We put on moisturizer so her skin does not become dry. Almost more than the pain, this is one of the most difficult aspects of burn recovery.

She has also felt discomfort with her running shoes; there is a part of her heel that hurts and the shoe feels tight. I bought them a size bigger but she still has a problem; so we'll try one of the other pairs, the New Balance high-top walkers, which were wider; these may help. With her physical therapy, she may be walking down the hall, but what she is really doing is climbing a mountain—and she needs good shoes!

Then there was the room change. Lauren's condition was extremely critical when she first arrived at the Burn Center, and she spent ten weeks placed in a room directly opposite the nurses' station. It was well situated for coming and going, well lit and bright. But it is usually used for patients who are more acute than Lauren is now.

She was supposed to move down the hall to the corner room, a huge, sun-filled suite with southern exposure and a panoramic river view. But there is a young baby in that room now; so when it came time to move, Lauren got a spot two doors down the hall from there. The new room is as wide as her old one, but a foot shorter, and has two fewer window panels, making it seem much smaller. It has a river view, though from the bed the patient can see only a sliver of water. Still, when Lauren spends her hours in the chair, she will be looking south along the East River, seeing Manhattan, Brooklyn, and the 59th

Street Bridge. From the bed, at night, she will see the top of the Chrysler Building. And since the room is a distance away from the nurses' station, it can be made darker and quieter.

Since she'd just been moved, of course, her cards and pictures were not on the wall, so it felt more institutional. This was enhanced in an odd way by Harry Waizer's discharge to rehab earlier that day. It was as if all the routines we'd built up, all the familiar landmarks, and the people, had been stripped away at once.

But that's the fact of the hospital; those familiars were an illusion, built up over time, that the place was hospitable. It's not. It's a grisly place to have to be, and being there was all about saving Lauren's life. The best way to keep saving that life is to get out. Lauren needs to be here up until the moment she can leave, and not a moment longer.

The doctors and nurses haven't changed; they're still as dedicated as they were. But the emotional burden is now on her family. The medical staff has new critical patients who continue to come in, because fires have no respect for dates or events, and people who were not at the World Trade Center on September 11 can be burned just as badly. In fact, there are quite a few children on the unit; to see them in their beds as we walk by is heartbreaking. The OR is still busy, though not as busy as it was then; and there is a new group of patients who need to be monitored 24/7 as they navigate their own drug-induced sleep.

I helped straighten out her new room, tried to help with her itching. I fed her dinner, got her settled with her relief companion. I ran the videotape of people I made at the party saying hello to her. She smiled throughout, but misted when her close friend Debra said that she and Lauren would someday run the New York City Marathon together; and she cried for a moment when her mother spoke beautiful words about the renewed depth of the bond between them. The rest of the tape featured Tyler's birthday extravaganzas and a couple of play dates; I think watching him on a twenty-five-inch TV screen brought her a lot of peace.

I felt much better when I left around midnight; Lauren was very relaxed, ready to sleep; the river was still flowing outside her window; and Tuesday the cards and photos will go back on her wall.

Monday was my first time back at work—actually my second, since I had visited there on October 2. I walked through the office to the relocated executive area, past long tables with bottled water and coffee urns, baskets of pastry that took the place of our destroyed kitchen, past the rows and rows of workstation positions for traders and sales-people, flanked by glass-windowed offices at the edges of the floor.

I met with Gil, who has been wonderful, and I told him so, and like so many people, he insisted that what he had done for me and my family was not that much, really (I begged to differ). We talked about Lauren and her coming transition to rehab. Inevitably, we spoke about how strong she was; he, like so many others, said she was going to make it. He told me about the crisis support that continues to be made available, and encouraged me to meet with the on-site person in charge of trauma counseling and related services.

I then met with the other executives, all of whom shook my hand and gave a warm welcome. I am the straggler here; they have been coping with the loss of colleagues for two and a half months, going to scores of funerals and tributes, and rebuilding a company. In fact, the rebuilding looks like it's working; there was a distinctly different tone to the place than there had been weeks earlier, when I visited for the first time.

I made this observation to our director of human resources, who has also been wonderful, and she said that people had been in shock. When I'd first stopped by, I'd been watching a group of people still in the midst of trauma, many of whom had struggled to escape the buildings themselves, all essentially wandering in a communal daze. She says that when people return for the first time—such as myself—they still wander about in what is clearly the same daze, though they get better as each day goes by and eventually regain their regular stride. I am sure that the on-site trauma counseling has helped move this process along.

People have their bearings now; they are back at their workstations taking phone calls, shouting bids and offers, the usual background noise of a brokerage shop. If anything, the tech staff works even harder, around the clock, trying to rebuild the infrastructure that supports these operations. But they all remember that there are sixty people who should be sitting here who aren't, and so the dedication to the firm—to rebuilding every aspect of the business—is probably seated at a much deeper emotional level than it was before the attacks. Euro Brokers is more than a company now; it is a monument.

I found out about a T-shirt being sold to raise money for the Euro Brokers fund. The front of the T-shirt says "EB—Never Forget." The back is a waving American flag; the red stripes are formed entirely from the names of the lost employees. I bought one immediately.

I spent some time with the trauma counselor, who told me that writing these e-mails, and being at Lauren's side, were actually choices that I had made, no matter how compelled I may have felt to do both. He talked about how impossible it is to integrate a tragedy of this size, and said that no matter how much I had expressed my emotions, and how much I had done to cope, I shouldn't be surprised, and therefore alarmed, if I noticed a "delayed reaction" of some sort; a mood swing, irritability, fatigue, anxiety, anything. It is entirely normal, and the way to cope hasn't changed: eat, sleep, and do something meaningful to move on.

As you all know, I am doing two meaningful things; I am being there for Tyler and Lauren (with an enormous assist from her mother and father), and I am writing these e-mails, which represents, after caring for my family, the most valuable thing I have ever done. Aside from its value in getting my thoughts out of my head and onto paper, I have wanted it to build a network of love for Lauren so that when she heeds it, the embrace that will take her in will encircle the globe. I have also appreciated hearing from people that my words have been inspiring; it is equally inspiring to have them read. But the soul of inspiration in this story is, of course, Lauren.

Since she is having major surgery Wednesday, the office understood that I would really be coming in in another week to do something useful. I was told to pick a workstation location, then just talk to people, so that's what I did, and I will write more about those conversations tomorrow. I grabbed some KFC from a huge order that had just come in, packed away my new T-shirt, and headed out to see Lauren; I got delayed on the way, and so I made her sad. But I will be on time Tuesday.

Love,
Greg & Lauren

I did get to the hospital on time today, and Lauren was glad to see me. She was far from alone; her mom and dad were there, as were a physical and occupational therapist and the staff psychologist.

Last night, when she was hurt and upset, she'd told me she so looks forward to seeing me that she was devastated when I didn't get there. That was what was behind her anger. This resurfaced for a moment today, while the psychologist was there. The psychologist pointed out that the two of us need to be able to talk about such feelings and it seemed that we had, and Lauren agreed.

But this was just a detail; big things had already happened.

Lauren walked unassisted today (again, I missed it). She went down the hall with the walker, then returned with slight support from the physical therapists. And then she headed down the hall, and came back, without any support.

My contribution was the sneakers; she used the New Balance today, and they were exactly what she needed—wider, with comfort and stability.

That was before I arrived. At 3:30, a meeting convened at Lauren's bedside; our group was joined by the staff social worker and Lauren's doctor. The purpose of the meeting was to make a decision about rehab facilities and discuss Lauren's longer-term prognosis and long-term planning for her recovery.

We all stood around her bed in our yellow hospital gowns and blue caps; all of us wore the bouffant style except for Lauren's doctor, who wore the tieback. Lauren herself lay in bed, her upper body and head raised, wearing her blue patient gown and an NYFD cap given to her by her nurse some days before. The late afternoon sun streamed in under the half-lowered window curtain; she had just taken off her sunglasses.

Her doctor began by saying it was good that we were having the meeting because it meant that Lauren was getting out of this place.

He explained that she would be having the surgery tomorrow and would need five days to recover from that. He then saw her staying another two weeks, and finally moving on to a rehab facility.

The two that were discussed were Rusk, at NYU, and Burke, in Westchester. The features of each were described to Lauren; both are among the best rehab facilities in the country, with the major difference being location: Burke is a sixty-acre facility in White Plains, Westchester County; Rusk is at 34th Street and First Avenue in Manhattan.

Until this meeting, Lauren and I had been leaning toward Rusk (I have heard very good things about it), because of its proximity to our home and our friends for visiting purposes. But we learned several things that made us decide on Burke as the first choice.

New York-Presbyterian has a close affiliation with Burke, and has offices nearby. Neither Rusk nor Burke has a special reputation as a burn rehabilitation center, but this is because burns themselves are not a statistically noteworthy rehabilitation category. There are nowhere near as many burn patients as there are stroke victims or spinal cord injuries. But both facilities are more than capable with regard to the type of rehab Lauren will require.

She can walk. But she can't really do that reliably; in her own words, she can't get out of bed herself, she can't right herself, and she can't do anything when she gets where she is going because both of her hands are still so compromised. That is what her rehab will focus on—regaining strength, so that she can walk for herself, and starting her on the road to regaining hand function. No matter how much progress she makes in rehab, she is likely to need a home care aide for some months afterward, to assist with grooming, getting dressed, and doing things around the house.

The discussion then turned to Lauren's surgery tomorrow. This is the difficult one.

Her doctor repeated something in the meeting that he had said to me several times before; that her hand could wait until now because it was not a life-threatening situation. Her early surgeries were performed to save her life. Tomorrow's operation is being performed to preserve function. (He did not see her having another surgery after that for six to twelve months; that is when the cosmetic procedures can begin.)

Tomorrow he will amputate the full third segment of the index finger on her left hand, and remove a smaller amount of tissue from the middle finger, ring finger, and pinkie. It has been clear since the beginning that some degree of amputation would be necessary. The surgery was postponed as long as possible to give her fingers a chance to heal further, and thus better define the areas that were viable and those that would have to be removed. This has now happened.

Lauren has heard about this during the past week; but tomorrow it will actually take place, and there remains nothing I can do to save or protect her from it.

Our hands are an enormous part of our expressiveness—they are what we use to communicate with the world, to function: to play sports, to express love, to create art. We need fingers to grasp a golf club, we need fingers to pick up a baby. Lauren is a talented artist. We have beautiful framed etchings on our walls that she created in college. The dexterity of her left hand, which produced that art, may be lost.

Yesterday, in fact, there were tears over this; she wanted to keep the dexterity to do the simple things in life, like dial a phone number, sign her name, change Tyler. It will be a struggle for her to regain it, and she will have to rely greatly on her right hand.

Today she asked why the full third segment of her left index finger had to be removed. Her doctor explained that a lesser amount might leave it nonfunctional; it might draw down into a claw tip and actually be a hindrance. So she asked that whatever was done be as cosmetically appealing as possible.

I am not given to too much wailing in my writing about Lauren, but on this one I say I feel so sorry for her, my beautiful angel, so ravaged by this horror. And so tough and honorable and gentle in facing it. I doubt I could ever be half as strong as she is proving to be. And I am praying even now that it will be easy on her, and that she will regain more left-hand function than anyone thinks possible. She has already done that in other areas; but there are limitations to everything.

The doctor will also graft a six-square-inch area of her buttocks that has not yet healed; this will finally close her wounds there. This has been the hardest area to graft; the buttocks are the hardest area on any patient. They are, as she said, "her Achilles' heel." She is looking forward to that being fixed, but the surgery will require her to be in bed, and not bend her hips, for five days.

So these five days, this Thanksgiving holiday, are going to be brutal; there is no other way to look at it. The best thing that can be said is that it will last only five days, and then she will be past them. And we will be there to help.

The doctor asked her where she would like the donor skin to be harvested from; he noted that if he took it from her foot, "she would have to wear socks instead of underwear." It was a joke on a grim topic; it made Lauren laugh.

And then she herself summed up the action items: the social worker would apply to Burke and to Rusk, and her doctor would do the best job he could to repair her. From the back, her father saluted these marching orders and everyone laughed, because she had basically given us all our assignments. This seemed so incongruous coming from the patient, lying in a hospital bed, but it was a brilliant testament to the take-charge attitude that has brought Lauren through this.

Following the big meeting, Lauren got to give her own consent to her surgery for the first time. (I signed all the previous consents even after she had awakened, so long as she was still on narcotic medications.) This time, I witnessed her approval.

The occupational therapist showed us the samples of compression garments that Lauren will be wearing for scar control for the next year. She will need to wear them twenty-three hours a day. The pressure controls and smoothes scars for a better long-term cosmetic result. Special pads can be placed underneath the garments to apply spot treatment to specific points. For much of the next year she will need to wear a full body suit of such clothing. She will also receive a clear, silicone-lined mask that will be custom-fit to her face using computer scanning technology. The silicone breaks down and softens the scar tissue; the computer scan will permit the mask to be so accurately machined that it will provide equal pressure at all points on her face.

In many ways, it is proper to dread tomorrow; but tomorrow is also the passageway, finally, to the future. I will be with her, as always, before she goes into the OR.

With luck, when she comes out of the OR she will be going into the big corner suite after all. I hope she does; then she can watch the river as she heals; and then we can turn our backs on this era of grafts and helplessness, this eon in the ICU. Five days from now, I think we will be out of the woods.

Good luck, Lauren.

Love,
Greg & Lauren

On the day of Lauren's final surgery at the Burn Center, I arrived at 7:20 AM, just as she was called for the OR. She was resting as I reached her room, eyes closed, face peaceful. I sat down and looked at her for a few moments. I was glad that she was relaxed enough to sleep, though this was probably assisted by medication. This was her big day: the last big day of its kind, the one we have been aiming toward since she was brought to the hospital on September 11. The one, after which, once she healed, she would be "closed"; her wounds controlled, her skin regrafted, her injury contained, her prognosis, finally, optimistic.

Kareen came in and told me Lauren had been looking for me at 7 AM; it was comforting to know that I would be there when she opened her eyes before they brought her down.

When she did open her eyes, she smiled.

I told her that she would do fine; that she has always sailed through surgery and healing.

She asked if I would be there when she woke up; I said I would, but that I would also be there the whole time she was in the OR.

She told me that I had been in a dream; we had been driving down a country road. I told her that I'd had a dream about the Princess of Perry Street, reigning peacefully over her domain. She knew I made this up, but she smiled.

The orderly came to transport Lauren down to the OR. In the past, it had taken four people to wheel her down; two to control the bed, one to wheel the IV trees, and one to pump the blue vent bag to feed air into her lungs. Today she was free of everything except a single IV drip, which was laid on her bed beside her head. Only one transport person was necessary to wheel the bed.

Also different this time, she was awake; she could be nervous and anxious despite her medication. So I walked beside her bed all the way to the elevator, talking to her, telling her again that she would be fine. At the vestibule by the elevator, she said, growing a bit emotional, "Pray for my hands, that what they do looks good."

I told her I'd been praying for her fingers and toes since September 12.

As she entered the elevator, I helped wheel her in, and I told her if she opened her eyes, I would still be standing in the gap as the doors slid closed. She did, and I waved, and she blew me a kiss. After the doors closed, I felt myself fighting back tears.

I think I am having one of those delayed reactions the trauma counselor spoke of, and not because he mentioned it just two days ago. I find myself unexpectedly on the verge of tears now as I look at her, in a way that I was not in prior weeks.

It is the real sadness over her condition, over the change in our lives, over the gritty struggle she has waged and the singular trip she will now be making back from injuries that most people simply do not survive. Just as she is a miracle to make it this far, the road she must travel to return to a normal life is that much longer. I am sharing Lauren's sadness at what has happened to the ends of her arms, to her fingers; I am sharing her pain as she experiences the cold truth.

That truth is unavoidable, and it is unfolding as slowly as the initial injury was sudden, violent, and traumatic. The residual savagery of that violence echoes even in the softest of statements. Last night I missed reporting some details of her pre-surgery conversation with the doctor yesterday, because I was in a rush to get to sleep so I could be back at the hospital by seven this morning. He had said, gently, to explain why he had to take so much from her left index and middle fingers, that those areas were "not alive." There really was no other way that he could put it; the truth had been dictated in the lobby of 1 World Trade Center at 8:48 AM on September 11, and today it has become reality.

After Lauren went down, I headed downstairs to get some coffee and a scone. Kareen accompanied me; she says every day that she loves Lauren, looks forward to seeing her and wants to help her.

She knows all of Lauren's requirements; how she likes her room kept clean, how she wakes at 6 AM and wants her juice, over shaved ice. She intends to work for Lauren throughout the Thanksgiving holiday, to get her through this tough period, which is a beautiful gift. She is not taking a day off; her holiday will be devoted to making Lauren's a kind and peaceful one. So the decision of someone who entered our lives only days ago will be perhaps the most important one to make our Thanksgiving holiday enjoyable. As we parted just outside the Starbucks-run Patio coffee shop by the main entrance, she said Lauren would be fine: "Just trust in the Almighty."

I returned to the waiting room, always sparsely occupied at this early hour, where I trusted to the hands of God, as present in the skill of Lauren's surgeon.

This is the first, and I hope only, day that she will lose a part of herself. None of us should ever have to go through this; it is, on top of everything else, the slap in the face before the final exit to safety. But she has so many people who care about her, so many now who love her, that perhaps that love will balance the pain.

Yesterday the occupational therapist, the queen of the splints, worked to demonstrate how Lauren's left hand would be able to function despite the amputations. We were talking about what she would be able to do in the future. (Swing a golf club? Oh, sure, but she may need surgery on that ribbon scar under her arm that we pointed out to her this morning.) The therapist said to Lauren, "I've been trying to see how you would function. That's because I think about you all the time. Here"—and she opposed her thumb to just the bottom segment of her index finger—"you'll be able to write, to pick things up. You'll be fine."

Today's surgery took four hours. Just after 11:30, Lauren's doctor came to the waiting room and gave me the report. Once again, he was pleased; not over what he'd had to do, this time, but over what it had meant.

He'd had to remove the third segment of the index and middle fingers, as expected. He'd grafted skin onto several fingers of the left hand and the pinkie of the right hand. He had been forced to place pins in the joints of her left thumb and to leave the pins in the joints of her other left fingers, all to preserve a functional position and prevent unopposed tendon function (the palm side of her hands was not badly burned) from drawing her fingers into a nonfunctional claw position. He had harvested skin from the top of her thigh and used it for the graft on her left buttock, then sewn the dressings on, rather than stapling them, to give a better chance of healing.

To prevent her flexing her left leg, and therefore the hip, possibly ruining the new graft, her left knee was immobilized using a plastic splint wrapped in Ace bandages. Her right hand had also lapsed, in a matter of hours the night before, into a nonfunctional position. To permit her to regain full function of that hand, it needs more time in a good position; so she would have a cast there, too, for the next five days.

This would all be very restrictive. But there was one simple, over-riding question: once this surgery healed, was Lauren really out of the woods? Had she reached the stage where her prognosis had significantly improved? She had entered the hospital absolutely critical, in danger of dying from her wounds or an opportunistic infection. She had been expected to need eighty-three days to be "closed"—long, difficult days, with major surgeries, repeated infections, and her major organ systems in overdrive; one day for each percentage of total body surface area the burns covered. But she needed only seventy-one days.

Her doctor cited two caveats: the remaining, though healing, tracheostomy opening, and a lingering immunosuppression over the next month. But then he said, "Yes, she's out of the woods," with a quickening and lightening of his voice.

OUT OF THE WOODS!!! The odds have finally changed.

On one level, I felt as if I had found the Holy Grail. On another, my elation was muffled by the difficulty of this particular recovery. This time, in what should be her great triumph, her World Series trophy, she will be highly conscious of the pain and restricted mobility.

I asked the doctor if the medical report was over, there was something I wanted to add. Informed that it was, I told him thank you, that I couldn't believe we'd made it. I told him that he had certainly saved her life. I said, "You and the guy who rescued her were the two people she needed to meet so that she could live."

He said, "Thank you for saying that."

In the past, Lauren had been brought straight back to her room after surgery, because she had remained on a ventilator and wouldn't be waking up. This time she was taken to the recovery room like a typical surgical patient. I went down to the surgical floor for the first time (I had always waited at the Burn Center), and found her in a large room lined on four sides by ten beds, each of the patients recovering from surgery, with nurses watching monitors and administering medication as the patients shook off the effects of anesthesia. Lauren was in the far corner, awake and suffering. She felt pain, and her mouth was dry. I sat with her for ninety minutes, feeding her shaved ice from a cup and dabbing water on her lips as the nurse gave her IV morphine.

When she was brought back upstairs, she did have the corner suite.

The new room is almost twice the size of the small room she'd had the last two nights, even the room in which she'd spent the previous ten weeks. There are two windows with southern exposure, and because the room is so large, her bed can be oriented so that she can look south along the river. The sun is bright, streaming in; there may be too much light, but she has two pairs of sunglasses to cope with it.

She even has a guest chair that can be reclined to permit sleep—I will use this feature.

Once in the room, Lauren became much more aware of itching and the restrictions on her movement. The right-hand cast was actually added there. All these things together made it difficult for her; at one point she turned to me and said she was scared about how restrained her movements were.

That was when I gently repeated that she had to do this; the point of it all was to prevent her from ever again needing a similar surgery, to load her up with healing on both hands and on her buttocks so that she was launched into the rehab phase of her recovery. I acknowledged that this was easier for me to say, harder for her to do. But it's five days. They will seem long and difficult, but in five days they'll be over. Then, barring a contracture (skin tightening that poses a permanent threat to the range of motion of a joint, and cannot be overcome through physical therapy), she should be free of surgery for at least six months.

Kareen returned promptly at 7:30, saying she'd left home early to be back with Lauren. She asked me when I'd gone home, and that's when we both realized I'd been there for a full shift. Lauren was glad to see her, and she started off collecting supplies for the evening hours—juice, ice, fresh bedding.

As much as morphine and anti-anxiety medication, the salve that would prove most effective through the subsequent evening was a videotape: five classic episodes of "I Love Lucy." (As Lauren watched it, the I Love Lauren show unfolded by her own bedside.)

When I headed down to the staff lounge to put the tape in one of the two VCRs, Lauren's doctor was there, reviewing charts. As I fiddled with the VCR, he told me that he had been down to Ground Zero for the first time several days earlier. He went with a friend who had been the facilities manager for American Express. The friend had retired, but had gone back to help with repair to the building, which is part of the World Financial Center. They were able to look down at

Ground Zero from fifty-one floors up, a view that had been only halfway up the towers. Then they had walked among the wreckage. He said that the scale of chaos was simply enormous. He said, We're used to seeing a scene like that where they're building something; but this was all destruction.

I added that the incredible thing to me was that there were people to whom this brought a smile.

He said that it had affected him deeply, even though he had nowhere near the personal involvement of someone such as Lauren or me, while noting the unit had treated so many people who had come from there. And again I made the observation that probably no one had done as much to save people's lives in the wake of that as he had, he and the two other attendings on the unit. Probably no one is as familiar with the intimate details of the personal destruction and injury of those terrible moments as these three doctors: the chaos of Ground Zero on a human, biological scale. They had been waging their own rescue effort for many weeks longer, in the theater of the OR, and that morning had probably achieved one of their more noteworthy successes.

The family of the Burn Center, so long and closely involved with the NYC Fire Department, had suffered losses too; while Lauren was down in the OR that morning, I'd spoken with the social worker in the hallway about Lauren's rehab applications. She told me about one woman's husband, a firefighter, who'd been lost. He'd been on the walkie-talkie from inside the doomed buildings. The firefighters had known something bad was happening, but they had said, We have injured people here, we can't leave them.

There were so many more who deserved to be saved, but we have one who was, and she was declared out of the woods the day before Thanksgiving. When we look back on this day from the distance of time, we may realize we have had no more powerful Thanksgiving than the one we are about to share.

Love,
Greg & Lauren

I spent Thanksgiving morning with Tyler. I've mentioned that his mom made him dance when they were reunited at the hospital, but I haven't discussed how much he likes it. It takes only a few notes and he starts to rock back and forth, in rhythm; he'll be able to lay down a foundation like his bass-playing dad, that's for sure.

Tyler's mom had a pleasant Thanksgiving. It was a sunny day, so her room was bright and expansive. Since I couldn't be there in the morning (I'd decided not to bring Tyler because I didn't want him to be down the hall from her and have her not able to see him up close), I sent waves of family up there. Her mom and dad were there at their usual 10 o'clock time; then at 11 my sister and brother-in-law arrived with our niece, who of course had to stay in the waiting room, and my mother and her husband at 1. Lauren's sister also came by, so by the time I got there at 2:30, she'd had company all day.

Her bed was oriented toward the window, so she could see the river while lying down. She was wearing the NYPD cap my sister gave her, and she put on her sunglasses. She looked hip, or, as she'd said just the day before, like someone who's just had a facial peel.

What she's had was more of a body peel; she is covered in new skin. She has lost most of her muscle tone; when she lifts her arms to exercise them, you can see where the tone is gone. One hazard, apparently, is that as the muscles heal, they can be out of alignment; where the fibers were previously all in one direction, as the body rushes to heal from such an injury, the fibers may become somewhat tangled. Lauren has a lot of physical work ahead to regain normal function, but almost every moment you look at her she is doing the maximum exercise that she can do given the position she is in. This is the definition of motivation.

For lunch, she had shrimp cocktail and some crab salad. Later the unit had another catered Thanksgiving buffet, this time provided by Christine, the singer-songwriter, only recently returned from accompanying the stock trader patient to Chicago. This time he was taping "Oprah" (for the episode of November 29).

I went down and fixed Lauren a plate of Thanksgiving dinner and brought it back to her room. When I headed back to the buffet to grab a bite, I ran into the stock trader patient himself. He had returned for Thanksgiving, looking healthy, vigorous, and cheerful. His pressure sleeves were a stylish black. He reported on his Chicago experience, offered me some Ben & Jerry's ice cream. The broad selection was actually provided by Ben & Jerry's themselves. He is beginning to work on various projects, and they are a sponsor of some sort, and I can't say that today I absorbed exactly what these projects are. But he is busy and in the public eye, and he intends to do something with his newfound renown. And why not? His is a compelling story, just as Lauren's is; but he himself says his is not nearly as long, nor as arduous.

Lauren is the miracle girl, lying in her hospital bed now, with less than four full days of immobility remaining. Her hands are healing, her wounds are closed, and those around her know that they can begin to focus on a longer-term future.

I told her she was out of the woods without realizing what I was saying. She hadn't known she was still in them. But I explained that I was referring to the chance of infection that had lurked as long as her wounds were still open. With her trache due to heal within days, Lauren soon will be "closed." For the first time, really, she is closer to her life back outside the unit than to the day she was injured.

She was grateful for all the company on Thanksgiving. She had thought she'd just see her mom and dad in the morning, and then be on her own for the rest of the day except for me. Instead, she had waves of visitors, staggered; and her sister brought her a small wood wreath garlanded with autumn leaves, which was standing on a rolling table just below her picture gallery.

I told her this was a great Thanksgiving because she had done so well; because she was still here. She was in tears suddenly, saying she felt "so blessed." As I was about to leave, I told her again that she was a miracle; that God's hand had touched her, that angels' wings had enfolded her, and that I loved her.

She was looking forward to watching *Miracle on 34th Street,* which would be shown twice on AMC that evening and was just right for the mood. The end of the movie features a moment very similar to the way we bought our country home in Pine Plains. At the end, Natalie Wood insists they stop the car as they are driving down a suburban lane, and then she runs into a house, shouting I knew it! or something to that effect. Her Christmas wish to Santa Claus was for a private house of her own, and Edmund Gwenn, who it turns out really was Santa Claus, has indeed left it for her.

Lauren did the same thing in 1998; we were driving up a country road in Pine Plains, and she said, That's it, stop the car. She had recognized a house at the side of the road from a search she had done on the Internet. The realtor, in the car right behind us, hadn't even meant to show it to us because it was new construction, but she had the keys to go inside. The view of neighboring horse farms and mountains was so breathtaking, and the house so beautiful, Lauren decided to buy it. The only difference between the movie and our lives was that Lauren was her own Santa Claus—she made her own miracle, just as she is doing again. The next time she walks through the door of our country house, she will be further narrowing the difference between the movie and her life. (How different would it be from the next day, when Natalie Wood, John Payne, and Maureen O'Hara presumably moved in?)

Lauren's doctor certainly has the appropriate silver hair and kindly manner, though he is far too thin, clean-shaven, and dresses in a white lab coat rather than a fur-lined red jacket. And Lauren certainly gets enough bags of cards from children, all wishing her well and giving her God's blessing. For all of you doubters, we would call it Miracle on 68th Street (I'm sure the numerologists among you have already noticed that 68 is *exactly* two times 34).

We left the hospital and headed to my friend Kitty's for Thanksgiving. About five years ago, this became a new family tradition, and we needed to preserve it, at least I did. Lauren and I had gone there with her sister for the past three years. Last year Tyler had been one month old, and spent more than an hour in Kitty's arms. A year later and it is his first trip facing forward in his car seat; he was fascinated to see where he was going. We brought Lauren's mom and dad, my mom and her husband, and my sister, brother-in-law, and our twenty-month-old niece; ten people, counting the kids. Not the Manning family, but the Manning clan.

We arrived fifteen minutes late, and with Kitty's usual military precision, dinner was aready waiting: the turkey was already carved, and there were mashed potatoes, gravy, delicious stuffing, sweet potatoes, glazed carrots, and, of course, cranberry sauce. There was Kitty's full crew of Scot (back for the weekend from Japan), sister Gwyneth, brother-in-law, niece, childhood friend from Philadelphia, and tall, lanky theater friend (who has sent Lauren several beautiful cards). I was met shortly after entering the dining room by a stem glass of dry sherry, and then we all sat down to the feast. (I opened Tyler's portable crib and the two little ones spent some time in it during dinner so that the grown-ups could relax. For a very little while.)

I was suddenly very explicitly aware that while Lauren had survived, she was still missing at the table, a feeling I had not had so powerfully since Rosh Hashanah, the Jewish New Year, a mere six days after September 11. This was more than two months later. Sitting there, I felt as if there was nothing I could talk about other than her condition, but they had all read the e-mails, and there was nothing to add. I felt a huge emptiness. Normally fairly talkative (you can stop laughing now), I could think of nothing new to say. Burns and wars are not holiday-table conversation.

Feeling ever more subdued, I went to the sofa and fed Tyler his dinner on my lap, and I understood that this was the first traditional holiday I'd been through with Tyler, without Lauren. We weren't splitting the watching duties, sharing holding him, changing him; it was down to me alone. Even though we all held Lauren close to our hearts and drank to her good health and long life, she was far away from joining us. I felt such a mix of emotions: joy at Tyler's presence, loneliness at Lauren's absence, sadness at the violent changes to our lives, dread as I caught just a glimpse of the abyss looming before all those whose spouses died September 11.

Fortunately, I rallied; I went downstairs and wrote part of this e-mail, and having done my bit to recount Lauren's Thanksgiving, the one that brought her to tears of joy, I felt as if I could go back upstairs and revive my social skills a bit. Dessert, featuring Lauren's mom's perfect pecan pie, cranberry-pear upside-down cake (I think), and a sponsor-worthy collection of Ben & Jerry's, was excellent.

Then it was time to return home; and Tyler, as ever, was a perfect metaphor. He was facing forward, as were we all; and though he fell asleep early on his journey, he could trust us to get him home safely. That is our Thanksgiving wish to Lauren: get home safe.

Love,
Greg & Lauren

From: Greg
To: Everyone
Date: Saturday, November 24, 2001 7:09 AM
Subject: Lauren Update for Nov 23 (Friday)

When I arrived at the hospital, Lauren told me she was really glad to see me; she'd had a rough day. She was having an impossible time finding a comfortable position. The immobilizing brace was off her left knee, which surprised me; but I was assured by the nurses that this would not affect the adherence of the L-shaped graft on her left buttock.

Lauren spent a lot of time shifting between lying on her back and lying on her right side. Pillows would go in to prop her up, then come out when she wanted to lie back down. We would roll up the blanket and sheet to keep her warm, then roll it down when she got too hot.

This type of discomfort is exhausting, and she was showing some real fatigue when I reached her in the late afternoon. The duty nurse at the Burn Center (in charge of the shift on that wing) had done us a big favor, however; he'd arranged for the hospital to provide a day companion for Lauren for several days, in addition to the night companion she already has, and this woman was sitting in the room with Lauren when I arrived.

The nurse explained it this way: following her surgery, Lauren has needed a lot of help repositioning herself, help with the blanket, help eating, help turning the TV on or off or playing her boom box as she tries to get comfortable. These are all legitimate needs, but they do not require a nurse, so the unit can't assign an additional nurse just to meet them. So the duty nurse decided to see if he could get Lauren a day companion from the hospital.

When he called the nursing shift supervisor, he said, he got the woman who is the top nurse in the hospital, and she understood the situation and saw to it that someone was sent over. This is the type of courtesy you would not necessarily expect of a hospital, but it is not a surprise coming from the nurses at the Burn Center, who have formed a strong bond with Lauren, part pride in contributing to such a brilliant recovery, part genuine affection for who she is, how well she has done, and how she is handling herself.

There are two other September 11 patients still at the Burn Center with serious burns who have not done as well. Much of it is the seriousness of their lung injuries (one man has been plagued by recurring pneumonia). I have seen the faces of these patients. Their eyes are open, they are aware, but they seem disconsolate, lethargic. The frustration of being harmed by this evil must be overwhelming.

Lauren is not a superwoman, of course—she, too, can be disconsolate. Today we spoke about more people from Cantor Fitzgerald. She asked me about one guy, and I was pleased to be able to report that his name was on the "safe and accounted for" list. But then she asked me about another man, and his name was not on the list. Having put another face to life, she almost immediately put a new face to death, and began mourning anew. I told her that the odds were very difficult, and suggested that she not keep naming people one after the other, but try to give herself some rest and a chance to heal without focusing on the tragedy.

We talked again about how many people were praying for her. Shortly after this, she started to sing "Day by Day," the song from *Godspell*. I helped her set the melody, but then she told me to stop singing; I don't have much of a voice. Teary, with uneven tone, and air still hissing through her tracheostomy, she worked through the song several times. She said she wanted to sing; she wanted to make some noise. It seemed she wanted to alter the experience of lying in that bed, and hearing the relentless progression of bad news, by singing a prayer. She asked Kareen, her overnight companion, to teach her a gospel song.

We tried to get her settled, and we had some success. When the nursing shifts changed, she got more pain medication, more anti-itch medication; we got her started watching *Play It Again, Sam* on TCM. Kareen was feeding her a lemonade frozen fruit bar. When it was time for me to leave, Lauren didn't want me to go, so I stayed for another hour until she felt a little better.

Still, she looks good to me; she is moving more, and more easily; her facial expressions are much the same as they were, just a little sadder, with less laughter. The contrast with other patients who've been admitted over the past several weeks and are as acute as Lauren once was is striking; I walk by their rooms, and I never see any of them moving, not a limb, not a hand. Lauren spent weeks in that condition. I understand that I am looking at something that we recently experienced ourselves, but even so I feel a bleakness when I walk by.

I notice new faces in the waiting room, though now I spend almost no time there. I see families navigating the same difficult course, but with less support of numbers. I hope this translates into less communal tragedy to deal with as their fights progress. But I also understand the emotions that they are feeling, and that these can emerge in any number of ways: anger, faith, resolve.

I met two women in the gown room last night; their family had lost three children in a Brooklyn house fire, and a brother of one of them was lying down the hall, 50 percent burned. I think they were from the same family as two women I'd met the night before who'd been fighting over blame for the same fire. Two very diverse responses to the same tragedy. The singular lesson is that we are healed only when we remember to find love in the face of evil and hate. I found a lot of love yesterday, and not just with the Princess of Perry Street.

Yesterday morning I played host to another wing of the Manning clan; this one my cousin, her husband, and four children from Israel, my cousin being the daughter of my uncle who sent me the book of Scottish songs (hence the Manning clan). My sister, brother-in-law, and niece also joined us, as did my mother.

I remember this cousin as the happiest baby I'd ever seen (until Tyler), a little girl who never stopped laughing, to the point of hyperactivity; yet while I can't remember how much older I am than she is, it's only maybe five years. But here she is now with four children of her own, her oldest about thirteen or fourteen. They have been living in Boston for the past year and a half, and they've wanted to come down since September 11 to be with us.

They finally made it. They brought a white wagon for Tyler, and a baby doll in a convertible swing/high chair for my niece. My cousin's children played with Tyler, who laughed and laughed, though with a bit more control than my cousin had shown at his age. He danced, did his thing.

We had a great visit, sharing a post-Thanksgiving pizza feast, laughing at the antics of the kids, speaking more solemnly when discussing Lauren's situation. We spent the full day together, and then I went to the hospital.

Lauren was relaxed, doing well, so when I left the hospital, I went to a late dinner with another childhood friend, the son of one of my mom's friends from her own long-ago childhood in Vienna. He and I had been on a couple of ski trips together with our fathers when we were in high school; we'd been to each other's houses many times as kids but hadn't seen each other for probably thirty years, not since a memorable trip to Lake Placid and Whiteface Mountain.

He is now in biological research at Stanford. We spent about two hours together, the conversation never flagging. I am amazed at how much I still have in common with people I knew when I was a kid, and how easy it is to resume the contacts, even now that we are fairly grizzled adults.

We grow apart for ordinary reasons: time, distance, a memory of awkwardness at a certain age. This terrible tragedy has called all that distance into question. We all really share the same journey from birth, and it turns out that we never lose the time we've spent together, no matter how many years go by, or the shared perspective that being the same age brings.

It was a very enjoyable time; we reminisced, we caught up, and we marveled together at how Lauren has rallied since this terrible tragedy that changed our lives, and the world.

So many of us have come back together; the distance of decades has been wiped away. All that exists now is support, and a love that has become far easier to express. If I needed a refueling in that department so that I have more to give to Lauren, then I got it yesterday.

Love,
Greg & Lauren

I am sitting in the corner of Lauren's room, watching the dark eddies of the East River flow over the edges of Roosevelt Island and Manhattan. Three towers of the Queensboro Bridge string curved ribbons of suspended lights above its roadway; below me, cars with their lights on drive north and south on the FDR.

The scene here is gentle. Vivaldi is playing on the CD player.

My love lies sleeping in her bed, turned slightly to her right. Both hands, wrapped in dressings and bandages, lie across her midsection. The fluffed sheet is tucked up to her collarbone. Behind and above her, the clear numbers on the monitor convey her heart rate and her last measured blood pressure (she has not worn the cuff full-time for several weeks).

Get Well Soon, We Love You, and Hope You're Feeling Better balloons wave gently above the nurse's computer where I sit, nudged by the imperceptible breeze of the ventilation system. I am on the raised swivel chair typing quietly at a muffled keyboard (there is a soft, clear, sanitizing cover over the keys); Lauren is dreaming of music, I hope, in a bejeweled nighttime landscape.

Standing sentry around the room are the stolid soldiers of recovery. The IV tree, with its base power supply, stands denuded, for the first time since September 11, of any fluids or feeds. A lonely stethoscope hangs from the highest branch. Her walker rests against the wall between the south-facing windows. Beside it, the rolling patient tray table holds an open container of Kozy Shack chocolate pudding; apple juice; a pink plastic pitcher of ice water; tiny, square hospital tissue boxes; a stack of three Styrofoam cups; a package of SnackWell banana cookies; and a tin containing a small cranberry-pear upside-down cake.

There is a rolling pedestal of nursing supplies: 4" x 4" gauze pads, clear dressing tape, syringes, A & D ointment, petroleum jelly, scheduled medications; a rolling laundry hamper for discarded gowns; a stainless steel trash container for bio-waste; a square low-riding disposal bucket for sharps.

On the windowsills are "Spandage" webbed bandages, which once wrapped Lauren from her shoulders to her toes, plus Ace bandages, strips of Dermabond, splints that are awaiting reuse or discard. There are bags of videotapes, personal hygiene supplies that matter again, such as toothpaste, toothbrush, Oil of Olay lotion. There are boxes stuffed with books of poetry and prose, and an overflowing CD collection. There are cards on the wall, from family and friends, from strangers; hand-painted cards from schoolchildren and handwritten notes from adults. There are pictures of family members, friends, nieces and nephews, and a healthy, smiling Lauren Manning with her husband, and with her son.

For close to four hours now, with a break for a dinner of fish filet, Tater Tots, and green beans, she has been sleeping in half-hour shifts. The curtain is drawn and the room is dark, the only lights the computer screen and a couple of blinking green dots at the base of her hospital bed.

The most beautiful sight in the room is her face; slightly reddened, as if from exercise, but free, finally, of tape and tubes. Today, after "cycling" Lauren for a couple of days (turning off the feeds at night), her doctor wrote the order to remove the feeding tube. At about 7 PM, just a short while ago, her nurse flushed the tube with clear water, lifted the tape from her nose, and then drew out the feeding tube. It took about six seconds. So ends an era.

Lauren's face is back to being hers; her nose has stopped being a path to her stomach. She has one lingering IV in her left arm, which will be gone in a day or so (they are still using it to give postsurgical analgesics intravenously). Her family hopes she will have an appetite tomorrow; I think it will be enormous, and I am contemplating which restaurant to tap for a meal of true haute cuisine that we can order in and serve to her as she sits before her panoramic view.

Her legs are swathed in Tubi grips, tight elastic wraps that compress her healing skin. This was the third day post-op, so the doctors took down the dressings and assessed her left hand and the graft on her buttocks; there was good news on both fronts. She seemed pleased with the cosmetic appearance of her left hand; the black fingertips that peeked out from beneath her Spandage dressings since September 11 are finally, and forever, gone.

Whether it is the boredom of my company, the serenity from having yet another invasive line removed, or the lingering effects of the pain-relieving drug she was given at 3 PM, she is sleeping more peacefully, on her own, than she has since she was first sedated and sent on a long journey into a netherworld of unconsciousness.

This calm scene is a sharp contrast to the celebration that ensued when the tube was taken out, when I started jumping up and down and waving my arms like a hyped-up cheerleader, when Lauren remarked, in a tired but amused voice, "You're happier than I am."

I told her I was cheering the way she would if she had the energy. "Your face is yours again," I said. "You're ready to go to Bloomingdale's."

Around the world, a war is being waged against evil; anyone who doubts the justness of that conflict should study why a scene in an ICU, where a woman faces years of rehab to regain use of her hands, strength in her arms and legs, normal posture, and, somewhere in the middle of all of these, happiness, can be so sweet and serene.

Love,
Greg & Lauren

P.S. There is an issue on the way, one that may be far less poetic but is no less crucial to Lauren's recovery: the long-term financial implications of rehabilitation and treatment. Once she returns home and is no longer under the care of an RN, she may not be reimbursed for the daily costs of her care. Home care aides are typically not paid for by insurance; neither are additional child care expenses, or any number of ancillary costs that are impossible to anticipate now. Her overnight companion now is not a covered cost.

I have been concerned since September 11, and may have written about it, that our true needs are in the future, and ongoing; also that by surviving, with grave injuries, Lauren and her fellow patients have fallen into a small category that has not been central to the news coverage or political discussion, but is likeliest to require great long-term financial and emotional support. I don't believe for a moment that Lauren or her fellow patients will be ignored, but there is probably a need to get us organized, and I am trying to take some steps in that direction.

I don't know enough about the road back to know the steps we will need to take; I am continually surprised by the milestones, even now, and I won't wait any longer to be surprised by the obstacles. The woman sleeping in the bed asks no less.

As yesterday's sojourn with Lauren was quiet, today's was filled with conversation. She was awake the entire time. And battling discomfort, but only the way any one of us would if forced to spend five days on our back in a hospital bed while an L-shaped wound healed on our backside.

As has happened following each of Lauren's surgeries, tomorrow is the day that the dressings will be taken down and the grafts assessed by her doctor. We are hoping these adhered; I saw the site tonight and it looked as if they had, but what do I know? She has already seen how her left hand looks, and it was better than she expected. The trauma is cleaned up, and all that is left is healthy tissue.

This is the first time that can be said of her since September 11—all that's left is healthy tissue. If these last grafts have taken—in addition to the L-shaped site, she received very small grafts to clean up bad spots on the fingers and thumb of her left hand—she will have won the battle to survive, and she will then turn toward a longer and slower war against scarring and physical limitations.

(She was concerned that her visit to the tank tomorrow be a gentle one, and one of her former nurses, who stopped by the room, suggested asking for four to six milligrams of morphine half an hour before she goes in.)

Today I read her some get-well cards and notes from friends and strangers. To each of them she wants to send a thank-you. She is deeply touched, she is so grateful for the love and the prayers. It makes her cry, but it makes her happy. She says it is all overwhelming.

Several days ago she asked to see *The New York Times* story about her, so today I brought it in. I told her, Here is the front page, and here is the story about you. I also showed her the inside jump in the B section, which featured a picture of me looking pensive. She thought it was a good one; others are not so sure. All I know is, the photographer had shot two rolls of film. Thinking the shoot was over, I put my hand on the metal fence behind me and relaxed for a moment; and she photographed a genuine moment of thoughtfulness.

Rather than hold the newspaper, with its smaller print, in front of Lauren, I held up the printout of the online version of the story, which was easier for her to read. She scanned it from top to bottom, reading that she was one of the worst injured, that her chances of survival were very slim, that her friends hoped the story would lead more people to pray for her, and the quote from Howard Lutnick which became the quote of the day: "She's got to pull through, because she's got 700 families' worth of love. It's not fair, but she's part of their hope."

She may not think that she deserves all this love. I told her that she does; she has earned it by reaching this point, just by making it here, just by being herself and continuing to live her life.

She also read the story's last quote, the one that said, "I pray for Lauren to be happy again. I don't know what form that will take. But I do believe good things will happen to her—and she will deserve every one of them." She asked who said that; that one was mine.

Lauren will want to tell more; in a very emotional voice she said: "I want the world to know my story, so it can do some good. Hang on to what you have. Be strong. Protect your country. Because you never know what will happen."

She is asking to see the footage of the plane crashes and the collapse of the towers. I said to her that it would be difficult to watch, but she wants to see it. She asked me if I had seen it, and I told her that there was little else on television for three weeks after the attacks. I did tell her that I saw most of it out of the corner of my eye, shots of Ground Zero, of planes hitting buildings, of Giuliani at a press conference. I was too focused on the horror, and the heroism, in front of me.

Lauren said, after reading the *Times* story, that she never prayed to die; but that is what she told me at St. Vincent's. I pointed out to her that she had changed her mind pretty quickly. She spoke a little more about the attacks, and Kareen asked her what floor she'd been on. Lauren explained that she'd been in the lobby. So I asked her if she was in the airlock, or the lobby proper?

Let me explain: at both street entrances the World Trade Center had a double set of doors. Four exterior revolving doors, with panic-bar fire exits between, led to a vestibule sixty feet wide and ten feet deep (I'm guessing) from which swinging glass doors permitted access to the main lobby and the elevators. This vestibule is what I call the airlock. I have wondered since September 11 how Lauren could have survived the fireball if she was already inside the main lobby, especially how she could still be physically intact if she was all the way inside and the explosion was powerful enough to blow out successive sets of doors. It seemed to me that the only chance for survival would have been in the airlock/vestibule, rather than all the way inside.

But she was all the way inside; this is how she explained it yesterday:

"I had just entered the lobby proper. I saw the fireball coming. I felt it; it pushed me out. I was not under my own power. It blew me through the doors. There was propulsion in the outer lobby, toward the outer door. I half pushed it, it half pushed itself, and I was outside.

"I ran screaming across the street. I ran to the median to put myself out. That's where [her rescuer] found me. The fireball followed me. It came outside the building. It was terrible. The heat was so intense. It was so hot. I ran across the street. I had to keep running.

"I kept saying, The building's going to fall, we have to move."

She seemed ready to go on, but this was more than I had expected, so I told her she could stop if she wanted to, and she did.

We've all seen the fireball that burst from Tower Two. The plane that hit Tower One sent a similar blast out the back of that building, and an arm of that explosion reached down the elevator shafts, killing and burning people in the lobby. I have one friend who saw it coming and froze, only to have it dissipate and its heat pass over him, like fingertips grazing but unable to grasp. Where Lauren stood, the full force of the explosion was concentrated but found a way outside. She was carried by its venting energy. I cannot help thinking, What if she had been ten feet to the left or right, and not in front of the exit doors? The fire would have pressed her into a wall and that would have been it.

Instead, it pushed and pursued her out of the building. The fact that it had that exit valve may have saved my friend from serious injury, but it also saved Lauren. I wrote yesterday that she had surfed the wave of severe burn; it turns out she surfed the fire itself. You can say that the fire lifted her, or you can say that the hand of an angel grasped her and carried her before it. Either way, she has certainly been to the door of hell, and lived to tell her tale.

Love,
Greg & Lauren

From: Greg
To: Everyone
Date: Tuesday, November 27, 2001 2:29 PM
Subject: Lauren Update for Nov 26 (Monday)

Lauren's grafts adhered 100 percent, the best possible news, so she is now due to leave for rehab in at most two weeks.

Tomorrow is day seventy-seven. Ten days from now, a week and a half, will be pretty much on target for the length of stay in the ICU predicted by her percentage burn.

Of course, it's like saying let's go survive the battle of Omaha Beach; all we have to do is make it to the top of the cliffs. There were no guarantees, simply an objective criterion by which we would be able to recognize the battle was won.

It's won.

Perhaps because of this, Lauren was very emotional today. When I got to the hospital, after my first day at work trying to actually work, she said, "I missed you." She was crying a bit. She said she'd been on the verge of tears all day, and she didn't know why.

I told her I thought it was because she was out of the woods, truly; if her grafts have adhered 100 percent, she is "closed." It's over, the door to infection has been shut. It will be locked in another month or so, when her immune system recovers more fully; but there is already a strong barrier to opportunistic infection.

I told her, now is when she can take a breath; now is when she knows that she made it. And she understood that, saying in a voice still choked with emotion, "I'm out of the woods, out of the woods." But coming from her it was a very different thing than coming from me; she was speaking it, she was alive, and she knew that if she hadn't made it out of the woods, she wouldn't be here at all.

It had also been a trying day; the anticipation of the tank room, some fear of pain, the questions about her grafts, the looming rehab, needing to remain on her back through tomorrow. It was only yesterday that she recited for the first time the story about how the fireball had literally pushed her out of the building. After such a day, I would be drained.

She had a to-do list for me; things to do with our finances, various things she had obsessed about that were largely done or in the process of being completed. She was very much on edge, but she knew it. She

243

said she was due for her anti-anxiety medication, and she needed it to calm down.

"Even though I'm out of the woods and I have people around, it's hard being confined to my bed, not having use of my hands; it can get very lonely," she said. "I get very claustrophobic."

We got her the anti-anxiety medication, and we watched the Little Rascals on AMC, then, later, "Seinfeld"; and soon enough we were laughing and relaxing, and she felt reassured. Reassured enough that she grew tired, so that by 9:30 PM, she was ready for her sleep medication.

I had just been busted for using the computer workstation in Lauren's room, which the nurses use to enter chart data. It's also possible to open a browser, and to send and receive browser-based e-mail, but you're not supposed to do it. Patient families are not supposed to touch the computer at all. But when the nurses aren't in the room, they log off, and some nurses—I will never say who—had let me use the computer if I did so unobtrusively.

Tonight Lauren wanted me to stay, so I used the nurse's computer to start writing this update. Unfortunately, we had pressed the call button to find out when Lauren was going to get certain medications, and all of a sudden not only the nurse but the charge nurse came in. And I kept typing! He looked at me and said, "Sir, you're not supposed to use the computers." There was nothing to do but log off, and that meant it was a suitable time to say good night.

So I did.

Love,
Greg & Lauren

Lauren greeted me with a smile this afternoon, but some very complex emotions were roiling her. She told me she was having a very emotional day. At 10 o'clock in the morning, she had seen *Life* magazine's commemorative issue about the September 11 attacks.

She had seen the planes being crashed into the buildings, the fires and smoke, the people jumping, the towers collapsing, the horrified onlookers, the enveloping clouds of dust that left people covered in funereal ashes. She had known about the deaths, she had known about the collapse, but she had not truly imagined the horror and destruction.

We have all known that someday she would see the images and learn everything; I knew that she would have to cope with the same horror that had left the entire world stunned and groping for solace, and that we could not cushion it in any way. The strategy has been to provide information in stages so that it would not overwhelm her; but it is different to hear about a nightmare, and then to see it.

And she is not just seeing it; she was in it, she was buffeted by the very fuel explosions that so horrified us as they seemed to burst from some terrible apocalyptic movie we could not turn off. Those explosions haunt every one of us, but the fingers of the very first explosion actually reached out to grab her, as if a hurricane of flames—literally that—lifted her and flung her aside.

Today her anger and pain boiled over. She seems to have met the truth full force, as cold and merciless as the fire that burned her was hot. She has seen, without an intellectual filter, how horrible the destruction was; she saw what happened to people, and she knows she survived the worst of it. She knows that she stood at the border of life and death, at the farthest limit of where one could go and still come back alive.

"Why, why, why!" she wept. "My friends, my friends. My people. I knew them for ten years. My friends are in that rubble. My friends are buried beneath there."

She started saying individual names, her boss, her CEO's brother, the head of Cantor's agency desk, asking again about the head of taxable fixed income. She is under the impression that everyone at Cantor was killed instantly, which isn't the case, but no one is going to correct her now. She knows who was pregnant, who was engaged, who had young children.

"They really got us. They came back and got us. We kept going back into those buildings every day like they weren't going to try again. Why, why did they do it!"

She asked for Ativan, the anti-anxiety medication to calm her down; they had spaced the dosage a little wider, weaning her, but her psychologist had suggested, for today at least, having it with the previous level of frequency to handle all that she had seen. In a bizarre twist, her nurse for the day had slipped in the tank room and blown out his knee, so she was being taken care of by the charge nurse, one of the guys I had met that very first night, who is now an acting nurse manager on the unit.

He returned with the Ativan, and while he was administering it, she began sobbing again, then became very angry. She asked again why they had done it. And we told her, there was no reason, none at all. She didn't have to retaliate because the U.S. military was fighting for her. She didn't need to worry about revenge, just about getting better.

"Evil popped its head out and had its way on September 11," she said.

When I arrived, she'd been seated in her rolling chair, and she'd been a little cynical. She'd been accepted to the Burke rehab facility; good news, but mentally she resented having to go there. "I got accepted to Burke. I should be saying I got accepted to Harvard, for the graduate program. But I'm saying I got accepted to Burke, for rehab."

She was being fitted for a compression bandage that would wrap around her face, from under her chin to above her head. The occupational therapist was cutting ear holes for her; this was a generic garment, but she will have custom-fitted ones soon, to wear over most of her body.

Earlier, she'd gotten back on her feet; she'd walked the length of the unit, to the Christmas tree and back, a round trip of more than two hundred feet, an enormous achievement after being on her back for five days. I asked her how it had been. She'd said difficult, painful; she'd lost a lot of strength in just a week. But the pain came from muscular weakness, which she can reverse.

She'd been uncomfortable sitting, so she'd been moved back to her bed. Now her anger turned to the state she'd been left in by these terrible attacks, and how bad it had been to be set back a week; she does not have the perspective of seeing the speed of her own recovery during the time she was sedated.

"I want to be out of this," she said. "I want to be done with this as fast as possible."

But of course, she can't rush things.

That's when the nurse said, "We haven't had this conversation yet. But for all you've been through here, rehab will be harder. Rehab depends on you, how hard you can push yourself. There will be good days, and there will be bad days. There will be days when you surprise yourself by doing more than you ever thought you could do; two days later, you won't be able to do anything. The good days are never as good as they seem, the bad days are never as bad. But you will get better."

I told her she'd done an amazing job from the very beginning. Lauren said that one of the other nurses had told her he felt from the moment she was brought there that she was going to survive, and, turning to the nurse, she asked if that was true.

"We got an inkling," he said. "We thought you were going to be our miracle girl."

She really has made a miraculous recovery. She has reached the stage where she is conscious of how far she still has to go, so the miracle is far from over; but she's still here.

Between the medication, the pep talk, and deeper breathing, she seemed to calm down.

She had grown close to Howard Lutnick's brother Gary over the summer, and she repeated his name several times. "I feel so sorry for Howard," she said, and decided she wanted to write him an e-mail, and send it immediately. So she dictated a thoughtful and heartfelt message and I sent it from my BlackBerry.

"OK, enough," she said. "I don't need to cry now, they're in heaven. I have my job to do here."

And that is Lauren's fighting spirit, shining in the midst of her grief. I have called her the Princess of Perry Street, but the word "warrior" belongs at the front of that title (Xena, stand aside). She told me she got the toughness from her paternal grandfather and her father, who, she said, would always say, Quit your bellyaching. That's where she found the strength to fight this. Her father always faced things down and dealt with them, and he continues to do so today. He exhausts me because he is so efficient; I don't know if I will ever have that level of motivation. But Lauren does, and she knows that her determination, her sheer tenacity, are what pulled her through.

She asked me to spin the Dwight Yoakam CD. I can't explain why, but that particular album, "Just Lookin' for a Hit," has always seemed to have healing properties, or at least rejuvenating ones; it is great to drive to, great to sing to, and great to sing along to with someone else. It has great guitar work, great fiddles, a great rhythm section. Those tunes must have made for a hell of a time in the studio.

Lauren and I sang "I Got You" to each other, and then she sang along to a few others with her eyes closed, probably remembering all those trips up the Taconic to Pine Plains, or the time she'd been driving and played "I Got You" over her cell phone to me.

And I just watched her, and the pleasure she had singing. She always had a good voice, but this was different; she's still recovering her ability to speak. She's singing now, when she couldn't even vocalize three weeks ago. For her, it's more than just cutting loose; for her, right now, it is the ultimate affirmation of life.

Later on, Kareen arrived, poking her head through the door before she put on her uniform, saying, "How are you, my love? How are you doing today?"

Lauren gave an account of her day, all that she had done, and then she mentioned that she had seen the pictures of September 11, and she started to become upset again.

Kareen said to her, "You are blessed, you have your son, you have your husband. You have your limbs, you have your eyes, you have your face. It could have been much worse. You should be thankful. You can walk, you have everything. You are blessed."

All true.

Love,
Greg & Lauren

Today, for the first time, I saw Lauren's left middle finger and parts of her left hand. As in almost every other instance of seeing a graft or a burn site, it was not as bad as I'd imagined. I'd known that several knuckles had been pinned to preserve functional position during healing; the pins were actually visible, like a needle or tiny brad nail that protruded from either end of the pinned joint. The pins will be removed at some point in the future, and then, if the knuckles cannot recover function, they can be fused in functional position.

Lauren remains pleased with the way her fingers turned out. Her left middle finger was badly swollen, but it looked OK to both of us. While she lost a part of it, it seems as though she retains more than enough for the finger to remain useful. The other fingers on her left hand were wrapped in a newer type of dressing that was supposed to promote better healing by permitting air to permeate the barrier.

Lauren's biggest disappointment was that she did not walk today; she spent more than two hours in the tank, and this was the first time it felt particularly clinical to her. She had a full crew of seven, nurses, techs, and doctors, working on her. Throughout this lengthy process, she was lying in a stainless steel tub, without her gown, and she felt very much the patient. The tank can be very painful, and she had a healthy dose of morphine as they gave her a new local treatment to close some small spots that are not fully healed.

These are locations, the biggest the size of a Snickers bar, where the graft is experiencing hypertrophic growth, healing so much more quickly than the neighboring skin is growing that the two do not join. There is a layer of new tissue on top of the graft, but it will not fully close unless it joins with her skin.

The newest attending at the Burn Center, the doctor who joined just a week prior to September 11, has brought some new techniques, and had these areas treated with silver nitrate, which burns off the hypertrophic layer and permits the newly healing graft to bond more cleanly with the neighboring tissue.

Since she missed her walk today, Lauren intends to walk twice tomorrow, and she laid down the law to every nurse who came into her room afterward.

Shortly after I arrived, the Burn Center's psychologist stepped into the room for her daily visit. She was holding the commemorative issue of *Life* magazine that she had shown Lauren yesterday. I had somehow deleted the reference to this in yesterday's e-mail; Lauren did not look at the September 11 pictures herself on Tuesday. She was shown them by the psychologist.

This was done as part of a "desensitization" therapy: gradual exposure to something that causes fear or stress, with the goal of reducing sensitivity to the stimulus. Images and memories of the September 11 attacks will be unavoidable, if not overpowering, so Lauren needs to develop a means of learning about and coping with them. Through gradual exposure to all the facts, traumatic images and stories can be dealt with in a clinical setting where she has twenty-four-hour professional support and the emotional impact can be muted. But the pictures still have the capacity to shock. Until Tuesday, Lauren did not know that hijacked planes had also hit the Pentagon and been crashed in Pennsylvania.

The psychologist asked Lauren how she had done yesterday, and Lauren recounted how she had cried to me and to the nurse in the evening about the loss of so many friends and the inexplicable evil of the attacks. The hardest pictures to look at had been the ones of people covered in ashes and dust walking home after the towers' collapse. After seeing these and others, as she put it, she had been "feeling a bit low."

Today the psychologist wanted to focus on uplifting stories from the disaster, specifically on one account of six firemen who lived through the collapse because they were with a woman who had slowed down their descent to safety, and they were therefore in the single precise location, at about the second floor of the fire stairwell, that was spared from being crushed. Ten feet farther along or ten feet behind, and they would not have made it. Lauren will see the video of the news report on that incident in the next few days. The hope is to show that not just sadness came from the attacks.

The psychologist also asked Lauren about her fears. Her main fear was not about her injuries. No, she was afraid that our apartment might not be ready for her return. (Our master bedroom has been awaiting some major renovation since last year, and I am trying to have it completed before she is released from rehab.) I had suggested some days ago that if the renovation was not finished, she could stay with a friend of ours on Long Island (along with Tyler, Caleigh, and me), but she did not like plan B. So there is only plan A: when rehab is over, she comes home.

We got a bit tense discussing the renovation (what couple doesn't?) and the psychologist helped us through that, noting that we were having an escalation of tension in an extraordinary situation, and we needed to learn how to recognize this and step back from it. We will need to focus on how we communicate, so that when stresses find their way in, we can release them instead of turning on each other.

Lauren is filled with very strong emotions, and she observed that she can go from a mild statement to tears in seconds. When she does that, she is "peaking," going to extremes, which is a common hazard of being so emotionally traumatized. (The medication she receives helps deal with this.) And really, it is hard to think of a tougher road to travel than the one she is on. She has had to deal with a horrible injury, amputations, the loss of hundreds of friends, her own miraculous escape from death, and, in her own words, disfigurement. Through all this, she remains herself; she is still the same person.

When Lauren asked the psychologist how she was doing, the psychologist said, "Amazing."

Lauren's perspective, and the speed of her recovery, are indeed amazing; it is hard to remember where she was only a month ago. But then I walked past the room of another September 11 patient who is still struggling to heal and who remains sedated, is still on a ventilator through a tracheostomy, still has two trees with four Baxter pumps sending in intravenous drugs, and has a heat shield, a glass rectangle the size of the mattress, suspended several feet above the bed. These rooms are still about silent vigils and difficult communication; these patients are still deep in the woods.

By contrast, Lauren is fully alert and communicative, she has completed the necessary surgeries, and she is able to engage in diverting conversations with the nurses who cared for her while she was sleeping for weeks on end.

At one point, she asked for a blanket and the floor had run out of them; they were awaiting the evening shipment from housekeeping. The nurse came back to the room with two more sheets and explained the situation to Lauren. Then he spent time explaining the facts of hypertrophic growth and the uses of silver nitrate. As the nurses say, he'd "had Lauren before," meaning he had cared for her during her long sedation and sleep. It was quite a journey from those days to these, where all he has to do is give her medication and take her vital signs once an hour.

Lauren asked him, "How do you deal with it, these terrible injuries, disfigurement?" He thought she was asking how he thought she should deal with her own, but she made it clear she was asking about him. He admitted that it was very stressful work. What makes it worthwhile, he told her, is when a patient walks out of the unit, and then comes back six months or a year later and is doing fine. Lauren asked him whether he had any hobbies. He gave a confessional smile, sat down, and we started just to talk. (His hobby is playing Dungeons and Dragons.)

The contrast in demeanor since October, from lifesaving mode to casual chitchat, could not have been more extreme.

At one point after this conversation, I heard someone call my name from the hallway, and it was Christine, the karaoke queen. She had just dropped off bags full of pastries for the nursing staff. I asked her if she wanted to meet someone, and then I introduced her to Lauren.

Over the weeks when she and her crew of volunteers were bringing dinner three times a week, Christine was one of many people who heard Lauren's story and spoke of wanting to meet her. Tonight she put on a gown, hat, and gloves, and came in.

She told Lauren that she had been an inspiration; that when Christine, who'd sacrificed training to do her volunteer work, ran the marathon, every time she flagged she thought, "If Lauren is hanging in there, so can I." Lauren thanked her, but Christine said, "No, you're my personal hero."

Lauren asked what had led Christine to volunteer, and she explained how the hospital had saved her boyfriend's life three years earlier after he'd been run down by an SUV, and as she'd spent a two-month vigil at his bedside during his barbiturate coma, she'd noticed how hard the nurses and doctors worked to keep him alive. She had intermittently brought food to other units over the years. After September 11, she made feeding the medical staff of the Burn Center her personal mission, and she wound up feeding a lot of patient families as well.

She stayed and talked for a while more; she and Lauren were both all smiles.

I enjoyed listening to these conversations; they meant that Lauren was indeed coming back, that she was managing the news of tragedy but not letting it prevent her from moving on with her life, from asking others about themselves and focusing on something other than her injuries. That's how she is going to continue to make it: just keep taking those baby steps, one after the other.

Love,
Greg & Lauren

From: Greg
To: Everyone
Date: Friday, November 30, 2001 12:17 AM
Subject: Lauren Update for Nov 29 (Thursday)

Lauren walked to the gym today unassisted; it is at the far end of the Burn Center, down the hall to reception, and then down the hall again, past the waiting room, down the corridor lined with handwritten cards from around the country and the world.

She climbed the stairs, really four steps to a wooden platform, and then back down. She did well, but when the occupational therapists had her try to grasp the railing with her right hand, the pain made her black out. This tells you what she is capable of, how hard she is pushing herself, and what her limitations are.

She was so proud of her achievements today; she makes such an effort to reconnect with her life, never knowing how much of it she will be able to take back. She has to have faith in the future, she has to be patient, to believe in herself, and I am there, a calm voice of reassurance saying these things; but I can never shake how easy these things are for me to say, how hard they are for her to do.

Her hands, for example; the worst is over, yet it is only beginning. She receives a new cast almost every day; she has received new splints, new dressings; at times, she holds her hands up and simply stares at them, trying to believe in their potential to heal. And it is there; we just don't know to what extent.

There are days when the weight of this burden is heavier than the day before.

I have often referred to burn care, the process of taking down dressings, cleaning wounds, and then replacing the bandages. I have seen instances of this through a gap in the drawn curtain to her room, but I was never there for the entire process until today. Lauren asked me to stay for moral support, so I did. She has undergone this twice a day for seventy-nine days; for the past few weeks, she has been awake for it.

The nurse told me, "If you faint, I'm just stepping over you; I'm not picking you up." She said this with a smile, but of course it is a real hazard. I told her I'd seen everything, and she said, "You only think you've seen everything." She was right.

I have seen Lauren's legs and her back and her buttocks and her arms; but never all at once, never together. I never saw how they massacred her body.

Today I saw the full extent of her injuries, and of course, parts of them have been healed for two months. But others are only a week old; her hands, for example, looked the worst and have the furthest to go to be normal, or as normal as possible. I saw the state of the grafts that run from her heels to her shoulders, and the state of the donor sites on the fronts of her legs. Before, I could think only of how much better she was than she had been. Now I can see only how hard it will be for her to cope. Yet she copes.

The nurses remove Lauren's gown and then all her dressings, and the doctors doing rounds come in; today that meant her doctor, a fellow, and two residents. In the past, when Lauren was sedated, the nurses would roll her, but today she did it herself, slowly and with great effort, as the doctors inspected the state of healing of all her wounds. In the past she would be silent as they fought to keep her alive; today she would offer her insights, and remind them of things that were important to her (such as putting on certain dressings with the proper padding to minimize pain).

She lay there on the bed, illuminated by bright fluorescent lights and an overhead heat lamp. The nurses put a towel on her body for modesty as she spoke to the doctors, and after an area had been checked, the nurses bathed her gently with warm towels.

In September, burn care took two hours because dressings needed to be removed and reapplied for almost her entire body, and she would emerge wrapped in white webbed bandages as if cocooned by some giant silk spider. Today burn care took no more than fifteen minutes, and dressings were applied only to small areas on her buttocks and her hands.

Her doctor also discussed other events of the day, about her blacking out on the stairs; he joked that the way he heard it, the physical therapists had pushed Lauren off. Regarding one particular procedure, Lauren suggested putting it to a vote, and he turned to the gathered staff, said, "OK, let's see who works for me," and tallying the voters, said, "That's six, and Greg doesn't count."

I watched and listened from a chair at the other end of the room, and once they were done, I stood up to speak with her doctor as well. We discussed Lauren's discharge date; the hospital is thinking as early as next Tuesday, but it seemed to me that she should have another week (meaning a week from Monday) to complete the healing of the remaining stubborn areas.

As emotional as I have been about all of this in the eleven weeks and two days since the world changed, there is always a chance to feel sorrow anew. But however I am affected cannot compare to what she feels, and she wants to live; she is thankful that she lived; and she can live a good life, though it will be vastly different.

It will not be a good idea for her to go out in the sun again without full coverings and wraparound sunglasses. She will not be able to work in a normal office for quite some time; we do not know when she will be able to type on a keyboard. She will need help at home for many months. There will be no more long afternoons at the beach or by the pool; there will be no carefree days for a long, long time. But her greatest yearning, the one that brings tears to her eyes, will happen. "I want to hold my son. I want to hold him so badly."

We are really preparing ourselves for battle. Nature is without mercy; what we face is relentless work, and we need to have the strength for it. I think we do; I think that we can get discouraged as the shocks follow one after another. But I feel as if we can shake them off.

I am not afraid. Not of this. I am not afraid of anything if she needs me to be strong for her. She escaped alive from an inferno. She expected me to be there on the other side. And I am.

We have always been a powerful team, and we will triumph.

Love,
Greg & Lauren

"The age of wireless has begun," Lauren said early this evening. "I have no lines in me." It took me a second to register what she meant and then she made it clear; her catheter had been removed, and she was finally completely unconnected to any external devices; she was back in charge of every one of her bodily functions.

I haven't mentioned much of this, because it doesn't change day to day and was not a complicated management issue when compared to skin grafts and infections; but of course her kidneys and digestive system are just as important as her breathing and her heart rate. The output of her kidneys is measured around the clock, and any drop in fluid rate is cause for concern. Lauren had only a few episodes of insufficient output in her first crisis weeks; her kidneys have been doing well since. Yet this is the last line to go because its absence would most often require her to climb out of bed.

While the other lines (IVs, electrodes, oxygen monitors, arterial lines, heart lines) are much more closely related to acute-care needs, this is a major milestone in her physical recovery, because it means she is strong enough to get up and use a commode. She had to retrain to ensure she would not be incontinent, and then she had to prove she could perform on her own, but she did this in a day; and now she is no longer bothered by any tubes. I think it's hard to measure how much more comfortable this makes her, in addition to making her feel that much closer to being a healthy person.

Lauren made the announcement on my second trip to the hospital, in the evening. The first trip was just as noteworthy, for an entirely different reason.

Tyler paid his second visit to the hospital today, arriving in the midst of a nap. He fell asleep in the car, and after opening his eyes for a moment as he was transferred from the car seat to the stroller, he fell back asleep with his head slightly to one side. The Quiet Room was already open when we reached the 8th floor, so Joyce and I wheeled the stroller in and I went to check on Lauren.

She was having a new set of dressings applied to her left hand by the occupational therapists, and then she was ready to have a seat in her rolling chair (a chair old enough that one of the nurses said Florence Nightingale herself had probably used it). It was time for lipstick and the FDNY hat. They gave her a new gel seat cushion to make the chair comfortable, and two of the therapists "jumped" her into it: one took her by the thighs above her knees, the other under her arms, and at the count of three lifted her so that she was seated far back on the chair and did not have to slide her rear end across. She still has some open spots, and wriggling backward might irritate the new grafts.

She wore the new Easy Spirit lace boots I'd bought her; the New Balance shoes had a double tongue for waterproofing that was giving her a one-and-a-half inch blister on the front of her right foot at the ankle, where she had received a skin graft.

I wheeled her out to the Quiet Room and set her chair opposite Tyler's stroller, where we all admired his peaceful sleep. His eyes were closed, of course, and he had on a denim jacket over blue denim overalls, a shirt with red and yellow balloons, and his cool black sneakers.

We were joined by the nurse who'd given Lauren the FDNY hat; he was there "not wearing scrubs," just checking in while taking a few days off, and of course he wanted to meet Tyler.

It was all very emotional for Lauren, as you would expect; looking at Tyler, she said how much she loved her little angel. She thanked Joyce for all her help, and cried a bit as Joyce gave her a hug. Joyce gave Lauren a framed "penny" prayer from Hallmark and a signed get-well card from Tyler (his writing skills are extraordinarily advanced, but he does this only when Joyce is around).

As babies will, Tyler woke up, and the rules were a little more relaxed this time; we could hold him close enough for Lauren to kiss him (we just needed to move the bill of her cap a bit), and so she got to kiss her baby, the first time she had touched him since September 11. She sang to him again, barely making it through her favorite ditty.

When we held him close to her, he didn't cry, though he was a bit contemplative; he has seen her only twice in eleven and a half weeks, and she does not look the same; her face is different, her hair is short and under a baseball cap, her voice is a little hoarse, and she cannot pick him up. He did recognize her, but she is not the center of his universe these days. For now, he spends the most time with his nanny and his grandparents.

That's the real crime. There is no getting around the change in our lives, or in his. We are just thankful that a year from now, when the major battles have been fought, Lauren can reestablish herself where she should be.

There is a very odd parallel in this to my own life. My father reminded me of it when he was up here in November. When I was two years old, my mother was in New York Hospital for three weeks with nephritis. Her window overlooked the courtyard where they have since built their new entry corridor and chapel and coffee shop. One day he took me down to the hospital so she could see me, but I was too young to be brought to her room; so she looked out the window as I played on the sidewalk outside, and while I do not remember doing this, I have seen pictures. Sometimes it does seem as if fate is running out of original ideas.

Soon enough Tyler became impatient with being kept in one place, so we gave him his lawn mower and he was off. Lauren said she wanted to go with him, so I turned her chair and wheeled her out to the hallway, and we started to follow our one-year-old as he motored his way down the hallway toward the gym.

I pressed the square plate on the wall that opens the doors automatically, and Tyler went straight through and right into the open doors of the gym, where we surprised eight physical therapists in the midst of their lunch, some holding sandwiches to their mouths.

To say that Tyler was welcome in this environment would be too slight; he was a conquering hero returning in triumph, and became the immediate focus of approximately ten adults, attentive to his every movement. (Probably a better analogy is that he received instant VIP treatment, as if he were a movie star entering a trendy nightclub.)

I took several photographs of Lauren and the therapists, and of Tyler with a couple of them. He wandered around (we kept him away from anything dangerous, of course). He remained unflappable. Instead of being scared or reaching for his mom and dad, he becomes thoughtful; he looks at people and sizes them up very contemplatively, then decides on a course of action and pursues it with vigor. When he approached a children's rehab device with white and black triangles, squares, and circles, the therapists all kept observing how calm he was.

We had a great time there until Lauren began to tire and we had to leave. We pointed Tyler out of the room, and he headed straight out the door, through the open double doors, and made a left up the corridor lined with get-well cards, as Lauren followed on her rolling chair.

When you're with a young and newly mobile child, one of the most enjoyable parts is to follow him as he experiences the world. Lauren cannot do this yet on her own, but through the miracle of Florence Nightingale's chair, she was able to keep up with him, so my family moved about and had fun as we used to. It was a far, far cry from the old way, but it was real enough.

I wheeled Lauren back to her room and helped get her back into bed; this time the nurse and I helped her stand up from the chair, and then she lay down on the bed and rolled, taking a couple of minutes to maneuver herself into the center. The effort involved in all this was exhausting and left her moaning, though she recovered well.

I got her set, then drove home with Tyler and Joyce.

There had been another milestone very early this (Friday) morning; at about 7:30 I received a telephone call from Lauren. As her companion held the phone, Lauren said good morning and asked me to send up some regular clothes for her to wear during Tyler's visit. She is taking more and more control of her life. Given who she is, she has been trying to manage things almost from the moment she reawakened; but she now needs fewer and fewer intermediaries to get her messages across.

While the visit with Tyler was going on, electricians were at the apartment moving several electrical outlets in the den so that we could finally have our custom-built home office installed. I had called the building superintendent before I left for the hospital, and asked him to plaster the openings they'd made in the walls to thread the cables through the studs. By the time we arrived home, the electricians were done and the plaster was drying. This was certainly the best luck I've had with a renovation project in a long, long time.

When I returned to the hospital, I discovered that Christine had paid Lauren a visit and delivered some pastries and slices of Starbucks cakes. She brought a copy of her own self-titled CD, a copy of her demo of a song she wrote in August called "One World," and a second copy of the Eva Cassidy CD "Songbird," which we'd received from a friend of Lauren's the day before.

I fed Lauren her dinner and helped her sample the broad range of desserts she had in her room. Afterward, we relaxed and listened to "Songbird."

It begins with a beautiful version of "Fields of Gold," and the last song on it is a slow, haunting rendition of "Over the Rainbow." These days Lauren takes great pleasure in singing along to songs that she likes, and she sang along with "Fields of Gold." We let the CD play, I read her some e-mails and cards people had sent, and then I stepped out to check on something. When I came back, she had her eyes closed and was singing along to "Over the Rainbow." It was a pure moment of joy, and it brought tears to my eyes. I had to compose myself for a moment before I spoke to her, and showed her the pictures Joyce had brought of Tyler and a friend of his in their Halloween costumes.

We both fell asleep for an hour; then I kissed her good night and it was time to go play a gig.

I went to Le Bar Bat, and the place was packed because this was a benefit performance. Again, I dedicated "Wild Horses" to Lauren. What I said, as briefly as possible: "Since September 11, my wife has been in the burn unit; for two and a half months, we didn't know if she was going to make it. Well, last week, we found out she was going to live." The place broke out in applause.

At the bar after we were done, our drummer was talking with an attractive young woman from his office who'd come to the benefit. She wore a beautiful engagement ring with a huge round-cut diamond flanked by two more that were just a little less huge. I told her, "Nice ring," and she said in a quiet voice, "My fiancé died September 11."

He worked on the 89th floor of Tower Two, my building, five floors up. He'd left for work that day and she remembers everything he was wearing; she can't believe that she lost him. We talked for a while, and mostly I tried to reassure her. We drank to each other's sorrows, the memory of her fiancé, and Lauren's miracle, and then she told me I was really lucky, and I couldn't disagree.

I had seen Lauren with Tyler only hours before.

Love,
Greg & Lauren

Saturday afternoon Lauren was sleeping after a rough day; she had been walking and been to the tank, and she had not felt good during most of this activity. When I got there, she was fast asleep, while a Bill Moyers program played on her television. Joseph Campbell, I believe, was discussing the resurrection myths of the Egyptians, and Lauren lay in her bed, swathed in white cloth, arms crossed on her chest, wrapped in white casts, a towel draped over her head for warmth, seeming very much like an ancient head covering for a princess who will be reborn.

The peaceful scene gave me a moment to think of how much it contrasted with so much of our lives. Once we are past the central point that Lauren survived, and it is the major point, there are many frustrations.

There is the frustration of never being able to go back to what we had. There is the frustration that Lauren faces in every step she takes. There are no choices in this; the only successful long-term strategy is acceptance and coping.

In that, she is quite skilled, far better than I am; she has always had a gift for dwelling in the actual, and accomplishing the full measure of what she is capable of within whatever constraints truly exist. I have dwelled much more in unrealistic dreams.

When this disaster took place, I had to believe that she would survive, no matter how unrealistic the prospect might have seemed. I had to have the faith that it was possible for her to sneak through the gaps in the statistics. One way I did this at the time was to avoid learning the statistics. Her job, and mine with her, was to survive. Now the job is to set goals and work toward them through the thousands of challenges that remain, and without anger.

When I got there today, a number of relief nurses were seated behind the main desk at the nurses' station waiting for patients to arrive. There had been an explosion in a cooling and ventilation unit in lower Manhattan, and the Burn Center went into disaster mode after hearing early reports that there were more than thirty casualties.

Fortunately, of the thirty-eight firefighters injured in the blast, there were fewer major burns than anticipated. Many injuries were minor traumas for which the patients were treated and released. Three firefighters were brought to the Burn Center, though none with burns in excess of 50 to 60 percent. While those could be grimly critical injuries, we can be thankful that no one was quite as critical as so many of the September 11 patients.

Yet even though it was not an act of terror, in Lauren's memorably whispered words, there were two eerie links between the explosion and September 11.

Later in the evening I was speaking to the chaplain about the incident. Her position is funded by the Fire Department, so she was called when the explosion occurred and there were burn injuries. But having been there for some hours, she was preparing to leave because the toll of serious burns was less than expected. As I stood in her doorway, Lauren's doctor stopped by.

The chaplain had told me a fact that revealed the first eerie coincidence; the explosion occurred in the basement of One New York Plaza—the building where Euro Brokers has temporarily moved. I don't know whether there will be more limited access to the building; I don't know how serious the damage is. But I'm sure it will be disconcerting to many people there, non–Euro Brokers employees as well. The *Times* story on the explosion closed by saying, "Despite the severity of the blast, fire officials said there were no immediate signs of structural damage to the building."

Lauren's doctor revealed the second coincidence. On September 11, he had been driving to give a lecture on disaster management in New Jersey when he was paged that there'd been an attack on the World Trade Center. Saturday, he was similarly about to stand up and speak, again at a lecture in New Jersey, when he was paged about the explosion at One New York Plaza. "I'm not giving any more lectures in New Jersey," he said.

There is no real link, of course, except in our psyches, but the stresses of living in a strange and more foreboding world continue to accumulate.

When Lauren awoke, we watched *Please Don't Eat the Daisies,* a harmless romantic comedy starring Doris Day and David Niven. I remember loving the movie when I was young; this time Lauren noticed that the dog they were hoping would not eat the daisies was a wheaten, the same breed as Caleigh.

The healing skin on her face is still thin, so when she becomes emotional, her face glows crimson; but when she is relaxed and enjoying herself, her skin tone begins to resemble the way she looked before this, and will look again.

As she watched the movie, I was looking at her, noticing how much more normal she looked, and still how pretty. She turned to me and asked why I was looking at her; she said it made her a little self-conscious. I told her it was because her eyes were so beautiful, and her face. She started to smile, and it was a real one; she said it was nice to be told she was beautiful, and she is.

Love,
Greg & Lauren

From: Greg
To: Everyone
Date: Monday, December 3, 2001 9:08 AM
Subject: Lauren Update for Dec 2 (Sunday)

If it were possible to say that nothing new happened, today would be the day to say it. Lauren walked from her room to the waiting room and back, she sat up in the chair for a few hours, and she wore the pressure garment for her face for close to ten hours. All greater accomplishments than the day before, so this was a good day; but less dramatic, somehow, when there is not as much danger. Now a bad day means a setback in her energy level or her strength: but it does not mean that she risks losing her battle forever. It just means we'll get 'em tomorrow. I am not nostalgic for those bad old days; entering a phase where what happens can seem routine, not extraordinary, is actually an amazing milestone.

As I've noted, the pressure garment for Lauren's face is a generic version of the pressure body suit she will wear on her entire body for the next year to control scarring. She will be measured for the full suit tomorrow; she will also be measured for a silicone-rubber-lined clear plastic mask that will be contoured to fit her face and apply even pressure. (The silicone lining moisturizes the healing tissue and prevents it from becoming so hard.)

The garment she has worn tonight and for the last few days wraps above her head and under her chin while applying pressure to the sides of her face. It can't be called a hood or a mask because it is entirely open in the front and does not cover the back of her head; it is really just a five-inch band wrapped vertically around her face (like the toothache dressings you might see in an old comedy, though this one is not funny). There are holes cut for her ears, and the two sides sweep back behind her ears to a Velcro closure at the base of her skull. Strips of silicone gel are placed underneath the covering at the left side of her chin to further assist in the breaking down of scar tissue.

She is building up the amount of time she keeps this pressure dressing on; the goal for today was twelve hours. The problem is that the bottom, underneath her chin, is a little tight against her neck when on correctly, so is not that comfortable. It is our hope that the custom-tailored garments will be easier to wear.

In addition to the pressure garments, she still needs high levels of protein and calories to keep healing. She is off the 6,000-calorie-a-day tube feedings, but her appetite is still moderate and she does not finish her meals (which of course are hospital food). So on the way to the hospital, I bought her two cases of Ensure, a liquid, high-calorie supplement that will provide additional energy and protein for healing. She had the strawberry flavor over ice, and drank it down. One can has as many calories as a slice of pecan pie; it doesn't taste as good but is better for her.

At around 6 PM we caught *Charley Varrick,* a 1973 Don Siegel film starring Walter Matthau. After that, we watched *Butch Cassidy and the Sundance Kid.* AMC has been doing us a real escapist favor the last couple of nights.

Lauren had Kareen back tonight (she's had a relief companion the last two nights), so she was quite comfortable, and I left as she received her sleep medication at her routine time of 10 PM.

Then again, maybe not everything was routine. I remembered a quote, "God is in the details," and the Internet permits me to report that it was written by Ludwig Mies van der Rohe in the June 28, 1959, *New York Herald Tribune.* It may be the only aspect of modern architecture that I agree with, based on something that happened on December 2, 2001, on Central Park West.

I had gone shopping on the Upper West Side after a friend gave me a lift there; that's where I bought the Ensure, at the Food Emporium. I tried to hail a cab at about 4:45 PM so I could head over to see Lauren. Unfortunately, this was the witching hour, when all cabs on the East Side or West Side (but not in the Village?) are either carrying passengers or off duty. The number of new people seeking cabs remains steady, until every block has three or four parties waiting; but there are no cabs, so the odds of getting one are reduced to less than zero, especially when one factors in anxiety. Nowhere, as far as the eye can see, is there a vacant cab to be had.

I felt helpless. I needed to get across Manhattan to the hospital and it looked as though I would be forced to walk. I headed along 69th Street from Columbus Avenue toward Central Park, because I figured at worst, I could cross the park at 72nd Street, and see Lauren in around thirty to forty minutes. I turned north on Central Park West and was walking along the southbound lane when a bus simply stopped next to me.

I walked past the door; I wasn't at a bus stop, and I fully expected someone to be getting off. No one did, but I had a flash and ran to get on. It was a crosstown bus marked 72nd and York. The driver confirmed that he was headed toward the East Side, so I dipped my MetroCard and sat down. I read some e-mails on my BlackBerry, noticed we had made the left onto the 66th Street transverse, and realized, moments later, that we were already across the park and past Fifth Avenue. I could not imagine how a bus had made the trip so fast. He cruised across the East Side just as quickly, and we reached York and 72nd in about ten minutes, as fast as a cab would have.

As we slowed at the last stop, I asked the driver why he'd stopped for me; after all, I hadn't hailed him and I wasn't at a bus stop, I was just walking up the street. Somehow, driving his bus in the gathering darkness, he'd read my mind.

He said, "You looked lost."

I told him I didn't know how often he gets thanked, but I wanted to thank him; and I reached out to shake his hand. I think he was startled, but he returned the handshake, gave me a real smile for one or two seconds, and I was off, walking the four very short blocks south to the hospital.

I had no sooner despaired of assistance than a New York City bus was sent to pluck me from the night and get me to my destination (if not God in the details, then certainly a Harry Potter moment from *Prisoner of Azkaban*). We seemed to cruise magically through traffic lights and past bus stops, and long before I thought I would, I was saying hello to Lauren.

Love,
Greg & Lauren

From: Greg
To: Everyone
Date: Tuesday, December 4, 2001 1:06 AM
Subject: Lauren Update for Dec. 3 (Monday)

Lauren was worn out by a rough day of walking and range-of-motion work. She is due to get the cast off her right hand tomorrow, which she is looking forward to. She went to the tank late, just as I got there, so when she was returned to her room the nurses scrambled to put her pressure dressings back on, the Tubi grips for her legs, and I took the small blow dryer and dried her hair (it is still so short that this took about twenty seconds). Underneath her gown, on her back, she was wearing a pressure dressing that resembled Iron Man's chest plate, or some form of beige plastic body armor.

We helped her as she rolled to a sitting position on the bed (she needed a slight boost; she did not quite have the strength to get her torso vertical). Then she stood up and turned to sit on the chair. The nurses helped jump her back to a proper seated position and she asked for her NYPD cap to be placed on her head.

She was scheduled to attend her first meeting of a weekly burn support group held in the Burn Center's gym at 5:30. It had been canceled and then uncanceled, so the expected attendance would be smaller than usual. This would be Lauren's first appearance as a person since September 11. Until now, she's been the patient, attended by doctors, nurses, therapists, and family. Today she would be seated among a group of people who'd suffered similar injuries, and she would be speaking for herself.

I wheeled her down the corridor to the Burn Center, then down the hall of get-well cards to the gym.

The most prominent piece of equipment in the gym is the stairs, those four steps up to a platform and four steps down; there are mat beds, arm machines, and other devices to help burn patients stretch their skin and muscles and attempt to regain normal function. There were twelve people already gathered around the large conference table at the rear: three occupational and physical therapists, two physical therapy students, and seven burn patients.

They welcomed Lauren to the table, making space for her at the head, and offered us coffee cake and cookies.

The session began with everyone introducing themselves; my entire introduction was "My name is Greg, I'm Lauren's husband," and turning to her. Lauren's was longer.

She spoke in her soft, deliberate voice, with increasing emotion as she neared the end. As close as I can remember it, she said: "My name is Lauren. I was burned on September 11 in the lobby of the World Trade Center. I had just gotten out of a cab. I heard a loud whistling noise, and I didn't know what it was. I went into the lobby and a fireball of jet fuel came from the elevators. It engulfed me. It pushed me back out the door. When I touched the door, that is when I burned my hands. It was terrible. I ran across the street to the grass, where a man came and helped me. If I'd been two minutes earlier, I'd have died. Most of the people at my company died; seven hundred of them. I was there ten years, so I lost a lot of friends. I've had a lot of grafts, and according to my doctors and my husband, I've been a good healer. I'm scheduled to be released from the hospital next Monday, to rehab at Burke in Westchester. I'm glad to be alive." She composed herself for a moment. "I'm optimistic, but one of the hardest things has been knowing that this is not just a recovery of two months but two years."

She simply came to a stop; and for a moment, no one spoke.

There were other, equally horrible stories. There were two other patients from September 11, both with burns of under 40 percent, who are already home with their families. One of them complained about severe, intolerable itching; another said that the pressure garments were too tight to sleep in comfortably, and was teased and told, "You'll learn." One woman told a brutal story of having been burned deliberately by her husband over 70 percent of her body; her sister was killed in the same attack. One man had been burned ten years ago; another woman had been burned thirty years ago.

Lauren was by far the most acute case at this point, and had the greatest percentage burn of anyone in the room, but otherwise she shared all of their concerns, and they had been down the same road that she will travel.

One woman in particular, the one with the 70 percent burn, told a gripping story of progress from almost complete immobility three years earlier to a very normal and functional situation today. Following her injury she had been unable to move her right hand; but through sheer hard work, it was now fully functional. At first glance it appeared entirely normal, though a second glance showed that it had been completely grafted. Her face had been unharmed, but underneath her clothes she carried heavy scars over most of her body. Yet she was very upbeat, very independent; she spoke of her injuries matter-of-factly, without self-pity, just self-awareness. It was not hard to see how she had made it back this far. She still wears her pressure garments after three years.

The functioning of this woman's right hand was the most encouraging thing Lauren could have seen; she moved her fingers with normal dexterity and energy.

Lauren asked and received answers to questions regarding pressure garments, silicone-lined face masks, itching, long-term therapy and rehab, drug treatments—the works. Patients discussed body image; one woman burned last April told of her return to the pool at NYU, and of how she had bravely donned a bathing suit and gone back to her regular exercise program. She said she'd received only one comment, a positive one; the person said, "Looks like you had a rough year."

All the patients discussed the tightening of their skin, and how sometimes it seemed as if they had to stretch every ten minutes to overcome the feeling of constriction. One woman said, "It seems like your skin will just tear open," but one of the therapists said, "But it doesn't tear, does it?" and the woman answered, "No, it does not." One woman pulled up her sleeve to show Lauren the healing from a thirty-year-old burn; another man showed an almost invisible graft of ten years ago.

It was a sobering experience but an encouraging one; these people had all been badly injured and affected for life, and had come here to share their feelings with the small group of patients and professionals who could understand what they lived with. Yet they were all "normal," meaning they did not pity themselves; they dealt with it. All of them had moments, if not lengthy periods, of despair; but the conclusion to be drawn from them is that the despair can be coped with.

The woman with the 70 percent burn said she suffered terrible flashbacks after the World Trade Center attacks; she dreamed that Osama Bin Laden was chasing her with gasoline and a match. But this woman also said that she'd forgotten the pain, and the constriction, of her injuries; she had clearly rebuilt her life.

One of the therapists wanted Lauren to reflect on this woman's example: "She's being modest. Three years ago she couldn't move at all; now she's living by herself, doing everything herself."

One woman had suffered a 30 percent burn on the 78th floor of Tower Two, my building. She normally worked on 86, which means she would have used the same bank of elevators that rose to Euro Brokers. The plane hit 78 directly; it is a miracle that she survived.

The 78th floor was known as the Skylobby; those who worked on the very highest floors would take express elevators to 78, where there were further banks of elevators that went to six-floor sections of the next twenty-seven stories. Throughout the day, there would typically be at least twenty people in the Skylobby waiting for elevators; at rush hour, there could be a hundred. The large express elevators from the ground floor could easily hold twenty-five people at once, and there were at least ten of them feeding just the 78th floor. I had assumed, since that entire floor was open from one end to another, that once the plane hit, no one on 78 could have survived.

But this woman did, along with two other people; a commercial jet under full power hit less than a hundred feet away from her on the same level, but somehow she was standing in the one spot that was spared. She descended the same staircase that my friend Brian Clark took down from the 84th floor, also commenting that it appeared empty.

Lauren grew fatigued and had to leave before the group session was over; she was asked how she felt after attending it and she said, "Encouraged."

As I wheeled her from the room, the particularly kind man who'd sat next to us and cut our pieces of cake got up to open the door for us, giving Lauren closing advice: "The Jobst [the pressure garments, pronounced biblically] will be your best friend" and "Stay out of the sun, even though it's winter."

And then I was wheeling her back; my intrepid hero, who will rise out of that chair and begin striding purposefully through her life as she works with focused determination over the next two years.

Love,
Greg & Lauren

From: Greg
To: Everyone
Date: Wednesday, December 5, 2001 9:04 AM
Subject: Lauren Update for Dec 4 (Tuesday)

Lauren wore regular clothes for the first time today; Burn Center scrubs, gray top and pants with the Burn Center insignia. They were her workout clothes for the most strenuous physical activity she has experienced in twelve weeks.

And yes, it has been twelve weeks; I started by taking this thing in hours, then twelve-hour shifts, then days, then weeks, and now even longer. Until this week I would never have missed counting the days, and that's the odd part, because these are the exact days—eighty-two, eighty-three, eighty-four—that we have been aiming for since September 11. I had always said it would be a journey of eighty-three miles through enemy territory before Lauren would be out of the woods, and that date passed Monday without our marking it. But we can mark it now, knowing she beat it by at least ten days. I missed that artificial target date because I am looking toward the future. For so long the future was inconceivable because I did not know if Lauren would share it. Now I know she will.

When I reached her today, after going clothes shopping for her (more on that later), Lauren was wearing her scrubs top as she lay in bed. The Queen of the Splints was with her, finishing wrapping the newest splint onto Lauren's right hand (the cast had come off this morning as scheduled, and had successfully stretched the inner tendons). I suggested that she and Lauren could form a rock band: Lauren and the Splinters. Lauren proceeded to talk about her day with some pride.

Dressed in her scrubs, she'd walked to the gym, and back at the end of her workout. She'd done three minutes on the treadmill; then she sat on the mat and did torso twists and leans; she stretched her arms, her legs, her neck, her back, her shoulders. The physical therapist said she'd gotten Lauren to roll forward on one of those big inflatable workout balls, which Lauren didn't like but rolled anyway.

"I'm tired," she said. "I did a lot of work today."

"She really pushed herself," the therapist said. "Through the pain. Even when it hurt, she kept going."

"She's a pretty determined lady," I said.

"I think it also helped that she heard the other patients in the group talk about how they'd pushed through," the therapist added.

While Lauren is a person of singular determination, listening to the other patients probably did help; it was encouraging to see people who'd been through hell but come back to be normal, and to hear that her skin wouldn't tear open and her joints pop if she pushed herself gradually to regain her full range of motion and flexibility.

She will be having a minor procedure tomorrow; they will be removing the pins from the knuckles of her left hand.

Some areas, notably her left arm and her hands, will be harder to rehabilitate, and may require additional surgeries to correct or fix limitations or lingering injury. But there is hope there too; the woman with the 70 percent burn had only recently had a surgery to loosen the scars that had constrained her right arm, and was happy at the range of motion she'd regained (though she will have to wear pressure garments for another year on that specific area to control the postsurgical scarring.

There was also a brief fashion show. I'd gone to Paragon to buy Lauren loose-fitting drawstring pants with no elastic in the waist, and relaxed shirts that she would be able to put on even with splints on her arms. Yoga pants fit the bill perfectly. I purchased some in gray, black, green, and red. I was a little concerned that they might not be stylish enough, though Lauren liked the selection. These clothes were important to her, and it's not a mystery why; about the group the other night, she'd said, "Everyone there was dressed as a normal person—I was the only one wearing a robe over a hospital gown." Her mother had also had some success shopping for her at Eddie Bauer; so Lauren's fashion needs are met for the time being.

Also tonight she asked to watch the news, and, for the first time, unexpectedly, she saw the footage of the towers collapsing. There was a story about some firefighters, and suddenly, there was Tower One imploding, with the swirling cascade of dust and twelve-foot-long structural steel members that looked like matchsticks bursting outside the gray cloud. I moved to turn it off, but she said, Leave it, I want to see it. They showed only about six seconds. She was OK with it; it did not seem to affect her, probably due to a combination of her own strength and the successful "desensitization" process she'd undergone regarding the events of September 11. (I hope this is still true overnight.)

Since Lauren cannot do much for herself, she requires a lot of minor, trivial, but necessary assistance: straightening out her sheets, pulling down her scrubs top when it rides up on her, Vaseline for her lips, Oil of Olay for her face, putting on and taking off the facial pressure bandage; helping her sip juice or water, feeding her her dinner, giving her a scheduled medication by mouth; pulling down or raising the blankets to help her when she is hot or cold, "itching" her (tapping or massaging an itch), caressing or massaging her scalp.

I was massaging her scalp and the back of her head, where her hair has been slow to grow back because she has been lying on it (though it has started). After doing this awhile, I moved down the bed, and caressed her right leg, gently drawing my fingers down the outside of the ribbed elastic Tubi grip that circled her leg like a beige leg warmer from the middle of her thigh to her heels. She looked at me and said with the accent on SO, "That feels so nice," and then she was crying.

"No one has touched me like that in so long," she said. "Everyone has just flipped me over, put things on, and taken things off. It hurts and it's so rough. No one has touched me like that. Thank you, honey, thank you."

I said, For God's sake, please don't thank me.

It was a pleasure to continue doing it; she had not felt a loving touch in so long, except lightly on her arm or when someone stroked her hair, or when I was first able to give her a gentle hug. And there were some good reasons why, which are more heartbreaking than thinking abstractly about how long she'd had to wait for this.

It wouldn't have been possible to stroke her like this immediately after September 11, or even two weeks ago; she wasn't strong enough, she was too sensitive, and it would have caused her pain. Three months ago, the skin beneath the Tubi grips hadn't even been there; the fronts of her legs had been harvested perhaps four times for donor skin, and the backs of her legs had entirely new skin that had healed from grafts performed within her first week at the Burn Center. The muscles, and the contours, were the same; and I believe our skin cells recycle completely every three months (I expect the doctors who receive this update to correct me if I am wrong); so maybe it wasn't that much different from normal, except that we don't typically remove the skin in order to replace it.

She had her eyes closed, relaxing, soothed, and she didn't even know how extensive the grafts were—she didn't realize that the fronts of her feet (the areas that would be covered by spats, if she were in the mood to wear them) had been grafted. Her body was fighting its way back, and it had come far enough that it could be touched as if she were a whole person again; an amazing achievement, and frankly an inconceivable outcome back on September 16 or 17, when the surgery took place. There could be no sense, then, that in December she would be lying in a bed, eyes closed, sinking in to the feeling of the first loving caress since the night of September 10.

On October 2, the day of the Cantor Fitzgerald firm-wide memorial service, she had a 100 percent injury. There was not a spot on her body that wasn't a recovering burn, donor site, or graft. Those few days were among her toughest, when her prognosis would have been its most bleak. And it was on that day—I did not write of this at the time, but here it is—that the priest giving the closing prayer told a parable that ended with a child saying, "I want my love with the skin on."

The moment the priest said that, I stifled my own involuntary yelp, but the people immediately around me heard it and knew why. As the priest repeated the line six more times—"That's what we want today, our love with the skin on"—I could only flash back to Lauren, at that very moment with her eyes swollen shut, her body, even her head, wrapped in white webbing and Biobrane, with a breathing tube between her teeth running down into her lungs, the hissing of the ventilator accompanied by the beeping of her blood pressure and heart monitors.

I covered my face with my hands and I was sobbing over her state and her helplessness. Five pairs of hands reached out to hold me: one widow who had just beautifully eulogized her husband, the wife of my friend who'd been called downstairs by security two minutes before the first plane struck, that friend himself, the Cantor general counsel, and his wife. None of them let go of me until the final repetition of the phrase had finished echoing.

But the echoes have never truly died—they were heard again tonight, when I had my love, with the skin on.

Love,
Greg & Lauren

From: Greg
To: Everyone
Date: Thursday, December 6, 2001 10:20 AM
Subject: Lauren Update for Dec 5 (Wednesday)

Lauren's day began with the placement of an IV line in her right fore-arm. Her minor surgical procedure was scheduled for noon; the pins would be removed from the knuckles of her left hand. It took the doc-tors and nurses a long time to find a good vein, and this left her feeling stressed and lonely until her parents arrived at around 10 AM. In addi-tion, she had not eaten since midnight the night before, which was a requirement before surgery.

Right around 10, she was seen by a hand surgeon whom her doc-tor had called for a consult, something he does not typically do while a patient is still in the acute stage. (Normally such a consult would come after he or she has been through rehab.) The consulting sur-geon was unable to check Lauren's right hand because it was wrapped in a splint, but he did check her left hand. He told her that she would recover the dexterity in that hand, which I have to say is simply remarkable news. She will not have full function because she is missing parts of her fingertips; but he confirmed that she will be able to grasp objects, to write, and to do most things one does with a hand. I couldn't have been happier for her; from the beginning I have feared that the injuries to her left hand would be far more severe than this. It will take a long time, but we have now heard learned opinion that she will regain good, functional use of that hand.

She was also finally measured for her permanent pressure garments.

She had to wait until 2 o'clock to go down to the OR (which all the staff says is "up," because the OR used to be on a higher floor than the Burn Center). I told her that delays happen when you're not the first case in the morning, but the two-hour wait made her anxious, and since she couldn't eat, hungry. She instructed me to have a toasted bagel with light butter, scrambled eggs, Swiss cheese, and bacon ready for her when she returned.

As she was about to be wheeled out of her room for the trip downstairs, I saw one of the other burn patients we'd met, the electrician who suffered the 65 percent burn in June but had survived and become somewhat of an inspirational speaker to other patients. I introduced Lauren to him as he approached and regretted that we would miss the chance to talk to him some more. But then Lauren's bed had to be parked in the hall for five minutes, with the two transport attendants standing by, while her nurse got Lauren an ID bracelet. This gave her time to talk to the other patient.

He stood by her side for that entire period, talking about his experience and encouraging her to be optimistic about her own. He'd suffered severe burns to his face and his vocal cords had been badly damaged; but in a hoarse whisper he told of how hard he had worked and was still working. He told Lauren to accept help from all who offered; he talked about disliking wearing the pressure garments but then coming to terms with them and growing comfortable wearing them. Underneath his baseball cap, ski jacket, plaid shirt, and black jeans, he was wearing a full face mask with eye, nostril, and mouth openings, a zip-up turtleneck undershirt with long pressure sleeves, gloves, and presumably leggings. Lauren smiled broadly at him and thanked him for speaking with her; they wished each other the best.

And then it was finally time for her to go to the OR. Once again I walked her to the elevator and stood at the door as it closed, waving to her and wishing her good luck. Then I headed off to fetch the toxic bagel.

The procedure was successful. The pins came out of the fingers on her left hand but stayed in her left thumb because the knuckle joint there seemed as if it was still at risk of opening. (The joint could part and the skin would split above the knuckle.)

She had some apple juice as soon as she returned, and then about half an hour later, sampled the scrambled egg, cheese, and bacon bagel. It met with her initial approval, though she ate only half of it and her stomach was a bit unsettled as the evening came on.

Just before 8 o'clock, one of the nurses advised me that someone wanted to drop something off for Lauren; it was Gary Lambert, her office mate from work. I told Lauren he was in the waiting room but had not asked to see her, and she said, "I'll see him." Kareen, who'd just arrived, made Lauren a new bed with fresh sheets, put a new gown on her, and got her ready to receive her first nonfamily, non-burn-community visitor.

I went down and told him what was about to happen, and he was thrilled. I showed him how to put on the cap, gown, and gloves, and brought him down the hall. He'd been in Lauren's room once, just days after September 11, so he had seen her during the most difficult part of her fight, but she had not been aware of him. This time she was in her bed, smiling, wearing the NYPD cap on her head. She had a nickname for him: "Guy," the French guy (and the French pronunciation).

She said "Guy," and then she started to cry, saying she was so happy to see him. She was very emotional, telling him she'd missed him; he was a bit emotional too, speaking of how touched he'd been that she'd asked about him during the early hours at St. Vincent's.

"We lost so many friends," she said, "so many friends," and she was sobbing for a bit; but she was also happy to see him, so then she relaxed. She learned he'd just gotten off an express bus at Vesey Street and was a block away from the building; just a brief walk from being where she was when the plane hit.

"Two minutes, for me," she said. "Two more minutes and I would have been dead. And five minutes for you."

I told him he could rest his gloved hand on her right forearm as they spoke, and I placed his hand there, below the splint and above the IV needle. He kept his hand there for the entire fifty minutes they talked.

He told her that all the market data people ask about her, and all the traders at other firms, too, as well as everyone at Cantor. He told her that he is completely dedicated to building on the business plan and strategy she laid out; he said he realized how much he learned from working with her the past few years, and especially during the past few months.

"You gave me a great foundation," he said.

In fact, the business that Lauren was preparing to lead will be huge. Among the many things she's lost was the business opportunity of her lifetime: to be the lead player in generating huge new revenues in market data sales to replace the old business that came to an end in the summer of 2001 with the bankruptcy of Bridge and the sale of Tele-rate. She had the contacts and the vision; and it is probably not an exaggeration to say that she set things up so well that all Gary had to do was execute. And that he does, working twelve hours a day every day. He is on a mission to make things work, on his own behalf as well as Lauren's.

They talked at length about their close friends who'd been lost and there were more tears over those, a couple of whom she hadn't thought of yet; but they also talked about Cantor's rebuilding, how former employees and new employees had come to work for the firm in memory of those who had been lost, how some of the biggest businesses had not only survived but thrived.

(This has also been true of Euro Brokers' customers; there has been tremendous support from the Street, though there are also competitors who have always wanted to take away Cantor's and Euro Brokers' businesses and haven't stopped trying now. No one expected the competition to stop; this is not a warm and fuzzy industry. But there are also many who have decided to support their team, or join it, to help it survive.)

Gary also talked about Howard Lutnick's dedication to the Cantor families, how hard he is working on their behalf, how every evening this week is being spent meeting with the families at convenient locations throughout the New York area to explain what Cantor Fitzgerald will be doing to help them. Howard has also been waiting to see Lauren; now that she has chosen to see one friend, I hope that she will have the strength to see more.

The conversation ended with Lauren telling him again how happy she was to be alive, and saying about all of those who care about her and pray for her, "I won't let you down."

And he told her she shouldn't worry about any of that. "You're alive, I'm alive. We have you—I have you, your family has you,

Greg has you. Tyler has you. We all have you. That's all that matters."

Love,
Greg & Lauren

If you were outside in New York today, then maybe you were touched by the same breezes that touched Lauren as she sat in her wheelchair at the main entrance to New York-Presbyterian Hospital, out by the black steel benches and the grass and the tree-lined traffic circle.

"I was outside, I breathed fresh air," she said. "And it gave me a sense that there's a whole world out there that I want to reconnect to."

It is hard to convey how she sometimes says these things. She starts out speaking normally and then she becomes more and more emotional and there may be tears; but they are the result of particularly intense emotion, not sadness, and they subside. She wants her life back, and she said exactly that tonight.

"I realized how far I have to go" is another thing she said.

She walked to and from the gym three times today; she did more torso stretches and she did more hand work. It is the hand work especially that tells her the distance she has to travel to get back to a space near where she was. That's why her rehab is expected to take one to two years; her hands are her real challenge. The occupational therapists have rigged up a pulley system for her fingers that I will have to help her use. I will also be helping her on and off with splints that will hold her hands and arms in different positions during different times of the day. There will be a lot of effort, but for a good cause.

While the hands will take the longest to come back, her whole body will require work, and she is already on record as wanting it to be a "work of art." Today, for the first time, she was wearing a pressure glove on her right hand (with the pinkie cut off because her right

278

pinkie still has two pins). She also had a pink silicone oval applied to her neck and the underside of her chin to soften the scar tissue; this area is beginning to harden a bit.

She will be receiving her first Jobst pressure garments in ten to fourteen days. She will also receive the face mask, which they will measure for on Monday; she will have inserts that will smooth small areas just above and just below her lips on the left side of her face. She intends to be very conscientious about this; the goal is, as she says, "a perfect face."

One of the most important things is to soften and stretch areas where scar tissue begins to build, and this is true all over her body. There are areas that were grafted almost three months ago that have had a chance to tighten, and she does stretches to break these up. I felt one such spot on her tailbone today when she asked me to knead her back.

She is able to roll on her side more easily; this is one reason the raw spots on her buttocks are healing up, finally, and closing. I stood behind her and kneaded my fingers up and down either side of her spine, very, very gently. I could tell that the muscles were not strong; her skin seemed fragile as well, newly healed there over the past three months. But with proper treatment with pressure garments and stretching, she will clearly recover. Underneath, the muscles seem healthy. So, incredibly, on December 6 I was giving her a backrub. If anything, this was more encouraging than the day before, when I touched her leg; this was the single largest graft she had received, and it was entirely closed and healed.

Earlier, during one walk to the gym, Lauren saw a friend of hers sitting in the waiting room. This is a woman who has come by the hospital and sat with me, though mostly with Lauren's parents (because they are on the day shift), since early October. She has written me beautiful letters; she has bought CDs and books for Lauren to keep in her room. She has also volunteered extensively at the Cantor Relief Fund, while trying to rebuild her own independent business.

She is a headhunter. She lost over a hundred candidates in the attacks, and she lost clients: firms that had their offices destroyed, as well as key contacts at those firms. She has been in the midst of the tragedy, seeking largely on her own to rebuild her life and her income; but she has still found the time to reach out to me and to so many others.

It seems especially fitting, therefore, that Lauren was sent past her on the way to the gym today, so she saw her. Lauren was surprised;

I've seen people I knew turn up in the waiting room for months now, but for Lauren this was an entirely new experience. She was overjoyed to see her friend and they spoke for a while; this, too, gave Lauren pangs about rejoining the world, and her life. The nice part is that the world is out there, and her life is still waiting for her.

Lauren misses Tyler a lot; she's seen him only twice, and now that she is so aware and active, she is more and more conscious that he is out there, but not with her. I reminded her that she has a lifetime ahead with him; and within a couple of months, she will be back with him for much more time than she had before, when she was both a devoted mother and a driven career woman.

We used to rush home at 5:30 to be with Tyler by 6, and every night was a three-hour love fest. Lauren would cook beautiful dinners, or we would take Tyler to a neighborhood restaurant, where he would sit in his high chair and play with a couple of teaspoons as people stopped to tell us how well behaved he was. Back home, when it came time, Lauren would take him into his room and in the darkness feed him his bottle as his eyes closed and his arms went limp and he was ready for bed. Even if he wasn't fully asleep, she would set him down and give him his blanket, and he would rock himself to sleep.

But for most of the day she'd be high up at the World Trade Center, working hard, the two of us more than eight hundred feet up in what is now blue sky. At some point, she will be able to return to work. But soon, and for a long time to come, she will be able to be with Tyler almost around the clock. I cannot think of anything more likely to provide real fuel for a speedy recovery.

She already talks of the walks they will take, Tyler and Joyce and Lauren and Kareen (to whom she said, "I want to take you out for a cup of coffee and pay for it with my own hands").

I have said many, many times since September 11 that there can be no such thing as a silver lining after such horrific events. But good things can happen afterward; you just have to mine reality long enough to find them: the tiny glimmer that tells you that a deeply held dream, not even hoped for, has finally panned out.

Love,
Greg & Lauren

(Be prepared, maybe grab a coffee; this is a long, long one.)

Lauren looked great tonight; healthy, relaxed, smiling, herself; everyone who came into the room saw the same thing. I am already so used to the pressure bandage she wears around the sides of her face that I don't really see it. But even so, she looked completely natural; free from hazard, stress, and, it seemed, from fear. And everyone who came into the room saw the same thing; her companion, her nurse, and Karen Waizer, who stopped by since Harry is back in the hospital for a couple of days for a minor procedure.

Events are speeding up now that Lauren is about to make her move; just as we are looking to leave, we are more and more active at our present location.

She was outside yesterday for the first time in eighty-six days, and now that she's had a taste of fresh air, she's ready for a real lungful. One of the most attractive things about Burke is that it is in the country (well, at least the suburbs), so when she goes outside, she will be able to relax, free of the stresses of an urban environment.

Not that she's wasting time in dreamy anticipation. As I said, a lot went on today, on both fronts, the hospital and the domestic.

Lauren's face was scanned for the clear plastic mask, the one that will be designed to fit her face exactly, to apply even pressure at all points to best fight scarring. There was a slight problem when they took the measurements, however, so she will be measured again on Monday.

She took her longest walk yet today, in the company of two of the physical therapists, wandering down the endless corridors of the hospital. I don't know exactly where she went, but this was another taste of freedom. She did the treadmill for three minutes. She did more work on her hands; she was encouraged by the way the right-hand splint had straightened her fingers the previous night.

Because of the weakness of the top of the fingers versus the inner side, her right fingertips have shown a tendency to bend at 90-degree angles while the rest of the finger remains straight. This is not a movement we can make naturally, and such damage is a key reason that the rehab of her hands will take so long: between one and two years. But just from yesterday to today she had more movement and more control. Her determination reaches from her toes to her fingertips, literally. (Because she was wearing sensible shoes on September 11, her toes were not hurt.)

The splints she is wearing now hold her fingers in a swan position (pointing straight, bent close to 90 degrees at the base knuckle—just make a swan with your hand), with the thumb free. Both her hands were loosely wrapped in dressings tonight, and I learned how to apply the two-part overnight splints. These are two plastic sleeves that surround and position her hands; they are secured with white gauze, which is wrapped onto them, starting at the middle, and then out to each end, to apply the strongest and most even pressure.

Lauren's social schedule also included a visit from the NY Firefighters Burn Center Foundation, who came by to drop off an apron, baseball cap, tennis shirt, and sweatshirt. The firefighters stayed for forty minutes, talking to Lauren about September 11; they too had lost so many friends and colleagues.

Shortly after I got there, we had the visit from Karen Waizer. Just like me, she lived at the Burn Center after September 11, the linchpin of a support group of family and friends who began with a vigil by the sedated patient's bedside, praying for his survival, and ended with relief at his imminent discharge and simultaneous apprehensiveness at the long road ahead. She also did it with three kids!

Harry, who has been at Burke, will be here only briefly; he is not even staying in the burn ward. But neither he nor Lauren will sever their connections with the Burn Center for quite some time. Lauren will be returning for clinic to have her progress assessed by her doctor, and she will do so with regularity, if decreasing frequency, for years to come.

Lauren and Karen had a lengthy conversation about Burke. The rooms are on the small side, but the care is excellent; the doctors are committed, the therapists maintain the proper balance between pushing to the limit and not exceeding it. There are many patients there who are dealing with severe problems, but it is apparently a place where they all feel at home, and encouraged.

Harry is looking forward to having Lauren there and she is looking forward to hanging out with him, and it will be great for the two of them to sit together and realize they both made it. Both are emblems of hope for Cantor Fitzgerald, and they share a singular level of traumatic experience.

Harry was on an elevator that reopened on 78 once the plane hit. Since the elevators were programmed to return to their base floor, this means he had to have been on the elevator from the 78th floor Skylobby to 105. And this also means he was seconds away—seconds—from being above the plane with no chance of escape.

Imagine being in a closed box such as this when it drops and then bursts into flame with you in it. Then imagine reacting as Harry apparently did, screaming and cursing at the fire as he tried to put it out with his hands, "You're not going to get me, you're not going to get me!" until the doors opened, breathing in the smoke of a jet fuel fire as it consumed industrial carpeting, laminated plywood, and your own clothing. Then imagine walking down seventy-eight flights of stairs before you can receive help.

In Lauren's case, imagine pushing glass and metal doors open and running outside in flames, screaming, "I'm not going to die, I'm not going to die, I'm going to live for Tyler and for Greg!"

And then dissolve to three months later, among the trees in Westchester County; as the breezes blow over you, catching a moment of quiet with someone who was truly there with you, in awe at the wonderment of your own survival and the fact that you can take this breath, smell the grass, see this blue sky.

I think it will be good for both of them.

Regarding the Burn Center, Harry shared certain likes and dislikes with Lauren, mainly for the tank. Both found the tank demeaning because of the nature of it; you are naked, in a metal tub, while teams of nurses clean and debride you and flip you over.

To top this off, at the end of the process, the patient is typically shivering with cold, and when the nurses dry you, as Lauren said, "There are never enough warm towels." As a result, the patient can lose a couple of degrees of body temperature. When Lauren was heavily sedated and this happened, they might put a heat screen above her, or a "Bair Hugger," a forced-air warming blanket where heated air is blown into ducts inside the blanket to warm the patient through convection. But once she woke up, they tended to just wrap her in ordinary blankets, and she would shiver until she warmed up.

Several days ago, Andrew was her nurse again, and he got her a Bair Hugger and left it in her room; so for the remainder of her stay we have that option to warm her.

A quick digression: the nurses told me early on that one of the things they truly look forward to is meeting the most acute patients as they are awakened from their sedation. So in recent days there has been a virtual parade into Lauren's room, on a nightly basis, of bright and smiling faces who "had her" when she faced her toughest spots, and who now come in to joke around with her. They tell her she looks great. She tells them to quit smoking, or hooks them up with real estate brokers, or tries to set them up; she is unbelievable.

I think that for the nurses, having such a directed personality appear from beneath the bandages and the bacitracin with a strong sense of humor and motivation has to be extremely rewarding. When Lauren addresses them and cracks a joke, you can see them visibly brighten and relax. It doesn't mean that she is not demanding; but it does mean that for a brief moment the nurses can legitimately enjoy laughing with someone whose life they saved.

Anyway—taking a breath—Lauren was so tired, she fell asleep at 8:30 PM. I was probably just as tired after my own day.

First, one of the bright spots: late in the afternoon I took Tyler to a birthday party in the toddler gym at Chelsea Piers. Once again there were hordes of one-year-olds, a couple more of them standing, a couple walking, crawling up the ramps and throwing the rubber balls, falling on the padded floor or knocking down structures built from multicolored paper bricks.

Tyler had two favorite toys, one a large green exercise ball, which he rolled, as if Indiana Jones had decided to start pushing around the boulder from the beginning of *Raiders of the Lost Ark*. At one point, Tyler was drumming on the green ball with both hands in a clear rhythm. I leaned over and played "Wipeout," and he started drumming with alternate hands, still keeping time.

The other favorite was a red balloon he held and bounced repeatedly off my face as I carried him around and spoke to the other parents. They were all very happy to hear the good news about Lauren and all sent her their best, even though she has yet to meet most of them.

Tyler made his usual impression; this is a direct quote and I am not making it up: one of the women said, "He looks like he could be a politician; he looks senatorial."

Speaking of government, my day began with a visit to the office of Eliot Spitzer, the New York State Attorney General. In this case, that is a literal statement. He had been forced to go to California, but he hoped that I would still meet with two aides from his office through whom I had sought the meeting. I was happy to do so, and I met the aides in the conference area of his office. My purpose was to express the needs of those critically injured on September 11, and discuss my experience, since his office was involved with making recommendations regarding the administration of government entitlements in the wake of the disaster. I met with a First Deputy Attorney General and the NY State crime victims advocate. Both women were focused and responsive. They treated me with respect and gave valuable guidance and recommendations.

Let me also tell you of my visit to the office. It is a corner suite on a twenty-something floor with a panoramic view of Ground Zero, which sits right across the street.

Since it had rained earlier, much of Ground Zero was an expanse of black mud. The wreckage has been cleared well below grade in many spots. Cracked levels of the subterranean parking garage stretch like geological layers along one side of the pit. The backhoe excavators stand with their huge grabbing shovels scratching at their feet; the dump trucks drive right to the center of the pit to be loaded with debris. Damaged buildings loom on the sides; the site looks more like pictures of the Center's early construction than it does anything else, as if we have time-traveled back thirty years, except that while towers may rise again, the people will not.

Towers One and Two have been cleared to grade, including the burnt skeletons of the lobby floors. When I was here on October 3, these same areas were solid mounds of compacted rubble rising forty to seventy feet above ground.

One office building, which used to be across from Tower Two, has a ten-foot-wide section carved out of its northern face, as if a dentist were cutting away the decay; it will be patched with metal and brick. Damage to the corner of the American Express Building in the World Financial Center caused by falling debris has been similarly trimmed.

Of course, I shouldn't have been able to see the American Express Building at all. What used to loom in front of this office window was a mass of steel and glass that towered eighty stories higher. These windows did not even look to the knees of the towers, and now they are looking to their foundations, just as they did when the towers were built.

Lauren and Harry survived forces powerful enough to bring these structures down. So did the other thousands who made it, but they were shielded; Lauren and Harry were at the edge, and, remarkably, lived to tell about it.

On the way home I tracked the perimeter of Ground Zero, wading through the crowds gathering at each offshoot west of Broadway, one hundred, two hundred people milling at each one, holding up cameras, camcorders, periscopes. The fences lining the site were covered with messages and banners with signatures just like the hall of get-well cards at the Burn Center. Further along, the top of the hurricane fence sprouted a bouquet of flowers every three feet.

I was on a cell phone call, so I was barely registering these details; I had made the walk a thousand times before, but there had always been the Trade Center there. I almost didn't realize, because my walk was relatively unimpeded, what was going on. The streets had always been similarly crowded, but with people going to work. Now they were dressed casually, and they were standing there, straining for a glimpse of history.

The madmen who did this have made this place the center of the world for a time; and all of civilization understands that what our enemies want is for all of our homes, our centers of government and culture, to resemble this blackened pit of destruction.

Not going to happen.

Love,
Greg & Lauren

Lauren and I had a date to take a walk in the afternoon. As women will, she was running a bit late getting dressed.

When I arrived, the head occupational therapist was wrapping her hands in self-adhering stretch tape. Each finger is individually wrapped, with a ridge like a Chinese dumpling; then her hands and wrist are wrapped, with web dividers between the fingers. We helped her into her American flag T-shirt and her red Eddie Bauer drawstring pants. We pulled the NYPD cap over her head, and she was ready to roll.

She stood up, and we were off to traverse the entire Burn Center. She walked with a good pace, not a full, normal stride but a steady one, distinctly not a shuffle step. Her room is at the southwest corner of the unit. With me on one side and her sister on the other, neither of us touching her, Lauren headed east along the corridor of the Burn Center, toward the southeast corner about 150 feet away.

As we passed the staff room on our right, halfway down the hall, I looked down at her feet, walking in her regular running shoes (in the end, none of the size-bigger high-tops worked).

"Honey, you beat Tyler," I said.

"I beat Tyler," she said, laughing.

We reached the end of the hall and turned north. There was another wing of rooms here, identical to the hall that Lauren had been on. There are twenty critical-care beds, for a total of forty beds in the burn ICU.

There were even more children on this wing, so we passed strollers in the halls and stuffed animals on the nurses' station as we walked toward the end of the hall, zigzagged left past the entrance to the Burn Center's gym, and continued down the hall of get-well cards.

"That's the room where my mom, my dad, you guys waited, isn't it?" she said as we passed the waiting room that had been so central to our experience when love lay sleeping, as it were, down the hall.

We turned left into the main entrance to the Burn Center,

pressed the square on the wall for the automatic doors to open, walked past the gown room, and stopped to inspect the Christmas tree, festooned with hanging ornamental cards written by school-children in that same earnest, youthful, "hope you're feeling better" penmanship.

The clerk behind the front desk was looking at us with a smile, and I realized that though he'd been there the night of September 11, had given us mail, offered us coffee, played tapes on the VCR, called in orders to change the temperature in her room, and given us an extra sheet and blanket for Lauren whenever we asked, he'd never met her. So I introduced them and he said, "Good to see you up and around."

"It's nice to meet you," she said to him as we continued down the hall past her first room, right across from the nurses' station, where she'd spent weeks with her eyes shut, not moving, webs of clear plastic lines threaded into her body, stacks of Baxter pumps feeding measured amounts of drugs and nutrition into her system, displaying the flow on their LCD screens, and monitors constantly beeping as they tracked the wave motions of her heart, her blood pressure, and her oxygen content.

Then we continued past the tank room and completed the last lap to her corner suite. Her sister stepped down the hall for something, and Lauren and I were looking at each other.

"Not bad, huh," she said.

And then she started to dance.

She moved her hips a little and her shoulders at the same time, her eyes down and a soft smile on her face, as if she were on the dance floor. Christine's CD was playing in the background with an easy dance rhythm. I started dancing too. I couldn't help thinking about the last time we'd danced; she'd been lying in bed, unable to speak or to sit up on her own, but she'd started to move her head to the music, as a form of exercise the therapists had recommended to her. The expression on her face was the same then as now, but otherwise we had come a million miles.

One of the wraps on Lauren's hand was tight, so the physical therapist came back to redo it. As she was sitting, watching her hand be rewrapped, she started to say, "I can't stand this. I can't live like this. I can't do anything for myself. I can't dress myself. I can't do anything."

And then she shook her head and went "Aaaaaaaaaah" in almost a normal tone of voice, though this was clearly a primal scream of frustration.

The therapist told her, "You couldn't walk, you couldn't talk," by way of indicating how far she'd come. I told her that she would be able to do everything she wanted but had to give it time. She'll be able to do everything she wants to do, just not by 6 PM tonight. She calmed down, though she did ask for some anti-anxiety medication.

Just after 5 PM, Howard Lutnick stopped by to see Lauren, awake, for the first time. (He'd come once a couple of weeks ago, before she moved her room, but she was not yet seeing anyone outside her family. This time he came by invitation.) The last time he saw her, two weeks earlier, she was still sedated; he'd stood by her bed, leaned down, and found ten different ways to say he and everyone at Cantor Fitzgerald loved her. This time he appeared in the doorway in surgical cap and hospital gown, and Lauren said hi, and I waved him in, and he leaned over Lauren's bed and she leaned up to hug him, and cried into his shoulder.

He stepped back and showed her a new baseball cap he'd brought her. On the front it said "Cantor Fitzgerald," on the back, "United We Stand."

"I read that you were wearing FDNY and NYPD caps, and I had to bring you a Cantor one," he said.

Lauren put it on and said, "Check this out," and she rolled a bit to her side, sat up, and stood on the floor.

"Well, you're better." He looked at me, and he was laughing. "This is a lot better."

Lauren hugged him and thanked him for standing by her, and she cried very hard again; this would happen several times in the next hour, though there were also moments of laughter.

He said he really missed her; the market data business could certainly use her, especially now, when it is really beginning to move. She said, "I waited years—years!—for the market data opportunity, and I built it all up to get it ready, and then this happened."

They remembered Howard's brother, who died on September 11, Lauren saying how she and Gary had grown much closer over the past year, and he had really "settled into himself."

Howard talked about succeeding in the initial stages of rebuilding Cantor; it was working because he was willing to accept a smaller firm with a narrower focus. His priorities are his family, his employees, and the families of the people he lost, and the only way he can help them is if he keeps the company a going concern—and not just able to survive, but to thrive. (He has received thousands of resumés from people seeking to work at Cantor; but of course has practically no one to review them for him.)

He talked, as I have, about how terrific an environment the World Trade Center had become. Their offices were beautiful, the stores and the area were great, the view was spectacular even on a bad day. But now, through this disaster, he said, Cantor has been knocked off the top of the mountain, quite literally.

"Well, you have a choice," he said. "You can either try to climb back up the mountain, and maybe in five years you'll be where you were; or you can strap on skis and ski on down."

The second way is definitely easier.

He spoke in some depth about the success of the Cantor Relief Fund, but since I don't remember all the facts or the numbers, I don't want to get any of them wrong. He is making the effort to help the families that he promised to make. I have always strongly believed that he would fulfill those commitments.

We did talk a bit of the hard road Lauren faces, and he said to her, "It's hard to say you're lucky, but think of how many people would love to be in your position right now. You can see Tyler, and he will see you, forever. That's a gift."

Lauren said, "I won't fail. My life is going to mean something."

Howard told her, "When you're ready to come back, I'll have a desk all shined up and ready for you. It doesn't matter when it is—don't worry about that. You're mine."

In 1993, Lauren recalled, things had gone a bit differently. Howard had kept her waiting an hour and a half to be interviewed. She'd decided she'd had enough, stood up, and walked out. Howard ran after her and caught her at the elevator; the same elevator shaft through which the fireball descended in 2001. If he doesn't catch her at that moment, none of this happens; we're not married, there's no Tyler. A tiny event that I wasn't even aware of seems to have determined the course of all our lives.

Many of you may have read last week's *New York* magazine article, where Howard was quoted as celebrating that "Lauren Manning walked forty feet."

Lauren had heard about this; so tonight, when it was time for him to leave, she stood up and we walked him all the way to the visitor elevators, more than two hundred feet away. After they had hugged and he had gotten on the elevator to go down, she quipped, "I wanted him to see that I can walk more than forty feet."

That is the combativeness, playful this time, that's gotten her this far, and she had enough of it left to make it back to her room. But she was a bit fatigued, so the nurse came in to help her and to give her some scheduled medication. There was an old woman in the room next door to Lauren, Harry's old room; she had been cooking one night and her clothes caught fire. She'd been fighting a hard battle but had seemed to be losing. Burns are just very hard on the elderly, and she was eighty-eight or eighty-nine years old. The curtain to her room had been closed most of the day.

Lauren asked how the woman was, and in a quiet voice, the nurse said, "She passed away."

Lauren began to cry. "Someone died right next door to me," she said.

I thought immediately that I had seen it happen a number of times before; if not next door, then certainly just a few rooms down; but of course I couldn't tell her that. The nurse explained that the woman had tried, but she was very old and burns were very tough. The woman's family had written a DNR, so when she entered a life-threatening crisis, she was allowed to slip away. I had heard one of the attendings paged earlier; I had seen doctors go in and out of the room; it had seemed that something not good was going on, but I felt it was none of my business.

It is my business only in one sense; we can be fooled by the spectacular East River view, by Lauren's progress, and by the love that so many on the unit feel for her, into thinking that this has become a benign place for her to be. It's not. She does not belong here a moment longer than she needs to be.

Exhausted by her most active day yet, Lauren fell fast asleep, and I headed home for my first night alone in my apartment since September 11. Lauren's parents are staying elsewhere in the New York area for her final few days at the Burn Center.

Tyler was there, of course, but otherwise it was just me; no one else in the bedroom. The place seemed bigger and a lot more lonely. I don't think I could have handled it on September 11, or anytime soon thereafter. Three months later, I was subdued but OK. It was also the first time I'd slept in a real bed since September 11—I've been sleeping on the sofa bed in the den.

It was quiet, but I knew that soon enough it would be crowded, that Lauren would be here with Tyler, and the sound of laughter would echo off the walls. She had prayed to survive; her prayers had been answered.

Last night, I thought of how many prayers of how many other victims would never be answered, and I understood that what was lurking all around me, the looming presence in the dark rooms lit only by the streetlights outside, the sense that suffused the bedroom when I finally closed my eyes and slept in my own bed, was hope.

Love,
Greg & Lauren

From: Greg
To: Everyone
Date: Monday, December 10, 2001 1:28 AM
Subject: Lauren Update for Dec 9 (Sunday)

The process of moving out has begun and it's more substantial than you would expect. Lauren has accumulated a fair bit of stuff over the previous three months; CDs, cassettes, videos, books, various sundries, pajamas, T-shirts, baseball caps, posters, photographs, and hundreds of cards and notes.

We did some packing; the cards came down today, leaving the walls bare; the videotapes and the books came home, along with some of the loose-fitting clothing she will be wearing at Burke.

So much of the world has moved on since September 11, but in so many ways I haven't. I have thought of it, often, as a "bipolar" disorder; I have existed in two distinct places, the hospital and my apartment, for twelve weeks, driving my car from parking garage to parking garage with a few detours, and losing track of almost everything but news about the war, the Yankees, and Lauren.

I have gotten to know the security guards at the hospital, and the parking attendants. I know most of the nurses on the ward and most of the doctors; I have gotten used to things that would have been overwhelming and unimaginable on September 10, and are now part of our lives. Contact precautions (gowns, gloves, caps), burn pathology, the coming and going of critically ill patients, the sensation of walking by room after room where patients lie sedated and unaware as their bodies fight to live.

I cannot even remember how I felt on September 10; I can barely remember that world. While I can recall what happened the day and the night before the attacks, those moments seem to have come from another era. All I am aware of is going to the hospital and spending weeks trying to figure out the fastest route across town. Now that I have it figured out, the logistics of Westchester will be entirely different. But Lauren is back; she will walk out of the ward, and when she does, she will be a miracle. Finally, we get to move on.

Lauren had an eventful day, but I was home doing laundry so I missed most of it; a friend dropped by with a gift, and a couple who had sent Lauren American flag T-shirts but had never met her before came. I'm sorry I missed seeing them, but at least I know where those T-shirts have been coming from. She did her hand work and did some walking; by the time I got there, she was cocooned under a blanket and ready to rest for a bit.

We've had dinner together every day for the past month; much of the time I've shared her hospital meal, though the past few evenings we've ordered in, like any New York couple.

Tonight we got Japanese. Lauren had a craving for sushi, but raw fish is out of the question; so we settled for shrimp and vegetable tempura, stir-fried vegetables and dumplings. The previous two nights we ordered in from Brunelli's, an Italian restaurant at 75th and York that has donated a lot of food to Christine's volunteer effort. It was her idea, but it was their pastafagiole; and I highly recommend it.

Later we watched *Giant*, on TCM, and it held Lauren's interest for the full three and a half hours.

Before the movie Lauren and I did a lot of talking, mostly her giving me a to-do list (train schedules, packing of clothing and sundries, the logistics of who rides in the ambulance with her and who follows in the car). If it weren't for the hospital gowns and bouffant caps, you could have mistaken it for a typical domestic scene. In the middle of it all, though, I looked at her; I'd just fed her the tempura and helped her take some pills by mouth; and I looked down at her face, and I said to her, "You are amazing. Just amazing. You are so beautiful."

I got a beautiful smile back.

I told her, I didn't want to wear her out with it, but again, I loved her. I have already confessed I didn't do this enough before the terrible disaster that brought her here; but now I get such joy out of it, because it is not only fun to say, it is also fun to be able to say it and to have her hear me.

I said, "You're my wife."

"Yeah, a wife who can't dress herself or feed herself."

"But you will, you will. You will get all of that back."

"Yeah, in a year."

"But we know that. We just have to gut it out, and a year from now, maybe that's when the fun starts. Not before. But you have no idea how far you will go in the next year. You have really been so lucky."

She agreed, talking about how she has her sight, her hearing, her sense of smell, the ability to taste, to speak, to walk; she will come out of this with all of those intact.

"I've been here every day," I said.

"I know. Thank you for staying by my side," she said, and the emotions welled over again.

"Of course," I said. "I'll always be by your side; I'll take care of you, I'll protect you."

"Oh, Greg, I love you so much," she said. "We have to stay together, we have to grow old and die together in a bed someday."

"Let's not rush that day," I said, "but yes, we will."

Love,
Greg & Lauren

I got to the hospital today at 9:45 AM, because this time I was going to experience all of Lauren's day; instead of missing it, I would see every aspect of her rehab exercises. Also there to observe, dressed in gray Burn Center scrubs and taking detailed notes, were two occupational therapists from Burke, who had driven down for a day-long training session in Lauren's rehab. They will be responsible for this work for at least the next month.

As I have noted, Burke does not specialize in burn rehab per se; it is an acute medical rehabilitation facility that treats a wide variety of traumatic injuries, including spinal cord trauma and stroke. Burn patients are not a large category for them; but their rehab is very demanding. The Burke staff may be aware of the full list of things that need to be done but may not have had many patients who need all of it at once, like Lauren. This may be analogous to the situation when St. Vincent's, after admitting her, had to research the steps of burn protocol because it is not something they do every day. Also, the Burke therapists may not realize how far Lauren is willing to push herself, or how far through pain it is all right to let her push; so the training session will help by establishing the norms for her and clearly delineating the goals.

Lauren's injury is so widespread that it involves most of what the physical and occupational therapists do at the Burn Center. A couple of the most acute things she doesn't need: help with swallowing, for example. But others she does; she did suffer partial finger amputations, and she was burned on every limb and the entire back of her body. She needs arm work, leg work, hand work, torso work, range-of-motion exercises on every limb and joint except her knees; she needs to improve her stamina (she has already recovered her balance), and she needs to correct her posture where the scar tissue limits it. She has to do so many things that, as the occupational therapist said, Lauren has come to take up the largest part of her day.

Today I would see the full extent of that work.

Before Lauren gets out of bed to walk, the therapists help stretch her legs and ankles. She then sits up under her own power, using her elbows to prop her and the weight of her legs as a counterbalance to reach a sitting position. She then slides her feet onto the floor, stands, and walks.

The first step on today's itinerary was on the 18th floor of the main hospital building, in the hospital's main PT gym, an aerie of healing with a three-sided panoramic view of Manhattan. To get there, Lauren led us down the hall from the Burn Center, around several bends, to an elevator with a blue door and the words "Patients Only" stenciled in white block capitals. She did this with her steady gait, resolute, in expansive good humor. We took the elevator up the ten floors to the gym.

Sunlight filled the room, giving a very cheerful character to the mat beds and exercise equipment that various patients, dressed in sweats, worked at. Lauren was wearing her black Danskin yoga pants with a gray terry-cloth waistband and drawstrings, Lycra yoga top with wide, three-quarter-length sleeves, and her tan baseball cap with a blue and black Cantor Fitzgerald logo.

In a small office at the back of this room, Lauren again had her face optically scanned for the silicone-lined mask she will wear to control facial scarring. This time the scans went well.

While we waited for this to be completed, I recognized one of the physical therapists who'd been on the burn unit until two weeks earlier. She'd said good-bye and wished us well; it was good to see her here. She gave me a hug, and said Lauren looked terrific.

"I remember the first day, when she came in," the therapist said. "I have to tell you, I didn't think she was going to make it. And now look at her."

"I never lost faith," I said.

"No, you didn't, and neither did she."

Lauren did some brief work on her legs, and then stood up to head out. As she did, another therapist, also from the burn unit, came in, sporting a dark tan from a week in Aruba. She was the woman who had run the New York City Marathon in honor of Lauren, and she brought us pictures. In one, she stands next to another woman; both are wearing red T-shirts. Across the back of her shoulders, the therapist had a white banner saying "In Honor of Lauren Manning, WTC Survivor." The other woman wore a similar white banner, this one reading "9-11-01."

After this session it was back to the Burn Center. When we reached Lauren's room, it was time for lunch, so we took a break.

She asked me to run out and get the lunch she was craving: one hot dog with mustard, one with mustard and relish, a knish with mustard, and a ginger ale. I headed downstairs to the corner hot dog guy.

As I stepped out of the main entrance to the hospital, I ran into a man who'd visited Lauren in the early days; he'd worked in Cantor's deposits business, and been let go in August. When I last saw him, he had been on the verge of tears in the waiting room; deeply religious, he had come to give me Lauren's first mass card, and told me that she'd been chosen to survive. (He was trying to come to grips with the feeling that he, too, had been so chosen, because if he'd still worked at Cantor, he'd have been at his desk and died on September 11.) This time he was wearing a suit and looked more relaxed. I asked him to walk me across the street; he wound up buying Lauren's lunch.

I brought the hot dogs upstairs and asked him to wait in the waiting room; I said Lauren might want to see him if she knew he was there. He was surprised; he'd really come to see me, since Lauren has seen only a few close friends outside her family. He had not thought there would be an opportunity to see her. I left him with his own two hot dogs and told him I'd check and see how Lauren felt about it.

When I got to her room, she already had a visitor, the woman from Milwaukee who'd come by the day before. This time I remembered who the woman was; she and her husband run a camp for children who have survived being burned. After reading Lauren's story in *The New York Times,* they had sent two American flag T-shirts along with the copy of their photo book showing beautiful pictures of these children.

The woman had been scheduled on a morning flight home, but had woken up at 3 AM certain that she had to see Lauren one more time. She'd gone to Tiffany's and bought two silver bracelets, each with an oval American flag pendant. She gave one to Lauren, and told her that she would wear the other one until Lauren returns home.

Lauren wore hers all day, even under her splints.

As the woman was preparing to leave for the airport, I started feeding Lauren her lunch, building up in fat content from the single hot dog with mustard to the deep-fried knish. Since her metabolism is still so elevated—her heart rate dwells in the high nineties—and she is still rebuilding so much tissue, she can eat anything she wants, and does. I told Lauren her friend from Cantor was in the waiting room, and she said she would see him, so I asked the woman if she would mind sending him in on her way out.

He came in, and again there was sadness; Lauren learned of the death of a man she'd known at work whose daughter had died of cancer in the past year. Lauren burst into tears at the news. But the visitor was able to say that the man's wife has been amazing; she has a surviving daughter, and she has been steadfast through the tragedy. After losing two out of four members of her family in less than a year, she takes comfort in her faith, though the pain must be immense.

They talked more about the tragedy that hit Cantor Fitzgerald on that grim day; and Lauren said, as she has before, "I dedicate my life to everyone who died. I won't fail."

"You were chosen, I have no doubt about it," he said.

Being a man of such deep faith himself, he asked for permission to pray by Lauren's side. He knelt by her bed; I placed his hand on her arm, and he started softly reciting a prayer. Her eyes were closed. She listened to the entire prayer and with a relaxed smile told him that it had been beautiful.

After lunch, Lauren took a ten-minute nap; she told me she had never done this in the afternoon and was actually starting to really fall asleep, but we were due back in the gym for part two of her rehab.

This was the hand work. She sits in a chair and places her forearms and hands on a small therapy table in front of her. The OT sits on the opposite side and starts to work with each finger, each knuckle joint, stretching and limbering them, massaging the wrist, working, increment by increment, to help Lauren recover full dexterity. More than any other exercise, the pain involved with this brings moans of pain and tears to her eyes.

Before she sat down for this, Lauren said, "Let the torture begin."

It took an hour. Some fingers needed the bend improved; others needed straightening. The work is very delicate, yet it is among the most important of any Lauren does.

We use our hands constantly, every moment of every day from infancy onward. We type, we pick up the phone; we tap our fingers together, grab change out of our pocket. Beyond the basics such as dressing ourselves and grooming, our hands do the subtlest work, and make almost everything possible.

Lauren has practically none of this capability now; her hands are by far her worst injury, suffered, she thinks, as she pushed superheated metal doors open to get outside and escape the flames. What she touched was hotter than a branding iron; it's a miracle that she may recover to the extent they expect.

Just a small window into what she faces opened when the OT sought to bend the big knuckle at the base of each finger to 90 degrees; the skin on the back of Lauren's right hand actually blanches; She has to fight tightness and trauma in the tendon and the healing skin in order to permit the small muscles of her fingers to do their work.

One contraption that looks like the misplaced hand of a robotic marionette is a splint with individual wire pulleys for each finger on her right hand. This instrument permits the therapist to set a graduated constant tension to limber Lauren's fingers over some fixed period of time. The therapist described it as a specialized torture device.

After the hand rehab, Lauren worked on her torso; this will be a real challenge as well, since her back, she says, is "starting to feel like armor." Scar tissue grows for a year to a year and a half, like a long echo of a cataclysmic bang; but Lauren is going to be conscientious and fight it every step of the way. At one point, one of the therapists kneeled on the mat behind Lauren and placed the top of her head against Lauren's spine, helping Lauren to bend forward to stretch the skin on the base of her back.

When the session was over, Lauren walked back to her room, exhausted, and proceeded to catch a one-hour nap.

For dinner we decided to have the pastafagiole from Brunelli's, and we were about to order it at around 5:45 PM, when Christine showed up with a Starbucks shopping bag and three fresh croissants. She told me she would be bringing pastafagiole; I told her we were just about to order it for dinner. She said don't, she would take care of it; and about half an hour later, she returned with five cups of it.

I fed Lauren spoonfuls, alternating with spoonfuls to myself, making sure that Lauren always had some pasta; she doesn't like it when it's all beans. I got to thinking about what a coincidence it was that the soup had been delivered to us, and then I remembered the magical crosstown bus, and I thought about how God is in every one of the details in this story.

God brought us Lauren's fiery exit from the building, still alive, with a chance to survive; he brought her the man who rescued her and put her on the ambulance; he brought us her doctor, who performed eight surgeries to graft her skin, close her wounds, and preserve as much hand function as he could. I stroke and caress areas where he excised burned tissue, stripping it away like a damaged film, and reapplied enough of her healthy skin for it to adhere, grow, and cover her, so that she could become whole again.

God brought us the nurses on the unit who managed to follow her twenty-four hours a day, every second, catching every emergency before it became lethal. God brought us the love, support, and prayers of our families, friends, and coworkers, and then larger and larger segments of the world; God brought us Lauren's overnight companion, Kareen, who entered our lives the very evening that Lauren's eyes were wide with terror at the thought of spending another night alone in this ICU to which she'd only just awakened.

Tonight God, seeing much of his work done, brought us pastafagiole.

Later on, several nurses stopped in to start saying good-byes; one of them, the Dungeons and Dragons guy, told her with a very broad smile, "You've overstayed your welcome."

I think she has, but only at the ICU, not on earth. I have to echo what her visitor said today: she was chosen, somehow, and has inspired so many, starting with me. And that may be all she has to do; there is no requirement that she go on to be anything other than what she was when she entered that building on September 11—a loving wife and mother, a determined businesswoman. I do not intend to claim any divine knowledge; I don't have the experience. But I know how I feel.

I forgot to write, yesterday, one of the most emotional things Lauren and I said to each other:

"Of all the people on earth, Lauren, God chose you that day."

"I know, I know," she said, tears of joy and gratitude welling from her eyes. "Thank you, God, thank you for my life."

Love,
Greg & Lauren

This was a historic day, and began that way with a worldwide moment of silence. Lauren had the TV on and, because she could not get to the remote, found herself watching the national and global commemorative services of the September 11 evil.

I entered her room to find her crying, saying, "They're doing it again."

I looked at the screen and saw a bombed-out Pentagon, then President Bush speaking, and for a moment I thought there had been another attack. But the images of the Pentagon were from September 11, and President Bush was speaking at today's service.

Lauren was very agitated as she watched the world commemorate the moment she was so savagely attacked.

I asked her, "Do you have to watch this?"

"I want to," she said.

"But you don't have to," I said. "We can get the tape." And I switched it off.

Her mood improved immediately, and we set about the business of packing the last of her things, because today was the day she was scheduled to leave the hospital.

We were busy in her room, helping to dress her. It had rained on my drive to the hospital, but the sun was back out and the view of the East River must have been beautiful; but none of us was looking at it. She chose a white T-shirt, red drawstring yoga pants, and her tan Cantor hat. She was wearing the custom-fitted pressure bandage that encircled her face (and it was still very tight; all these will take some getting used to), with a clear silicone rubber insert underneath to soften the scar tissue beneath her lower lip and under the left side of her chin. Underneath her T-shirt she wore a cerulean blue Jobst vest, a very Jetsons palette that she did not choose herself.

In an early, quiet moment shortly after I got there, Lauren's doctor had come in to say good-bye (at least until her clinic appointment back at the hospital next Monday). He saved her life, and he did it methodically, in the OR, and during rounds on the Burn Center floor. He managed her medications, and her antibiotics; he managed the hiring of the nurses and therapists who worked with her; but most of all, he stood in the operating room and cut away the bad and rebuilt the good, bit by laborious bit. She is the shining example of his finest work.

She knows this. Today she said to him, "Thank you. Thank you for saving my life."

Her face turned a deep red, as it does now when she is experiencing strong emotions, and she was sobbing; and he put his gloved hand on her shoulder, comforting her in one of the kindest gestures I've seen a doctor perform.

Later, he sent me an e-mail, writing that the empty room meant success, but also sadness that there was no one in there to spar with. "At multidisciplinary rounds on Monday there was a spontaneous round of applause when it was announced that Lauren would be going to Burke the following day. I suppose that each member of the team was applauding each other. Thanks to your support and Lauren's fortitude, we are all proud."

Now we were packing her things; one brown paper shopping bag was filled with wound care supplies, bandages, bacitracin, special nonstick dressings; another bag was filled with scar management items, Tubi Grips, silicone rubber, Elta moisturizing cream. Her yoga fashions were in a red SportSac; her sundries in a smaller plaid bag, some other supplies in a brand-new Swiss Army knapsack her friend from Milwaukee had also brought her the day before. All of this was loaded on a wheelchair as if it were an airport luggage cart, because Lauren wasn't being wheeled out, she was walking out.

Lauren's nurse today was Andrew, the first person I saw on the Burn Center floor on September 11, who watched Lauren's gurney arrive and shouted "Next!" Today he wrote up Lauren's discharge papers, reviewed them with me, and for the final time at New York-Presbyterian Hospital, I signed on her behalf.

We milled for a bit outside her room. I said good-bye to the chaplain. Lauren's doctor returned, because we'd asked him to come back just before we left; we thanked him again and Lauren had tears in her eyes, though this time she stood and hugged him. The three of us spoke a bit more and he said to me, "This is a long way from the time we stood in the waiting room and I told you what to expect in her burn care."

The two EMTs came down the hall in their dark blue uniforms, soft-spoken and considerate, the same manners and competence as so many rescuers who were lost. Lauren introduced herself. They brought over a gurney, because they would need to strap her into it to take her through the doors of the hospital and load her in the ambulance; but she would walk out the front door of the Burn Center.

And no sooner had the moment come than she raised her arms and said, "That's it. Ninety days to the day, and we're getting out of here."

And she started walking down the hall, accompanied by one of the EMTs as the other one followed with the gurney. I trailed, pushing the wheelchair, and suddenly tears filled my eyes. Lauren had lain in bed for weeks, but I'd walked these halls hundreds of times; so the departure hit me not in the room, but as I headed down the main corridor past the two nurses' stations. There were scores of people I should be saying good-bye to, scores who'd saved Lauren, who'd consoled me, who'd told me the truth but given me reasons to hope, from the resolute associate director of the unit who'd said they didn't want the bastards of September 11 to get another victim, to all the nurses who'd lovingly cared for her.

I was overcome. I'd expected joy, but instead, it all came rushing back to me, how unlikely an outcome this was; Lauren literally walking out, refusing the gurney, leading her entourage into the future. We were leaving. We'll be back but it will be different; she'll be a recovering patient, my miracle, their miracle. All embodied in this five-foot-four-inch lady with her pressure garments, yoga outfit, and Cantor hat.

In the end, I turned toward Andrew to shake his hand, and suddenly I gave him a powerful hug, and said thank you for everything. He wished us good luck. He was standing less than thirty feet away from where he'd been standing on that long-ago evening.

I continued down the hall. The physical and occupational therapists were gathered at the front desk, and Lauren stopped to hug each of them; and then she walked out the front door into the hall of get-well cards. We followed her to the patient elevators.

I remember entering the Burn Center through the same inner hallways, following her gurney, thinking she would not make it, having the weight hit me as she was finally in the care of the only people who could save her. Now she led us out, and then we were riding down in possibly the same elevator car. I reached across and gave her a gentle high-five.

She left the hospital the same way she'd entered, through the ambulance bay, where on September 11 people stood in stunned silence as Lauren was unloaded and rolled into the door amid a quiet so complete, you could hear the wheels creaking. This time as she lay in the back of the ambulance, she was waving joyfully and calling people's names.

I remembered Jennieann, Inga, Dolores, René, and the others who did not make it, who came through that same door in the same way as Lauren, with loving, desperate families fervently hoping for the impossible, for all of them to survive. How hard each of them had wished for a day like this.

I followed the ambulance out of the hospital entrance and onto the FDR. The ambulance drove with its lights flashing but no siren; I rode behind it with my headlights on and hazards blinking. Three cars still managed to cut between us as we drove north to White Plains, and after waiting for the ambulance to start the siren and cut through traffic so they could illegally follow it, they gave up and went around it. We arrived at Burke, and Lauren was in her room shortly before noon.

Burke's sixty-acre campus is fronted by a grand redbrick building in the Federal style, with six white columns and a bell tower above. Behind this research facility stands the hospital, a three-story structure with long, long arms. Inside, it is clean and bright; patients in wheelchairs sit in the hallways, older people with walkers amble slowly through the corridors. As Lauren was wheeled in, the staff stopped as we passed and said, "Welcome to Burke."

Lauren's room was indeed small, reminding me of a college dorm room ready for its new occupant. It has a vanity sink, a large mirror above it, a bathroom with a toilet and a shower; there is also a hospital bed, a pedestal dresser, a closet with sliding plastic shelves, and a regular coat closet. Lauren has given up the East River view but looks out on a lawn and a playground and gets good afternoon sun.

The nurses wear varied jackets, no more gray scrubs. They are reassuringly attentive and responsive. They know that they have a bit to learn about Lauren's burn care, and expect to master this quickly. (It was fortunate that Kareen was there overnight, because she had to show the night nurses how to do Lauren's dressings.) They have made life far easier for Lauren; within an hour, there was a technician in to set up a device that permitted her to control the television, call for the nurse, and even answer the phone, by puffing on a straw. Such a device is used by people with irreversible spinal cord injuries; fortunately, thanking God again, in Lauren's case it is only for a few days, or weeks, at most. Now she can change the channel herself.

There is a library downstairs, and they gave Lauren a device that props up a book and permits her to turn the pages so that she can read, something she has missed. She picked a Kay Scarpetta mystery she hadn't yet read, and was starting it when I left in the evening.

Her new doctor, the rehab specialist, came by shortly after we were settled in the room, and reviewed Lauren's medical history and chart. He is extremely genial, and seems quite dedicated; when she had a craving for french fries, he picked up the phone and ordered them delivered to her room. He wanted to review her medications with her, and what her physical requirements are; he talked about the staff there coming up to speed, and reassured her that they would learn everything they needed to about her special case, and would be completely dedicated to her rehabilitation.

I met him in the hallway sometime later, and we had a long and good discussion. Lauren is the second September 11 patient they've admitted, the first being Harry Waizer.

Later that night the doctor examined Lauren fully, and said of the work done to fix her at the Burn Center: "Simply remarkable."

I was cheered by my first impressions of the facility. Lauren and I took a pleasant walk to the library, and to a sunlit sitting room with a huge bay window overlooking trees and grass. It was the two of us, out for a stroll. We had left the acute care facility for a place where everyone was expected to last through the night. The Burn Center is about life and death. This place is about making it back all the way.

I mentioned that Lauren's room has a mirror. Today she saw her reflection for the first time. The occupational therapist at the Burn Center had urged her to do this soon, so she would understand what she faces in scar management. Her face is not dis-figured, but the formation of small scars is dragging a bit at her lower lip. I have said it is the same face, and it will be; but she had not seen it since she finished putting on her makeup on September 11.

Her reaction was simply to ask for the silicone gel band that she needed to wear over her upper lip. She saw where it would help her; as predicted, she saw what she was up against. Her hair is darker than its normal shade, as a result of the trauma. Her skin is far more pink than it was. She does not have all of her left ear. But the expression in her eyes is the same; her smile is the same. So there were no tears; if anything, there was just a touch more resolve.

She is on the road now. From September 11 to December 11, Tuesday to Tuesday, Lauren never stopped fighting. She says the battle continues; I tell her the war's over, and she's won; she is now the conquering hero.

Over dinner tonight in Westchester, Lauren and I spoke again of September 11. She knew I was originally going to the conference at Windows on the World on the 11th. She knew that she ran late the morning of the fateful day.

"Thank God you didn't go to that meeting," she said, referring to the conference at Windows. "We would have gone in together. We would have shared a cab. I would have been on 105, you'd have been on 107, and we'd both be dead, and our little boy—our little boy wouldn't have any parents."

Even now I cannot stop the tears; I've written about it, talked about it. But today she and I shared the thought; I looked at her, and she looked at me, and we were both alive, and our little boy has both of us.

The most horrible visions of which I am capable certainly happened to people I knew and that Lauren knew; we cannot stop thinking of what might have been.

But I didn't go that morning, and she did run late; and I did find her. A tag team of angels brought her back to me and kept her alive for our boy.

"I just love you, Lauren. You don't know."

She looked at me and started to cry again; neither of us can help ourselves these days.

"I'm so glad we found each other," she said.

"You're here," I said. "You're safe. And you're not going anywhere."
She said, "Except home."

Love,
Greg and Lauren

From: Greg
To: Everyone
Date: Tuesday, December 18, 2001 12:05 AM
Subject: A Note from Lauren

Hello Everyone.

Finally, a word from the patient.

I'm struggling right now to find words because it's impossible to really put on paper the gratitude I feel for the love, the caring, the support, and the prayers that you have all provided.

My very existence has been buoyed by the wonderful messages and gifts that you have sent.

I love you all, and everything that you have done for me, and continue to do, helps make each day be a bit easier to take.

As you know, I am at Burke. We are working on my rehab very vigorously. Although I will never look quite the same, I know in my heart that I had a calling to live, and with that I will strive to help others who have endured similar struggles.

God bless and keep each one of you in good health—

All my love,
Lauren

Afterword

"I WISH MY TEARS COULD
WASH AWAY MY SCARS"

Burke Rehabilitation Hospital in suburban White Plains, New York, sits on the top of a high green hill that rises gently for more than a quarter of a mile from Mamaroneck Avenue. The main building, the one in the brochure photograph, contains research offices and laboratories, and fronts a colonnade that connects to Building 7, the patient hospital, on the other side of a green parade ground.

The hospital is a more modern, rectangular building. The ground floor houses some administrative offices, the department for therapeutic recreation, the occupational and physical therapy departments, and the patient gymnasium. There is a coffee shop down the hall from the security desk, and a library where patients can check out books or use a PC to access the Internet or send e-mail. One flight up are three long wings of patient rooms, each a distinct unit with its own staff of nurses, techs, and nursing aides, anchored at the south end by a fourth wing containing the cafeteria and the hospital kitchen. The sitting room is just to the left of the elevators.

Lauren's room was one of the six private rooms at the far end of the west wing, and I found her there at the end of her first full day. She had been in therapy from 8 in the morning until 4. She was very tired, and by the time I arrived, she'd had dinner and was resting.

Since she could not use her hands for any but the most rudimentary activities, I offered to help her change out of her clothes. When I was taking off the light blue Jobst vest she was wearing, I accidentally snagged the pin that still remained in her right pinkie.

I saw her flinch. The pin was sticking up like a blunt needle. Since September 11, I had tried to protect her from anything that might cause her pain or compound her injuries; now it seemed as if I'd done exactly that myself.

The doctors examined Lauren and did not think it was serious, but they said she would need an X ray and would have to go back to Manhattan to see Dr. Yurt. She stayed calm, reassuring me that it didn't hurt, but she was anxious about missing a day of rehab. Fortunately, that didn't happen. Instead, Dr. Yurt came up to Burke himself the following evening, sparing her the ambulance ride and saving her the therapy day. He took a look at the X rays, examined her finger, and asked if she was having any pain. As she said no, he took the protruding end of the pin in his fingertips and pulled it out.

"It looks stable to me; I think it will be OK," he said. "We'll see you in clinic on Monday." A grateful Lauren walked him to the elevator, the mini-crisis averted.

Dr. Richard S. Novitch, director of pulmonary rehabilitation at Burke, was the doctor in charge of Lauren's care. He admitted her to Burke's Pulmonary Service, where the four patients from the Burn Center who came to Burke were all treated. He was amazed that she had not had more medical complications. He remembered feeling empathy for Lauren from the moment of their very first meeting, and recognized from the start that she was ready to take an active role in her recovery. "We could go right into her therapy," he said. "She was really game."

She would be busy six days a week, with Sundays off. Every weekday she would spend two hours in occupational therapy, break for lunch, then spend two more hours in physical therapy. On Saturday this was cut back to one hour each for PT and OT, though the OT always ran long. Often she would have relaxation therapy in her room at the end of the day, and every night Kareen would be there to help with wound care and her nightly routine.

Because Lauren's injuries were so extensive, the occupational and physical therapy departments both took extraordinary steps to prepare for her arrival, starting on December 9, when two occupational therapists came down to the Burn Center at New York-Presbyterian for a detailed briefing. They were Rob Young, OTR (Occupational Therapy Registered), who was to be her primary occupational therapist at Burke, and Corina Hall, OTR, the occupational therapy supervisor. When they returned to Burke, Corina assigned Rob and Tina Forenz, COTA (Certified Occupational Therapy Assistant), to handle Lauren's treatment.

The fact that she was a September 11 patient was additional motivation, for, like the caregivers at the Burn Center, the entire staff at Burke—doctors, nurses, therapists, and aides—felt a special concern for those victims.

A few days after Lauren's arrival, the full PT staff attended an in-service lecture by Hope Laznick, the assistant chief of physical therapy at the Burn Center, who came up to Burke to discuss the care of burn patients, including treatment techniques, the use of pressure garments, scar management, typical issues burn patients encounter, and what to expect during the healing process. Lauren was there too, and received a demonstration paraffin wax treatment as part of the session; she also talked to the staff about her concern that pressure and silicone were being properly applied to her wounds. She was at ease when she spoke, and even got a few laughs.

Lauren's primary physical therapist was Elizabeth Mallon, MSPT. Liz and the two occupational therapists were immediately impressed with her courage and resilience. They could see how energized she was, and how determined. The three of them consulted textbooks and reviewed her chart from the Burn Center, further educating themselves about burn protocol, range-of-motion treatments, and skin care. Skin and wound care are usually nursing functions, but because they would have to remove Lauren's bandages and compression garments to treat her, her OTs and PTs would be involved with cleansing, debridement, reapplication of ointments, and bandaging.

We knew from the Burn Center that the objective of occupational therapy was to make it possible for someone who had been severely compromised or disabled to function independently. Her therapy would focus on fine motor skills, the intricate movement of the hands and the wrists, and on the activities of daily living ("ADL"—a term we had first learned about on November 7): personal grooming, dressing, feeding herself, sitting down and standing up, climbing into and out of the shower or the bath or the seat of a car. For someone who has been forced out of society by a severe injury, part of the OT cure is also to go out in public, to visit the mall, to see a movie, to eat in a restaurant; to learn how to handle the daily pace of life, to regain the ability, and the confidence, to do the normal things we take for granted.

Lauren had been deprived of all these things, and the time ahead was structured to help her recover them to the greatest extent possible. First and foremost came regaining the dexterity in her hands through the ranging and joint mobilizations I had first seen at the Burn Center. These involved manipulation to break down the internal and external scar tissue and loosen everything so that the healing skin would be flexible, the ligaments would permit joint extension, the tendons would glide as they were meant to, and hand function could slowly be regained.

Ranging was a three-step process: active assist, fatigue, and then passive stretch. First Lauren received assistance in achieving a particular movement, possibly increasing its range slightly. She would then attempt the same movement against resistance until the muscle group being worked was fatigued. Next came the passive stretch, in which the therapist provided all the impulsion. With the initial range of motion established through the active assist, and with the fatigued muscle group unable to inhibit the range of movement, the passive stretch would go farther than the assisted stretch; there was a discernible release. Thus, one degree at a time, the range of motion would be regained.

Fortunately, Lauren's OT also featured pleasurable activities, including dancing, cooking, potting a plant. There was a specialized video game station with a series of interchangeable hand pieces, each of which duplicated a hand or arm movement: turning a key in a lock, turning a doorknob, opening a bottle or jar, rotating the throttle forward on a motorcycle. It was an ingenious setup, allowing her to work on her fine motor skills while having fun.

Lauren also treasured the companionship of her therapists. "They were a great lifeline to the outside world on a daily basis," she says of Rob and Tina. "Smiling, full of fun, they became my friends. I looked forward to going to therapy in the morning."

This was remarkable, because so much of the process was very difficult. The ranging and mobilizations were painful. Her hands were still very sensitive, blistering easily, and she faced continuing challenges from skin contractures. In the evenings she needed to wear splints: C-splints to reestablish the webbing between her thumb and her index finger so that she could extend her thumb a normal 90 degrees; and robotic marionette splints, which used high-load-capacity fishing line to apply steady, directed pressure to help bring her fingers to her palm and eventually make a fist.

It was all as complicated as it sounds.

I was trained to range her myself, to supplement her daily OT with additional work at night and on weekends, and for a while, this became our intimacy, the first chance I had to touch her body for long periods of time. It wasn't intimate in the usual sense, but the closeness made a difference because it was one of the few things I could do for her. Disease and injury can hijack the intimacy between two people, who go in a moment from partners to dependent and a caregiver. I wanted to be of help to her.

Physical therapy was, if anything, even more strenuous. Liz was very committed and organized, Lauren said. She admired Liz's warmth and skills, her willingness to take things to the limit, and the creative ways she devised to stretch and strengthen Lauren's body. As Liz worked Lauren's ankles, knees, and hamstrings, then her arms, elbows, and shoulders, she recognized Lauren's readiness to try anything she devised. Even when Lauren arrived in pain from an OT session, she shook it off. However hard or exhausting the work, she never backed off. She had a vision of what she wanted to do and be able to do, and this drove her always.

Where special skills were needed, Liz did not hesitate to bring in others to help. At one point, Lauren was walking around with one shoulder raised and her back in an awkward position, and Liz sought out Jennifer Hogan, the assistant director of OT, for a treatment that helped Lauren assume a more normal position. Lauren was enormously grateful. "Jen saw how awkward I was with my shoulder and sprang things back into place," she recalls. "That was a watershed, the day that I got my back into shape, back into alignment." And there were also the other OTs and PTs who would treat her on the weekends with equal dedication and skill.

Just as important as the flexibility and strengthening exercises was Liz's work on scar management: the heavy massage to break up and properly align the fibers so that Lauren's skin would be supple and soft. When I noticed that her back felt far softer to the touch, it was very much the result of Liz's hard work. Much of this work was done behind a privacy curtain, and if I came in during a session, I could hear Lauren's voice, joking away while Liz painstakingly massaged every inch of her back and legs.

We had learned that scars continue to mature for one to one and a half years. New scar tissue is very red, the sign of heavy vascularization—the presence of blood vessels that bring a copious blood supply to the tissue. The tissue will "blanch," or lighten, where pressure is applied and turn red again when it is is removed. Scar growth is at its most aggressive during the first six months. Compression garments are a vital tool in scar management because they provide sustained pressure across the entire area of the scar, squeezing out the blood and thus slowing tissue growth. (Silicone inserts are also used beneath compression garments as an aid to healing.) If compression has been used conscientiously, when the scar matures and hypertrophic growth stops, the skin can heal into a smoother, more pliable surface with good tone and flexibility.

Lauren had a graphic example of this the very first weekend she was at Burke, when two women came to visit her: Natasha, a former burn patient who'd been through the Burn Center and Burke in 1999, and Erin, who had worked for Lauren at Cantor in New York.

Natasha had been burned over more than 50 percent of her body in a bad automobile accident and had undergone extensive grafts. Before the visit ended, she changed into shorts to show Lauren how her legs had healed. She was an invaluable demonstration of the benefits of compression because she'd been more conscientious wearing the Jobst compression garments on her left ankle and foot than she had on her right knee. Lauren could clearly see that the healed grafts on her left ankle were smooth, and had a supple texture—"like butter," said Natasha—while her right knee still showed the mesh pattern of the graft and was not as clean and smooth. The benefits of compression were clearly visible to our eyes.

Lauren received her first compression garments at the Burn Clinic at New York-Presbyterian on December 19. (She realized on the ride down that this was her first trip in a vehicle since September 11 in which she could look out the window and see the world; ambulances have no views.) The clinic was on the seventh floor of the hospital's main building, away from the west wing where the Burn Center was located. When Dr. Yurt examined her, he was pleased to see that the grafts on her buttocks that had been slow to close were almost completely healed.

She had been fitted for her Jobst garments before leaving the Burn Center, and they were now ready for her: leggings that resembled heavy-duty pantyhose, a long-sleeved top with zippers running the length of each arm and up the front to a high neck, and two fabric hoods and a plastic face mask. Together, these items would provide compression for everything except her hands, which were not yet strong enough to tolerate Jobst gloves.

This was her first time wearing full-body compression. Knowing this was to come had made her anxious, fearful, sad—she knew she would need to wear it twenty-three hours a day for at least a year. A patient with a lesser burn might need to wear only a compression shirt or sleeves or leggings, but Lauren had to wear all three, plus the face mask. Even those areas that were not injured or only mildly burned, such as the front of her torso and the fronts of her legs, had to be covered to ensure that pressure could be applied to the injured areas.

The face mask took time because it had to be fitted on her directly—holes needed to be cut for her eyes, mouth, and nose, and the edges buffed. But a couple of hours later, we were done.

As I helped her eat her lunch in the hospital cafeteria before we headed back to Burke, Lauren recalled our first meeting, in 1995, and I saw her eyes fill. "Who knew, when you met me, that it would come to this?" she said. "Who knew?"

Lauren was becoming apprehensive about how she would ultimately look. She was understandably mourning the loss of the person she had been and trying to come to terms with the gravity of her injuries. And she was becoming conscious of how much she missed being a beautiful woman, which is what she was when she entered One World Trade Center on September 11. She confessed to an utterly human vanity, entirely normal in the past but painful to her now. She had always taken such good care of herself, always looked out for her health, always had an extraordinary fashion sense. And then the day came when she was in the line of fire—and she knew the consequences would always be with her.

In late December she got a long look at her back in the mirror and saw the full extent of the grafts below her shoulder line. Only one portion of her back had been spared. Everything else was new—the grafts that were now her skin. "I just can't believe this is me," she said sadly. "I keep wishing less had been burned, more left undamaged." Later she said, "I keep thinking this is a dream, and that I will wake up and it won't have happened."

Mostly, she would say, "I can't believe this is my body."

But the difficulty of these realizations did not impede Lauren's determination; discouraging as they were, they motivated her even more strongly to wear the pressure garments. She knew what she had to do and was driven to do it. At one point Dr. Novitch, just back from a vacation, told her that the doctors often had to find ways to motivate some of their patients. "But that's not an issue with you," he said to her. This was true, but she still had to learn how to be patient, to accept that the process would take time, to keep the faith. My job, as I saw it, was to reinforce that faith and to rekindle it when it flagged.

I was pleased to be able to make one gesture that I thought might help. I had lost my wedding band in a taxi prior to September 11. Finding myself with some unexpected free time on December 17, I

317

headed over to Tiffany's in the Westchester Mall for a "power-shop": in and out in five minutes with a wedding band just like the one I'd lost. When I came back from my brief expedition Lauren noticed the ring right away. She smiled.

Her progress was steady. Because I was there every day, I didn't notice every step, but when I stopped to reflect on the stages she had already gone through, I realized how far she had come.

By December 23, less than two weeks after coming to Burke, Lauren was feeding herself with a regular plastic fork and could pick up a telephone receiver carefully with her right hand. She was using that hand for almost everything, including writing her name in a childish but legible script. Moreover, her left hand, which been operated on just before Thanksgiving, was coming along, and she was able to use it together with her right hand to pick up papers or a dinner plate.

At dinner on December 29, she reached up with her left hand and was able to touch her face. She blew a kiss; she kissed her own left fingers. It was a huge milestone, the result of weeks of arduous work, but it made her cry because it reminded her how far she still was from normal.

"I just want to get better," she said. "My hands. Everything."

But she *was* getting better. She could do twenty minutes on the treadmill at a level-four incline, and the therapists had told her the swing was back in her step.

On January 5 she bent down and picked up a towel that was lying flat on the floor, to the applause of her fellow patients.

In the second week of January, she went down to the city to the Burn Clinic, and everyone remarked on how great she looked. She could raise her right arm vertically. She did a little ski move, jumping in place while twisting her knees, like a slalom racer. And there was another difference, possibly even more striking.

"Want to keep from crying? Get some new makeup," Lauren had said to me on January 11. Earlier in the day, Corina had found her crying and asked how she would feel about going off to the cosmetics counter at Bloomingdale's.

Four of them had gone shopping, and Lauren looked wonderful now. The makeup had completely changed her appearance. She appeared more in command of herself, healthier, more normal. And with her increased dexterity she was able to apply it herself, comb her own hair, take charge of her appearance at last. It was a welcome milestone, and similar ones were to follow.

On January 26, she got her first real haircut. She had been left with uneven hair since September 25, when her scalp had served as a donor site, and she now found her "tufted" look unacceptable. A hairstylist came to Burke once a week to give haircuts to the male and female patients in a basement room set up with a shampoo station, a barber's chair, a large mirror, and old magazines. Lauren told him she wanted a cut like Sharon Stone's, and that's what he gave her, gently cutting, drying, and shaping her hair. When he was done she looked much more like herself, just as she had the day she resumed wearing makeup. Her hair had been a persistent reminder of being forced to neglect her appearance; it had a proper cut at last.

On February 20, her hair received its professional coming-out party. I was present at the occasion; I went with Lauren to the Simon Salon, on 66th Street between Madison and Fifth Avenue.

When she walked through the door, her hairdresser embraced her with such warmth and sincerity that I was moved to tears. He held her for a very long time, and she cried; she was so happy to be back, and so sad to be hurt. They took her to the rear of the salon, where there would be more privacy. He cut her hair and showed her pictures of his pets and gossiped, and she talked to other women who were having their hair done. She looked wonderful.

This was her world, an outpost of style where I felt like a foreigner. But I could see how overjoyed she was to be back, her palpable sense of belonging. I was thrilled that they really seemed to love her. I had been apprehensive about the visit; the last time she had been there, she had certainly been one of the most beautiful women in the place, and whatever you could say about her appearance, her strength, and her character—which was a lot—she was not, at that moment, conventionally beautiful. But she was perfectly at home there and this enhanced her loveliness. Her injuries were more than balanced by her grace, her goodness, and her happiness at being alive.

On January 27 Rob set her up with a roll-out practice putting green and Lauren held a golf club again. She couldn't wrap her fingers around it yet, but she could squeeze enough to hold the weight. She lined up a putt and hit it, right on target but not hard enough. While she could perform the motion, the amount of strength she was projecting was less than she expected. She took some more practice shots, finally sinking one—and before she left Burke she successfully chipped on the grass outside.

Later that week a friend brought Japanese food for dinner. I expected Lauren to eat it with a fork, but instead, she broke apart a set of chopsticks. With unexpected ease, she plucked a piece of beef negi-maki, raised it to her mouth, and ate it.

Then there was the roadwork.

In addition to his daily rounds Monday through Friday, Dr. Novitch held weekly team meetings where each patient's case was discussed. Lauren's case would be presented by her nurses, her OTs, and her PTs, her progress measured and the next week's goals set. One of the evaluations was a six-minute walking test given to pulmonary patients.

Once a week Liz and Lauren would set off down the hallways with a pedometer to measure how much ground Lauren covered in the allotted time. Most pulmonary patients are lucky to travel several hundred feet. Lauren's lung injuries had been real but relatively minor, and her recovery excellent from the pneumonia she'd suffered at the Burn Center. "Lauren was doing more than two thousand feet with no problem," Liz said. "We'd go tearing off around the building, people would be bolting out of our way. They were used to seeing us. She would be doing a brisk walk, bordering on a jog, and talking the whole time. After six weeks, the doctors said we didn't need to do it anymore."

On a springlike day in late January Lauren told me she was ready to take a walk around the grounds. We headed downhill along the blacktop path beside the long driveway, enjoying the sunset in front of us, the rolling lawn to our right, the trees that lined the road to our left. We turned around just short of the front gate and headed back up the hill, a walk of more than half a mile. Lauren later told me that this had been one of the high points of her stay at Burke.

There was progress of all kinds. She enjoyed going out. Rob and Tina would take her to Dunkin Donuts, and there were other expeditions. On January 31, I met her at Nordstrom's in the Westchester Mall, where she was already shopping, accompanied by Deirdre from the department of therapeutic recreation. She bought a pair of boots and we headed up to the second floor to buy her an elegant jacket and top. It was a highly satisfactory day; she paid for everything with her own credit card and signed with a graceful, carefully wrought new signature.

On February 16, Lauren drove our car again, with an OT in the passenger seat. She started in the visitor parking lot, drove up to the outpatient hospital, and went around the front of the hospital to the research building, finally returning to Building 7. Her grip on the steering wheel wasn't perfect because the Jobst gloves she now wore were a fine mesh fabric and slippery, but the ride was smooth.

There was no longer any comparison between the Lauren who had checked into Burke on December 11 and the woman who walked the halls with such authority, her trademark black tote bag on her arm.

We continued to return to New York for monthly appointments at the Burn Clinic, where Dr. Yurt would check her burn sites. He continued to find her progress impressive, and his reassurances that she was doing well, and that the areas that were still healing would see sustained improvement, helped to ease her doubts. In February he said that her back was looking even better than he had expected.

We also traveled to the city once a month to see Lauren's hand surgeon, Dr. Andrew Weiland, who first saw her during a visit to her Burn Center room on December 5, when she had been unable to move the fingers of her left hand. When we went to him next on January 16, Lauren raised her hands in their Isotoner gloves and moved her fingers to demonstrate the range of motion.

"The progress you've made in six weeks, less, is amazing," he said. "You're a hard worker!"

X rays showed that the internal anatomy of her wrists and hands was mostly healthy. Because the fingertips of her left index and middle fingers had been amputated, she would have a permanent deficit, but it was one she could adapt to. It would not prevent her from writing; in fact, she had started writing with her left hand, very slowly and deliberately, only two days earlier. Her surviving fingertips on both hands would have permanent losses in range of motion, but they remained in functional position. The index finger is responsible for 40 percent of hand function. Her right index finger was in the best condition, the finger in which she would see the greatest recovery of range.

On February 20, Dr. Weiland echoed his previous comments. Lauren had increased all her ranges, and could almost make a fist. "You're unbelievable," he told her, and hugged her as she left. Describing her level of motivation, he would call her a "quadruple A personality."

One more factor during these weeks that reinforced this motivation and brought her great joy: once she was at Burke, no longer at serious risk of infection, we were able to bring Tyler to be with her more often. The financial support of the Red Cross and other agencies enabled us to have a second nanny on weekends, when Joyce was off, and this made it possible to bring Tyler there not only more frequently, but for hours at a time. When he grew restless his nannies would take him for walks down the hallways, or to the sitting room if he got cranky. They were devoted to him, and they shared the same intense motivation to bring mother and son back together.

Tyler has always been an adaptable little guy, and he took to the new travel schedule, new faces, and new locations with aplomb. Lauren was overjoyed. The two of them lived a shared adventure during her time at Burke, reintegrating their lives at last.

He had seen his mother only twice while she was at the Burn Center. We were eager to have him really know her again. Starting with his first visit to the Burn Center, we had begun pointing at Lauren and telling him, "This is Mommy," so that when we asked him, "Where's Mommy?" he would look at her. But it was clear that he didn't know this emotionally in the same way he knew that I was Daddy.

The first time Tyler truly focused on Lauren was December 16, when he began to play a long game of peek-a-boo with her, laughing in delight. With an assist from me, she could even hug him for a moment, and I saw her tears of joy. Two days later, while I was at Burke and he was at home with Joyce, he figured out that he could walk. I missed his first moment of deliberate perambulation, but he soon brought hs new skills to Burke, and we scrambled to baby-proof Lauren's hospital room.

On Christmas Day, he woke up crying with an ear infection. Despite the holiday, the pediatrician generously made time to check him and prescribe an antibiotic; but I was alone with him that day and assumed this would interrupt my unbroken streak of Lauren visits since September 11. Instead, my brother-in-law's wonderful aunt Charlotte stepped into the breach, hopped into a cab in Sheepshead Bay, and came to babysit, so at 5:15 PM, I was on the road north to spend the holiday evening with Lauren.

The day after Christmas, Tyler said his first sentence. At least it sounded like a sentence to me; I heard his voice drop at the end.

I said, "Hi, Tyler."

He said, "Hi, Dad."

I couldn't wait to tell Lauren.

A week later he seemed better. Early on New Year's Eve I brought him to Burke, and Lauren pushed his stroller down the hall. "I'm so proud when I push him," she told me, and I didn't ask if the pride was at how wonderful a little boy he was, or at simply being able to push a stroller at all.

Our friends Mike and Ellen Wlody came to pick him up. He was to spend the night at their house (I would go over there too, after celebrating with Lauren), but first they took him along with them to a New Year's Eve party, where all the mothers fought over who would rock him to sleep. On New Year's morning we all sat around lazily in the living room until I looked at Tyler's ear and noticed a discharge. Packing up all the kids, we went off to see the Wlodys' pediatrician, who told us that Tyler had suffered a ruptured eardrum. He carefully cleaned the ear and prescribed antibiotics and ear drops, but noted that since Tyler didn't seem to be in pain, we should just keep him on his medication and let him get better. He was smiling again within three days, and this time he stayed healthy.

By late January he was far better with his mother, often smiling at her, developing a clearer and clearer idea that she was someone special. He was fascinated by her plastic face mask, patting it when she was close to him or reaching out to undo one of the Velcro strips that held it to her face. And one evening while we were having dinner in the patient dining room, she sat at the piano while he stood next to her and banged on the keys. When he was done, she picked him up, holding him around the chest in a bit of a rescue carry but bringing him all the way across the dining room to me.

He especially enjoyed being with his mother in the OT gym. "The gym was like a playland," Lauren remembered. "Big balls to play with, room to run around. He loved falling and rolling on the mats."

When she hit her golf shots on January 27, it would have been far easier if Tyler had not been wandering around, picking up and trying to eat the golf balls.

Finally that night, her fondest dream was realized. She held Tyler— not in a rescue carry, or for a few seconds, but at her shoulder, with her arms supporting him.

By Presidents' Day weekend he was the star of the hospital, his reputation preceding him wherever he went. If I was walking down the hall by myself, someone, a patient, a family member, a staffer, would invariably say to me, "Where's Tyler?"

Probably in another hallway. He loved the halls and thought nothing of charging along them on his own, a fearless adventurer. Sometimes he'd be uncertain and stop and look to one of us for approval be-fore he continued on; but at other times he'd stamp his feet and laugh in sheer fun as we walked together from Lauren's room to the sitting room and back, a grand hike for a fifteen-month-old.

In the last week of February something seemed to change in Tyler, as if he finally truly understood who Lauren was. He began to choose her out of all the people in a room, walking over and hugging her, or wrapping his arms around her legs if she was standing. She would pick him up and say, "Give Mommy a kiss," and he would lean forward and kiss her right on the mouth. When she held him in her arms, he would relax and lay his head on her shoulder. This meant more to her than even we can comprehend. We would have to have come back ourselves from as great a distance as she did. She would look at him with love so intense that sometimes her face would redden and she would start to weep.

One night when Lauren was feeling a bit blue after a visit to the Burn Clinic—it had been a day full of small frustrations—the phone rang. Someone was calling from New York. Lauren picked up, and Tyler said, "Hi, Mommy."

Lauren asked him, "What does the tiger say?" and he growled.

I credit Joyce with perfect timing.

"I loved it when you and Tyler were there," Lauren says, remem-bering. "I was so proud when everyone said how cute he was, flirting with all the other patients. That little boy is the light of my life."

Throughout her three months at Burke, visits from friends helped her get through her days.

On December 21, Lauren met Harry Waizer's rabbi, who had come into her room to pray in her presence on September 16, when we didn't even know whether she could hear the words. I thought back to that dark time when I looked at his broad smile now. Later that day our friends Debra and Mark arrived bearing gifts. Lauren walked up to Debra, hugging her and saying amid tears, "I love you—it's so good to see you."

We spent an hour talking, first in Lauren's room, then in the sitting room. Lauren recalled how we'd all hung out on Labor Day in the summer house we'd shared—who could have known that this was where we were headed? Holding up her bandaged arms to Debra,

Lauren cried. "I want you to come over and to be able to serve you a glass of wine with my own hands," she said.

Tears and hugs marked most of the times she saw her friends. She could be fragile, emotionally volatile, whenever a new visitor arrived. Some things were easy to talk about—friends and family, business, real estate, her exercises—and others were much harder: the length of the rehab that lay ahead, her first days in the hospital, and the inevitable discovery that someone else she knew had died. Today Debra told her about the loss of the husband of a friend of ours, and she grieved.

On December 24, Debra and Mark returned for a more festive visit, wearing red reindeer antlers and bearing a pint-size Christmas tree in a flowerpot and a sleigh's worth of gifts for Tyler and his mom. Lauren's friend Judy had arranged for us to buy entrees at Mulino's of Westchester, so we set up our holiday dinner in the patient dining room and raised our glasses to a beautiful Christmas Eve.

We had many such dinners with friends in the patient dining room. They all brought feasts, and I would be the busy host, running back and forth from the two microwave ovens, serving their largesse on our finest black Styrofoam plates with our best white plastic silverware. Lauren was immensely cheered by these visits; they made the long, hard days and evenings more tolerable.

There was also the devoted cast of regulars from Lauren's months at the Burn Unit: her parents, who returned for a week-long visit in February and were amazed by her progress; her sister Glynis; my stepsister Laura; and my father, who drove down to Burke twice a week from Fleischmanns, in upstate New York, where he was spending his annual two-month hiatus from Florida as an eighty-year-old ski bum. Glynis often brought us wonderful meals, and she helped organize the burgeoning collection of cards and gifts, placing the cards in plastic sleeves in a loose-leaf binder. She also brought back the photo gallery, so that Lauren's favorite snapshots formed a phalanx on a side table.

A special adornment went up on her wall the very first week she was at Burke. When she was at the Burn Center she had received a framed poster from the New York City Ballet, a portrait of Darci Kistler in Central Park, signed by all the members of the ballet company in silver ink. Lauren had been a member of the Junior Committee of the New York City Ballet since 1998, and she had planned to be more active in the fall. The poster arrived with a beautiful cover letter from Peter Martins, the director of the company, but there had been no space to hang it until now.

And on Christmas morning, Lauren and Harry Waizer took a long walk together. Both from Cantor Fitzgerald, they were also becoming colleagues in their shared effort to make it all the way back. Lauren called the two of them the "Burnies." One thing was true; each was becoming an inspiration to the other. Harry told her she was giving him the heart to try harder in his recovery.

When I walked into Lauren's room on Christmas night, I held her close to me, unable to let go. I felt again that since September 11 my life had been recast; I had no regrets, though I had once had many. I felt as if all my mistakes had been redeemed, that I was fulfilling the destiny I was born for. As I held her and looked into her eyes, I was boundlessly grateful that she was alive. She told me later, "I always told you we were meant to be."

Glynis had brought us a holiday dinner, and my father joined us. Once again we loaded Lauren's wheelchair with the fixings, and it was off to the dining room for another feast, followed by desserts provided by the Waizers. They had just brought them; Harry had gone AWOL, going home for the first time since September 11 to his own house with his own family, returning only a short time before.

I arrived at Burke the next evening to find Lauren with Harry and Karen, who were talking about Jobst garments and a surgical procedure Harry had undergone. He told us that there was a concert in the patient dining room, so off the four of us went to hear a harpist and a flautist who were already playing for an audience of about twenty people.

The harpist was a woman playing a harp with a mahogany-colored body; the flautist was a man with short hair dressed in a royal blue shirt. They played beautifully for forty-five minutes, the harpist speaking between selections with warmhearted humor. When they were done, Lauren asked her how heavy the harp was. About seventy pounds, we learned, but it fit in a large station wagon.

As we walked back to the rooms, Harry turned to us and said, "I don't know about you guys, but that was our first date in three and a half months."

And then came New Year's Eve, and saying good-bye to 2001, so strange and terrible a year. I had long looked toward it, to the new century, as a glamorous adventure. Instead, it brought madness, mass murder, and war. The morning of September 11 ended with deaths too horrible to imagine. I should have been there; Lauren was. Our friends died. But Lauren ran out of the flames to survive, and thus define forever a message of struggle, hope, renewal, and love.

We had found ourselves at the center of the world when the attacks came, our family and our companies devastated. We found ourselves at the center of another world now, in which love and prayers flowed unceasingly from our friends, our family, and strangers around the globe.

I was in debt to everyone who wrote or who came by the hospital, expressing support; I was also in debt to everyone who had entered a place of worship and prayed for Lauren and for Tyler. May they all find peace and happiness, and most of all, health in coming years; may the kindness they have shown reflect back onto them.

Joyce had driven up with me on New Year's Eve so she could spend time talking to Lauren before heading home on the train. We had a Chinese feast with the Waizers in a cordoned-off section of the dining room at about seven. Howard and Alison Lutnick called and Lauren told them how happy she was to be saying Happy New Year to them; Howard said they had to do it every year from now on.

When midnight came, and we left 2001 behind, it was a New Year's Eve like no other. I held Lauren close; we were both in tears. She said, "We made it, we're here."

"You're here," I said.

"It's just the beginning," she told me. "I'll be by your side for years, my angel."

On television we watched the revelers in Times Square celebrating, and the strength, the optimism, and the faith we saw in the huge, festive, and orderly crowd made me proud to be a New Yorker and proud to be helping Lauren in her fight to return to her life. I told her once again that she was my hero, and I thanked her for fighting so hard to make it. "I did fight hard," she said through her tears. "I decided I was going to make it, and I did."

It stayed tough, though. There was always pain, frustration, the knowledge that she would not like the way she looked. She had some nightmares, too, including a terrible one in which she dreamed she had brought Tyler with her to work on September 11. She was fearful whenever she thought about going home, worried about not having all the support she had come to rely on. But Dr. Novitch reassured her she needn't be, that she should look forward to it, that Burke would grow stale, and that when it was time for her to go home she would be ready.

I was sure she would be, too; she hadn't wanted to leave the Burn Center a moment too early either, but when it came time to go, she walked through the front door without a second's hesitation.

Lauren had become a truly inspiring symbol for almost everyone at Burke, patients and staff, just as she had at the Burn Center. Late one evening in mid-January she had stepped out of her room and when I went to look for her I found her in the hall talking to a ninety-four-year-old man who was sitting in a wheelchair in the middle of the hall. She had been walking by when he'd said to her, "You're from the building, aren't you? You made it. God bless you."

Every night we would have dinner together in the patient dining room. Even at Burke, I told her, we were always having dinner out, and she laughed. "That's because we're New Yorkers," she said.

Often Dr. Novitch would stop by in the evening. He lived nearby, and he introduced us to his family. After Lauren went home, we came back one day for a choral performance by his eldest son's cross-district choral group, dedicated to the September 11 patients who had come to Burke. Lauren liked him: his readiness to listen, his caring, his sense of humor. "He always said he did not have a lot to do for me physically," she told me, "that it was the PTs and OTs who were doing all the work. But he truly did a great deal, and he was great to have around."

Given all that was going on and all that lay ahead, on January 23 I decided to take an indefinite leave of absence from work, at least until after Lauren came home. I went into the office to talk to Gil, who graciously agreed. It was another example of Euro Brokers' supportiveness; I was disappointed that I had been able to contribute so little to the firm's rebuilding, but I hoped to have an opportunity down the road.

Elaine Duch arrived at Burke after four and a half months in the Burn Center. Her recovery had moved more slowly than Lauren's. As with the Maffeos and the Waizers, we had gotten to know her family, but Elaine herself was still sedated when we left. Now at last she was getting better, and she was enthusiastic about coming to Burke because Lauren and Harry were already there.

Early on the evening of January 29, Harry and Lauren went to her room to welcome her. It was a lively encounter—a reunion for the family members, a first meeting for the patients. "Remember how we always talked about this?" Elaine's sister Marianne said to me. "Now we're here."

Harry went home on February 13. No longer upstairs from a full-therapy gym, he was down the hall from his children, in the same room, at last, where his wife slept. I learned about Harry's arrival home not from Lauren but from an e-mail, short and cheerful, signed "Harry." His hospital room was empty, but that meant nothing. His home was once again full.

That is all everyone really wanted to live for: to make it home.

At the end of January, I had noted to myself that the patient families had moved from hugging one another, in the first days after the attacks, to hugging the patients, and that in Lauren's case, I no longer had to worry that I might hurt her. She was strong and returned the embrace. And of course, Lauren and Harry had hugged each other. They were still injured and they were often unhappy, but happiness had intruded now.

In early February I saw this play out. Lauren was healthier, freer to think about what she'd survived, and it upset her. She struggled with a surge of anger. She told me she needed to talk to a fellow patient, and we went down the hall to Harry's room. Lauren said, "I'm just so angry that I was burned!" and burst into tears.

Karen Waizer hugged Lauren, comforting her.

Then Harry said a wonderful thing. "I have the same feelings," he told Lauren. "I get angry, frustrated, and whenever I feel like that, I always think of the widows. They would give anything on earth to have what Karen and Greg have. So I'm grateful."

I said to Lauren, "Now say thank you to the nice man," and everyone laughed. And so we achieved one small moment of coping, among the thousands to come.

Lauren needed moments like these to get her past the dark ones. One day in February she had been crying in occupational therapy over the injuries to her hands, and the therapists had gathered around her and tried to comfort her to no avail. Dr. Novitch came by later to see how she was doing, and she talked about her hands, and how deeply she wanted her face to recover fully, how much she still had to overcome. I was sad as I drove home, but minutes after I walked in, the telephone rang.

"I bounced back; I rallied," she said, her mood clearly lighter than when I'd left.

I had to think this was Kareen's doing. Kareen was still there almost every night, coming up to Westchester now, instead of to the Burn Center. She remained a beautiful, wonderful constant, someone Lauren trusted to be there with her all night long. In the background through all these months her presence could be felt; she helped Lauren every night with her wound care, her Jobst garments, her nightly shower, with conversation and humor. Lauren called her "Madame Curie," and she called Lauren "Madame Fury." Lauren's stay would have been so very different without her. Kareen's near-constant presence gave me serenity. I knew she was watching lovingly over Lauren.

The nurses and the aides were also taking wonderful care of her. "They eased my pain," Lauren said. "They would come into my room and listen and talk. They were a very integral part. Whenever I needed help, or was having a bad moment, they gave me support." This included small, unobtrusive touches; when Lauren and I had our dinners together in the dining room, for example, without fail, as their shift was ending, one of her nurses would wander down to make sure she received her evening medication.

On Saturday morning, February 9, Lauren and I met Senator Hillary Clinton at Burke, in a meeting arranged by Geri Shapiro, Mrs. Clinton's Westchester County coordinator and a Waizer neighbor. Geri had made a significant effort to become acquainted with Lauren and Harry's situation, the plight of the critically injured in general, and the fact that the seriously injured had not been directly addressed by the legislative or regulatory remedies that had been undertaken to assist the families and loved ones of the deceased.

Mrs. Clinton was warm and attentive to all: relaxed, direct, unpretentious. She seemed committed to addressing these issues; she had visited other injured victims and was keeping in touch with them. It was a good discussion, and we took some snapshots. But my lasting memory is of Lauren's approach to this meeting. She stood up and spoke forcefully and directly to a United States senator, brimming with determination and clarity even when on the verge of tears.

On Valentine's Day, I again power-shopped at Tiffany's, buying Lauren a silver necklace with rose quartz stones so that she would always have a bouquet of roses around her neck. The day after that, February 15, was her birthday and the party was at Chez Waizer.

In addition to the large Waizer family, the guest list included Glynis; Lauren's parents, who were up for a visit; my father, down from Fleischmanns; Rob Young and his wife, Cara; Corina; and Geri Shapiro.

We entered to a long table covered with trays of hors d'oeuvres and a banquet set for twenty. Pots simmered on the stove, glasses of wine awaited us, and Harry, wearing a normal shirt, was standing in his own house, smiling. There was really nothing like being able to take a shower in your own shower, he said, to rest in your own bed. The things that he'd thought would be difficult once he came home weren't as bad as he'd feared, and the things he'd thought would be good were far better.

Lauren made a toast. Tyler did laps around the table, then sat happily in his stroller through the superb meal. Lauren enjoyed it immensely. Howard Lutnick had sent a bottle of fine champagne, but Lauren and Harry decided to save it for a larger celebration, after Lauren returned home. We returned to the hospital late, just missing a call from Senator Clinton.

February was a birthday month, and the 26th was Harry's. Lauren threw a surprise party for him at Burke, and when he walked into the room where we were all hiding, he gave a huge smile. He offered a beautiful toast, and we all shared the cake. His children were there, and some of his friends, and the therapists and Dr. Novitch and others on the hospital staff. But the most noteworthy thing about the guest list is that it included the last four World Trade Center burn patients to be released from the Burn Center: Harry, Lauren, Elaine, and Donovan Cowan, who had arrived at Burke just days before.

The end of the month meant that the book's publication was only a short time away, and we did some taping for the Oprah Winfrey show. Lauren was wonderful: dignified, soft-spoken, and direct; courageous, intelligent, immensely lovable. She was someone for whom you felt sorrow but whom you did not pity.

She was professionally made up for her appearance, but all the makeup did was to give her an even skin tone. I was pleased to be able to point out to her that once her scars matured and her color evened out, this was exactly how she would look. In other words, I said, she was still beautiful. I realize I said that to her all the time, but it was nice to have objective proof.

We were approaching the end of Lauren's stay in the hospital, and we were on the brink of a great change in our lives: she would be home, and I would be published. It was one of my fondest dreams, but even more, it was a unique opportunity to tell Lauren's story, to show her courage and tenderness to the world. If I had a skill that permitted me to do that and do it well, I was certainly grateful.

We celebrated our wedding anniversary on March 8. I brought a very special dinner from Philip Marie, the restaurant where I first told Lauren that I loved her, and where I proposed to her. Understandably, she was full of conflicting emotions; happy to be celebrating, sad over all she'd been forced to endure and at the fact that we had to do our celebrating in a hospital. But we both realized we really had made it, and that was reason enough for joy.

And then it was the six-month anniversary of September 11. Half a year had actually passed. Once again, a story about Lauren was on the front page of *The New York Times*, and that afternoon, we were on "Oprah."

We watched the show, for which the final taping had been completed a few days earlier. The producers did a wonderful job of framing the story, and Oprah herself did an extraordinary job of telling it.

That night Lauren and I attended the Women's Bond Club dinner, at which Lauren was one of six people, including Dr. Yurt, honored for the roles they played on and after September 11. When she was introduced she received a lengthy standing ovation, and I was immensely proud of her. Both featured speakers later wrote her beautiful notes saluting her courage. These were the women of her industry, and they were cheering for her.

Tuesday morning on the "Today Show," Katie Couric told viewers that Lauren was one of the most remarkable women she had ever met. This was her introduction to the first of two features on Lauren's recovery and on the book. The second segment ran the next morning.

Between Monday, March 11, and Friday, March 15, the work on our apartment was completed, the painting done, the closets installed. On Thursday night Christine and her friend Carlo helped unpack everything that had been stowed in boxes. They were the Manhattan crew. In Westchester, Mike Wlody and Gene Ambrosio, the first nurse (or staff member) at the Burn Center to tell me that he thought Lauren would make it, helped box Lauren's books, CDs, medical supplies, clothes, and cards.

That day the therapists at Burke threw Lauren a huge farewell party. "My best moment there was that party," Lauren says, "how they were all there to wish me goodbye." She told me her worst moments were Sunday mornings before I got there with Tyler, when she said she would lie in her bed "feeling very physically hurt, so alone, so far from being back. But every day when you walked in the door was so wonderful. I loved it when you and Tyler were there."

Now, at last, we would be there all the time. On Friday, the Princess of Perry Street returned home, completing a journey that had lasted six months and four days. She left for work at 8:30 AM on September 11, 2001, and returned at 11:45 AM on March 15, 2002.

As she left Burke, the nurses streamed into her room to say goodbye, hugging her, wishing her well, and giving her some lovely gifts. Other patients stopped her in the hallway to say farewell. Rob and Tina walked us to our car, and Lauren climbed in. We sailed down the Hutchinson River Parkway to the Cross County Parkway, down the West Side Highway to the Village, and I stopped in front of our building with the hazard lights blinking.

I held Lauren's door open as she slid out on her own and walked over the cobblestones to the sidewalk and into the entrance to our building. The elevator came and we rode up, went down the hall, and into our home.

Joyce and Tyler were there; Joyce had decorated the apartment with signs saying "Welcome Home, Love You." There were beautiful bouquets of flowers from Joyce and the other nannies, and from other parents. (The nannies had the advance notice our neighbors didn't even have, so of course the parents found out too.)

Lauren gave Joyce a huge hug, both of them crying. As I stood watching them, I realized this was the last big step, and emotions that I thought had moderated came flooding back.

I remembered when Lauren was so swollen I did not recognize her, when it was still less than forty-eight hours since the world had gone so tragically wrong. I remembered all the milestones, large and small, but the biggest of all would be this one—the transition from the world of the ill to the world of the normal.

She had so much more work to do that it was daunting. She would be returning to New York-Presbyterian five days a week for one hour each of PT and OT. We had twenty-four-hour companion care, which was a godsend; Lauren needed help getting into and out of her compression garments and managing many other tasks, and with Tyler around, there was no way I could take care of both of them.

Lauren had wanted our dog, Caleigh, there for her arrival but we couldn't arrange that, so at one o'clock I went over to the apartment where Caleigh was staying and brought her back to see Lauren. Caleigh went airborne immediately, but she calmed down quickly and spent the next four hours by Lauren's side, sleeping beside the sofa in the den as Lauren napped.

Lauren and Tyler were together again, and she would look at him and sometimes just cry; and then he would laugh and she would laugh right back. When mealtimes came, there was no journey to the cafeteria. Every night, when she watched a sleepy Tyler finish his bottle in his stroller, instead of his being wheeled to the car for a long ride home, she knew he would be wheeled ten feet down the hall and into his crib.

We spent our first night and every night since in our beautiful king-size bed, the ceiling fan above us circling at low. There were no nurses coming in, no PA announcements, and no loneliness, because I was there, too.

Still, it was quite an adjustment. Hospitals are designed to heal the sick, and as much as they are about confronting and treating suffering, they are also cocoons compared to the outside world. Despite the pain she endured, Lauren's hospital memories were all of improvement; the present was almost always better than the past, and her progress was always close to miraculous. But back in our neighborhood, she also had to confront memories of being ablebodied, of a world before September 11. She could finally face just how profoundly she had been changed, and how much work lay ahead to make it back to the way she had been.

"I wish my tears could wash away my scars," she said.

On March 31, 2002, *Love, Greg & Lauren* debuted at number 4 on The *New York Times* Hardcover Nonfiction Bestseller List.

The book contained a special e-mail address, and every day brought e-mails from readers as young as eleven to those in their nineties, telling me that Lauren was their hero, that her struggle had placed their own lives in perspective, helping them to face their problems and to heal their own wounds of September 11. A doctor wrote that the book forever changed his view of the ICU in which he worked, and his understanding of the patient families who mount their anxious vigils in every ICU waiting room. A nurse wrote that she was returning to the profession after reading and understanding that her skills were invaluable in saving lives. One woman reconciled with a sister to whom she rarely spoke; another, who cared for an ill husband, said that she had learned that she could take care of herself on occasion, even have fun, without guilt or shame.

I had spent my life wishing, but never expecting, that I could write a book that would have a positive impact on someone's life. Through

Lauren's survival, and with the love and support of countless friends and colleagues, Lauren's family and mine, I had been privileged to witness and report on a slice of history that permitted me to realize my highest hope. Maybe not my wildest one, but certainly the one that was most worthwhile.

I am not grateful to the madmen who perpetrated this genocidal tragedy, and I still reject the idea that any such event can have a silver lining. But in this damaged time, when all of us are all left fighting for the preservation of our families and our freedom in a world brimming with so much hate and madness, I have been given the chance to tell a story of great sadness and much joy. The sad parts were those that were not up to us.

I have told the truth; Lauren has lived it. So let me end with this: Lauren gave me love and a home that I realized, in an instant on September 11, were what I wanted to live for.

We love and remember the dead, but we love and embrace the living. It is always possible, even with her grievous injury, to put matters into perspective; the wind blows, the sounds echo, the seasons return, and we take a breath and realize that we are so very blessed to have her, and to have each other, even to be sad together, because to feel is to be alive. Tyler was waiting for her, and there is far more laughter now than there are tears. Lauren is back; she is home.

ACKNOWLEDGMENTS

I wrote this book late at night and in the early mornings; I wrote most of it on my own computer, but also on the computers of friends; I wrote parts of it from a handheld BlackBerry pager in the waiting room of New York-Presbyterian Hospital. It began as e-mails advising our friends on Lauren's condition; it grew into a diary of our lives. In many instances I did not name the people who performed countless acts of courage, bravery, and generosity. But the book would never have been written, or would have been a very different work, if Lauren had not made it; so as a husband, even more than as a writer, I would like to take this opportunity to thank the Burn Team at the Weill Cornell Burn Center, the doctors, nurses, physical and occupational therapists, psychologists, and social workers who cared for Lauren and made it possible for her to survive.

I wish to thank Dr. Roger Yurt, the director of the burn unit and Lauren's doctor, who performed the crucial surgeries and directed her care; he proved equally skillful at communication and compassion. Thanks also to his colleagues, associate director Dr. Palmer Bessey (known to others, but not to me, as Joe) and attending surgeon Dr. Gregory Bauer, burn fellows Dr. Jason Rolls and Dr. Joseph Turkowski, and the other fellows and residents who supervised Lauren's care for the ninety-one days she was at the Burn Center.

I offer a very special thanks to the burn nurses who cared for Lauren. Some, who cared for her through her most difficult days, she met only briefly. Others, who cared for her as she awakened and began to fight her way back in earnest, she came to know quite well. I met them all, and they all did their share, tracking every heartbeat and every breath as Lauren fought for her life, and managing her through every crisis.

Richard Thalman was her day nurse through her first days, and the first to play her classical music; Lars Updale saw Lauren through her first night, and Pauline Lee the following nights, as she survived the resuscitation phase. They were followed by many who cared for Lauren with equal dedication and compassion; listed alphabetically they are: Jill Abshire, Nicole Alden, Eugene Ambrosio, Alex Baguio, Dawn Battle-Massey, Virginia Bentley, Jennifer Bianchi, Edna Blaise, Zenon Borawski, Andre Cesarski, Nicole Cole, Mervin David, Bobby Dixon, Hantz Dumont, Judith Dziuba, Monica England, Jennifer Estes, Faith Fajarito, Jennifer Forsberg, Marjorie Fortin, Debra Fox, Polly Frank, Sandra Garraway, Michael Geremia, Jonathan Gilbride, Ellen Gilley, Kelly Giudice, Andrew Greenway, Daniel Haughie, Diana Kraus, Jo Kraynick, Gregory Lee, Holly Macklay, Bernadette Maguire, Alison Malarkey, Barbara McGee, Charles Mitchell, Peggy Mitchell, Chanita Montgomery, Oscar Nagrampa, Kenneth Osorio, Arti Panchal, Rafael Portales, Theresa Potocki, Kathleen Pry, Linda Quintiliani, Barbara Ritchwood, Elvira Robateau, Kelly Russell, Meredith Santiago, Sarah Seiler, Roger Tague, Hayes Vargo, Susan Vinge, Tanya Walker, Rhonda Wilson, and Svetlana Zavuroua. Thanks, Dan and Gene.

Thanks also to the patient care technicians who assisted with Lauren's burn care and visits to the tank room, and to the nurse managers and clinicians.

The physical and occupational therapists provided intensive rehabilitative care with similar assiduousness. Thanks are due to Hope Laznick, Assistant Chief of Physical Therapy, and Robin Silver, Senior Occupational Therapist, as well as to Kimberly Broderick, PT, Jennifer Gilbert, OTR, Kimberly Hill, OTA, Rita Ingram, OTR, Tracy Maltz, PT, Maureen Marren, PT, Ivette Mayo, PT, Alyssa Padial, PT, Kerrie Schryver, OTR, Malvina Sher, PT, Samuel Yohannan, PT. Thanks also to Tracy for running the New York City Marathon in Lauren's honor.

Jennifer Roberts, PhD, the Burn Center's psychologist, worked with the patient families as they first arrived at the Burn Center, and then with recovering patients, helping all to cope; social workers Joyce Scheimberg, MSW, and Nancy Li, MSW, assisted with planning and placement for rehabilitative care. Reverend Carolyn Yard, the Burn Center chaplain, provided spiritual and corporeal sustenance with the same generosity.

On September 19 I had no thought of a book, but as time passed and I kept writing, others saw the potential. My friend Dan Gold forwarded some of my e-mails to Stephen Fried, accomplished investigative reporter and author, and with Dan, a fellow college journalist (Dan and Steve were the editors of *34th Street Magazine* at the University of Pennsylvania the year before I served as executive editor of *The*

Daily Pennsylvanian). Steve put me in touch with his editor, Ann Harris, at Bantam Dell.

I sat down with Ann for the first time in late October, and she moved quickly to arrange for publication of the manuscript, once it was completed. I will always be grateful to Ann for her judgment, her faith, and her discerning eye; she made the process of turning the e-mail diary into a book not just exciting but also a learning experience. Ann brought to this project the highest degree of professional commitment, personal sensitivity, and grace. My thanks also to Irwyn Applebaum, the president and publisher of Bantam Dell, for whose kind words, support, and continuing personal involvement I am truly grateful, and to Barb Burg, director of publicity, for her creativity and her commitment to making sure that Lauren's story was not only told, but heard. From the earliest moments, she did this with the greatest sensitivity to Lauren's recovery, and the greatest care that Lauren's experience would be a positive and enjoyable one.

I would like to thank my agent, Loretta Fidel, who helped me navigate my newfound business and literary affairs with clarity and professionalism, and with a powerful personal commitment.

I am grateful to the friends and the business associates who rushed to be with us in those first terrible days and have remained stalwart sources of support, There is not space to thank them sufficiently; there is not a hug big enough to return all their kind wishes and prayers, though I would offer a special hug to Mary White and Chris Flowers, who helped so much in the very first days after September 11, and to Kitty Leech, whose lifelong support has always meant so much.

I am grateful to Howard Lutnick, CEO of Cantor Fitzgerald, who hurried to Lauren's side to express his love and who, with his wife, Allison, has never wavered in his support; and to Gil Scharf, whose only instruction to me after the events that devastated our firm was to stay by my wife's side and to pull her, and my family, through this.

Some rock and roll thanks go to Mick Jagger for his wishing Lauren the best and for signing the beautiful red Telecaster guitar that I received on the "Oprah" show, so I could play the songs "a bit better"; it was played and immediately retired on a memorable night for the Rolling Bones.

I would like to thank the entire team at Burke for their knowledge, skill, and dedication: all the members of the medical staff, the nursing staff, the aides, and especially the physical and occupational therapists who cared for Lauren. When their hospital had to serve as our second home, they made it a most welcoming one.

There are many medical facts discussed in this book, and I would like to thank all the doctors, nurses, and physical and occupational therapists for their patience in explaining them to me. It goes without saying, but should be said anyway, that any errors are mine and mine alone.

Finally, I would like to thank Aneita Reid-Parnell, who joined with Joyce in taking wonderful care of Tyler, and who made many trips to Burke; and Lesma Williams, who was there when Kareen was not to make sure that Lauren always had a companion. Thanks to Lauren's family, and to my family, for always being there; and thanks most of all to Lauren for continuing her fight, for Tyler and me.

ABOUT THE AUTHOR

Greg Manning is a graduate of the University of Pennsylvania. He has worked as a reporter, an editor, and in senior marketing positions in the financial information industry since 1984. He is now Director, Information Sales and Marketing, at Euro Brokers, which was also based at the World Trade Center. He lives in New York with his wife, Lauren, and their young son.

gregandlauren@aol.com